ENCYCLOPEDIA OF COLD WAR POLITICS

ENCYCLOPEDIA OF COLD WAR POLITICS

BRANDON TOROPOV

ELIN WOODGER
Special Research Assistant

Facts On File, Inc.

Encyclopedia of Cold War Politics

Facts On File, Inc.
11 Penn Plaza
New York NY 10001

Library of Congress Cataloging-in-Publication Data
Torpov, Brandon.
Encyclopedia of coldwar politics / by Brandon Toropov.
p.   cm.
Includes bibliographical references and index.
ISBN 0-8160-3574-1
1. United States—Foreign relations—1945–1989—Encyclopedias. 2. United
States—Politics and government—1945–1989—Enclyclopedias. 3. Cold
War—Encyclopedias. I. Title.
E840.T57 2000
973.92'03—dc21   99-056805

Facts On File books are available at special discounts when purchased in bulk quantities for businesses, associations, institutions or sales promotions. Please call our Special Sales Department in New York at 212/967-8800 or 800/322-8755.

You can find Facts On File on the World Wide Web at
http://www.factsonfile.com.

Text design by Cathy Rincon
Cover design by Steve Monosson

Printed in the United States of America.

VB Hermitage 10 9 8 7 6 5 4 3 2 1

This book is printed on acid-free paper.

CONTENTS

LIST OF ENTRIES

INTRODUCTION

Few Americans realized in the aftermath of World War II that they were about to embark on yet another conflict, one that would last for 45 years and change the domestic political landscape in unimaginable ways. The conflict took many forms and involved innumerable battles, both physical and psychological, that left many scars but also taught many lessons.

The era that would be called the Cold War lasted from 1945 to 1990. The expression "cold war" had previously been used to describe any state of tension or hostility between two opposing sides, but it was in the postwar years that the phrase acquired capital letters and came to characterize the most intense and mutable struggle of the 20th century. Pulitzer Prize winner Herbert Bayard Swope first used the term in a speech written for presidential economic adviser Bernard Baruch, but it was journalist and political commentator Walter Lippmann who brought it into popular use. Initially, "cold war" was thought to be too harsh a description of the relations between the United States and the Soviet Union, but the name stuck. Even the Soviets began to use the phrase in the mid-1950s.

Who or what was responsible for the drastic reshaping of the domestic political landscape that accompanied the Cold War? It is still difficult to say. Certainly the global conflict had its roots in interactions and occurrences that took place on the global stage during and even prior to the Second World War. In the late 1940s tensions accelerated, leading to a sustained competition between diametrically opposed sociopolitical systems that would imprint itself indelibly on the American political scene. Only with the collapse of Soviet communism in 1990 could the war be said to have been "won," and for many American politicians, analysts, and voters, it is still difficult to determine the nature and significance of that victory.

For Americans, the Cold War was fought in many arenas. First and foremost, immediately following the war, they found themselves faced with the rise of a Soviet communist state deeply hostile to American interests. As a result, the U.S. government began a sustained campaign to counter communist influence and to form alliances with other nations equally dedicated to checking communist expansion—in essence, implementing the policy that came to be known as containment. Thus was born (among others) the Truman Doctrine (1947), the North Atlantic Treaty Organization (1949), the Southeast Asia Treaty Organization (1954), the Manila Pact (1954), and the Carter Doctrine (1980). In seeking to fulfill such commitments to contain communism, the United States played a complex and constantly evolving role. That role ultimately led to four and a half decades of intricate diplomatic and intelligence initiatives, involvement in two direct armed conflicts with communist forces (the Korean War and the Vietnam War), and a seemingly endless series of shocks, adjustments, and readjustments within its domestic political system. This volume aims to chronicle these transitions, and focuses on those involving U.S. political events. References to international personages and events are to be found under the topic or topics that most affected the American political scene.

At home, the fear of Soviet domination led many Americans to look among themselves for spies and subversives who might have destroyed domestic peace and stability. Fears often gave way to unwarranted accusations and hysteria, which led to Senator Joseph McCarthy's rise to power and the anticommunist "witch hunts" of the 1950s.

Americans also found themselves drawn into a race for nuclear superiority. The explosion of the world's first atomic bomb at the conclusion of World War II set off a period of research and development that resulted in an immense stockpiling of weapons of mass destruction that in turn threatened to destroy the planet if used unwisely. Fears regarding those who had their fingers on the nuclear trigger eventually led to innumerable treaties in the hopes of regulating, if not dismantling, nuclear armaments. Nevertheless, the struggle between the United States and the Soviet Union to maintain a nuclear advantage continued, and for many became the central issue of the Cold War. (Indeed, it was the proposed U.S. development of the Strategic Defense Initiative that many credit with toppling the Soviet Union.)

The political, social, and economic landscape of the United States was transformed irrevocably during the Cold War years, and it is probably fair to say that no sector of American society was entirely unaffected by the events of the Cold War. Of particular note during this time was the rise of three great movements: the antiwar movement, the civil rights movement, and the women's movement. All three were closely linked to each other, and all three challenged American political systems and social institutions to live up to the promises of democracy. Indeed, the viability of such promises was one of the central issues of the Cold War. Thus the U.S. political system saw tested its adaptability, its accessibility, its progressive nature, and even its democratic character. These challenges within the American system held, in an era of competition between nuclear superpowers, both domestic priority and significant geopolitical implications.

The focus in this book, however, is on domestic events and issues. Those of an international nature are touched upon to the degree that they directly affected the U.S. political scene (i.e., the Berlin blockade and the Korean and Vietnam wars). Included are biographies of the major and lesser-known American personalities of the era, from the presidents who formulated foreign policy and therefore directed the course of the Cold War (Harry Truman through George Bush) to the activists who often opposed them (A. J. Muste, the Berrigan brothers); from policy makers (John Foster Dulles, Henry L. Stimson) to civil rights leaders (Jesse Jackson, Martin Luther King, Jr.); from the infamous (Alger Hiss, Julius and Ethel Rosenberg) to the respected (Henry Cabot Lodge, Ellsworth Bunker); from the newsmakers (Jane Fonda, Jerry Rubin) to the news reporters (Walter Cronkite, Edward R. Murrow).

In addition, other entries cover the groups that often wielded power and influence, both publicly (American Civil Liberties Union, House Un-American Activities Committee) and behind the scenes (Central Intelligence Agency, Federal Bureau of Investigation), as well as certain key events that affected the nation as a whole (Kent State massacre, Watergate) or on specific groups of affected people (the COINTELPRO operation, blacklisting). Also covered are many of the catchphrases that marked the Cold War decades ("America, love it or leave it," "Hell, no, we won't go!") and broad definitions of many of the words and terms that characterized the Cold War era (flexible response, pacification, civil disobedience).

The Cold War officially came to an end years ago, but its effects live on in the American consciousness. For the student who must research notable events or personalities of the time, or for the reader who simply wishes to refresh his or her memory, this encyclopedia provides a previously unavailable resource that will serve as a springboard to further research and discussion about an era that shaped a nation.

ENCYCLOPEDIA OF
COLD WAR POLITICS

Acheson, Dean (1893–1971)

U.S. secretary of state from 1949 to 1953 and adviser to four presidents, Dean Acheson was a principal creator of U.S. foreign policy in the Cold War period. Following his graduation from Yale University and Harvard Law School, he became a private secretary to Supreme Court justice Louis Brandeis. In 1921, he joined a law firm in Washington, D.C., where he stayed for several years before receiving his first government appointment, in 1933, as undersecretary of the Treasury under President Franklin D. Roosevelt. In 1941, he joined the Department of State, first as an assistant secretary and subsequently as an undersecretary (1945–47), in which position he provided support for the development of the MARSHALL PLAN.

After securing Senate approval for U.S. membership in the United Nations in 1945, Acheson, who already had a strong distrust of the Soviet Union, developed a fervent anticommunist attitude that would strongly influence how he later conducted foreign policy. His shaping of the TRUMAN DOCTRINE in 1947 was developed to counter anticipated Soviet expansion in the Middle East. Subsequent to being appointed secretary of state under President Harry TRUMAN in 1949, Acheson promoted the formation of the NORTH ATLANTIC TREATY ORGANIZATION (NATO), which had also been specifically designed for the CONTAINMENT of communism.

Acheson became embroiled in controversy after the entry of Communist China into the KOREAN WAR and the subsequent removal of Douglas MACARTHUR as commander of U.S. forces in Korea. He established the policy of nonrecognition of China, and promoted aid to Chiang Kai-shek's Nationalist Party in Taiwan (although he also suffered some public criticism when China succumbed to communist control in 1949). He also helped to supply military assistance to the French colonial regime in Indochina in their battle against Ho Chi Minh.

Despite his anticommunist stance, Acheson was strongly supportive of his State Department subordinates during the McCarthy congressional hearings, refusing to fire any under suspicion—including Alger HISS, who was later convicted of perjury. Because of this, Senator Joseph MCCARTHY accused Acheson of shielding communists within the State Department.

After leaving the State Department in 1953, Acheson returned to private law practice, but also continued to serve as a foreign policy adviser to Presidents John F. KENNEDY, Lyndon JOHNSON, and Richard NIXON. Acheson's recommendation that Johnson pull

1

Dean Acheson is sworn in as secretary of state as President Harry Truman looks on. (TRUMAN LIBRARY)

U.S. forces out of Vietnam helped to halt U.S. bombing there in 1968. (During the speech in which he announced the bombing halt, Johnson also stunned the nation by declining to seek reelection).

Acheson's book describing his years in the State Department, *Present at the Creation,* won the Pulitzer Prize for history in 1970.

Agee, Philip (1939–   )

Philip Agee is a former CENTRAL INTELLIGENCE AGENCY (CIA) officer whose exposure of covert operations conducted by the CIA has gained him both applause and censure. The son of a successful Southern businessman, Agee was raised as a Catholic in a conservative environment. He graduated from the University of Notre Dame in 1956, and in 1957 was recruited to become an intelligence operative for the CIA. From 1960 to 1968, he operated in Ecuador, Uruguay, and Mexico, during which time he became disillusioned with U.S. policy in Latin America. He resigned from the CIA in 1968, and three years later began a crusade against the agency that took the form of lectures, magazines, and books in which he exposed covert operations and misconduct by CIA officers. Agee described the CIA as "nothing more than the secret police of American capitalism, plugging up leaks in the political dam . . . so that shareholders of U.S. companies operating in poor countries can continue enjoying their ripoff." His best-known book, *Inside the Company: CIA Diary,* created a sensation when it was published in

1975. In it he described details of various agency abuses, especially in Latin America.

Agee's exposé of the CIA and its operatives, as well as his alleged contacts with various foreign governments, led to his public censure and persecution. He fled the United States and lived in several European countries, including Great Britain, from which he was deported in 1977 for national security reasons. For a brief time, he returned to the United States and attempted a career as a campus lecturer, but the effort was not successful. He currently lives with his wife in Germany, where he continues his campaign against the U.S. government and his avowed support of the goals of COMMUNISM.

Agnew, Spiro (1918–1996)

Spiro Theodore Agnew was the 39th vice president of the United States, serving under Richard M. NIXON. He was also the second person in the history of the office to resign (the first being John C. Calhoun, in 1832), and the first to do so in disgrace.

Agnew was born in Baltimore, Maryland, the son of a Greek immigrant who had shortened his name from Anagnostopoulos. He earned his law degree from the University of Baltimore in 1947; 10 years later, he began his career in political office with his appointment to the Baltimore County Executive Zoning Board of Appeals. He was elected governor of Maryland in 1967. Agnew had little public recognition when Richard Nixon chose him to be the vice presidential candidate in 1968, but he quickly established himself as a memorably blunt orator. (He called Nixon's opponent, Hubert HUMPHREY (a Democrat), "squishy soft on Communism.") After his election, he achieved notoriety for his colorful speeches supporting Nixon's policies in Vietnam and attacking radical dissidents and members of the MEDIA. In 1973, he faced federal indictments on charges of extortion, bribery, and income tax violations incurred during his tenure as Maryland's governor. On October 10, 1973, he pleaded nolo contendere to a single count of failing to report income on his tax return. That same day, declaring it to be in the national interest, he resigned as vice president. He was fined $10,000 and sentenced to three years of unsupervised probation. Agnew was disbarred in 1974, after which he became a foreign business consultant to private U.S. firms. He published several books, and his 1980 book, *Go Quietly . . . Or Else,* provides a defense of his political career, in addition to exposing and attacking certain officials of the Nixon administration.

Allen, Richard (1936–)

Richard Allen has long been active in right-wing politics, having been a foreign policy adviser to Richard NIXON, Ronald REAGAN, and the Republican Party, in addition to serving for nearly two years as national security advisor under President Reagan. Allen graduated from the University of Notre Dame and subsequently received his doctorate from the University of Munich. During the 1960s, he worked at the Center for Strategic and International Studies at Georgetown University, and the Hoover Institution on War, Revolution, and Peace at Stanford University. In 1966, he published *Peace or Peaceful Coexistence.*

Allen became involved in politics in 1968, when he was recruited to be a foreign policy coordinator during Richard Nixon's campaign for president. In that capacity, he met with Henry KISSINGER (then working for Nelson ROCKEFELLER) to help draft a position on the VIETNAM WAR for the Republican National Convention. When Kissinger was appointed national security advisor under President Nixon, Allen became one of the former's principal associates. However, the two men clashed, both personally and professionally, and Allen left the NATIONAL SECURITY COUNCIL to become a deputy to international economic aide Peter Peterson. Allen would later say that Kissinger had "open[ed] the bowels of the administration to the NEW LEFT."

After leaving Nixon's administration, Allen founded Potomac International, a firm that advised foreign businesses and governments on Washington interactions, and he continued to remain active in right-wing politics. He served as chairman of the Republican National Committee's intelligence subcommittee, in which capacity he conducted analyses of the threat from the Soviet Union. He also helped to found the COMMITTEE ON THE PRESENT DANGER, a group strongly opposed to any cuts in military spending and to SALT II (see STRATEGIC ARMS LIMITATION TREATIES). In 1978, he began advising Ronald Reagan on issues of national security. Subsequently, in 1980, he participated in drafting the foreign policy plank for the Republican National Convention, focusing on what he described as the "unilateral disarming of our intelligence agencies" and the need to strengthen rather than weaken U.S. intelligence overseas.

Allen resigned as presidential candidate Reagan's chief foreign policy adviser when the *Wall Street Journal* accused him of using his connections at the White House to gain contracts and political favors for friends and himself. However, a supportive Reagan appointed Allen to his staff immediately after the election, and in December 1980 named him national security advisor. In this capacity, Allen's strongly hawkish viewpoints proved to be at odds with other members of the Reagan administration, particularly Secretary of State Alexander HAIG. He and Haig clashed frequently, and in 1981 Haig made an announcement that a White House aide was engaging in "guerrilla warfare" against him; it was widely supposed that he was referring to Allen. Later that same year, reports surfaced that Allen had allegedly accepted gifts from Japanese journalists and businessmen but had not reported them; furthermore, he had reportedly continued to be paid for work from Potomac International. As a result, shortly before Christmas in 1981, he went on "administrative leave." He resigned as national security advisor on January 4, 1982, even though investigations by the Justice Department and the White House failed to determine any wrongdoing on Allen's part. After that, he continued to serve on a part-time basis as a foreign policy adviser to both President Reagan and to the Republican National Committee, in addition to which he founded a private consulting firm.

Alliance for Progress

The Alliance for Progress was the name given to a program developed by President John F. KENNEDY to promote and develop U.S. relations with Latin American countries (all except Cuba) and provide support for economic development and the democratic process in those countries. The name was originally derived from the Spanish word *alianza.* As Kennedy envisioned it, the Alliance would be "a vast cooperative effort, unparalleled in magnitude and nobility of purpose, to satisfy the basic needs of the American people for homes, work and land, health and schools." In essence, the idea was to aid in the implementation of social and agrarian reforms that would make the Latin American nations more appealing to foreign investors and thus ward off the possible spread of Castro-style communism into those countries. The program was informally launched by President Kennedy on March 13, 1961, but received official recognition in August that year at a special meeting of the Inter-American Economic and Social Council in Punta del Este, Uruguay. In time its lofty goals became lost in a maze of criticism, bureaucratic red tape, and squabbling, both in the U.S. Congress and in the countries the program was meant to benefit. Thus, although the program was extended indefinitely in 1965, appropriations for the Alliance gradually declined throughout President Lyndon B. JOHNSON's administration. By 1971, although it was acknowledged that there had been general improvements in economic growth, health, education, and housing, no clear or tangible results supporting the program's original ambitious goals could be identified, and the Alliance for Progress was finally phased out entirely.

Amerasia affair   See SERVICE, John Stewart.

"America, love it or leave it"

A popular catchphrase of the 1960s, this was the favorite response of those in the conservative right (especially the "HARD HATS" and members of the AMERICAN LEGION) to students and liberals who protested American involvement in the VIETNAM WAR. "America, love it or leave it" was also used as an attack on anybody who criticized the government and its decisions. Those who loved their country supported it; others could and should go elsewhere.

American Civil Liberties Union (ACLU)

The ACLU is a nonprofit organization dedicated to serving the public interest by protecting and preserving individual rights and civil liberties according to the Bill of Rights. Their mandate states: "To understand the ACLU's purpose, it is important to distinguish between the Constitution and the Bill of Rights. The Constitution . . . authorizes the government to act. The Bill of Rights limits that authority." The ACLU is the best-known human rights advocacy group in the United States. Nonpartisan in orientation, the ACLU does not provide direct litigation services per se, but does step in with legal assistance whenever there is a perception that individual rights are being violated or the civil liberties of groups are being abused. This wide-ranging scope of purpose has frequently provoked controversy for the organization, as it did during the CIVIL RIGHTS MOVEMENT of the 1950s and 1960s, when many conservatives (and, later, members of the NEW RIGHT) associated the ACLU with leftist causes. The implication of such accusations as "card-carrying member of the ACLU" was that the organization was procommunist. Some years later, when the ACLU defended the American Nazi Party's right to march in Skokie, Illinois, even more controversy ensued.

Originally called the National Civil Liberties Union, the ACLU was founded in 1917 (by A. J. MUSTE, among others) and renamed itself in 1920. Its original stated goal was to protect the free speech rights of U.S. citizens who openly criticized American participation in World War I, but this position was eventually expanded to include the protection of all liberties guaranteed by the Bill of Rights. There is a national board to determine the organization's overall policy and state affiliates that are self-determining. The services provided by the ACLU focus on litigation (it has filed more briefs in Supreme Court cases than any other organization), lobbying for legislation that preserves civil rights and against legislation that violates them, and educating the public by way of advertising and publications. The ACLU currently boasts more than 275,000 members; its national headquarters is located in New York City.

American Friends Service Committee (AFSC)

The American Friends Service Committee (AFSC) is an organization founded in 1917 by the Religious Society of Friends (Quakers) to promote peace and justice throughout the world through acts of public service and education. Although Quaker-based, the AFSC involves people of many religious faiths in its goals of overcoming violence and injustice. According to its mission statement, the organization "seeks in its works and witness to draw on the transforming power of love, human and divine. This AFSC community works to transform conditions and relationships both in the world and in ourselves which threaten to overwhelm what is precious in human beings. . . . We believe that ultimately goodness can prevail over evil, and oppression in all its many forms can give way."

The AFSC was originally founded as a way for CONSCIENTIOUS OBJECTORS to make contributions to the war effort without enlisting, specifically by aiding civilian victims of World War I. The organization has grown since then to focus on goals and missions that encompass such issues as peace advocacy, demilitarization, economic and social justice, aiding those in poverty, overcoming the problems of minority groups, and supporting and guiding the world's youth. Throughout the years, the AFSC has participated in many arenas where the cause of peace and the protection of human rights are paramount. It was an especially strong presence during the CIVIL RIGHTS MOVEMENT of the 1950s and 1960s. Among its many proponents have been renowned pacifists. A. J. MUSTE and journalist Drew PEARSON. In 1947, the AFSC was awarded the Nobel Peace Prize jointly with its British counterpart, the Friends Service Council.

American Legion

The American Legion is an organization dedicated to the concerns of U.S. veterans of war. With a membership of over 2.7 million, it is the largest such organization in the world. Created by an act of Congress following World War I, in September 1919, the American Legion focuses on four primary goals: the rehabilitation of veterans, the welfare of children, issues of national security, and the concept of AMERICANISM. To accomplish its goals, the legion employs a number of tactics, including legislative lobbying (their work resulted in the formation of the Veterans Administration in 1930 and the GI Bill of Rights in 1944), community services, fund-raising, advertising, public relations work, and educational activities (including scholarships). The organization is steadfast in its support of U.S. foreign policy and promotes the maintenance of armed and ready military troops to ensure an adequate CIVIL DEFENSE for the nation.

The Legion has frequently been associated with the conservative right due to what some see as its "*America,* LOVE IT OR LEAVE IT" attitude. It has also been a supporter and promoter of the RESERVE OFFICER TRAINING CORPS (ROTC); during the VIETNAM WAR, the legion drew the ire of antiwar protestors for its efforts to forestall elimination of Junior ROTC programs. Frequently embroiled in controversy, the American Legion nevertheless remains best known and respected for its many veteran-based services and its fight to protect the rights and needs of the country's war veterans.

Americanism

While *Americanism* can rightly be defined as a word or phrase that expresses an American mood or point of view, in the context of the Cold War it is considered to be an attitude that reflects love and pride in the United States. Although the word has been in use since the 1700s, its current popular concept was first introduced in the 20th century by President Theodore Roosevelt, who said "Americanism means that virtues of courage, honor, justice, truth, sincerity, and hardihood—the virtues that made America." Americanism provides a

basic tenet for the goals of the AMERICAN LEGION, which promotes its principles in the organization's work with the country's youth and in its support of patriotic causes.

Americans for Democratic Action (ADA)

Americans for Democratic Action (ADA) is the oldest and perhaps best-known liberal political organization, its stated aim being a dedication "to individual liberty and building economic and social justice at home and abroad." The ADA was founded in 1947 by a number of prominent political, union, and intellectual figures of the day, including Hubert HUMPHREY, Eleanor ROOSEVELT, Walter REUTHER, Arthur SCHLESINGER, Jr., and John Kenneth GALBRAITH. In its representation of liberal causes and ideologies, the ADA has been actively involved in legislative lobbying, building coalitions for social and economic change, and leading many public fights having to do with domestic and foreign issues, as well as the environment. Although intended to be a nonpartisan organization, it is associated with the Democratic Party because of its goals and liberal leanings. In 1948, the ADA lobbied successfully for the adoption of a civil rights plank in the Democrats' electoral platform; this led the Democrats to take the lead in civil rights legislation over the next several decades. The ADA has also taken prominent (and sometimes unpopular) stands on such issues as American policy during the VIETNAM WAR, impeaching President Richard M. NIXON during the WATERGATE scandal, women's liberation, workers' rights (including increase of the minimum wage), and federal tax policy.

Anderson, Jack (1922–)

Jack Northman Anderson, a newspaper columnist and investigative reporter, started his career as a Mormon missionary in the southern United States (1941–44). In 1945, he worked for a brief time as a war correspondent. Two years later, he joined the staff of "Washington Merry-Go-Round," the muckraking column written by Drew PEARSON. He and Pearson collaborated on a book, *The Case Against Congress,* in 1968. After Pearson died in 1969, Anderson took over the column. In 1972, he won a Pulitzer Prize for national reporting after he exposed U.S. intervention in the India-Pakistan War. He was also lauded for his reports on the WATERGATE affair. However, he drew criticism for his treatment of Senator Thomas Eagleton, George

MCGOVERN's vice presidential candidate, in 1972. He also aroused the ire of the Nixon administration when he printed the name of an overseas intelligence source, prompting G. Gordon LIDDY to volunteer to assassinate the columnist. In addition to his journalistic activities, Anderson has written several books, including *The Anderson Papers* (1973) and *Alice in Blunderland* (1983).

Anderson, John (1922–)

John Bayard Anderson was a politician best known for his unsuccessful independent run for the U.S. presidency in 1980. He graduated from the University of Illinois in 1942, then continued his studies there, earning a law degree in 1946. He subsequently received another law degree in 1949 from Harvard Law School. Anderson entered the foreign service in 1952. In 1956, he began his career in Illinois state politics when he won election as the state's attorney in Winnebago County. He was elected to Congress in 1960. From 1969 to 1979, he served as chairman of the House Republican Conference. He was one of the first Republicans to call for Richard NIXON's resignation in the wake of the WATERGATE scandal. In 1979, he declared his candidacy for president and withdrew from any reelection bids for the House of Representatives after having served 10 terms. Although he lost the Republican nomination to Ronald REAGAN, Anderson ran as an independent candidate and gained national prominence for his views, which differed greatly from those of other Republicans in his unorthodox stances on such issues as the social security system. He managed to win about 7% of the popular vote. His books include *Between Two Worlds: A Congressman's Choice* (1970) and *Vision and Betrayal in America* (1975).

antiwar movement

Of all the major developments of the Cold War years, the antiwar movement may have had the greatest impact on the national consciousness. Effectively, it forced the U.S. government into a change in foreign policy. Peace activists had long been a part of the American political scene (see CONSCIENTIOUS OBJECTORS), but it was during the 1960s and early 1970s that their movement achieved an unparalleled influence on ordinary citizens and political leaders alike. In fact, the demonstrations for peace and clashes (often violent) between authorities and antiwar activists dur-

Military police hold back antiwar demonstrators at the entrance to the Pentagon. (NARA STILL PHOTOS DIVISION)

ing this time were in themselves a sort of war, albeit one that was fought on the home front.

The antiwar movement was composed of many differing factions that were all united in their opposition to the VIETNAM WAR. This opposition stemmed from a growing public disillusionment with decisions made and actions taken by the U.S. government that seemed to many to accomplish nothing other than losing American lives to a hopeless cause. The movement was also closely tied to the antinuclear movement, which was opposed to the creation of weapons of mass destruction that threatened global security. Earliest leaders of the movement included such prominent citizens as Dr. Benjamin Spock, the popular pediatrician and author, who was a member of the National Committee for a Sane Nuclear Policy (SANE). In 1959, the Student Peace Union (SPU) was formed, sparking the initial wave of discontent on college campuses that would reach its apogee 10 years later. The goals and activities of the SPU (which disbanded in 1964) would quickly give way, however, to the better-known and more controversial STUDENTS FOR A DEMOCRATIC SOCIETY (SDS), founded in 1960. The early mission of the SDS centered around the goals of the CIVIL RIGHTS MOVEMENT rather than on American involvement in Vietnam, which had not yet became a major issue. However, the focus of the SDS did begin to change with the emergence of the Free Speech movement, which also arose initially out of civil rights activism. The Free Speech movement began in late 1964 at the University of California at Berkeley as a consequence of students asserting their rights to engage in political protests and activities. As this ran counter to established university policy at the time, clashes between students and administrators inevitably ensued. Consequently, proponents of Free Speech began emerging on college campuses around the country, and were soon turning their attention to other major issues in addition to civil rights, particularly as regarded the U.S. government.

The antiwar movement coalesced in February 1965, when the United States commenced widespread bombing in North Vietnam. The SDS immediately began organizing a series of SIT-INS and demonstrations protesting the government's actions. Teachers soon followed suit, and before long "teach-ins" were being held to provide previously unreleased data on the war in Vietnam to students and citizens. In April 1965, an SDS-organized march on Washington brought together approximately 20,000 protesters, an unexpectedly high

number that galvanized the movement. More demonstrations began to crop up around the country, with the majority of the activity taking place on college campuses. Meanwhile, civil rights leaders such as Martin Luther KING, Jr., openly expressed their support for the antiwar movement, giving it even greater credibility.

In October 1967, antiwar activists gained widespread MEDIA attention with a two-day march on the Pentagon. All around the country, draft card burnings and massive demonstrations emphasized increasing public discontent with government policy. By early 1968, even President Lyndon JOHNSON had begun to listen to members of his administration who had become opposed to the war. Members of the NEW RIGHT remained unequivocal in their support of U.S. foreign policy, and many believed the antiwar protests were hurting the country, both domestically and internationally; in essence, they felt that if one was antiwar,

Protesters against the Vietnam War demonstrated in Wichita, Kansas, in 1967. (NARA CENTRAL PLAINS)

then one was anti-American. All the same, public sentiment by and large seemed to have gone against the war—and against the president. This became particularly true after the TET OFFENSIVE in late January of 1968. The horrors of that period, which were televised and broadcast into American homes, lent credence to the antiwar movement's message and irrevocably turned the tide of public opinion. Many political leaders now came out firmly against the war and government officials began discussing options for bringing about a "peace with honor."

The movement itself, however, began to suffer from a negative public image brought on by repeated, often violent, clashes with authority figures, as well as its association with HIPPIES and other anti-ESTABLISHMENT figures of the liberal COUNTERCULTURE with whom many mainstream Americans were decidedly uncomfortable. After President Richard NIXON took office (1969) and began implementing plans to de-escalate the war, the antiwar movement lost a certain amount of steam—but regained it in 1970, when U.S. troops invaded Cambodia, prompting renewed, more vigorous protests and demonstrations. (Early that same year, news of the My Lai massacre in Vietnam [see William CALLEY] had been released to the great outrage of the American public.) In May, the citizenry was further outraged when National Guard troops killed an antiwar protester at Kent State University in Ohio. (See KENT STATE MASSACRE.) The Nixon administration was not helped any by the publication of the PENTAGON PAPERS in 1971. They revealed many previously undisclosed details of the war, as well as the lies that had been told to American citizens, particularly with regard to the TONKIN GULF INCIDENTS that had supplied the United States with an excuse for escalating the war. All these events helped to galvanize the antiwar movement once again, and the pressure of public opinion became so great that President Nixon eventually bowed to it. In January of 1973, an armistice was signed and the withdrawal of U.S. troops from Vietnam began. Were it not for the energetic and singleminded movement that effectively shaped the public mind and forced the government into action, the outcome of the Vietnam War might very well have been quite different.

appeasement

An unpopular word among conservatives, *appeasement* denotes the policy of giving in to the demands of aggressors. The net result of appeasement is usually more demands and increased pressure from the enemy, which threaten the security of a nation. During the Cold War, while some Americans promoted appeasement as a means of avoiding nuclear confrontations and thus maintaining peace, others decried it, feeling that it would enfeeble the United States and its position as a world power. In time, the word came to be associated with weakness and fear, and was often used pejoratively by conservative leaders, among them Richard NIXON, in their arguments against liberal, antiwar positions.

Army-McCarthy Hearings   See MCCARTHY, Joseph.

Atlantic Charter

The Atlantic Charter was an informal document signed by Winston Churchill and Franklin D. Roosevelt in 1941 that later formed a partial base for the UNITED NATIONS Charter. The original intent of the agreement was to provide a set of principles that would serve as a guide to the Allies during their fight against Adolf Hitler and Nazism in World War II. Consisting of eight clauses, it encompassed such issues as the right of self-determination for the allied nations and "abandonment of the use of force" following the war. Signed before the United States had officially entered the war, the Atlantic Charter helped to ease the concerns of American citizens about what seemed to be eventual U.S. involvement in battle. It served effectively as propaganda against the Axis powers and its principles were endorsed within the United Nations Declaration issued on January 1, 1942, and frequently invoked after the war as a means of affirming the U.S. position on world affairs. As late as 1954, President Dwight D. EISENHOWER was restating the ideals of the Atlantic Charter in his formulation of foreign policy.

atomic bomb

The development of the atomic bomb in the 1940s would change the course of history and set the stage for the arms race of the Cold War that followed. A weapon of massive destructive power resulting from the fission (breaking in two) of atomic nuclei, the atomic bomb developed from research that was first begun in Germany in the late 1930s, when two physicists made the observation that a neutron could cause fission in the nucleus of a uranium atom. This discovery very quickly led to more breakthroughs by scientists around the world and the rapid publication of papers sharing some revolutionary findings in nuclear fission and atomic chain reactions. The potential uses of the technical advances being developed were clear, especially given the impending war in Europe. The race was on to develop an atomic bomb.

With the commencement of World War Il, the United States and Great Britain began to suppress publication of any new atomic research in an effort to prevent the Germans from gaining information that might assist them in building a bomb. Meanwhile, the U.S. government secretly organized a group of top scientists to research and build an atomic bomb; their mission was named the Manhattan Project, after the Manhattan Engineer District set up by the Army Corps of Engineers to construct the plants that would produce the necessary materials for the project. At first, three government-sponsored laboratories—at Columbia University, the University of Chicago, and the University of California—carried on the research that resulted in a decision to develop three major processes for producing fissionable materials. At that point, the project became centralized in a special laboratory at Los Alamos, New Mexico, for the purpose of designing and assembling the bomb under the supervision of J. Robert OPPENHEIMER. Meanwhile, Enrico Fermi directed the first self-sustaining atomic chain reaction in Chicago on December 2, 1942, thus paving the way for the creation of the first atomic bomb. In time, over 100,000 people were to work on the bomb.

Work on the bomb proceeded rapidly, and by February 1945, just before he left for the YALTA CONFERENCE, President Franklin D. Roosevelt was informed that a bomb would be ready for use by August of that year. On July 16, 1945, the first atomic bomb was successfully exploded at a site named Trinity, near Alamogordo, New Mexico. Creating a mushroom-shaped cloud that rose to 35,000 feet, the bomb's force was equivalent to 20,000 tons of TNT, and the devastation to the area around the explosion site was immense. President Harry TRUMAN received news of the explosion at the POTSDAM CONFERENCE, and after consultation with Winston Churchill, decided to issue an ultimatum to Japan to surrender or suffer the consequences.

Japan did not surrender. On August 6, 1945, a U.S. bomber bearing the name *Enola Gay* exploded a 15-kiloton atomic bomb over Hiroshima. Three days later, a 20-kiloton bomb was released over Nagasaki. The two cities were decimated and approximately 110,000

First successful test of the atomic bomb—Alamogordo, New Mexico, July 1945. (NARA STILL PHOTOS DIVISION)

people were killed, with injuries to thousands more. Within days, the Japanese government had surrendered and the war was finally over.

Truman's decision to drop the two bombs would be examined in detail over the years to come, but the fact remains that it brought about a quick conclusion to a war that could have dragged on for much longer. It also demonstrated the massive power and capability of atomic weaponry to the extent that no atomic bombs have been used in war since 1945. Indeed, many central points of discussion throughout the period of the Cold War have focused on the need to avoid using atomic bombs at all costs, as the danger they present to the safety of the entire world is too great to be ignored.

Nevertheless, development and testing of nuclear weaponry continued. Ironically, it was learned that the Germans had never developed a bomb, although U.S. fear of their doing so had been the primary motivation behind the Manhattan Project. However, shortly after the end of World War II, the Soviet Union successfully exploded its first atomic bomb, becoming the second superpower with nuclear capabilities and setting the arms race in motion. In 1946, the United States conducted "Operation Crossroads," a series of atomic tests in the Bikini atoll, a western section of the Marshall Islands located in the Pacific Ocean. Natives of the islands were evacuated and on July 1, 1946, a 20-kiloton bomb was exploded over a fleet of 75 empty and obsolete Japanese and American vessels. Damage to the ships was overwhelming. On July 25, a second bomb was exploded over 100 vessels. A column of radioactive water and steam rose nearly a mile into the air, several ships were sunk, and remarkably high levels of radioactivity were reported throughout the target area. The long-lasting effects of these explosions were such that island natives were not allowed to return until the late 1960s, only to be evacuated again in 1978, when it was determined that radiation levels were still too high for the islands to be habitable.

The design and force of atomic bombs have changed greatly since the 1940s, and humankind has found ways to use nuclear research in non-military areas like industry and medicine. Nevertheless, the words *atomic* and *nuclear* will remain forever associated with bombs, and many countries still engage in such research to develop their own bombs. In addition to the United States and Russia, France, Great Britain, China, India, and Pakistan have all built atomic bombs, and many more countries are now following suit. See also HYDROGEN BOMB.

An atomic cloud forms over the Bikini atoll. (NARA STILL PHOTOS DIVISION)

Atomic Energy Commission (AEC)

The Atomic Energy Commission (AEC) was the original agency established in 1947 by the federal government to monitor the development and use of weapons of mass destruction, as well as the disposal of nuclear materials. It was formed under the tenets of the Atomic Energy Act, the idea being that regulation of nuclear weaponry should be kept out of the hands of the military and in the control of civilians, to ensure that these weapons were not misused or abused in any way. The AEC reported directly to the president of the United States and was frequently embroiled in public debate when it made controversial decisions about what could or could not be revealed, not just to the American public but also to the president. The AEC was headed by political leaders and scientists; most notable were David LILIENTHAL (the first chairman) and J. Robert OPPENHEIMER, who for a time chaired the AEC's General Advisory Committee. (Oppenheimer later resigned when his opposition to the development of a hydrogen bomb was ignored.) The AEC was abolished in October 1974, and was superseded by the NUCLEAR REGULATORY COMMISSION.

Atoms for Peace

Atoms for Peace is a program whose main goal has been to engender a cooperative attitude among the world's nations in order to harness peaceful ways to use atomic energy. It was hoped that the arms race would be kept in check by the program's idealistic spirit. First proposed by President Dwight D. EISENHOWER in 1953, Atoms for Peace became a reality in 1954, with the creation of the Atomic Energy Act. As a result of this program, the United States negotiated numerous agreements with other nations that led to the development of peaceful uses of the atom in diverse areas, including medical research, agriculture, business, and technology. Atoms for Peace has encouraged the exchange of information and resources among cooperating nations, and has also paved the way for the establishment of such organizations as the INTERNATIONAL ATOMIC ENERGY AGENCY (IAEA), the European Nuclear Energy Agency (ENEA), and the Inter-American Nuclear Energy Commission (IANEC).

Baker, James Addison III (1930–)

The son of a lawyer from Houston, Texas, James Baker was a prominent government official and political manager who rose through numerous important posts in the Republican administrations of the 1970s and 1980s to eventually become U.S. secretary of state (1989–92).

Baker was a partner in a major Houston law firm when, in 1970, his longtime friend, George BUSH, asked him to run his campaign for the U.S. Senate in 1970. Bush lost, but the experience whetted Baker's appetite for politics. He subsequently served as under secretary of commerce in the administration of President Gerald FORD; as Ford's campaign manager in the 1976 presidential election; as director of George Bush's campaign for the 1980 nomination, and subsequently as a senior adviser to Ronald REAGAN's campaign; as White House chief of staff under Reagan; and as secretary of the treasury, a post to which he was appointed in 1985. In 1988, he again served as Bush's campaign manager, this time seeing his friend elected to the presidency. The campaign Baker had so carefully strategized benefited in no small measure from television advertising that caused voters to doubt Democratic candidate Michael DUKAKIS's qualifications as a poten-

tial commander-in-chief. (A spot featuring Dukakis riding inexpertly in a tank was particularly damaging.)

Baker was appointed secretary of state in the Bush administration. In this role, he proved to be influential in the reunification of East and West Germany in 1990, helping the United States to come to agreement with the Soviet Union on that issue. He subsequently assisted the direction of an international coalition opposed to Iraq's invasion of Kuwait (1990–91).

Baker resigned as secretary of state in 1992 in order to take on his old post of White House chief of staff, while also directing Bush's reelection campaign. After Bush's loss to Bill Clinton, Baker returned to private law practice and became a political consultant.

Ball, George Wildman (1909–1974)

George Ball was a lawyer and government official whose most noteworthy tenure was as undersecretary of state from 1961 to 1966, during the administrations of John F. KENNEDY and Lyndon B. JOHNSON. After earning his degree from Northwestern University, he practiced law in Chicago and became a supporter of Illinois governor Adlai Stevenson. His involvement in politics intensified when he served as national director of Volunteers for Stevenson during the presidential campaigns of 1952, 1956, and 1960. He received a post as undersecretary of state for economic affairs in the Kennedy administration, but was quickly promoted, and was a key adviser to Kennedy during the CUBAN MISSILE CRISIS of 1962.

Ball adamantly opposed increasing U.S. involvement in the VIETNAM WAR, telling both Presidents Kennedy and Johnson that a guerrilla war there could not be won. With the passage of time, he has emerged as one of the most important early opponents of the military buildup in Southeast Asia. His advice, however, was ignored, and in time the original 400 "advisers" sent to Vietnam escalated to some 500,000 U.S. ground troops. Ball resigned his post in 1966 to return to private law practice, but was called back to serve as U.S. ambassador to the UNITED NATIONS in 1968. He served as a principal foreign policy adviser to Democratic presidential nominee Hubert HUMPHREY in 1968; after Humphrey's defeat, Ball earned a reputation as one of the most vocal critics of President Nixon's Vietnam policy. In 1971, the publication of the PENTAGON PAPERS revealed the full extent of his early approach to Vietnam as a policymaker.

Ball published five books, including *Diplomacy for a Crowded World* (1976) and *Error and Betrayal in Lebanon* (1984).

Bay of Pigs invasion

Also called the "Bay of Pigs fiasco," the CIA-planned invasion of Cuba proved to be a disaster for newly elected president John F. KENNEDY, even though it was originally conceived during Dwight D. EISENHOWER's administration. In hopes of overthrowing the communist regime of Fidel Castro, the CENTRAL INTELLIGENCE AGENCY secretly trained over 1,300 Cuban refugees in Central America for an armed invasion of Cuba, which took place on April 17, 1961. The force was transported to the Bay of Pigs, on the south coast of Cuba, in American vessels accompanied by destroyers. At the last minute, President Kennedy rescinded a plan to provide air cover, which contributed to the disaster that followed. After landing, the Cubans had to force their way through the swamps covering the Peninsula de Zapata, giving Castro enough time to assemble a large military force to meet and conquer the would-be invaders, of whom 90 were killed and the rest captured; an uprising of the Cuban people in support of the invasion, which the CIA had been counting

on, never occurred. The outcome was calamitous for U.S. public relations and would only be set aright by Kennedy's cool handling of the CUBAN MISSILE CRISIS a year and a half later. Meanwhile, the prisoners taken by Castro's army during the invasion were ransomed in December 1962 for pharmaceutical supplies worth $53 million.

Berlin blockade

A key event of the Cold War, the Soviet Union's blockade of Berlin and the subsequent airlift of supplies into the city had its roots in the postwar question of what to do with Germany. The answer—which was determined at the POTSDAM CONFERENCE of 1945—was to divide the country into four zones, each to be occupied independently by the Soviet Union, France, Great Britain, and the United States. Although technically ruled by all four nations jointly, the city of Berlin lay completely within the Soviet sector of the country.

There were problems from the start of the arrangement, primarily of a political and ideological nature, and over the next three years a widening gulf formed between the Soviet Union and the other powers. In February 1948, the three democracies met in London without inviting the Soviets or informing them what the meeting was about, despite repeated demands to disclose the contents of the talks. The following month, in protest, the Soviet Union withdrew from a meeting of the Allied Control Council for Germany, effectively ending the governing partnership. The Soviets immediately began to impose regulations on persons entering and leaving Berlin, including military personnel. As a result, tensions mounted and then intensified when the agenda of the London Conference was finally revealed in early June. Although it was in direct violation of the Potsdam agreement, the allied nations had resolved to include Germany in the provisions of the MARSHALL PLAN and to create an independent West Germany with its own constitution and a stronger economy. Soviet ire was further aroused when, on June 18, the Allies announced plans to implement a currency reform in their sectors, essentially uniting the western part of the country against the communist-controlled east. To the Soviets, these moves signaled the end of joint control and the formation of an independent German state, which they opposed for fear of Germany's rearming and becoming a threat once again. On June 24, the Soviet Union registered its protest against the Allies by blocking land routes into the city from the west, as well as all rail traffic. On July 1, they officially withdrew from the Kommandatura, the joint council governing Berlin. The Cold War was now in full swing.

The Allied powers discussed making a challenge to the blockade, but it was overruled for fear of starting an undesired conflict. "If our actions should provoke war," said President Harry TRUMAN, "we must be sure that the fault is not ours." Consequently, the Western nations, led by the United States, commenced an airlift of supplies into their part of Berlin as well as a counter-blockade on the Soviet zone. The airlift began on June 25 and continued over the next 11 months. To be successful, 4,000 tons of supplies needed to be transported into Berlin on a daily basis. By the time a third airport was constructed in West Berlin, 600 planes a day were flying in, and near the end of the operation, 900 planes carrying almost 9,000 tons of supplies made deliveries of food, clothing, fuel, and other goods to Berlin citizens. The total number of flights over 11 months eventually reached a staggering 213,000.

On May 12, 1949, with the signing of the New York Agreement, the Soviet Union lifted its blockade of Berlin. By this time, separate governments had been established for the administration of East Berlin (under Soviet control) and West Berlin (under U.S., British, and French control). This was followed by the creation of East Germany (the German Democratic Republic) and West Germany (the Federal Republic of Germany, with its capital in Bonn).

One aftereffect of the Berlin blockade was the spirit of cooperation it engendered in the Allied nations, now bound together by a shared democratic philosophy and so united against the possibility of communist aggression that they would implement any appropriate measures to contain and deter it. This spiritual and political alliance led to the creation of the NORTH ATLANTIC TREATY ORGANIZATION (NATO), something for which the Soviets eventually had a more notorious response: the BERLIN WALL.

Berlin Wall

The Soviet Union's erection of the Berlin Wall in 1961 proved to be one of the defining moments in the Cold War, symbolizing as it did the barriers that lay between communist and democratic nations. After the BERLIN BLOCKADE of 1948–49 and the division of Germany into Soviet-ruled East Germany and Allied-ruled West Germany, German citizens seeking refuge from com-

munist oppression began pouring into West Berlin. By mid-1961, as many as 3.5 million citizens had left East Germany. On August 13, 1961, in an effort to "plug the dike," the Soviets closed all crossings between the east and west sections of Berlin and erected a barrier of trenches and barbed wire, which was soon replaced by a permanent concrete wall capped by barbed wire. Thereafter, all movement between East Germany and West Germany was vigorously monitored.

The building of the Berlin Wall aroused enormous protest and enmity from the Western nations, although no action was taken against it and it soon became an accepted, if detested, part of life in Berlin. It was also the scene of President John F. KENNEDY's last public triumph prior to his assassination. In June 1963 he gave a famous speech to a crowd of German citizens near the Berlin Wall, in which he expressed a spirit of solidarity by declaring "*Ich bin ein Berliner.*" (There was a brief moment of stunned silence before his audience burst into cheers; the reason for this became clear when a literal translation of his statement showed that he had actually said, "I am a sweet doughnut"—a gaffe that could have been avoided had he simply said, "*Ich bin Berliner.*" He meant, of course, to say "I am a Berliner.") Kennedy's speech was a signal for the increased power and prestige of the United States in its role as a world superpower and foe of COMMUNISM. Many years later, in 1987, President Ronald REAGAN foreshadowed the downfall of both the Berlin Wall and the Soviet Union when, in a similarly famous speech, he demanded, "Mr. Gorbachev, tear down this wall." Two years later, in November 1989, the wall came down, and in 1990 Germany became a unified, democratic nation.

Berrigan, Daniel (1921–   )

Daniel Berrigan is an American Jesuit priest and poet best known for his political activism during the 1960s. He is the older brother of Philip BERRIGAN, also a political activist. He chose not to fight during World War II, and instead entered the Jesuit order. After his ordination in 1952, he traveled to France, where he developed an admiration for the militant workers he met there. Upon his return to the United States, he taught at Brooklyn Preparatory School and subsequently at Le Moyne College. He made a second trip to France in 1963, and thereafter he devoted himself to the CIVIL RIGHTS MOVEMENT, the ANTIWAR MOVEMENT, and antipoverty work. In May 1968, he and his brother, along with seven other antiwar protestors, raided a

Selective Service office in Catonsville, Maryland, taking baskets of draft files into a parking lot and burning them with napalm. In 1970, he was sentenced to three years' imprisonment for these activities; attempts by the defense to justify the action by arguing that the war itself was immoral were unsuccessful. To escape punishment, Berrigan became a fugitive, but he was tracked down, captured, and imprisoned, then paroled in 1972. Since then, he has written numerous books, plays, and volumes of poems, as well as his prison memoirs, *Lights On in the House of the Dead* (1974). He also remained active in the peace movement. In 1980, he, his brother, and six other members of the PLOWSHARES MOVEMENT broke into the General Electric plant in King of Prussia, Pennsylvania, where they attempted to damage nose cones and blueprints for

President John F. Kennedy stands on a platform overlooking the Berlin Wall. (KENNEDY LIBRARY)

President Ronald Reagan speaks in front of the Brandenburg Gate at the Berlin Wall. (REAGAN LIBRARY)

nuclear warheads, using both hammers and their own blood. With the rise of AIDS in the 1980s, Berrigan began ministering to AIDS patients.

Berrigan, Philip (1923–)

Philip Francis Berrigan, a former Catholic priest, was a well-known antiwar activist of the 1960s. He and his brother, Daniel BERRIGAN, were part of a family of six sons. Unlike Daniel, Philip enlisted in the army during World War II. His wartime experiences were quite harsh, and he later remembered himself as being "a very good killer who knew no history or morality." After the war, he went to Holy Cross College; he was ordained after graduating in 1950, and subsequently joined the Josephite order. He and his brother were heavily influenced by the work of Dorothy DAY; they became active in the CIVIL RIGHTS MOVEMENT and the ANTIWAR MOVEMENT in the 1960s, joining Day's Catholic Worker movement and founding the Catholic Peace Fellowship. Berrigan was tried and convicted for

destroying Selective Service files in the late 1960s. In 1970, while he was imprisoned, Berrigan was convicted for smuggling mail out of the federal penitentiary at Lewisburg. His convictions were overturned in 1972 and he was paroled in December of that year. He spent his time in prison writing; his published works include *Prison Journals of a Revolutionary Priest* (1970) and *Widen the Prison Gates* (1973). He continues to wage protests against government policies, with his attention largely focused on disarmament. In this regard, he and his brother founded the PLOWSHARES MOVEMENT, with the aim of focusing attention on the continued production of nuclear weapons, despite the diminishment and subsequent end of the Cold War.

"Better dead than red"

This anticommunist slogan first saw life in the late 1950s as "Better red than dead," a catchphrase for the British nuclear disarmament movement. As espoused by philosopher Bertrand Russell, the feeling then was that communist domination was far preferable to annihilation of the human race by means of nuclear weapons, a sentiment in keeping with the hotly debated policy of APPEASEMENT. However, as the Cold War got even colder in the face of increased Soviet aggression, this point of view reversed itself, especially in the United States, where the feeling was such that any alternative was preferable to living in a communist state. "Better dead than red" thus became a maxim often used by the conservative right.

Bikini atoll   See ATOMIC BOMB.

Black Panthers

The Black Panthers were the best known and most prominent of the black liberation groups formed during the civil unrest of the 1960s. Originally dubbed the Black Panther Party for Self-Defense (BPP), the group was originally conceived in Oakland, California, in 1966 by cofounders Huey P. NEWTON and Bobby SEALE as a means of providing protection for black Americans in the nation's ghettos, as well as to counteract racism in the United States, particularly from policemen. The BPP also promoted principles of self-reliance. In pursuit of its goals, the group advocated the right of blacks to patrol neighborhoods, create schools, and bear arms. The Black Panthers were very successful in the beginning, and the party had attracted over 2,000 members by the late 1960s, in addition to forming affiliated chapters around the country.

The BPP very swiftly reached a position of political power and respectability among black Americans, and even brought about the election of Oakland's first black mayor. But erratic leadership, internal disputes over differing viewpoints regarding the use of violence or nonviolence to achieve its aims, and external pressures brought to bear on the organization by such measures as the COINTELPRO operation conducted by the FEDERAL BUREAU OF INVESTIGATION combined to bring about the disintegration of the BPP by the early 1980s.

black power

"Black Power!" was a rallying cry that came to be identified (perhaps unfairly) with the more violent element in the CIVIL RIGHTS MOVEMENT. The phrase had been in use by African Americans for decades, but it was in the 1960s that it became popularized by the likes of black activist Stokely Carmichael and the BLACK PANTHERS. During the 1966 March Against Fear in Mississippi, Carmichael and others began to use the expression in speeches to create a sense of solidarity in their audiences. Other civil rights leaders, such as Martin Luther KING, Jr., recognized the force of the two words, but refused to use it themselves for fear that it might alienate whites whose support they needed for the movement. Indeed, critics were quick to associate "Black Power" with black violence, and the MEDIA caught on to that point of view, which helped to create a negative reaction with the white public as well as dissension within the activist ranks. In time, African Americans fighting for civil rights could be considered as divided into two factions, one whose goals of achieving legal and social equality for blacks was exemplified by the slogan "FREEDOM NOW!", the other whose pent-up frustration with white persecution and impatience with the movement's slow progress was plainly expressed by "Black power!"

blacklisting

Blacklisting is the process of persecuting individuals who have fallen into disfavor by placing their names on a list to identify them as "enemies" of some sort. Persons on a blacklist are generally being punished for something the creator of the blacklist believes they have said or done, and more often than not the blacklist is used as a means of denying them privileges or rights they are otherwise due according to law. While blacklisting can occur in many arenas—business, labor, special interest groups, and political venues—the phrase took on special meaning for government employees and the entertainment industry during the so-called WITCH HUNTS of the McCarthy era. In the 1950s, as Senator Joseph MCCARTHY and the HOUSE UN-AMERICAN ACTIVITIES COMMITTEE conducted special investigations into communist infiltration into the fabric of American politics and society, hundreds of people came under attack for their suspected involvement with the Communist Party or their possible pro-communist sympathies. In many cases, the charges brought against these people were either distorted, exaggerated, or entirely unfounded. Nonetheless, once brought into the spotlight of suspicion, it was difficult if not impossible to prove one's innocence, and as a result, blacklists were created and those affected lost their jobs and, frequently, their reputations. For example, writers who were blacklisted during the McCarthy era, such as novelist and screenwriter Dalton Trumbo, were often forced to resort to subterfuge (using an alias or another writer for "cover") to make a living, or had to switch to new careers to survive. After the anticommunist hysteria began to die down in the late 1950s, the blacklists gradually disappeared, but not before doing irreparable damage to many lives.

Block, Herbert Lawrence (Herblock) (1909–)

Herblock is the pseudonym of Herbert Lawrence Block, a nationally-known editorial cartoonist and Pulitzer Prize winner. Born in Chicago, Illinois, Block attended Lake Forest College from 1927 to 1929, and also studied art on a part-time basis at the Chicago Art Institute. Herblock's first cartoons were published in 1929, in the *Chicago Daily News*. From 1933 to 1943, he worked for the Newspaper Enterprise Association, earning the first of his two Pulitzer Prizes in 1942 (the second was awarded in 1954). He served in the U.S. Army from 1943 to 1945. Upon his discharge, he was hired by the *Washington Post* in 1946. His contributions to the *Post's* editorial page drew great attention and applause, along with harsh reactions from his targets, and helped to gain a wide readership for the paper. The cartoons were of a decidedly liberal bent, attacking injustices in politics and business, as well as other areas affecting public attitudes and opinions. His best-known cartoons in the early 1950s vilified Senator Joseph MCCARTHY and what Herblock viewed as the incipient fascism he promoted. In a famous cartoon, Herblock depicted the GOP elephant being pushed toward a large barrel of tar labeled "McCarthyism." As a result of this, he is given credit for coinage of a term that defined an era.

Herblock won the "Reuben" award for Outstanding Cartoonist of the Year from the National Cartoonists Society in 1957. The attacks on McCarthy helped to define Herblock, as did his similarly pointed images during national debates over the VIETNAM WAR and WATERGATE (and, indeed, in relation to most of the critical events of Richard NIXON's political career). Over the years, Herblock has published numerous collections of his cartoons, as well as an autobiography entitled *Herblock: A Cartoonist's Life* (1993).

bomb shelters

A bomb shelter is a building or other structure designed to protect those inside it from the devastating effects of bombs. They are frequently used in wartime, but the building of civilian bomb shelters became especially

A private basement fallout shelter of the 1950s includes a 14-day supply of food and water, a battery-powered radio, auxiliary light sources, a first aid kit, and sanitary equipment. (NARA STILL PHOTOS DIVISION)

popular during the "red menace" scares of the 1950s, when U.S. citizens lived in seemingly constant fear of nuclear attack from the Soviet Union. Bomb shelters varied in size and construction, depending on the type of protection being sought. An outgrowth of bomb shelters were fallout shelters, which were designed as shields against radioactive fallout and debris.

Bowles, Chester (1901–1986)

Chester Bliss Bowles, a politician and diplomat who was to become well known for his liberal views, began his career as an advertising entrepreneur. After his graduation, in 1924, from Yale University, he worked for a year as a reporter, then took a job as a copywriter. In 1929, he joined forces with William Benton to create the successful advertising company of Benton and Bowles. He sold his interest in the firm in 1941 and went to work in Connecticut's wartime rationing administration, eventually becoming the state's director of price administration. He was appointed general manager of the Federal Price Administration in 1943 by President Franklin D. Roosevelt. After the war, he served as director of the office of economic stabilization for just a few months, resigning in protest over legislative curbs on his authority. He then made an unsuccessful bid for the Democratic nomination for governor of Connecticut, subsequently became a U.S. delegate to the first conference of the UNITED NATIONS Educational, Scientific, and Cultural Organizations, and later served a term as a special assistant to the UN secretary-general (1947–48).

In 1948, his second bid for the governorship met with success, but his bid for reelection in 1950 was defeated, primarily due to his strongly liberal politics. From 1951 to 1953, he served as ambassador to India for President Harry TRUMAN. In this position, he succeeded in securing aid for India through a $54 million POINT FOUR grant. Upon his return to the United States, he was elected in 1953 to the House of Representatives, where he served for three terms. In 1961, he was appointed undersecretary of state by President John F. KENNEDY, who later reappointed him ambassador to India in 1963. He held that post until 1969, during which time he intervened in disputes with Kashmir and China and tried without success to obtain U.S. military aid for India, which ultimately obtained assistance from the Soviet Union.

Bowles retired in 1969. In the course of his life in public service, Bowles wrote numerous books about his experiences as well as various other political treatises stressing his liberal viewpoint. These include his memoirs, *Promises to Keep: My Years in Public Life, 1941–1969* (published in 1971).

Bradlee, Ben (1921–)

Ben Bradlee is a nationally known journalist who, until 1991, was executive editor of the *Washington Post;* he continues to serve as that paper's vice president at large. Bradlee earned his bachelor's degree from Harvard University in 1942, and four years later was hired as a reporter by the *New Hampshire Sunday News.* In 1948, he started reporting for both *Newsweek* and the *Washington Post,* based first in Washington and subsequently in Europe. While working in Washington, he became friends with John F. KENNEDY, then a U.S. senator; they remained close friends until Kennedy's death.

In 1961, Bradlee became a senior editor at the *Washington Post,* then was named managing editor in 1965. He immediately set about to put the *Post* in the same league with the *New York Times* by recruiting distinguished reporters and promoting more in-depth investigative reporting. He was named vice president and executive editor in 1968, dual roles he held for the next 23 years.

Bradlee approved the publication of excerpts from the PENTAGON PAPERS on June 18, 1971, making the *Post* the second newspaper in the nation (after the *New York Times*) to publish the controversial documents describing U.S. policy in Vietnam since the Truman administration. Two years later, the *Post* led the way in uncovering the truth behind the WATERGATE scandal, when Bradlee approved and encouraged the investigations of reporters Bob Woodward and Carl Bernstein into the links between the 1972 burglary at the Democratic National Committee headquarters and the involvement of high-ranking officials in the Nixon administration. For a time, Republican defenders of the White House attacked Bradlee and cited his friendship with President Kennedy as proof that he was using the *Post* in a personal vendetta against the administration. However, the Woodward-Bernstein articles eventually uncovered a damning trail of evidence that led to the Oval Office, resulting in Senate hearings, investigations, and criminal proceedings, and finally forcing President Richard NIXON to resign from office.

Following his retirement as the *Post*'s executive editor in 1991, Bradlee set to work on his memoirs. *A Good Life: Newspapering and Other Adventures* was published in 1995.

Bradley, Omar Nelson (1893–1981)

General Omar Bradley achieved fame for his successful command of the 12th Army Group during World War II, thus ensuring the Allied victory over Germany. A 1915 graduate of the U.S. Military Academy, at West Point, he began his World War II service as commandant of the Infantry School at Fort Benning, Georgia, before going on to command the 82nd and 28th divisions. In 1943, he was made head of the II Corps for the North African campaign. His capture of Bizerte, Tunisia, led to that country's fall and the surrender of more than 250,000 Axis troops. His forces then went on to successfully invade Sicily in August 1943. Later that same year, he was transferred to England and put in command of the U.S. First Army. He was there with his troops when they invaded Normandy and fought German troops on the French mainland, as well as during the symbolic liberation of Paris in August 1944. He was also promoted to command the U.S. 12th Army Group, overseeing the largest force ever placed under an American commander. For the duration of the war, Bradley continued to carry out successful combat operations throughout Europe.

He returned to the United States after the German surrender, and served as administrator of veterans' affairs from 1945 to 1947, then as army chief of staff from 1948 to 1949. In 1949, he was named the first chairman of the

Joint Chiefs of Staff, and thus was one of the most important advisers to President Harry TRUMAN during the very early years of the Cold War. He was promoted to general of the army in 1950. In 1951, he was called to testify before the Senate with regard to the conflict in Korea. Bradley advised against increased military effort, noting that it "would involve us in the wrong war, at the wrong place, at the wrong time and with the wrong enemy." His advice was ignored, and the war escalated.

Bradley retired from the army in 1953, but remained active, primarily in private business concerns. He published his memoirs, *A Soldier's Story*, in 1951. In 1983, a follow-up, *A General's Life*, was published. In addition to his highly successful military career, Bradley achieved the distinction of being a general who was liked and respected by officers and enlisted men alike.

Bridges, Henry Styles (1898–1961)

Henry Styles Bridges was a five-time U.S. senator from New Hampshire who became known for his support of Senator Joseph MCCARTHY as well as other strong conservative stances during the earliest years of the Cold War. A 1918 graduate of the University of Maine, Bridges worked as an agricultural adviser for several years until his election in 1934 as New Hampshire's governor. He was elected to the Senate in 1936 and was an outspoken opponent of the New Deal during the Roosevelt administration. In 1940, he ran for and lost the Republican presidential nomination.

By the time Harry TRUMAN succeeded to the presidency in 1945, Bridges had become a leading conservative and powerful voice in the U.S. Senate. He was a sharp critic of President Truman and pressed for a strong anticommunist stance in foreign policy, believing that the Soviet Union was plotting a worldwide takeover. He succeeded in ending lend-lease supplies to the Soviets and vocally supported Chiang Kai-shek's nationalist movement in China. When Chiang and his followers were forced to flee to Taiwan in 1949, Bridges, who felt the Truman administration had essentially opened China to a communist takeover, accused U.S. diplomats of being behind Chiang's defeat and called for Secretary of State Dean Acheson's resignation.

As Senate minority leader in the 1950s, Bridges bitterly opposed the dismissal of General Douglas MACARTHUR, and supported a proposed invasion of mainland China by Chiang's nationalist armies. His virulent anticommunist stance continued into the Eisenhower administration, when he succeeded in blocking

Charles Bohlen's appointment as ambassador to the Soviet Union, his argument being that Bohlen had helped to negotiate the Yalta Agreement (a document he felt had contributed to a "traitorous mishandling of American foreign policy"). He opposed the 1954 Senate censure of Joseph McCarthy, whom he actively supported, as well as the 1955 Geneva summit conference, which he felt represented "appeasement, compromise, and weakness." (See APPEASEMENT.) Throughout the 1950s and until his death in 1961, he attempted to cut aid to or sever links with any country showing ties to communist nations or not aligned with U.S. policy. He attacked President Kennedy for what he perceived as a soft stance on COMMUNISM and pressed for resumption of nuclear testing, but supported Kennedy during the Berlin crisis, approving of the president's tough approach. Bridges died from the aftereffects of a heart attack, on November 26, 1961.

brinkmanship

A popular diplomatic term during the 1950s, brinkmanship was, as John Foster DULLES put it, "the ability to get to the verge without getting into war." As practiced by Dulles during his tenure as secretary of state, the policy entailed teetering on the brink of possible war while carrying out sensitive, potentially dangerous diplomatic goals in order to gain an advantage over the other side. That this put the nation at risk of full-scale war created tension and drew criticism from opponents of the tactic, especially Adlai STEVENSON, who attacked both Dulles and President Dwight EISENHOWER during the 1956 presidential election for their use of brinkmanship. Nevertheless, Dulles was a master of the tactic, and used it effectively to bring about an end to the KOREAN WAR as well as to resolve the Quemoy-Matsu crises of 1954 and 1958; as he put it, "We walked to the brink and we looked it in the face." Since Dulles' time, the term has been used with decreasing frequency, although it appeared during the 1964 Republican convention when supporters of Barry GOLDWATER displayed signs reading, "Better brinkmanship than chickenship." In recent years, brinkmanship has been used in other political arenas and has ceased to be associated exclusively with the threat of war.

Brown, Harold (1927–)

Harold Brown was one of the "whiz kids" brought to Washington, D.C., by Robert MCNAMARA during the Kennedy administration in the 1960s. He served as secretary of the air force under Lyndon JOHNSON from 1965 to 1969; later he was secretary of defense during the administration of President CARTER (1977–81). In between his political appointments, he was president of the California Institute of Technology (1969–77), in addition to serving as a delegate to the STRATEGIC ARMS LIMITATION TALKS (SALT) with the Soviet Union. During the latter phase of the Carter administration, he advocated Presidential Directive 59, calling for the broadening of U.S. missile targets.

Brzezinski, Zbigniew (1928–   )

A political scientist specializing in international relations, Zbigniew Kazimierz Brzezinski was born in Poland and became a U.S. citizen in 1958. He graduated from McGill University in 1949, and received his master's degree in 1950, then obtained his Ph.D. degree from Harvard University in 1953. He taught for a short time at Harvard before moving on to Columbia University, where he became a professor of international relations. In 1962, while still teaching at Columbia, he established the Research Institute on Communist Affairs (subsequently the Research Institute on International Change). During the intervening years, he became a respected expert on COMMUNISM and its inherent problems. From 1973 to 1977, he served as director of the Trilateral Commission, an organization devoted to the common concerns of the United States, Western Europe, and Japan.

In 1977, newly elected president Jimmy CARTER asked Brzezinski to become his U.S. national security advisor, in which capacity he served for four years. His policy of "architecture" was in sharp contrast to the approach previously taken by Henry KISSINGER. He also significantly reduced the size of the National Security staff from what it had been in Kissinger's time.

Although Brzezinski advocated constructive dialogue with the Soviet Union, he was pessimistic about

President Jimmy Carter and National Security Advisor Zbigniew Brzezinski (CARTER LIBRARY)

that country's intentions and consistently associated with a hard-line approach to international affairs. In fact, there had been speculation that his selection as national security advisor was intended to overcome possible criticism that the new president was SOFT ON COMMUNISM. Brzezinski argued forcefully that the United States could not be seen as abandoning its allies. He supported the SALT II treaty and worked to improve relations with communist China. He also played a key role in the negotiation of the Camp David accord between Egypt and Israel. Brzezinski was a strong supporter of the decision to admit the exiled Shah of Iran to the United States for medical treatment in 1979, which was one factor in the takeover of the U.S. embassy in Teheran. Despite Secretary of State Cyrus VANCE's opposition to the plan, Brzezinski subsequently threw his support behind the effort to rescue the Teheran hostages with U.S. commandos, which ended disastrously in 1980.

In 1981, Brzezinski returned to Columbia University; he also became a senior adviser at Georgetown University's Center for Strategic and International Studies and continued to express his opinion on U.S. foreign policy. Since 1989, he has been a professor at Johns Hopkins University's Nitze School. He is the author of several books on foreign policy, the Soviet Union, the Cold War, and the potential for global turmoil, including: *Soviet Bloc—Unity and Conflict* (1960); *Between Two Ages* (1970); *The Fragile Blossom* (1971); and his memoirs, *Power and Principle* (1983).

Buckley, William F., Jr. (1925–   )

William Frank Buckley, Jr. is a conservative editor, author, and gadfly who has exerted a profound intellectual influence on conservative politics in the United States Born into a wealthy family, he was raised in France, England, and Connecticut, and educated in his early years by private tutors. He later attended two English boys' schools and a preparatory school in New York, then spent a year at the University of Mexico before serving three years in the U.S. Army during World War II. After the war, he entered Yale University, where, among many other accomplishments, he taught Spanish, distinguished himself in debate, and served as chairman of the *Yale Daily News*. In time, he joined the staff of the *American Mercury*.

In 1955, Buckley founded and became editor in chief of the journal *National Review*, using it as a forum for conservative views and ideas. His column, "On the

Right," was syndicated in 1962 and for a time appeared regularly in more than 200 newspapers. In 1966, he began the first of many years serving as host of *Firing Line*, a weekly television program dealing with politics and public affairs. Over time, Buckley emerged as one of the nation's leading conservative polemicists and a formidable opponent of liberal ideologies. From 1969 to 1972, he served on the UNITED STATES INFORMATION AGENCY Advisory Commission, and in 1973 he was the U.S. delegate to the UNITED NATIONS General Assembly. Buckley was an ardent supporter of Ronald REAGAN in the 1980 and 1984 elections; he particularly endorsed Reagan's vigorous stand against communist regimes and his attempts to stem their global influences.

In addition to the work on the *National Review*, Buckley has written a large number of books and contributed to numerous magazines over the years. In the late 1970s, he added to his list of accomplishments when he began writing spy novels.

Bullitt, William C. (1891–1967)

A diplomat with a reputation as a nonconformist, William Christian Bullitt was the first ambassador to the Union of Soviet Socialist Republics. Born into a wealthy Philadelphia family, he graduated from Yale in 1912, spent one year at Harvard Law School, then went to work as a newspaper reporter in Europe. He joined the State Department in 1917 and became an attaché to the American delegation at the Paris Peace Conference. In early 1919, President Woodrow Wilson sent Bullitt on a secret mission to Russia to confer with Lenin and other communist leaders there. When he returned to the United States, he recommended recognition of the new Soviet government. However, after Wilson rejected his advice, Bullitt resigned from the Peace Commission and the State Department. Later in 1919, he testified before a Senate committee considering ratification of the Versailles treaty and, by virtue of his harsh criticism of the treaty, strongly influenced the decision to reject it.

After leaving the State Department, Bullitt pursued a variety of occupations in the early 1920s. For a short time he was managing editor of a motion picture company, and he also operated a New England farm. He then lived in Europe for a while, where he worked with Sigmund Freud on a biography of Woodrow Wilson (finally published in 1967). In 1926, he published a satirical novel, *It's Not Time*. In 1932, he was appointed as a special assistant to the secretary of the navy by president-elect Franklin D. Roosevelt, who then elevated him in 1933 to the position of first U.S. ambassador to the newly recognized USSR. Although initially a supporter of the Soviet government, Bullitt increasingly turned against COMMUNISM and became sharply critical of the Russian leaders. This had the effect of isolating him, and he was finally transferred to France, where he served as U.S. ambassador from 1936 to 1940. He subsequently became ambassador-at-large and carried out a number of diplomatic missions for the president.

For a time, Bullitt was one of Roosevelt's closest advisers, but in 1943 Bullitt decided to leave the administration. He worked briefly as a correspondent for *Life* magazine, then became a major in the Free French Army in 1944. After the war, he took on the role of elder statesman in international politics, becoming noted for his fervent anticommunism and his strong support for Chiang Kai-shek. Bullitt's views on foreign policy were outlined in two books, *Report to the American People* (1940) and *The Great Globe Itself* (1946).

Bundy, McGeorge (1919–1996)

A lifelong public official and influential educator, McGeorge Bundy was one of the principal architects of U.S. foreign policy during the administrations of Presidents John F. KENNEDY and his successor, Lyndon B. JOHNSON. He came by his credentials naturally; his father, Harvey H. Bundy, was an assistant secretary of state under Herbert Hoover.

As a boy, Bundy was one of Kennedy's classmates. He graduated from Groton Preparatory School in 1936 and from Yale University in 1940. Prior to World War II, he began postgraduate study at Harvard University, but suspended his studies when hostilities broke out. He served as an intelligence officer during the war, and participated in the planning for the invasion of Western Europe. After the war, he assisted in the preparation of Henry L. STIMSON's memoirs. He also served as a foreign policy adviser to Thomas E. Dewey, and worked as a political analyst for the Council on Foreign Relations. In 1949, he joined the Department of Government at Harvard, subsequently becoming dean of arts and sciences at that university in 1953.

Bundy's support of John F. Kennedy during the 1960 election led to his being named special assistant for national security affairs, a post he retained in the Johnson administration. He played a major role in the U.S. response to the CUBAN MISSILE CRISIS, and later in the decision to send in U.S. troops during the DOMINI-CAN CRISIS of 1965. He was also deeply involved in the

formulation of U.S. policy regarding the VIETNAM WAR, supporting among other things the bombing of North Vietnam in 1965. However, after he left government service in 1966, he advised Johnson against any further escalation of the war, which he had previously promoted and helped to plan.

Upon resigning his government post, Bundy became president of the Ford Foundation. He held this position until 1979, then went on to become a history professor at New York University (emeritus after 1989). He authored several books, and many of his speeches and essays were published as collections.

Bunker, Ellsworth (1894–1984)

Ellsworth Bunker was a businessman who became a respected U.S. diplomat with a reputation for skillful handling of numerous key crises during the Cold War as well as for his negotiation of the Panama Canal

Ellsworth Bunker (JOHNSON LIBRARY)

CIA director-designate George Bush confers with President Gerald Ford. (FORD LIBRARY)

Treaties. In 1916, immediately following his graduation from Yale University, he went to work for the National Sugar Refining Company, where he rose in position until becoming president in 1940 and board chairman in 1948. He also did work for Curtis Publishing Company, Lambert International Corporation, and Centennial Insurance Company. In 1951, he began a distinguished diplomatic career with his appointment as ambassador to Argentina, where he succeeded in easing U.S. relations with the Perónistas. He subsequently served as ambassador to Italy (1952–53), India (1956–61), and Nepal (1956–59). After successfully mediating a 1962 dispute between the Netherlands and Indonesia over West New Guinea, he began to earn more difficult assignments as a consultant to the State Department and as U.S. representative to the ORGANI-ZATION OF AMERICAN STATES. Among the many sensitive situations in which he intervened were the Panama crisis of 1964 and the DOMINICAN CRISIS of 1965; in the latter case, he was the principal mediator and is given chief credit for bringing about a peaceful solution to the

crisis. In 1967, he was appointed U.S. ambassador to South Vietnam, continuing in that position during the presidencies of both Lyndon JOHNSON and Richard NIXON. A strong supporter of the policy of VIETNAMIZA-TION, he helped to negotiate the 1973 cease-fire that resulted in the withdrawal of U.S. troops from the country. He was thereupon named ambassador-at-large, in which capacity he led the U.S. delegation for peace talks in the Middle East and also began complex negotiations for a new Panama Canal Treaty. The resulting treaties were signed in September 1977, and ratified by the U.S. Senate in 1978. Once again, Bunker was given the greatest credit for successfully resolving the disputes that had previously disrupted negotiations and bringing about a satisfactory settlement. Following this diplomatic triumph, Bunker retired; he died in 1984.

Bush, George (1924–)

George Herbert Walker Bush is the son of Dorothy Walker and Prescott Bush, the latter an investment

Bush, Reagan, and Gorbachev at the close of the Cold War era, New York Harbor (REAGAN LIBRARY)

banker and U.S. senator from Connecticut. In his youth, Bush attended private schools in Greenwich, Connecticut, and Andover, Massachusetts. After his graduation from Phillips Academy, he joined the U.S. Naval Reserve and served with distinction (1942–44) as a torpedo bomber pilot in the Pacific during World War II, earning the Distinguished Flying Cross. After the war, he enrolled in Yale University. He graduated in 1948, and later he moved to Texas and became a salesman of oil field supplies. In 1953, he cofounded the Zapata Petroleum Corporation, followed by the Zapata Off-Shore Company in 1954.

Bush began taking an interest in Republican politics in 1959. He lost a campaign for a U.S. Senate seat in 1964, due in part to his opponent's portrait of Bush as an extremist; the same strategy led Lyndon JOHNSON to a landslide victory over Arizona Republican Barry GOLDWATER in the general election. In 1966, Bush won a seat in the U.S. House of Representatives. He gave up that seat when he tried another run for the Senate in 1970, again without success. He was then chosen by President Richard NIXON to serve as U.S. ambassador to the UNITED NATIONS (1971–72). In 1973, he became chairman of the Republican National Committee. He stood by the president during the WATERGATE scandal until its end; in August 1974, he joined other Republicans in calling upon Nixon to resign. Later that year, President Gerald FORD appointed him chief of the U.S. Liaison Office in Peking. Two years later, he was brought back to the United States to head the CENTRAL INTELLIGENCE AGENCY (1976–77).

In 1980, Bush began a run for the presidency, but eventually abandoned it to throw his support to Ronald REAGAN, who consequently chose Bush as his running mate. The two were elected in November 1980, then reelected in 1984. Bush's eight years as vice president made him the logical choice in the 1988 presidential election. He easily defeated Democratic candidate Michael DUKAKIS, skillfully focusing voter attention on issues that galvanized voters, such as Dukakis's stand on whether public school students should be required to recite the Pledge of Allegiance.

As a moderate conservative, Bush did not depart too much from Reagan's policies as president. In December 1989, he ordered a military invasion of Panama that resulted in the arrest and eventual conviction of Panama's leader, General Manuel Antonio Noriega, on drug-trafficking charges. When Iraq invaded Kuwait in August 1990, Bush led a worldwide embargo against Iraq and sent U.S. military troops to Saudi Arabia as a safety measure. As he gradually increased the U.S. military presence in the Persian Gulf region, he also used considerable diplomatic skills to build a coalition of Western European and Arab states against Iraq. When that country failed to withdraw from Kuwait, Bush authorized a U.S.-led offensive beginning on January 16, 1991, first by air and subsequently by ground. The brief war destroyed most of Iraq's armies and liberated Kuwait.

Although he enjoyed great popularity because of his handling of the PERSIAN GULF WAR, and despite the fact that the Cold War concluded on his watch, Bush failed to respond effectively during and after a growing economic recession within the United States, and he was increasingly criticized for his lack of initiative in domestic affairs. It was largely due to the perception of his remoteness from average American voters that he lost his bid for reelection in 1992 to the Democratic challenger, Bill Clinton. The Bush campaign's attempts to cast doubt on Clinton's patriotism by citing his position on the VIETNAM WAR as a college student failed to resonate with voters. In addition, reports that Bush officials had investigated Clinton's mother in an attempt to locate left-wing sympathies backfired spectacularly. Bush retired from public life after leaving the White House.

Byrnes, James F. (1879–1972)

James Francis Byrnes was a Democratic politician best known for his service (1943–45) as director of war mobilization during World War II and as secretary of state under President Harry TRUMAN (1945–47). He began his career as a self-taught lawyer, turning to public life in 1908, when he became a public prosecu-

tor in South Carolina. From 1911 to 1925, he served in the U.S. House of Representatives. He was elected to the U.S. Senate in 1931, and quickly emerged as the majority leader. As a member of President Franklin D. Roosevelt's "Brain Trust," he helped push numerous New Deal measures through Congress, although he later rejected many of the administration's concepts as too radical. On the eve of World War II, he helped to launch defense preparedness legislation. He was appointed to the U.S. Supreme Court in 1941, but in 1942 was tapped to be director of economic stabilization, and subsequently to head the Office of War Mobilization. He was so effective and dominant in this position that he became popularly known as "assistant president of domestic affairs."

Byrnes resigned after attending the 1945 YALTA CONFERENCE with Roosevelt, but upon Roosevelt's death, he was asked by President Truman to take on the job of secretary of state. He accepted, and accompanied Truman to the POTSDAM CONFERENCE in 1945. Although he originally supported friendly cooperation with the Soviet Union over such issues as German reunification—he felt that compromise was necessary to maintaining the relationship established as a result of the wartime alliance—Byrnes' dealings with them eventually led to his becoming a hard-line anti-Soviet. Because of his concerns about Soviet expansion, he called for the United States to maintain a military presence in Western Europe. When the Soviets failed to withdraw from Iran by the agreed-upon deadline in

President Harry Truman and Secretary of State James Byrnes in an informal conference at Potsdam, 1945. (TRUMAN LIBRARY)

1946, Byrnes refused to compromise on any solution but an immediate withdrawal. Later that year, he gave a controversial speech in Stuttgart, Germany, in which he effectively delivered a strong warning to the Russians about American intentions in Germany.

Byrnes resigned as secretary of state in January 1947, largely due to his deteriorating relationship with Truman. He was subsequently elected governor of South Carolina, holding that post from 1951 to 1955 and in the process becoming an ardent supporter of racial segregation in the schools. He left politics after finishing his gubernatorial term in 1955. Byrnes published two books: *Speaking Frankly* (1947) and *All in One Lifetime* (1958).

Calley, William (1943–)

William Lawes Calley, Jr., is an American soldier renowned and reviled for his role in the 1968 massacre of Vietnamese citizens in My Lai. Born in Miami, Florida, Calley dropped out of college and worked as a dishwasher and a railroad switchman before enlisting in the U.S. Army in 1966. He was sent to Officers Training School and, upon being commissioned a lieutenant, was posted to South Vietnam. On March 16, 1968, his platoon entered the hamlet of My Lai and proceeded to indiscriminately kill the unarmed and unresisting inhabitants; estimates of the number killed ranged from 30 to 500 men, women, and children. When rumors of the massacre surfaced, the army investigated and subsequently charged 25 soldiers and officers for varying offenses. Calley was put on trial for the massacre of 109 Vietnamese citizens. In his defense, he argued that he was following orders. He also pointed out the difficulties of guerrilla warfare, which makes it difficult to distinguish between military and civilian combatants; clearly many American soldiers, frustrated with the difficulty of determining who the enemy actually was, often took matters into their own hands. Nevertheless, it was determined that he had grossly exceeded his orders, and in 1971 he was convicted on 22 counts of murder. Calley was sentenced to life in prison. However, his sentence was commuted by President Richard NIXON, initially to 20 years, then to time served in 1974.

National coverage of the massacre and the military's response to it was substantial, and was one of several factors contributing to public debate about the role of the U.S. military in Southeast Asia. Although others were implicated in the massacre, only Calley was convicted; the remainder were acquitted or had charges against them dropped. This led Calley's supporters to claim that he had been made a scapegoat for the overall horrors of the VIETNAM WAR. (Reports that the My Lai massacre was only one example of horrendous crimes against Vietnam civilians persist to this day.) Institutional failures were also identified as a result of the Calley affair, with critics concluding that he should never have been made an officer, and that both he and the army had been victimized by educational deferments that required the military services to lower their standards in selecting and training officers.

After his release from prison, Calley became an insurance agent and retreated quietly into civilian life.

campus activism   See ANTIWAR MOVEMENT; STUDENTS FOR A DEMOCRATIC SOCIETY.

Carter, Jimmy (1924–   )

The 39th president of the United States (1977–81) was born the son of a peanut warehouse owner and Georgia state legislator. James Earl Carter, Jr., graduated from the U.S. Naval Academy at Annapolis in 1946. Five of his seven years in the navy were served on nuclear submarines; he also worked with Admiral Hyman G. Rickover on the nuclear submarine program. Upon his father's death in 1953, he resigned his commission and returned to Georgia to manage the family peanut farm business. He soon became interested in Democratic politics, and he won election in 1962 to the Georgia State Senate, to which he was reelected in 1964. He then ran a successful campaign for governor of Georgia in 1970. As governor, he revolutionized the state bureaucracy by reorganizing state agencies and by naming blacks and women to many key posts.

Although not a nationally known figure at the time, Carter announced his candidacy for the Democratic

President Jimmy Carter (CARTER LIBRARY)

nomination for U.S. president in 1974. Through careful, skillful, and tireless campaigning, he managed to win the nomination in July 1976. Together with his running mate, Walter F. MONDALE, he defeated the incumbent, Gerald R. FORD, to become president. His style as president was decidedly informal and was seen to be much less pompous than that of his predecessors. However, despite a Democratic majority in the House and the Senate, he met with stiff opposition to his reform programs in social, administrative, and economic areas.

Carter's biggest achievements were in foreign affairs. In 1977, he obtained two treaties between the United States and Panama, giving the latter country full control over the Panama Canal by the end of 1999. In 1978, he brought Egyptian president Anwar Sadat and Israeli prime minister Menachem Begin together and guided the creation of the Camp David Accords, effectively ending the state of war that had existed between the two countries since 1948. On January 1, 1979, he established diplomatic relations between the United States and China while simultaneously severing diplomatic ties with Taiwan. The year 1979 also saw the signing of a new bilateral STRATEGIC ARMS LIMITATION TREATY (SALT II). After the Soviet Union invaded Afghanistan, however, Carter removed the treaty from Senate consideration for approval. He also placed an embargo on shipments of American grain to the USSR and initiated a U.S. boycott of the Moscow Olympics in 1980.

But this was not his biggest challenge; that occurred with the storming of the U.S. Embassy in Teheran by a mob of Iranian students in November 1979, and the seizure of American citizens as hostages. The subsequent standoff between the United States and the government of Iran, during which Carter attempted diplomatic means to achieve the release of the hostages and then agreed to a secret military rescue mission that failed, resulted in major political trouble for the president. Not even the issuance of the CARTER DOCTRINE, declaring the country's resolve to protect U.S. interests in the Persian Gulf region, was able to help the public image of him as a weak and indecisive leader. These crises, combined with economic problems on the domestic front and his failure to get legislative results for his ambitious ideas, led to a lack of confidence in Carter's presidency and to Ronald Reagan's defeat of him in the 1980 election. (It is worth noting that Reagan's

President Jimmy Carter often adopted an informal style as he worked. (CARTER LIBRARY)

primary attack on Carter had to do with the domestic economic agenda, and that issues related to the Cold War did not play a large role in the campaign.)

After leaving the presidency, Carter returned to Plains, Georgia, where he wrote his memoirs and numerous other books, and established the Carter Presidential Center in Atlanta with his wife, Rosalyn. He subsequently became a diplomat at large, serving to mediate the peaceful settlement of disputes in Nicaragua, Ethiopia, North Korea, Haiti, and Bosnia.

Carter Doctrine

In his State of the Union address of January 1980, President Jimmy CARTER announced his administration's newly formed doctrine: "Any attempt by any outside force to gain control of the Persian Gulf region will be regarded as an assault on the vital interests of the United States of America and such an assault will be repelled by any means necessary, including military force." These were strong words for the normally pacifist Carter, but necessary in the view of many, given the recent Soviet invasion of Afghanistan and the hostage crisis in Iran. Subsequent to the announcement of the doctrine, the Rapid Deployment Force was created to ensure military readiness in the event of a crisis. The doctrine that would bear Carter's name was subsequently endorsed by President Ronald REAGAN, who used it in negotiating and implementing foreign policy in the Middle East, and its warnings were acted upon by President George BUSH, who invoked it when justifying his decision to launch the PERSIAN GULF WAR of 1990.

Casey, William J. (1913–1987)

Best known as director of the CENTRAL INTELLIGENCE AGENCY (CIA) from 1981 to 1987, William Joseph Casey graduated from Fordham University in New York City in 1934, and, after a brief period at the Catholic University of America, received a law degree in 1937 from St. John's University in Jamaica, New York. Prior to World War II, he worked at the Research Institute of America in Washington, D.C. From 1941 to 1946, during and after the war, he served with the OFFICE OF STRATEGIC SERVICES (OSS—the CIA's forerunner), directing spies on the European continent from his London base. He went on to become a lecturer on tax law at New York University from 1948 to 1962. He also wrote several legal and business books and became wealthy through a number of sound investments. From 1957 to 1971, he was a partner in a New York law firm with Republican Party leader Leonard Hall and later became affiliated with the law firm of Rogers & Wells, from 1976 to 1981. After working on Richard NIXON's presidential compaign in 1968, Casey held a number of successive posts: chairman of the Securities and Exchange Commission (1971–73); undersecretary of state for economic affairs (1973–74); and member of the Foreign Intelligence Advisory Board (1976). He subsequently served as campaign manager for Ronald REAGAN's presidential run, and became director of the CIA in 1981.

Casey's years as CIA director were controversial. He increased covert CIA operations in Afghanistan, Central America, and Angola, among other areas, and increased support for certain anticommunist insurgent groups. His failure to notify Congress about the CIA's mining of Nicaraguan ports led to a conflict with the Senate and a search for alternate ways to fund covert operations in Nicaragua. When the IRAN-CONTRA AFFAIR came to light and the CIA's secret involvement in the sale of U.S. weapons to Iran in order to fund Nicaraguan rebels was revealed, Casey was seen to be a key figure in the scandal. He was scheduled to testify on the matter in December 1986, but shortly before his appearance, he suffered seizures and underwent brain surgery. A diagnosis of nervous system lymphoma was made, and he died without ever testifying about what he knew.

Catholic Worker   See DAY, DOROTHY.

Central Intelligence Agency (CIA)

The Central Intelligence Agency (CIA) was created in 1947 as part of the NATIONAL SECURITY ACT. Its predecessors as a security agency were the wartime OFFICE OF STRATEGIC SERVICES (OSS) and the postwar National Intelligence Authority and Central Intelligence Group. In addition to gathering and disseminating intelligence relating to the country's safety and security, the CIA's defined goals included performing "such additional services of common concern as the National Security Council determines can be more efficiently accomplished centrally." It is this directive that has often led the CIA to engage in covert and sometimes illegal activities for the presumed sake of national security, activities that were effectively endorsed by the Central Intelligence Agency Act of 1949, which exempted the CIA from requirements of public disclosure.

Although covert operations were not in the CIA's original directive, its supporters felt that they were a necessary part of the agency's mission to gather crucial information about the Soviet Union and Eastern Europe, as well as for fomenting dissension and rebellion in communist countries. However, detractors claim that such activities counteract the principles of a truly democratic society and tarnish the nation's reputation. Whichever point of view is taken, the agency has surely experienced its share of controversy as information about past and present clandestine operations comes to light and is subjected to public scrutiny. Some of the black marks against the agency include the disastrous BAY OF PIGS INVASION of Cuba in 1961, reports of assassination plots against communist and anti-American leaders of other nations, and the IRAN-CONTRA AFFAIR of 1986–87. Former CIA employees were also involved in the WATERGATE scandal that ended Richard NIXON's presidency. Nevertheless, the CIA maintains a worldwide network of operatives and continues to conduct illicit activities when deemed necessary for the security of the United States.

Central Treaty Organization (CENTO)

An organization that lasted only 20 years, from 1959 to 1979, the Central Treaty Organization (CENTO) was an alliance of three Middle Eastern nations (Turkey, Iran, and Pakistan) with Great Britain that was formed for reasons of mutual security. The United States became a "participating nonmember" of the alliance due to the crucial importance of the Middle East in international affairs, especially with the Soviet Union being so geographically close to member countries. Originally known as the Baghdad Pact, CENTO was poorly organized from the start, and had the loosely-defined goal of cooperation for the sake of security and defense. The organization was finally dissolved due to years of inactivity.

Chambers, Whittaker (1901–1961)

Born Jay Vivian Chambers, Whittaker took his mother's maiden name during the 1920s, when he became a member of the Communist Party. He studied at Columbia University, where he was an erratic student, but in time he became a journalist and editor. He joined the Communist Party in 1925 and worked as editor for the *New Masses* and the *Daily Worker.* Around 1932, he went underground and joined a Washington, D.C.-based spy ring. Chambers retained his party membership until 1938. From 1939 to 1948, he worked as a senior editor for *Time* magazine. It was in August 1948, after the statute of limitations had run out, that he testified before a congressional committee on communist activities, and named Alger HISS, a former employee of the State Department, as a fellow member of his spy ring during the 1930s. Hiss denied the charges and sued. Chambers then produced copies of State Department documents that had been typed on Hiss's typewriter as proof. He also led federal agents to microfilms of government documents that allegedly had been supplied by Hiss. As they had been hidden in a pumpkin on Chambers' farm, these microfilms were referred to as the "PUMPKIN PAPERS."

Hiss was eventually convicted of perjury—although he denied giving any documents to Chambers—and his career was over. The case was an important early triumph for Richard NIXON, then a congressman from California. Nixon had doggedly pursued the Chambers lead through the HOUSE UN-AMERICAN ACTIVITIES COMMITTEE, and cited the pumpkin papers as "definite proof of one of the most extensive espionage rings in the history of the United States."

After the controversy he provoked died down, Chambers became a senior editor of the *National Review,* a conservative magazine. His autobiography, *Witness,* was published in 1952. In 1964, three years after his death, selections from Chambers' letters and diaries were edited by Duncan Norton-Taylor and published as *Cold Friday.* Over 30 years later, in 1995, previously classified information from World War II, as well as research conducted in the newly-opened archives of the Soviet Union in Moscow, provided compelling support to Chambers' account of the KGB spy ring in the United States and Hiss's undeniable involvement.

Chaplin, Charles (1889–1977)

Charlie Chaplin, the son of British music-hall performers, first appeared on the stage at the age of eight in a clog-dancing act. His father died when he was young, and after that, his mother became subject to mental breakdowns. Charlie then entered a succession of boarding schools, the dreariness of which was broken only by stage engagements and those periods of time when he lived in the streets. When he was 17, his older half-brother secured a job for him with the Fred Karno Company, a vaudeville troupe. In 1913, after being spotted in a music hall by Mack Sennett, Chaplin was signed for the movies by the Keystone Company. He never worked on the stage again. He made his first silent film appearance in 1914; two years later, he had become one of the best-known personalities in the United States By the early 1920s, with both his talent and his salary on the rise, no studio could afford him, and he appeared only in films he directed. Although he made fewer movies after the advent of sound films in the late 1920s, his fame did not diminish—it only increased. With time, his films became recognized as classics. His most famous and profitable character was the Tramp, a sympathetic, mustachioed sad sack dressed in a derby hat, tight coat, baggy trousers, over-sized shoes, who carried a trademark cane. In 1919, with Mary Pickford, Douglas Fairbanks, and D.W. Griffith, Chaplin formed United Artists, a movie company created so that each actor could produce independent films. From 1923 on, Chaplin produced movies exclusively for United Artists.

Chaplin was married four times, the first three to leading ladies Mildred Harris, Lita Grey, and Paulette Goddard, and the fourth (in 1943) to Oona O'Neill, daughter of playwright Eugene O'Neill. Although he enjoyed a long and happy union with Oona, his personal life was often stormy; his first two divorces and a 1944 paternity suit yielded sensational headlines. He gained additional attention in 1942, when he called for a second front in the war against Germany. His left-wing views were criticized by many; his 1947 film,

Monsieur Verdoux, was attacked by the AMERICAN LEGION, among other groups. After being prosecuted by the government for back taxes owed, and attacked by politicians and newspaper columnists for his alleged links to various leftist causes, Chaplin left the United States in 1952. He surrendered his reentry permit at Geneva in 1953, and thereafter he lived with his family at Orsier-sur-Vevey, near Vevey, Switzerland. His 1957 film, *A King in New York,* took some satirical swipes at the HOUSE COMMITTEE ON UN-AMERICAN ACTIVITIES, as well as other aspects of American life, and brought on renewed accusations of his supposed procommunist stance. By 1972, however, he was able to return to the United States after a long exile abroad in order to receive a special award from the Academy of Motion Picture Arts and Sciences. He was knighted by Queen Elizabeth II in 1975. His autobiography was published in 1964.

Cheney, Richard Bruce (1941–)

Richard Bruce Cheney, known as Dick to friends and associates, was U.S. secretary of defense from 1989 to 1993, serving under President George BUSH. Born in Nebraska, he moved with his family to Wyoming when he was still quite young. He attended the University of Wyoming, and received his B.A. degree in 1965 and his master's degree in 1966. He arrived in Washington in 1969 as a congressional aide. A Republican, he held several appointed and advisory positions in President Richard NIXON's administration. He also served as chief of staff to President Gerald FORD, from 1975 to 1977. In 1978, he won election to Congress as a U.S. representative from Wyoming, and served until 1989; he was Republican whip for the last term. He was chosen by President Bush in 1989 to be secretary of defense and later played a key role in advising Bush on military strategy against Iraq during the PERSIAN GULF WAR of 1991. Cheney advocated reducing President Ronald REAGAN's proposed defense budget by $10 billion. He also believed that Congress played too prominent a role in the formulation of foreign policy, which he believed to be the president's responsibility.

Cheney resigned as secretary of defense in 1993. His wife, Lynne V. Cheney, is a Washington-based writer and editor who served as chairperson of the National Endowment for the Humanities from 1986 to 1993.

President Ford meets with Richard Cheney. (FORD LIBRARY)

Chicago Seven

The 1960s was a decade marked by civil unrest and tremendous excitement, both of which were reflected in the trial of the Chicago Seven in 1968. That year, a group of antiwar protesters—led by YIPPIES David DELLINGER, Abbie HOFFMAN, and Jerry RUBIN, and joined by BLACK PANTHER Bobby SEALE—disrupted the Democratic National Convention in Chicago with antiwar demonstrations to such an extent that Mayor Richard DALEY felt it necessary to call in troops to quell the disorder. The leaders behind the disturbances were arrested and subsequently brought to trial on charges of conspiracy to incite a riot. At first, there were eight defendants: Dellinger, Hoffman, Rubin, Seale, Rennie Davis, Tom Hayden, John Froines, and Lee Weiner. Seale's case was eventually separated from the others, creating the "Chicago Seven," who, with their lawyer, William KUNSTLER, would proceed to turn their trial into a MEDIA circus. In the end, Froines and Weiner were acquitted, while the others were found guilty only of crossing state lines with intent to incite a riot, for which they were sentenced to seven years in jail. However, their convictions were overturned upon appeal, and none of them served any time in jail for their parts in the Chicago riots. (Seale, who had contributed to the courtroom antics before his case was separated, was found guilty of contempt and sentenced to four years in prison.)

China Lobby

The China Lobby was an American political pressure group active from 1945 to 1955, formed in support of the nationalist regime of Chiang Kai-shek. The China Lobby was quick to blame and condemn the U.S. State Department for the ultimate triumph of Mao Zedong and the communists over the nationalists, who were forced to flee to the island of Formosa (later Taiwan) after their defeat in the Chinese civil war. The China Lobby also opposed the admission of the People's

Republic of China to the UNITED NATIONS. Fiercely anticommunist, the lobby was composed of a variety of individuals and organizations, with perhaps its best-known member being publisher Henry R. LUCE.

"A choice, not an echo"

"A choice, not an echo" was a popular phrase used to clearly define the ideological differences of political parties in the United States, particularly as it related to the presidential candidacy of Barry GOLDWATER. On January 3, 1964, Goldwater stated in a speech: "I will offer a choice, not an echo. This will not be an engagement of personalities. It will be an engagement of principles." At the Republican National Convention that year, Governor William Scranton of Pennsylvania played on that theme even further: "I reject the echo we have thus far been handed . . . the echo of fear, or reaction . . . the echo from the Never-Never Land that puts our nation backward to a lesser place in the world of free men." However, Goldwater's attempts to polarize his party's position met with failure at the electoral polls, which drowned him in a landslide loss to President Lyndon B. JOHNSON. That same year, Phyllis SCHLAFLY, an enthusiastic Goldwater supporter, published *A Choice Not an Echo,* a ringing endorsement of his policies.

Chomsky, Noam (1928–)

Avram Noam Chomsky is a linguist, writer, educator, and political activist who is best known as one of the founders of transformational (or generative) grammar. He became interested in linguistics through the influence of his father, a Hebrew scholar. After receiving his Ph.D. degree from the University of Pennsylvania in 1955, Chomsky taught modern languages and linguistics at the Massachusetts Institute of Technology, where he became a full professor in 1961.

Aside from his fame in the study of linguistics, Chomsky also gained national attention for his vocal opposition to U.S. involvement in the VIETNAM WAR. His political views were expressed in numerous lectures, books, and articles throughout the 1960s and 1970s. In addition, he spoke and wrote about social and economic issues. Some of his publications include *American Power and the New Mandarins* (1969); a two-volume set entitled *The Political Economy of Human Rights* (1979); and *Towards a New Cold War* (1982). His 1979 book, *Language and Responsibility,* discusses the relationship of language and politics, the history of ideas and science, and the consequences of generative grammar. These ideas were expanded and examined further in later books. Chomsky views language as the result of universal innate facility and considers his ideas about language to be related to those of the late 17th-century rationalist philosophers.

civil defense

Civil defense, also known as passive defense, is a centuries-old strategy that provides for protection of a population and its property against enemy aggression by nonmilitary means. In democratic nations, this has typically entailed maintenance of a system of law and order and the provision of food, shelter, and first aid and rescue operations as needed. In the Cold War era, a strong civil defense system also called for protection against nuclear attack and provisions for measures to be taken in the event of such an attack (i.e., BOMB SHELTERS). After the signing of the first and second STRATEGIC ARMS LIMITATION TREATIES (SALT), and the subsequent proposal that President Ronald REAGAN presented in 1983 for a STRATEGIC DEFENSE INITIATIVE, Americans were made even more aware of the possible consequences of nuclear attack and the need to prepare for it accordingly. However, opinions about methods of civil defense differed greatly, with right-wing HAWKS advocating a fully-prepared military defense system (i.e., Reagan's "Star Wars" system), while left-wing DOVES favored increased negotiations for complete nuclear disarmament worldwide.

civil disobedience

Civil disobedience is a strategy by which citizens register disapproval or protest of their government by means of a passive refusal to obey its laws or commands—in essence, nonviolent resistance. The concept of civil disobedience has been practiced for centuries, but it reached its apex during the CIVIL RIGHTS MOVEMENT of the 1960s, when it was put into practice by Martin Luther KING, Jr. Modeling his strategy on that employed by Mohandas Gandhi in his struggle to achieve independence for India, King created a prominent movement to advance the cause of equal rights for blacks in all sectors of society. Similarly, protesters in the ANTIWAR MOVEMENT frequently used civil disobedience to register their disapproval of the VIETNAM WAR and force public opinion against it. The tactics King and other protesters commonly used included "SIT-INS," boycotts, and massive demonstrations such as King's celebrated 1965 march in Alabama from Selma to Montgomery as well as the 1963 MARCH ON WASHINGTON. Because civil disobedience often calls for defiance of established laws, those who use it are frequently arrested or even injured in the civil conflicts that sometimes result. However, by bringing public attention to their causes through nonviolent means, practitioners of civil disobedience have frequently succeeded in effecting social and legislative reforms that have improved conditions for a group of people or brought about an end to a disputed or unpopular government policy.

civil rights acts

A direct result of the CIVIL RIGHTS MOVEMENT of the 1950s and 1960s was the passing of legislation in Congress designed to eliminate SEGREGATION and combat conditions that essentially discriminated against black Americans. Civil rights acts were passed by Congress in 1957, 1960, 1964, 1968, and 1991; of these, the 1964 act is perhaps the best-known as the one that

contained the most radical changes in legislation up to that time, fueling the civil rights movement to shoot for even higher goals in its fight for equal rights. In summary:

Civil Rights Act of 1957 Guided through Congress by then-Senator Lyndon B. johnson, this bill created the U.S. Commission on Civil Rights to investigate such problems as segregation practices in the South. It also tackled the problem of whites intimidating or harassing black voters at the polls, making it a federal crime to do so.

Civil Rights Act of 1960 This essentially introduced a means of enforcing the provisions of the previous bill, making federal courts responsible for complaints about voting rights. However, it did not address discriminatory eligibility requirements for new black voters.

Civil Rights Act of 1964 This groundbreaking legislation contained sweeping reforms that addressed segregation and discrimination in schools, hospitals, libraries, parks, and other public places, and also

President Lyndon Johnson signs the Civil Rights Act of 1964 as Martin Luther King, Jr. looks on. (JOHNSON LIBRARY)

addressed the problems of voting rights. In addition to providing the funding to bring businesses and institutions into compliance with the new law, the bill also ensured legal enforcement to investigate and prosecute those who continued to discriminate against others based on race, color, religion, or national origin. Title VII of the bill created the Equal Employment Opportunity Commission (EEOC) to assist in matters relating to the abolition of discrimination in employment. Many hailed the act, with Hubert HUMPHREY going so far as to say that it would eliminate poverty in the United States. Others protested loudly, some to the point of publicly defying the new law. This number included Alabama governor George WALLACE, whose previous actions in enforcing segregation in his state had, ironically, helped to set the wheels in motion for the bill's passage in Congress.

Civil Rights Act of 1968   This bill, also called the Fair Housing Act, addressed and attempted to correct discrimination in the sale and rental of housing to blacks and others. It also turned its attention to the problems of Native Americans, extending the Bill of Rights to that group.

Civil Rights Act of 1991   A series of amendments to the Civil Rights Act of 1964, this act tied into affirmative action and the 1990 Americans with Disabilities Act, making it easier for employees to bring suits against discriminatory employers and protecting against harassment on the job.

civil rights movement

The civil rights movement of the 1950s and 1960s took place at a time when the effort to achieve greater civil liberties for black Americans (and others of varying race, color, and creed), to put them on an equal footing with whites, was at its height. Composed of coalitions of individuals and organizations, the movement took many forms, from the passive CIVIL DISOBEDIENCE practiced by Martin Luther KING, Jr. and his followers to the more violent forms of confrontation espoused by MALCOLM X and the BLACK PANTHERS. Black Americans had long suffered from discrimination in the United States, and most felt that the concept of equal rights to all was not evenly applied to all citizens. Indeed, a more apt description of living conditions for many U.S. Negroes (as they were then called) was "separate but equal"—that is, they were equal in theory, but kept segregated in practice. The aim of the civil rights movement was to break down the barriers of SEGREGA-

The March on Washington was one of the civil rights movement's best-known efforts. (NARA STILL PHOTOS DIVISION)

TION to achieve true and full equality of freedom and opportunity for all blacks. In the view of many, this aim has not yet been achieved, although considerable progress has been made since the 1950s and 1960s through the efforts of many movement leaders such as King, Malcolm X, Medgar Evers, Eldridge CLEAVER, Jesse JACKSON, and others, as well as organizations such as the National Urban League, the National Association for the Advancement of Colored People (NAACP), the Congress of Racial Equality (CORE), and the STUDENT NONVIOLENT COORDINATING COMMITTEE (SNCC).

Although blacks in America had waged protests and fought battles against discrimination since Civil War days, many consider the modern civil rights movement to have been officially born on December 1, 1955, in Montgomery, Alabama. On that day, Rosa Parks, a black seamstress, refused to give up her seat on a public bus to a white passenger. For this act of defiance, she was arrested, and a boycott of the Montgomery bus system was subsequently organized and led by Reverend Martin Luther King, Jr., a Baptist minister new to the city. The boycott lasted nearly a year and was so successful that Montgomery officials, under pressure from the Supreme Court, finally desegregated the buses. King subsequently went on to become the most prominent and influential leader of the struggle for equal rights for African Americans throughout the country, but particularly in the South.

The tactics used by King and others in the civil rights movement included SIT-INS and organized demonstrations at colleges and urban locations around the country; the work of the FREEDOM RIDERS to test desegregation of interstate transportation; drives to register blacks to vote, thus influencing the electoral process; boycotts of buses, businesses, and products to bring attention to segregation and poor working conditions; lobbying for legislative reforms and new laws to protect civil rights; and mass marches to effect solidarity among blacks and, often, provoke confrontation with the white ESTABLISHMENT. Many times those confrontations became violent or resulted in arrests of those involved. Sometimes it even involved death—King, Malcolm X, and Evers were assassinated, and many others in the movement lost their lives for their cause. In addition, the progress for change was often frustratingly slow; for example, by 1964, only 1% of students in the South were enrolled in integrated schools. Nonetheless, the movement produced some positive results, specifically the CIVIL RIGHTS ACTS of 1957, 1960, 1964, 1968, and 1991, all of which helped to make greater strides toward a nation where, as Martin Luther King, Jr., once put it, "a man will be judged not by the color of his skin but by the content of his character."

Civil rights work weakened and slowly declined in the late 1960s due to internal strife between factions advocating violent and nonviolent approaches to problems, a decrease in public support for the cause (which some critics attributed to the so-called reverse discrimination perceived by some in the passage of affirmative action laws), and a broadening of discrimination definitions to encompass numerous other minority groups,

Leaders of the civil rights movement meet with government officials at the White House, June 22, 1963. (KENNEDY LIBRARY)

including Native Americans and women. That the movement reached its peak during some of the most intense years of the Cold War was not coincidental. For many blacks seeking an end to white oppression, the answer seemed to be contained within the tenets of COMMUNISM, which promised equal treatment for all people of all races. Some black Americans, such as Paul ROBESON, viewed communism as the answer to the problem of racial oppression. Others found the communist doctrine to be equally flawed, and perhaps even more oppressive. Thus was born the civil rights movement—a means of effecting positive change within the democratic system that has had lasting effects for African Americans in the social, political, educational, and industrial spheres. See also MARCH ON WASHINGTON.

Cleaver, Eldridge (1935–   )

Leroy Eldridge Cleaver, born in a small town near Little Rock, Arkansas, is perhaps best known for his autobiography, *Soul on Ice* (1968), which is considered to be a classic statement of black alienation in the United States. From his junior high school days until 1966, Cleaver spent a great deal of time in California correctional institutions for crimes ranging from bicycle theft to assault with intent to kill. He was an avid reader, and he became a follower of Malcolm X, a leader of the Black Muslim separatist movement. In time Cleaver became involved with the BLACK PANTHERS, for which group he eventually took on the role of minister of information. After a shoot-out with police in Los Angeles in 1968, Cleaver again faced the prospect of imprisonment; to avoid it, he jumped bail and fled to Cuba, then to Algiers, where he set up a headquarters for an international section of the Black Panthers. He voluntarily returned to the United States in November 1975. The charges against him were dropped in 1979, when he agreed to plead guilty to assault in the 1968 incident. He was placed on a five-year probation period consisting of community service. Around this time, he proclaimed himself to be a born-again Christian.

Clifford, Clark (1906–1998)

Clark McAdams Clifford was a lawyer and prominent Democrat who held several posts during the administrations of Presidents Harry TRUMAN, John F. KENNEDY, and Lyndon B. JOHNSON. Following his service in the U.S. Navy during World War II, he was named a naval aide to President Truman. Recognizing Clifford's talents, Truman appointed him as special counsel in 1946, in which capacity he assisted in initial developments leading to the MARSHALL PLAN, and also helped to draft the NATIONAL SECURITY ACT, which among other things established the new post of secretary of defense. Clifford was instrumental in Truman's successful election campaign, and became the president's close friend as well as adviser. He left government service in 1950 to return to private law practice, but continued to advise numerous political leaders, primarily Democrats. These included Senator John F. Kennedy, for whom he served as liaison with the outgoing Eisenhower administration after Kennedy's 1960 election as president.

Clifford was appointed chairman of the Foreign Intelligence Advisory Board in 1963. In 1968, President Johnson named Clifford secretary of defense. In this capacity, he proved to be highly influential in changing the direction of U.S. policy regarding the VIETNAM WAR. Although he was considered to be a HAWK and had previously supported the intensive bombing of North Vietnam then being waged, by 1968 he had become convinced that the war was unwinnable and bombing should be halted. On the day of Clifford's confirmation as defense secretary—January 30, 1968—the TET OFFENSIVE was launched, turning the American public's opinion firmly against the war. Johnson consequently announced that he would halt the bombing and begin peace negotiations—a major turning point in the course of the war that would be completed by his successor, Richard NIXON.

For his government services, Clifford was awarded the Medal of Freedom. In his later years, he became chairman of First American Bankshares, but he was forced out in the early 1990s due to a scandal connected with the Bank of Credit and Commerce International (BCCI). His autobiography, *Counsel to the President*, appeared in 1991, just before the BCCI scandal erupted. Although he was indicted for conspiracy to commit fraud, he evaded trial because of his ill health, and in 1998 came to a settlement with the Federal Reserve Bank. His final years were spent in quiet solitude, his long and distinguished service to the government obscured by the embarrassment of the BCCI scandal.

Cohn, Roy (1927–1986)

Lawyer Roy Cohn is perhaps best remembered for serving as chief counsel to Senator Joseph MCCARTHY during the infamous Army-McCarthy hearings of 1953–54. Prior to this, he had achieved some notoriety when he and a friend, G. David Schine, made a tour of U.S. State Department-run information libraries in Western Europe. Their purpose was to pick out procommunist books on the shelves and discredit those in charge of the information program.

During the hearings, Cohn could always be seen seated at McCarthy's right side. Their hysterical anticommunist "case" was eventually regarded as more dangerous than the people and activities they were investigating, and no concrete evidence was ever unearthed. The resulting disgrace effectively ended the Washington phase of Cohn's career. He went on to practice law in New York, and he wrote several books, one of which expounded the practical value of obnoxiousness. He eventually ran into serious legal and financial problems, and died in 1986 of complications relating to AIDS.

COINTELPRO

COINTELPRO (coined from "counter intelligence program") was a project conceived by J. Edgar HOOVER and executed by the FEDERAL BUREAU OF INVESTIGATION (FBI) as a means of destabilizing many organizations of the NEW LEFT and other groups that Hoover had determined to be subversive. Begun in October 1961, the project at first targeted such communist-affiliated groups as the Socialist Workers Party and the Young Socialist Alliance. Later, Hoover took aim at antiwar protesters and militant organizations such as the BLACK PANTHERS. To achieve their goals, FBI undercover agents infiltrated the targeted groups and worked from within to set up surveillance of leaders and to create dissension and discord. Although presumably carried out in the name of national security, COINTELPRO was in fact a controversial project that ignored civil liberties and broke numerous laws as operatives did their "dirty work." In many cases they succeeded; the Black Panthers, for example, disbanded as a result of COINTELPRO infiltration into their ranks.

Colby, William (1920–1996)

William E. Colby was a director of the CENTRAL INTELLIGENCE AGENCY (CIA) who revealed many of that agency's secret operations before a congressional committee, and was subsequently criticized for doing so.

He was born the son of an army colonel, Elbridge Colby, who badly damaged his military career by publicly decrying the acquittal of a murderer who had killed a black soldier in 1925. Colby's father's influence, as well as his religious upbringing, led to his becoming a liberal antifascist and an interventionist as a young man. He attended Princeton University and graduated in 1940.

After the United States entered World War II, Colby joined the OFFICE OF STRATEGIC SERVICES (OSS), an early precursor to the CIA. As a member of the OSS, he engaged in numerous acts of espionage and military daring, including parachuting behind enemy lines in Europe to work with resistance forces. After the war, he obtained his law degree from Columbia University, worked for approximately two years as a lawyer in the interests of labor organizations, then went on to the National Labor Relations Board before joining the CIA. He served for several years at embassies in Stockholm and Rome before going to Asia in 1959. In 1962, he became chief of the CIA's Far East division, where he exerted considerable control over operations in Vietnam, including directing the "secret war" against the North Vietnamese, in which Laotian tribal forces were used to attack North Vietnamese supply lines. He strongly advocated fighting the Vietcong with their own methods of guerrilla warfare, rather than traditional U.S. military methods. In 1968, he went to Saigon to direct OPERATION PHOENIX, a notorious program, supposedly for PACIFICATION, which in reality was an information-gathering operation used to root out suspected Vietcong operatives and arrange for their arrest, torture, or murder by South Vietnamese military and police forces. More than 20,000 suspected communists were killed as a result of this controversial operation.

In 1973, Colby was appointed director of the CIA by President Nixon. He immediately set to work "cleaning house" by writing a 693-page document that came to be known as the "family jewels," in which he exposed many of the agency's misdeeds and his own part in several of them. These incidents included bribery, plans to assassinate Fidel Castro and other communist leaders, mail interception, drugging, and various other covert operations. Colby was ousted in November 1975, and replaced by George BUSH in 1976. Colby's former CIA colleagues now viewed him as a traitor, although others felt Colby had saved the agency by coming clean about its operations before they were exposed by an independent investigation. He was accused of being a double agent for the Soviet Union, a charge that was never proven. He wrote about his experiences and his views of covert intelligence in his autobiography, *An Honorable Man: My Life in the CIA* (1978).

After he left the CIA, Colby practiced law in Washington and became a consultant for several firms in the Far East, as well as for the South Korean government. He also became a crusader for arms control and an outspoken opponent of the military buildup during the Reagan administration. In April 1996, he drowned during a solo canoeing trip on the Wicomico River in Maryland.

Colson, Charles (1931–)

Charles W. Colson is a former official of the administration of President NIXON and a key figure in the WATERGATE scandal of the 1970s. A native of Boston and a graduate of Brown University, Colson went on to earn his law degree at George Washington University, from which he graduated in 1959. He spent the next 10 years as an attorney before being recruited as special counsel to President Nixon in 1969. He soon developed a close and trusting relationship with the president. Colson left the White House in 1972, but continued to be employed by Nixon as an unpaid consultant. Prior to his departure, in 1971, he brought in former CIA operative E. Howard Hunt to join the White House staff. The following year, Hunt became known to the public as one of the "PLUMBERS" involved in the burglary of the Democratic National Committee headquarters at Watergate. Hunt had also been involved in the 1971 burglary of offices belonging to Daniel ELLSBERG's psychiatrist—Ellsberg, a Defense Department analyst, having provoked the ire of the White House by making the PENTAGON PAPERS available to journalists.

When Colson's involvement in the Watergate break-in was uncovered, he and six other men were indicted on perjury and conspiracy charges, on March 1, 1974. One week later, he was charged with obstruction of justice regarding the burglary of Ellsberg's psychiatrist's office. He pleaded guilty to the latter charge, whereupon all other charges against him were dropped. While serving a term of seven months in prison, he became a born-again Christian and started a ministry program called Prison Fellowship. This program has grown since its inception, and now has more than 40,000 volunteers participating in all 50 states.

Committee on the Present Danger

Founded by Tracy Voorhees, then undersecretary of the army, in 1950, the Committee on the Present Danger was originally intended to promote NSC-68, the plans for rearmament that Paul NITZE had drafter with Dean ACHESON. Voorhees eventually resigned his position in protest over cuts for military funding, but the committee continued on, expanding its focus to support the U.S. buildup of nuclear arms. It was dormant during the 1960s, then revived by Nitze and others in 1976; Nitze subsequently became its chairman of policy studies. Other members of the committee included Richard ALLEN, William CASEY, Jeane KIRKPATRICK, George SHULTZ, and Ronald REAGAN, who made the committee's philosophy a cornerstone of his presidency.

The committee was essentially an organization for HAWKS (both Republicans and Democrats) who rallied together against COMMUNISM and the SALT II agreement, and for increases in defense spending. The committee's greatest fear was that the United States was losing the Cold War and should take any necessary actions to maintain a strong CIVIL DEFENSE and a nuclear advantage over the Soviet Union in order to ward off attack and possible annihilation at Soviet hands.

communism

Rooted in theories developed by philosophers Karl Marx and Friedrich Engels that called for a social order in which all property was commonly owned, communism as it came to be known during the Cold War years was a political system whose primary purpose was the overthrow of capitalism and the establishment of a totalitarian regime in which individual thought and action were controlled by a single ruling entity. In an ideal socialist society, as Marx and Engels envisioned it, there would be no class divisions, and all citizens would work together for the common good, eschewing materialism in favor of the equal sharing of property and goods that would be achieved through the application of equal effort. In the mid-19th century, when the two philosophers proposed their theories, the Industrial Revolution was in full swing, and the great disparity that had emerged between owners and workers fueled their sense of injustice and seemed to signal a need for the more equitable system of government that they envisioned. Numerous incidents of labor unrest in the late 1800s and early 1900s also appeared to bolster their theories.

This, then, was the premise on which Leon Trotsky and Vladimir Lenin first established a communist government following the Russian Revolution of 1917. However, their socialist ideals were soon displaced by a struggle for power between the two leaders. Lenin prevailed and eventually established a dictatorship that was marked by repression of individual rights. Lenin also strove to suppress the basic freedoms that are taken for granted in democratic societies, where, ironically, the rise of the middle class soon obscured the owner-worker disparities and bolstered the growing effectiveness of capitalism. Such freedoms were not acceptable in a communist society where, in hopes of ensuring equal treatment for all, restrictions were placed on citizens' thoughts and actions. Such was the dichotomy of the Soviet system, which was originally based on socialist principles but soon became something quite different. For instance, instead of eliminating class distinctions, communist governments such as those established in Russia and China actually created a sharper division between workers ("the proletariat") and their leaders, resulting in a favored ruling class entitled to special privileges often denied the proletariat.

By 1927, when Joseph Stalin came to power in the Soviet Union, the communist mandate established by Lenin was no longer applied just to that country but to all countries that came within its sphere of influence and beyond—i.e., world domination. But for communism to succeed, it had to overcome the so-called greedy materialism of capitalism and implement a collective way of life to which all people would become subject. To accomplish this, all resistance had to be crushed, by violent means, if necessary—which was exactly what Stalin did, as did Mao Zedong in China some years later. Stalin, for instance, killed thousands of Russians in his quest to exert complete control over the country, so many that he actually handicapped himself when World War II broke out, for he had killed many of his best generals.

Ultimately, the original aims of communism and its subsequent applications in China, Cuba, and the Soviet Union proved to be paradoxical and self-defeating. Meanwhile, capitalist countries such as the United States came to fear the loss of freedom and individual expression that communism represented. This led to the rise of *anticommunism,* whose practitioners sometimes resorted to extreme measures to prevent communists from gaining any sort of a foothold. The WITCH HUNTS of the McCarthy era in the 1950s provided a particularly noteworthy example of anticommunism

gone haywire. It should be noted, however, that many anticommunists were politicians and intellectuals who found communism to be morally repugnant. Also falling under that rubric were members of any organized group fighting to expel communism from a country or region.

conscientious objectors

A natural outgrowth of PACIFISM, conscientious objection (CO) is practiced by those who oppose war on moral or religious grounds and is not to be confused with DRAFT RESISTANCE. In the United States, those individuals who are granted conscientious objector status are generally exempted from military enlistment, since, the reasoning goes, that government cannot morally compel them to do something that violates their personal beliefs. However, they are often required to serve their country in other ways. Prior to the KOREAN WAR, conscientious objectors usually cited the tenets of their religion as reasons for their refusal to fight. However, as the Cold War deepened, American citizens began to question U.S. involvement in the wars of other nations and whether the lives of their young men should be sacrificed for what many thought to be dubious causes. Consequently, there was a significant rise in applications for CO status, although the reasons given now went beyond the religious and into areas of personal philosophy and moral objection. The definition became even broader during the VIETNAM WAR era, when the U.S. Supreme Court began allowing exemptions for "beliefs that are purely ethical or moral in source." Many HAWKS deemed conscientious objectors to be cowards avoiding service to their country. However, since 1973, CO status is no longer an issue, as military conscription was eliminated at that time and the country's armed forces have become all-volunteer in nature.

containment

The diplomatic (and, in time, military) policy of containment was the best-known and most-used American response to communist expansion during the earliest years of the Cold War. The word was coined by diplomat and expert on Soviet issues George KENNAN, who recommended containment as a means of keeping the Soviet Union from taking over other vulnerable countries in Eastern Europe and Asia (and from there to other parts of the world). As originally conceived, the policy held that by limiting the expansion of COMMU-

NISM, the Soviet system would be weakened to the point of collapse. Initially this was to be obtained through diplomatic and educational measures, a result of which was the establishment of such alliances as the NORTH ATLANTIC TREATY ORGANIZATION (NATO) and the SOUTHEAST ASIA TREATY ORGANIZATION (SEATO). However, in time the United States began to resort to military measures, as in the establishment of U.S. bases in key locations around the world and increased American involvement in the Korean and Vietnam Wars.

Containment was practiced to its greatest degree in the 1950s during the tenure of John Foster DULLES as secretary of state. It lessened after that (even Kennan came to prefer a policy of disengagement over containment), although echoes of the policy resounded throughout the 1960s until rebounding briefly in the 1970s and 1980s. However, as the downfall of communism in the Soviet Union became inevitable, politicians began looking forward, to the point where George Bush's foreign policy as president would be labeled "beyond containment."

Contras

Contras was the name given to Nicaraguan rebel forces (originally members of the Nicaraguan National Guard under Anastasio Somoza, Jr.) opposed to the ruling Sandinista government. The name, which was drawn from the Spanish word for *counterrevolutionary,* became etched in the U.S. consciousness when details of the IRAN-CONTRA AFFAIR came to light in 1986.

counterculture

A rebellious response to the ESTABLISHMENT, the counterculture was an eclectic assortment of individuals whose views and actions generally ran counter to the prevailing mores of society, especially in the late 1960s, when they were at the forefront of many protest movements. Members of the counterculture could be professional agitators, antiwar demonstrators, college dropouts, anti-intellectuals, or dissidents; in the minds of the public, they were generally all associated with drug experimentation and alternate lifestyles. Another popular word for those in the counterculture was HIPPIES.

credibility gap

The "credibility gap" became a popular term in the mid- to late 1960s as cynical Americans increasingly came to distrust their political leaders, particularly in regard to the VIETNAM WAR. When public statements were belied by the facts, a politician was said to suffer from a credibility gap, the size of which was often determined by the scope of his or her statements. Lyndon JOHNSON was one at whom the credibility gap charge was frequently leveled. His former White House press secretary, Bill Moyers, commented on this when he said Johnson's credibility gap was "the difference between what the president says and what the people would like him to say or what they think he should say." Journalist Walter LIPPMANN saw it differently, feeling that the credibility gap in Johnson's administration was "the result of a deliberate policy of artificial manipulation of official news." The phrase became so prevalent that it became a major issue in the 1968 presidential campaign, and American GIs in South Vietnam even wore buttons that declared, "Ambushed at credibility gap."

Cronkite, Walter (1916–   )

After graduating from the University of Texas in 1935, Walter Leland Cronkite went to work as a reporter for the *Houston Post.* He worked briefly for Scripps-Howard before joining the United Press (UP) in 1939 as a news writer. When World War II erupted, Cronkite went to Europe as UP's war correspondent. He remained there after the war, first as UP's European correspondent, then as its Moscow bureau chief. In 1950, he joined the Columbia Broadcasting System (CBS) and became a Washington news correspondent. He was the anchorman of the *CBS Evening News* from 1962 to 1981, and also provided insightful news commentary on major stories during that time.

In his early years as a television anchorman, Cronkite was strongly supportive of the government and the Cold War. However, he became disillusioned by what he viewed as the American military's deception of the public, particularly after he visited Vietnam (following the TET OFFENSIVE). Cronkite's subsequent public criticism of U.S. policy in Vietnam was a major factor in the rise of mainstream opposition to American intervention in Indochina, and indirectly led to President Lyndon JOHNSON's decision not to run for reelection.

In addition to his journalistic responsibilities, Cronkite was host of the Emmy Award-winning television series *The 20th Century* from 1957 to 1966, and *The 21st Century* from 1967 to 1969. He won Peabody Awards in 1962 and 1981; received the George Polk

Journalism Award in 1971; and in January 1981 he was awarded the Medal of Freedom by President Jimmy Carter. Cronkite retired from newscasting in March 1981, but continued on with CBS as a special correspondent and has also worked on documentaries. In addition, he served on the network's board of directors from 1981 to 1991.

Cuban Missile Crisis

The events that transpired during the Cuban Missile Crisis in 1962 would prove to be one of the most defining moments of the Cold War, as well as a public relations triumph for President John F. KENNEDY. In

August 1962, U.S. intelligence discovered that the Soviet Union was building silos and storing nuclear missiles in Cuba. This was perceived to be a clear threat of possible attack on the United States, leaving President Kennedy and his advisers with a dilemma: Should they put the nation at further risk by responding with military measures, or were other, more diplomatic solutions possible? The crisis reached a climax in October of that year, when Kennedy, choosing to walk a fine line between the two options, instituted a "quarantine" on Cuba, establishing a military blockade of its ports and preventing any more missiles from being delivered. Furthermore, he demanded that the Soviet Union dismantle and remove all missiles already

Aerial photo showing Soviet missile installations in Cuba. (KENNEDY LIBRARY)

in Cuba. The standoff between Kennedy and Soviet premier Nikita Khrushchev lasted several days. In the end, Khrushchev agreed to Kennedy's demands. In return, Kennedy agreed to a pledge that the United States would not invade Cuba and that obsolete American missiles would be removed from Turkey.

The Cuban Missile Crisis has frequently been studied and debated by historians, and many have questioned Kennedy's decisions, even though they proved to be successful. On one point all are agreed, however: Without the very real threat of annihilation that nuclear weaponry and its use posed to the entire world, a war would almost certainly have occurred between the United States and the USSR. Thus, credence was given to the policy of nuclear DETERRENCE that would become the watchword of the later years of the Cold War. Another outcome of the crisis was an increase in the arms race between the world's two superpowers and the eventual signing of a limited nuclear test-ban treaty in 1963—as well as Khrushchev's downfall in the Soviet Union.

D

Daley, Richard (1902–1976)

Called "the last of the big-city bosses" because of his iron-fisted control of Chicago politics for over 20 years, Richard Joseph Daley served as mayor of Chicago from 1955 until his death. He also achieved great power in Democratic Party politics on a national scale.

Born and raised in Chicago, Daley was admitted to the bar in 1933 and quickly rose through the ranks of the Cook County Democratic club. He served in the state legislature, first as a representative and then as a senator, from 1936 to 1946. He was state director of revenue from 1940 to 1950, and served as clerk of Cook County (1950–55) before being elected mayor. After his election, he quickly consolidated his power and became the dominant force in Illinois Democratic politics, which he would influence for the rest of his life. He also gained the confidence of the business community through large-scale urban renewal and highway construction projects.

For years, Daley's support was considered critical by Democrats aspiring to the presidential nomination. Nevertheless, he was often subjected to harsh criticism for a number of failings in his administration, among them his reluctance to take action against racial segre-gation in housing and public schools, the unchecked construction of tall office buildings in the downtown area, and, perhaps most famously, the brutal measures taken by the police force against demonstrators protesting the VIETNAM WAR during the 1968 DEMO-CRATIC NATIONAL CONVENTION in Chicago. During the last years of Daley's administration, several of his officials became embroiled in accusations of wrongdoing, although Daley himself remained untouched by scandal. His eldest son, Richard M. Daley, was elected mayor of Chicago in 1989, and was reelected in 1991.

Davis, Angela (1944–)

Angela Yvonne Davis is a black activist who gained national and international attention in 1970–72 when she was charged with conspiracy. The daughter of Alabama schoolteachers, she studied both at home and abroad (1961–67) before entering the University of California at San Diego to study for her Ph.D. Her mentor there was Herbert Marcuse, a professor who espoused Marxism. Davis became a lecturer in philos-ophy, and acquired an excellent reputation for her teaching style and abilities. However, because of what they felt were her extreme political views, the

California Board of Regents refused to renew her appointment in 1970.

In time, Davis became a champion for the cause of black prisoners, and she grew especially close to one of the infamous Soledad (Prison) Brothers, a young revolutionary named George Jackson. On August 7, 1970, a botched kidnapping and escape attempt from the Hall of Justice in Marin County, California, resulted in the deaths of four persons, including the trial judge and Jackson's brother, Jonathan. Davis was suspected of complicity in the crime, and the subsequent search for her placed her on the FBI's "Most Wanted" list. She was finally located in New York City in October 1970, where she was arrested and returned to California to face charges of kidnapping, murder, and conspiracy. An all-white jury acquitted her of all charges. In 1980, she ran unsuccessfully for U.S. vice president on the Communist Party ticket. She has written several books, including *Angela Davis: An Autobiography* (1974); *Women, Race & Class* (1981); and *Women, Culture & Politics* (1989).

Day, Dorothy (1897–1980)

Dorothy Day was a Roman Catholic social activist, pacifist, and journalist best known for her efforts in helping to found the Catholic Worker movement in 1933. Born in Brooklyn, she spent two years at the University of Illinois before returning to New York as a social worker. She was an active member of the Socialist Party and closely involved with various Communist Party affiliates. As a journalist, she wrote primarily for socialist and communist publications. In 1927, she embraced Roman Catholicism, and on May 1, 1933, she and fellow writer Peter Maurin (1877–1949) launched the *Catholic Worker,* a newspaper devoted to social problems and the solutions provided by the Catholic Church; the title of the paper eventually became the name of her Christian movement for peace. Day also involved herself in charitable works, organizing hospitality houses for the homeless and hungry. She earned a reputation for her support of racial equality and organized labor, and for her calls for universal disarmament. She was a tireless antiwar protester, believing that there were absolutely no exceptions to the commandment "Thou shalt not kill." Day had her share of detractors, as she often held provocative views on such subjects as the ATOMIC BOMB, about which she said that it "is not just 'out there.' It is also within us. . . . It came from us and is now enthroned." Her

views heavily influenced such antiwar protesters as Daniel BERRIGAN and Philip BERRIGAN. Day's many books include *From Union Square to Rome* (1938); *House of Hospitality* (1939); *Loaves and Fishes* (1963); and her autobiography, *The Long Loneliness* (1981).

Dean, John (1938–)

John Wesley Dean III is a lawyer best known for the role he played during the WATERGATE scandal in the 1970s. Born in Ohio, he graduated from the College of Wooster in 1961, and went from there to Washington, where he received his law degree from Georgetown University in 1965. He worked as chief minority counsel to the House Judiciary Committee in 1966–67, then went on to a two-year term as associate director of the National Commission on Reform of Federal Criminal Laws. After Richard NIXON was elected president in 1968, Dean accepted an appointment as an associate attorney general. In 1970, Nixon selected Dean to be White House counsel.

On June 17, 1972, a break-in occurred at the Democratic National Committee headquarters in the Watergate Hotel. As implications of White House involvement became increasingly explicit, Dean began confessing what he knew to federal investigators. Nixon fired him on April 30, 1973. Two months later, Dean testified publicly before the Senate Select Committee on Presidential Campaign Activities, revealing how White House officials—including Dean and the president—had obstructed justice in order to cover up their participation in the Watergate break-in. The administration denied the charges (eventually corroborated on White House tapes) and attempted to focus public attention on various foreign policy initiatives, including the effort to develop DÉTENTE with Russia.

Dean was one of the most damaging witnesses to speak out against Nixon during the Watergate affair, which eventually resulted in Nixon's resignation. Several of Nixon's former top aides, including Dean himself, were imprisoned for their roles in Watergate. Dean wrote of his experiences in his book, *Blind Ambition* (1976).

Declaration of Conscience

By June 1950, Republican senator Joseph MCCARTHY was well into his campaign to ferret out supposed communist infiltration in the U.S. government. He had captured the public imagination with his crusade, as well as the support of a good portion of the Senate. However, several of his fellow Republicans, led by Senator Margaret Chase Smith of Maine, were appalled by his conduct and its effect on the national psyche. To express their moral outrage with his actions, they drew up a manifesto that they named their "Declaration of Conscience." Although McCarthy was never mentioned by name, it was clear that he was their target when they wrote: "Certain elements of the Republican Party have materially added to confusion . . . through the selfish political exploitation of fear, bigotry, ignorance, and intolerance. It is high time that we all stopped being tools and victims of totalitarian techniques . . . that if continued here unchecked will surely end what we have come to cherish as the American way." The document was signed by Smith and Senators George Aiken of Vermont, Robert Hendrickson of New Jersey, Irving Ives of New York, Wayne MORSE of Oregon, and Edward Thye of Minnesota. The document had little effect except to foreshadow the eventual national disgust that McCarthy would evoke two years later, when his investigations began to run completely out of control. Ultimately, he was censured by his former colleagues.

Dellinger, David (1915–   )

A member of one of New England's oldest families, David Dellinger is an author and editor who has affected the American social conscience with his pursuits as an activist for peace. He graduated from Yale University in 1936, and went on to further studies at Oxford University, Yale Divinity School, and, from 1939 to 1940, Union Theological Seminary. A confirmed pacifist, his resistance to being drafted into military service led to his being jailed in 1940 and again in 1943. He was released in 1945, and proceeded to found the Libertarian Press cooperative. In time, he came to be regarded as a leader in the radical PACIFISM movement, espousing nonviolent activism in the cause of peace. In 1956, he became the editor and publisher of the movement's major journal, *Liberation.* He became an outspoken opponent of the VIETNAM WAR, and worked with the North Vietnamese government to obtain the release of American prisoners of war. In 1968, at the Democratic National Convention in Chicago, he helped to lead an antiwar demonstration that erupted into a riot. He and others involved in this incident, including Jerry RUBIN and Abbie HOFFMAN, were put on trial as the "CHICAGO SEVEN." They

engaged in numerous courtroom antics during the trial and gained widespread MEDIA attention. Dellinger and the others were acquitted of charges of conspiracy to incite a riot, but were found guilty of crossing state lines with intent to incite a riot. The convictions were later overturned.

Dellinger remained true to his radical roots throughout his life, keeping himself outside the ESTABLISHMENT mainstream. He eventually became the editor of *Seven Days,* a magazine that stressed the need for nonviolent but radical change. In 1980, he left the magazine and moved to Vermont, where he taught and wrote books, the most recent being *From Yale to Jail* in 1993. His other books include *Revolutionary Nonviolence* (1970) and *More Power Than We Know* (1975).

Democratic Socialists of America   See HARRINGTON, Michael.

détente

Détente was the foreign policy put into practice by President Richard NIXON and his secretary of state, Henry KISSINGER, as they worked to develop a spirit of cooperation and normalcy between the United States and the Soviet Union. The definition of the French word reflected what they were trying to achieve—in essence: "A relaxing of tensions, especially between nations." Words used by political leaders that are similar to détente in definition and spirit include *accommodation* and *normalization* (of relations).

Although détente had been mentioned by previous presidents in dealing with specific situations, it was Nixon who put it to its severest test in a larger arena. His primary objectives were to come to agreement with the Soviet Union on arms control, ward off the possibility of future military confrontations, and work to forge closer economic and cultural ties between the two superpowers. While Nixon and Kissinger did succeed in achieving some victories in their efforts—most notably the SALT I treaty—ultimately they did nothing that helped to bring the Cold War to a speedier conclusion. Despite their efforts to curb the ARMS RACE, a strong rivalry centered around nuclear superiority would persist between the two nations for some time. In addition, in the course of improving relations with the Soviet Union and China, Nixon and Kissinger managed to offend many of their allies in NATO and other countries in the THIRD WORLD who felt either overlooked or ignored during negotiations. Détente was also criticized by hard-liners who saw it as "giving away the store" and getting nothing in return. Subsequently, President Gerald FORD did his best to distance himself from the policy, while President Jimmy CARTER tried to give it respectability by describing détente as "progress toward peace." President Ronald REAGAN had such contempt for détente that he and others in his administration would refer to it as "the d-word." Certainly it proved to be a useless policy following the 1979 Soviet invasion of Afghanistan, upon which hostile relations between the United States and the USSR intensified and alternative foreign policies had to be implemented.

deterrence

Deterrence is a means of protection against enemy attack through the capability of MASSIVE RETALIATION—in essence, military preparedness. In the Cold War age, deterrence came to be associated with nuclear arsenals; it was believed that a nation able to strike back instantly with weapons of mass destruction provided a very effective deterrent to war.

Dewey, Thomas (1901–1971)

A longtime Republican leader and U.S. prosecuting attorney, Thomas Edmund Dewey gained fame for his three successful terms as governor of New York (1943–55) and for his two failed bids for the U.S. presidency in 1944 and 1948. Dewey graduated from the University of Michigan in 1923 and received his law degree from Columbia University in 1925. He was admitted to the New York bar in 1926. Five years later, he launched his career in government service by serving as chief assistant to the U.S. attorney in the southern district of the state. He came to national attention during the years of 1935 to 1937, when he acted as special prosecutor in an investigation of organized crime in New York. Out of 73 prosecutions, he obtained 72 convictions. Having acquired a reputation for drive and integrity, Dewey was elected district attorney in 1937.

He first ran for governor of New York in 1938, and lost, but starting in 1942, he was elected for three successive terms. He became known and respected for his political moderation and administrative efficiency; among other accomplishments, he established the first state agency to eliminate discrimination in employment. In

1944, he was chosen as the Republican nominee for president. He was not expected to win against the powerful incumbent, Franklin D. Roosevelt, nor did he. In 1948, however, pollsters predicted an easy victory for Dewey over Harry TRUMAN, but Truman won a stunning upset, thanks to the loyalty of farm and labor supporters.

Having failed in his own bids for the presidency, Dewey nevertheless remained influential in national politics, and in 1952 he played a key role in securing the nominations of Dwight D. EISENHOWER and Richard NIXON for president and vice president. At the conclusion of his third term as governor, Dewey returned to private law practice, but remained a close adviser to Republican presidents. In 1968, Richard Nixon asked Dewey to serve as chief justice of the U.S. Supreme Court, but because of his age, Dewey refused the position.

dirty tricks

Although now commonly associated with the machinations of Richard Nixon's staff during his presidential campaign, "dirty tricks" have actually been employed by the CENTRAL INTELLIGENCE AGENCY (CIA) in many of their covert operations; in fact, during the 1960s and early 1970s, CIA operatives commonly referred to their "Department of Dirty Tricks." The term was acceptable at the time, for it was understood that the CIA often had to resort to extraordinary measures to achieve many of its objectives in gathering intelligence and protecting national security. However, as their activities were gradually revealed, especially during the waning years of the VIETNAM WAR, many critics found these tactics to be abhorrent and unethical.

Dirty tricks have also been used on occasion during presidential campaigns; they were, in fact, often thought of as "pranks" played by one candidate upon another. It was Richard Nixon and his staff who gave the term the criminal connotations it now has, due to many of the illegal activities employed by the tricksters, led by Donald Segretti, to undermine other candidates' campaigns during the 1972 election. Numerous details about the dirty tricks became known to the public as the WATERGATE scandal unfolded. Particularly notorious was the revelation of tactics employed to sabotage Edmund MUSKIE's campaign, including publication of false allegations that his wife had a drinking problem. Muskie became so emotional as he defended his wife that he began to cry on camera—and, later, withdrew from the race.

disengagement   See KENNAN, George

Dominican crisis (1965)

In 1965, the United States sent troops into the Dominican Republic, ostensibly to help quell a revolution against the military regime there and to protect American interests in the process. In reality, U.S. president Lyndon JOHNSON and his advisers feared the possible establishment of a communist government under former president Juan Bosch. After fighting broke out between the rebels and the government, the ORGANIZATION OF AMERICAN STATES met and approved the U.S. decision to import troops to control the fighting. They subsequently agreed to allow an inter-American peacekeeping force into the country to maintain control while a delegation headed by Ellsworth BUNKER was dispatched to negotiate a peace settlement. These actions, although successful in the end from the American point of view, tarnished U.S. relations with its Latin American allies as they belied the "good neighbor" status the United States had tried to achieve with such initiatives as the ALLIANCE FOR PROGRESS. In addition, many saw the Dominican intervention as a public relations tactic designed to offset the American diplomatic and military failures in Vietnam. The peacekeeping troops remained in the Dominican Republic until September 1966, by which time a stable government had been set up under the leadership of Joaquin Balaguer.

domino theory

The *domino theory* was a popular term often used to justify U.S. intervention in the conflicts of other countries. The theory held that if any one nation in a particular region fell under communist control (or control of any other repressive system), then other countries in the area would follow in quick succession, collapsing like dominoes, one after the next. The domino theory was first applied by the administration of President Harry TRUMAN in its response to possible communist threats in Greece and Turkey. Later attention focused on the perceived Soviet interest in Southeast Asia, and, acting on the possible scenarios posed by the domino theory, Presidents Dwight EISENHOWER, John F. KENNEDY, and Lyndon JOHNSON all committed to U.S. military involvement in South Vietnam, where it was believed the communist threat was greatest. The theory was later invoked by President Ronald REAGAN

with regard to the anticommunist efforts of his administration in Central America. However, the domino theory has had its critics. President Kennedy had his own doubts about it, while Senator J. William FULBRIGHT argued that "The inference we have drawn from this is that we must fight in one country in order to avoid having to fight in another, although we could with equal logic have inferred that it is useless to fight in one country when the same conditions are present in another." (Fulbright, *The Arrogance of Power.*)

Douglas, Helen Gahagan (1900–1980)

A notable figure in U.S. politics, Helen Gahagan started her career as an actress and achieved moderate success on Broadway in the 1920s. She then moved on to opera, touring with several European opera companies until 1930. In 1931, she married actor Melvyn Douglas. During the 1930s and later, during World War II, she worked as a high-profile volunteer and performed relief work related to the New Deal. Finding she had an affinity for politics, she ran for Congress from the 14th district in California and was elected in 1944. An unabashedly liberal Democrat, she served in the House of Representatives from 1945 to 1950, when she ran for the U.S. Senate against Richard M. NIXON, who had won national acclaim as a result of his investigation of Alger HISS. Nixon portrayed Douglas to voters as a communist sympathizer by circulating 580,000 pink sheets summing up similarities between her voting record and that of liberal New York congressman Vito Marcantonio, who was believed to be procommunist). The tactic worked; Nixon won by nearly 700,000 votes.

Embittered by her defeat, Douglas withdrew from politics for several years; but as the Cold War intensified and U.S. involvement in the VIETNAM WAR increased, she entered the peace movement. In 1964, she represented the Jane Addams Peace Association at the Soviet-American Women's Peace Conference in Moscow.

doves and hawks

Public opinion on U.S. involvement in the VIETNAM WAR and other world conflicts generally divided into two points of view: that of the hawks, who supported military intervention, and that of the doves, who lobbied for peace. Doves were believers in APPEASEMENT, accommodation, and conciliation as a means of settling hostilities between nations. Hawks—once called "warhawks"—

were those who believed aggressive action yielded better results than diplomatic "pussyfooting."

The two terms came to be used with increasing frequency during the Cold War. Their inherent divisiveness could be seen, for example, during the CUBAN MISSILE CRISIS, when President John F. KENNEDY's advisers split sharply in their opinions on how the United States should respond to the Soviet Union. Adlai STEVENSON took the dove's position, advocating a diplomatic solution to the crisis. He was opposed by McGeorge BUNDY, Robert KENNEDY, and Dean RUSK, all of whom sided with the hawk's preference for military retaliation. Stevenson and others who were identified in the press as doves were subsequently viewed as "soft," thus damaging their public image.

Doves were at the forefront of the ANTIWAR MOVEMENT during the 1960s and early 1970s, often leading demonstrations for peace. Hawks were generally members of the NEW RIGHT, hardline conservatives who supported the war in Vietnam and took an "AMERICA, LOVE IT OR LEAVE IT" attitude against the opposing doves.

draft resistance

A direct outgrowth of protest against the VIETNAM WAR in the 1960s was the resistance movement against being drafted into military service. Unlike CONSCIENTIOUS OBJECTORS, who could be exempted from combat duty on (largely) religious grounds, draft resisters simply objected to being conscripted against their will to fight a battle that they felt was not theirs to fight.

Military drafts are common in times of war, but the Selective Service Acts of 1940 and 1948 were established when the United States was at peace. Young men of predetermined ages were at certain times required to register with local draft boards, whereupon they might or might not be called for military service, according to world events and political circumstances. Inevitably, the men were called for duty in World War II, in the KOREAN WAR, in the Vietnam War, and also to serve in special crisis situations. The number of men drafted depended on the situation. In the case of the Vietnam War, huge numbers were forced into service for what turned out to be an unpopular conflict and the object of massive protests. Most soldiers accepted their lot and went to Vietnam. However, pockets of resisters around the country added fuel to the ANTIWAR MOVEMENT's fire at demonstrations with chants of "HELL, NO, WE WON'T GO!" as well as cries of "Make love, not war!" Other actions often taken included public burnings of draft cards, riots at induction centers, and, in some cases, flight to other countries, usually Canada or Sweden.

Due to pressure to reform the draft, the system was changed to a controversial "lottery" in 1969, which was refined in 1970. Draft inductions ceased in 1973 and registrations were suspended altogether from 1974 to 1980. In July 1980, a new registration system was instituted that remains in effect today. However, since 1973, the armed services have relied entirely on volunteers and reserve forces, thus making draft resistance a moot issue.

Dukakis, Michael (1933–)

A former governor of Massachusetts and the son of Greek immigrants, Michael Dukakis came to national attention in 1988, when he was selected to be the Democratic Party's nominee for president. After graduating from Swarthmore College in 1955, he entered the armed forces, and served in South Korea. In 1960, he earned his law degree from Harvard Law School, and almost immediately became involved in Massachusetts politics. From 1962 to 1970, he served in the state's House of Representatives. In 1970, he ran for lieutenant governor and lost, but in 1974 he won election as governor of Massachusetts. Faced with a serious budget crisis, Dukakis managed to restore the state's fiscal health. Despite this, he lost his bid for reelection in 1978. However, he was again elected governor in 1982, and enjoyed great popularity due to his strengthening of the state's economy by saving old industries and encouraging the growth of new ones. Partly because of his efforts, Massachusetts for a time enjoyed one of the nation's healthiest economies, and Dukakis was reelected by a wide margin in 1986.

Dukakis declared his candidacy for the U.S. presidency in April 1987. During the 1988 primaries, he emerged as the most popular Democratic candidate and won his party's nomination. However, he lost the election in November 1988 to George BUSH. A key point in the campaign was Bush's implication that Dukakis's patriotism was somehow suspect, given his administration's stand on the compulsory recitation of the Pledge of Allegiance in schools; the charge apparently resonated with voters, and Dukakis failed to launch an effective counterattack.

Dukakis did not run for reelection as governor of Massachusetts, and left office at the conclusion of his term in January 1991.

Dulles, Allen (1893–1969)

Allen Welsh Dulles was a U.S. diplomat and intelligence expert who directed the CENTRAL INTELLIGENCE AGENCY (CIA) during its earliest period of growth. The younger brother of John Foster DULLES, Allen Dulles received his M.A. degree from Princeton in 1926, then served in various diplomatic posts until 1922, when he was named chief of the State Department's Near Eastern Division. He received his law degree in 1926, upon which he served briefly as counselor to the U.S. delegation in Peking. He then joined his brother's New York law firm. After the United States entered World War II, Dulles was recruited for the OFFICE OF STRATEGIC SERVICES (OSS). He served as chief of the OSS office in Bern from October 1942 to May 1945, and played a major role in the events that led to the surrender of German troops in northern Italy.

In 1948, Dulles was designated chairman of a three-man committee whose purpose was to assess the U.S. intelligence system. Their conclusions led to the establishment of the CIA in 1947. Dulles served as the agency's deputy director under General Walter Bedell SMITH until he was appointed director in 1953 by President EISENHOWER. The CIA proved to be effective in a large number of overseas operations, including the overthrow of the government of Mohammed Mossadeq in Iran (1953) and Jacobo Arbenz in Guatemala (1954). The agency also managed to obtain a copy of Nikita Khrushchev's secret 1956 speech denouncing Stalin. However, the agency was put on the spot when a U-2 intelligence plane was shot down over the Soviet Union on the eve of a scheduled summit conference in June 1960. It was eventually revealed that many such espionage flights had taken place in recent years, despite earlier government announcements to the contrary.

Dulles was reappointed to his post by President John F. KENNEDY, but he soon incurred major embarrassment for the Kennedy administration with his role in the BAY OF PIGS fiasco in April 1961; Dulles resigned that autumn. He later served on the Warren Commission, which investigated Kennedy's 1963 assassination. He authored several books, including *Germany's Underground* (1947); *The Craft of Intelligence* (1963); and *The Secret Surrender* (1966).

Dulles, John Foster (1888–1959)

Known as a principal architect of U.S. foreign policy during the Cold War, John Foster Dulles was one of five children born into a distinguished family. His maternal grandfather was John Watson Foster, who served as secretary of state under President Benjamin Harrison. His younger brother was Allen DULLES, director of the CIA from 1953 to 1961; his uncle by marriage, Robert Lansing, was secretary of state under President Woodrow Wilson. Dulles himself was a brilliant student; he attended both Princeton and George Washington Universities, as well as the Sorbonne. In 1911, he joined the law firm of Sullivan and Cromwell as a specialist in international law, and by 1927 he had become the head of the firm.

His diplomatic career began early when, in 1907, at the age of 19, he accompanied his grandfather to the second international peace conference at The Hague. Upon the conclusion of World War I, when he was just 30, he was named by President Woodrow Wilson as legal counsel to the Versailles Peace Conference. He also served as a member of the war reparations commission. In 1945, Dulles served as a senior adviser at the San Francisco conference for the UNITED NATIONS, for which he had previously helped to prepare the charter. He was

John Foster Dulles, Adlai Stevenson, and Eleanor Roosevelt at the United Nations (ROOSEVELT LIBRARY)

also tapped by President Harry TRUMAN and Secretary of State Dean ACHESON to negotiate and conclude a peace treaty with Japan that was acceptable to the other nations involved. By 1951, the agreed-upon treaty was signed in San Francisco by Japan and 48 other nations.

In January 1953, Dulles became secretary of state under President Dwight D. EISENHOWER. With Eisenhower's confidence and support, foreign policy planning flourished under Dulles's direction. He initiated the Manila conference in 1954, which resulted in the SOUTHEAST ASIA TREATY ORGANIZATION (SEATO) pact, which united eight nations in a neutral defense agreement. (U.S.-SEATO commitments were a primary justification for U.S. involvement in Vietnam.) This was followed in 1955 by the Baghdad Pact, later called the CENTRAL TREATY ORGANIZATION (CENTO), which organized the so-called northern tier countries of the Middle East into a defense organization. Dulles was also instrumental in putting together the Austrian State Treaty of 1955, which restored Austria's pre-1938 frontiers and forbade any future union between Germany and Austria; and the Trieste Agreement of 1954, which provided for partition of the free territory between Italy and Yugoslavia.

Dulles's foreign policy was largely based on his opposition to violence, his strong belief in the value of treaties, and his profound distrust and dislike of the communist state. He coined the term *brinkmanship* in a 1956 magazine article, arguing that "the ability to get to the verge without getting into war is a necessary art." He was also a proponent of the concept of LIBERATION. A strong leader with a powerful personality, Dulles took special pride in pushing the Soviet Union as far to the brink as possible, and made effective use of the threat of MASSIVE RETALIATION. During the Austrian state treaty negotiations, he refused to compromise on some minor points, even though the Austrians were themselves willing to accede to the Soviets. Dulles maintained his position and the Soviets yielded to him.

Dulles is generally considered to be one of the most influential secretaries of state in American history. His books include *War, Peace, and Change* (1939) and *War or Peace* (1950).

Dylan, Bob (1941–)

Born Robert Zimmerman, Bob Dylan is a singer and songwriter who helped to shape the direction of the 1960s with his music. After an unhappy childhood in Duluth, Minnesota, Zimmerman changed his name in honor of the poet Dylan Thomas and began to travel around the country in frank imitation of folksinger Woody Guthrie. By the early 1960s, Dylan was singing in New York City in Greenwich Village coffeehouses and recording albums of Guthrie's songs as well as his own. Much of Dylan's early work was openly critical of militarism and racial discrimination, and it had a strong influence on thousands of young people, especially those involved in protest movements. Two of his songs, "Blowin' in the Wind" and "The Times They Are A-Changin'" were popular among antiwar protesters in the mid- to late 1960s, even though the VIETNAM WAR had not been a major national issue at the time of their composition.

Grounded in a tradition of social protest, Dylan's songs also employed metaphorical and allegorical lyrics that opened new territories in folk music. In 1965, he shocked fans by switching from solo acoustic guitar performances to electronically amplified band concerts, embracing the rhythms of rock and roll. His landmark albums *Highway 61 Revisited* (1965) and *Blonde on Blonde* (1966) heightened his popularity and went on to sell millions of copies. He went into seclusion after a motorcycle accident in 1966; when he emerged, he went through another musical transformation and surprised listeners with songs based in a country-and-western style. He continued to perform and to record throughout the 1970s, 1980s, and 1990s, and remains an influential artist in American music. Indeed, he is considered to be a major voice of his generation and one of the foremost representatives of the COUNTERCULTURE.

Joan Baez and Bob Dylan perform at the March on Washington. (NARA STILL PHOTOS DIVISION)

Eastland, James O. (1904–1986)

James Oliver Eastland was a Democratic politician known for his tireless opposition to civil rights legislation. Before being admitted to the bar in 1927, he attended the University of Mississippi, Vanderbilt University, and the University of Alabama. From 1928 to 1932, he served as a member of the Mississippi House of Representatives. In 1941, he was appointed to fill a vacant seat in the U.S. Senate. He subsequently ran for election, and was reelected as Mississippi's senator thereafter, serving from 1943 to 1978. He was consistently opposed to civil rights legislation and virulently denounced the 1954 decision by the U.S. Supreme Court to end SEGREGATION in public schools. An outspoken member of the Senate Judiciary Committee, he became its chairman in 1956. From 1972 until his retirement in 1978, he also served as president pro tempore of the Senate.

Eaton, Cyrus (1883–1979)

Founder of the Republic Steel Corporation, Cyrus Stephen Eaton owed his career as an industrialist and philanthropist to a fateful meeting with John D. Rockefeller. While still a student at McMaster University in Toronto, he met Rockefeller by chance. Rockefeller persuaded him to abandon his idea of joining the ministry and to become a businessman instead. He started in 1907, successfully completing some business transactions with his mentor that enabled him to build a series of power plants in Manitoba. In just a few years, he built several electric power plants in western Canada and had diversified into other utilities, as well as banking and steel in the United States. He became a U.S. citizen in 1913.

Eaton was a rigorous consolidator of the many companies that came under his control. In 1930, he amalgamated several of his steel companies into the Republic Steel Corporation, making it the third largest steel company in the United States. He lost most of his fortune during the Great Depression but he quickly built another business empire with his activities and investments in securities, banking, and railroads. At one time he was a director of approximately 40 companies in which he had holdings. At Eaton's death his fortune was estimated to be around $200 million.

Eaton became a nationally known figure in the 1950s and 1960s due to his calls for nuclear disarmament, as well as his advocacy of improved U.S.-Soviet relations. In the interests of promoting international understanding, he was one of the inaugurators of the Pugwash Conferences, originally held at his lodge in Nova Scotia, at which prominent scientists and scholars from around the world met to exchange views and ideas. His work on behalf of international peace was widely recognized: the USSR awarded him the Lenin Prize in 1960.

Ehrlichman, John (1925–)

A major figure in the WATERGATE scandal, John Daniel Ehrlichman grew up in Washington and California and held several jobs before enlisting in the U.S. Army Air Corps in 1943. He was discharged in 1945, after attaining the rank of first lieutenant, and went on to enroll in the University of California at Los Angeles in 1948. He subsequently went to Stanford University, where he obtained a law degree in 1951. After completing his education, he moved to Seattle, Washington, and established a law firm with several of his associates.

In 1969, President Richard NIXON tapped Ehrlichman to become his domestic affairs adviser. Together with H.R. HALDEMAN, he formed part of a "palace guard" meant to insulate the president from the public and from other members of the government. The two filtered information to and from the president, and exercised considerable authority in Nixon's name. Ehrlichman established a group called the "PLUMBERS," whose purpose was to acquire political intelligence and "repair" information leaks.

Ehrlichman approved covert measures meant to uncover incriminating facts about former federal official Daniel ELLSBERG, who had provided the *New York Times* with the classified history of the Vietnam War known as the PENTAGON PAPERS. On June 17, 1972, five members of Ehrlichman's group were caught at the headquarters of the Democratic National Committee in the Watergate complex. Although Ehrlichman initially suggested making a full public confession, he later became an active participant in the cover-up. After further disclosures revealed the depth of his involvement in the scandal, he resigned from the administration in April 1973. He went on trial the following year and was convicted on charges of conspiracy, perjury, and obstruction of justice He was released from prison in April 1978. He subsequently wrote several books about the scandal and his experiences.

Eisenhower, Dwight David (1890–1969)

Thirty-fourth president of the United States and supreme commander of the Allied Forces in Western Europe during World War II, Dwight David Eisenhower was the third of seven sons born into a poor, religious, and hardworking family. Young Dwight, who was nicknamed "Ike," was only a fair student whose preference was for sports. He graduated from Abilene (Kansas) High School in 1909, and in 1911 he entered the U.S. Military Academy at West Point. His remarkable class of 1915 would later produce 59 generals. Out of 164 graduates, Eisenhower ranked 61st academically and 125th in discipline. He was commissioned a second lieutenant and sent to San Antonio, Texas, where he met Mamie Geneva Doud. They married in 1916, and had two sons, the elder of whom died of scarlet fever in 1921.

During World War I, Eisenhower commanded a tank training center, was promoted to captain, and received the Distinguished Service Medal. From 1922 to 1924, he was assigned to the Panama Canal Zone. His commander, Brigadier General Fox Conner, became his mentor and influenced Eisenhower's selection for the army's command and general staff school at Ft. Leavenworth. In 1926, Eisenhower graduated first in a class of 275; two years later, he graduated from the Army War College. He went on to serve in France and in Washington, D.C., before becoming an aide to army chief of staff General Douglas MACARTHUR in 1933. He accompanied MacArthur to the Philippines in 1935, but returned to the United States shortly after Germany's invasion of Poland in 1939. After a previous series of small but steady promotions, he was swiftly and repeatedly raised in rank, attaining the rank of full colonel in March 1941. Three months later, he was made chief of staff of the Third Army, and soon gained the attention of army chief of staff General George C. MARSHALL for his role in planning war games for almost 500,000 troops.

By March 1942, with the United States now fully involved in World War II, Eisenhower had become a major general as well as head of the operations division of the War Department. In June 1942, Marshall selected him over 366 senior officers to be commander of U.S. troops in Europe. He was promoted to lieutenant general in July 1942, and named to head Operation Torch, the Allied invasion of French North Africa, which was concluded successfully in May 1943. By this time he was a full general, and he directed the amphibious assault on Sicily and the Italian mainland that resulted in the fall of Rome on June 4, 1944.

On December 24, 1943, Eisenhower was appointed supreme commander of the Allied Expeditionary Forces in preparation for an Allied invasion of France by way of the English Channel. The invasion took place on June 6, 1944, and on August 25 of that year, Paris was liberated. The war subsequently ended with the Germans' surrender on May 7, 1945. In the meantime, Eisenhower had been promoted to five-star general in December 1944. His plans to retire at the conclusion of the war were waylaid when President Harry TRUMAN named him to replace George Marshall as chief of staff. For more than two years, Eisenhower directed demobilization of the wartime army and worked to unify the armed services under a centralized command. In May 1948, he finally left active duty to become president of Columbia University. His book, *Crusade in Europe,* was published that fall.

Eisenhower's brief, uncomfortable career as an academic administrator was not very successful, and he was happy to accept President Truman's request to become supreme commander of the NORTH ATLANTIC TREATY ORGANIZATION (NATO) in the fall of 1950. He flew to Paris in early 1951, and for the next 15 months devoted himself to the task of creating a united military organization in Western Europe as a defense against the possibility of communist aggression.

In June 1952, Eisenhower officially retired from the army after 37 years of service. By this time it had become known that he was a Republican, and several members of the party, led by Governor Thomas E. DEWEY of New York, persuaded him to seek the presi-

President Harry Truman and General Dwight D. Eisenhower are jubilant after Allied victory in World War II. (TRUMAN LIBRARY)

dential nomination, running against the more conservative Robert TAFT of Ohio. Despite a rancorous fight with Taft supporters, Eisenhower won the nomination on the first ballot at the party convention in July. The young anticommunist crusader from California, Senator Richard M. NIXON, was picked to be his running mate.

Eisenhower was criticized for failing to take a stand against Joseph MCCARTHY by defending George C. Marshall, whom McCarthy had attacked. Late in the campaign, Eisenhower made an effective political appeal by vowing "I SHALL GO TO KOREA" to help resolve deadlocked negotiations to end the unpopular war. Subsequently, he and Nixon defeated Adlai STEVENSON and John Sparkman in the general election. Eisenhower later kept his promise and visited Korea.

As president, Eisenhower took a greater interest in foreign over domestic affairs, and he and his secretary of state, John Foster DULLES, worked hard to achieve peace and construct collective defense agreements designed to prevent the spread of communism. He negotiated a truce for the KOREAN WAR in July 1953, and in December proposed that countries of the world pool atomic information and materials under the auspices of an international agency. In 1957, his "ATOMS FOR PEACE" suggestion bore fruit when 62 countries formed the INTERNATIONAL ATOMIC ENERGY AGENCY. Eisenhower and Dulles also succeeded in creating the SOUTHEAST ASIA TREATY ORGANIZATION (SEATO).

Eisenhower suffered a heart attack in September 1955 and had an operation for ileitis in June 1956. Nevertheless, his party nominated him for a second term, and he and Nixon overwhelmingly defeated Adlai Stevenson and Estes Kefauver. Meanwhile, Egypt's seizure of the Suez Canal in 1956 resulted in the creation of the EISENHOWER DOCTRINE, a pledge to send U.S. armed forces to any Middle Eastern country requesting assistance against communist aggression. Domestically, Eisenhower had to deal with the effects of the U.S. Supreme Court's decision that racial segregation in public schools was unconstitutional; as a result, the CIVIL RIGHTS ACT of 1957 was born. After Sputnik was launched on October 4, 1957, steps were immediately taken to boost space research, and the National Aeronautics and Space Administration (NASA) was created in July of 1958. Meanwhile, the United States was suffering from an economic recession, for which Eisenhower was blamed.

After Dulles's death in the spring of 1959, Eisenhower assumed a more personal role in the direction of American foreign policy. To improve relations with the

President Dwight D. Eisenhower (EISENHOWER LIBRARY)

Soviet Union, he invited Nikita Khrushchev to visit the United States. The Soviet premier came in September 1959 and engaged in private talks with his American counterpart. Another summit meeting was planned, but in May 1960, a U.S. reconnaissance plane was shot down over the USSR. An angry Khrushchev immediately suspended the talks and rescinded his invitation to have Eisenhower visit the Soviet Union. (See U-2 AFFAIR.) In January 1961, during the final weeks of the Eisenhower administration, the United States also broke diplomatic relations with Cuba.

In his 1961 farewell address, Eisenhower warned that "the conjunction of an immense military establishment and a large arms industry is needed. . . . In the councils of government, we must guard against the acquisition of unwarranted influence, whether sought or unsought, by the military industrial complex. The potential for the disastrous rise of misplaced power exists and will persist."

Eisenhower Doctrine

A direct result of the Suez crisis, the Eisenhower Doctrine emphasized U.S. policy in the Middle East during the late 1950s. Congress issued a joint resolution authorizing President Eisenhower to defend Middle Eastern nations with military force against communist aggression, if such a defense was determined to be necessary. As drawn up by the secretary of state, John Foster DULLES, the doctrine had the approval and support of most of the affected countries in the Middle East. Consequently, the Eisenhower Doctrine was invoked (although not implemented) to lend support to King Hussein in Jordan. In May 1958, it was actually implemented when U.S. troops were sent into Lebanon to ward off a possible communist coup there. When the coup did not occur, the United States suffered some embarrassment internationally, as well as criticism at home.

Ellsberg, Daniel (1931–)

Political activist Daniel Ellsberg was a graduate of Columbia University, where he received his B.S. in 1952 and his Ph.D. in 1959. After a tour of duty with the U.S. Marine Corps, he worked for the Rand Corporation, conducting studies on defense policies, first from 1959 to 1964 and again from 1967 to 1970. Although he originally supported the U.S. role in Indochina, he eventually became a strong opponent of American involvement there. In 1971, he gave the *New York Times* access to a secret history of the VIETNAM WAR commissioned by Secretary of Defense Robert McNamara, which revealed that the government had repeatedly misled the American people about the escalation of the war. The report became known as the PENTAGON PAPERS. Among the report's explosive revelations was the disclosure that the TONKIN GULF RESOLUTION authorizing a U.S. military role in Vietnam had been drafted some months before the event that led to its being so named. Although the government attempted to prevent publication of the papers, the U.S. Supreme Court ruled that publication was in fact permissible. Nevertheless, the government attempted to prosecute Ellsberg for the release of the report. The charges were dismissed in 1973 after it was revealed that "PLUMBERS" working for President NIXON had burglarized the offices of Ellsberg's psychiatrist in an effort to find evidence that would discredit Ellsberg, in addition to conducting covert surveillance on Ellsberg himself.

Ervin, Sam (1896–1985)

Samuel James Ervin, Jr., was a U.S. senator from North Carolina best known as a stalwart defender of the Constitution and chairman of the committee investigating the WATERGATE scandal. The son of a lawyer, Ervin graduated from the University of North Carolina in 1917, then obtained his law degree from Harvard University in 1922, whereupon he returned to his home state to practice law. In time he held several state judicial posts, including a stint as justice of the North Carolina Supreme Court. He ran a successful campaign for the U.S. Senate in 1954, and quickly won respect and admiration from his colleagues for his constitutional expertise. He sat on the Senate committee that censured Joseph MCCARTHY, and helped to investigate labor racketeering in the late 1950s. During the 1960s, despite presenting himself as one of the leading champions of civil liberties, he fought vigorously against the CIVIL RIGHTS ACTS and often led Southern filibusters to strike them down.

Although Ervin supported President Richard NIXON's Vietnam policy, he strongly disagreed with the president's refusal to spend funds authorized by Congress for social programs. When Watergate broke, Ervin was chosen to head the seven-member Select Committee on Presidential Campaign Activities to investigate the scandal. The televised hearings turned him into a national celebrity due to his charm and humor, his distinctive accent, and his repeated denial of White House claims of executive privilege.

In 1974, after Nixon's resignation and after more than 20 years in the Senate, Ervin decided against running for reelection, and returned to Morganton, North Carolina, to resume his private law practice and to write.

escalation

A word that became a major part of the American cultural language due to its frequent use during the 1960s and early 1970s, *escalation* refers to a buildup in troops and arms in preparation for a possible conflict. It was also frequently used to describe an increase in military effort during an ongoing campaign, such as the war in Vietnam. Over the years, American intervention in that country escalated to the point where antiwar protesters were quick to use the term to point out the contradictions between America's stated policy and its actions; although presumably pledged to bring peace and stability to the area, in fact the increasing presence and participation of U.S. troops in Vietnam belied the government's objectives. Thus, policymakers were sensitive to the word, and avoided it as much as possible, while peace activists such as Martin Luther KING, Jr.,

used it ironically when they called for escalation of opposition to the war.

espionage

Issues and events related to espionage were often discussed during the Cold War. Spying in its many forms and purposes—whether it is the United States "gathering intelligence" or an enemy country "threatening national security"—is at once an accepted and a reviled part of modern mores. In fact, the practice goes back for centuries, and is considered a necessity for any organized government that needs to keep abreast of its adversaries' intentions in order to protect itself and its citizens.

The primary goal of any espionage operation is to gather relevant information that may be used in a country's defense or to formulate foreign policy. Often, however, it goes beyond this conduct to include secret activities designed to confuse, upset, or even destroy an enemy. Such activities might include funding military operations in other countries, disseminating propaganda in enemy nations, bribing foreign officials, stealing classified documents, or, most drastically, carrying out assassinations. Spying techniques can also include electronic "eavesdropping" in the form of wiretaps, surveillance cameras, and, in recent years, satellite technology. Counterintelligence, meanwhile, is often employed as a preventive measure against foreign nations thought to be infiltrating domestic institutions.

Revelations regarding espionage often present a dichotomy: it is often thought to be permissible for "us" to engage in it, but not for "them." In wartime, spies may be executed without benefit of trial. In times of peace, judgment on captured spies is harsh and punishment severe. All the same, it is an accepted part of any government's mandate that espionage activities carried out in the country"s best interests are excusable. Primary examples of this in the United States are found in the aftermath of the U-2 AFFAIR, when Henry Cabot LODGE countered Soviet anger over American spying with very clear evidence of Russian espionage.

Each country takes measures to counteract spying within its own borders, and the United States is no exception. In 1917, the Espionage Act was passed, and almost immediately was used to move against American communists, pacifists, and labor leaders, in addition to the primary target at the time, German spies. Twenty-one years later, in May 1938, the HOUSE UN-AMERICAN ACTIVITIES COMMITTEE (HUAC) was established for the purpose of monitoring Soviet and Nazi agents and to check subversion within U.S. borders. Given this mandate, the committee soon began to overstep its bounds, and in due time numerous blameless people were being investigated, including some members of the CIVIL RIGHTS MOVEMENT.

During World War II, the OFFICE OF STRATEGIC SERVICES (OSS) was established to handle intelligence-gathering operations. It was dissolved upon the war's conclusion, but as the Cold War began to intensify, the need for a similar office became clear and the CENTRAL INTELLIGENCE AGENCY (CIA) was set up to deal with the gathering of foreign intelligence. (The Federal Bureau of Investigation [FBI] handles counterintelligence matters in the domestic arena.) Both agencies have come under fire for their handling of certain matters—for example, the CIA's role in the botched BAY OF PIGS INVASION and its involvement in the IRAN-CONTRA AFFAIR.

Several cases of espionage grabbed the public's attention during the early 1950s. In 1951, Herbert PHILBRICK's role in bringing down leaders of the American Communist Party was treated sensationally in the newspapers that reported the story. At the time, the country was still reeling from the public investigation into suspected spy Alger HISS, an event that brought Richard NIXON to public prominence. Meanwhile, the trial and execution (in 1953) of Julius and Ethel ROSENBERG, who were convicted under the Espionage Act of 1917, incited tremendous controversy and debate among Americans, who were sharply divided on whether the Rosenbergs were guilty or innocent. However, evidence uncovered in the Soviet Union in 1990 revealed that the couple had indeed acted as spies for the communist nation.

Establishment, the

The phrase "the Establishment" was a popular capsule description of the established societal hierarchy—that is, those institutions, bureaucracies, and individuals that exercise control of any sort over a population. In the 1960s and early 1970s, this term was used in a pejorative fashion, mostly by HIPPIES, YIPPIES, and members of the COUNTERCULTURE. It most likely rose from the title of a 1961 essay in *American Scholar,* "The American Establishment," in which author Richard H. Rovere, with tongue partly in cheek, described the British NEW LEFT's attitude toward conservatives. It soon became a popular way of attacking any organized power structure that, for many of those who used the term, represented hypocrisy or oppression. Others impugned the Establishment simply for the fun of flouting mainstream societal rules.

European Recovery Plan   See MARSHALL PLAN

"evil empire"

An expression made popular by President Ronald REAGAN, the term *evil empire* refers to the Soviet Union and its aggressive reputation. Reagan first used the words in a talk given to the National Association of Evangelists in 1983, in which he spoke contemptuously of the Soviet system of government and oppression of other countries within its sphere of influence. Although critics decried the speech as extreme and detrimental to diplomatic relations with the Soviets, anticommunists grabbed at it eagerly, and the phrase soon entered the popular lexicon. While biblical sources can be cited for the expression's origins, it is possible that Reagan's speechwriter, Anthony R. Dolan, drew upon the *Star Wars* movies, in which "the Empire" is a villainous and tyrannical entity against which the forces of good must do battle, providing what was for many an apt metaphor for the United States's Cold War battles against the Soviet Union.

fail-safe

One of the most dramatic terms to come out of the Cold War era was *fail-safe*—a means of recalling a retaliatory strike or shutting down a nuclear system in the event of ambiguity, error, or unforeseen mishaps. *Fail-safe* also refers to a secondary mechanism by which a strike or system can be employed should the first fail to operate properly. When the principles and practice of fail-safe systems were first revealed to the American public, there was a sensational reaction as many realized that nuclear annihilation due to human error or an accident was a very real possibility. However, according to its creators, the object of fail-safe systems was to prevent that very thing from happening. For example, bomber planes responding to a perceived enemy attack might fly to a certain point but not proceed with their mission until they had received instructions to continue or return, allowing the home base to confirm the existence of the attack and the authorized response. If the bombers receive no instructions to proceed, they automatically return to base. Even so, critics have pointed out that any system has its flaws, a point made with seriocomic results in Stanley Kubrick's 1964 film *Dr. Strangelove, or How I Learned to Stop Worrying and Love the Bomb,* in which a fail-safe system ultimately fails, setting off an unwanted nuclear war.

Federal Bureau of Investigation (FBI)

The Federal Bureau of Investigation (FBI) is a special law enforcement organization attached to the U.S. Justice Department whose primary function is to investigate violations of federal laws that do not fall within the responsibilities of other government agencies. Of particular concern to FBI agents are crimes that affect national security (i.e., espionage) or the safety of government officials, in addition to which the organization investigates kidnappings, bank robberies, extortion, racketeering, and crimes that cross state boundaries (i.e., art thefts and other cases of stolen goods).

Prior to the bureau's creation, the Justice Department had no special investigation unit, and often had to "borrow" agents from the Treasury Service. Although Attorney General Charles Bonaparte (who served 1906–08) twice asked Congress to form an elite team of investigative agents, fears of creating a secret police force prevented Congress from doing so. Undaunted, in 1908 Bonaparte used discretionary funds to put together an initial team of nine agents from the Treasury Department. His successor, George Wickersham, retained the force, which he called the Bureau of Investigation. In 1935, the group became officially recognized as the Federal Bureau of Investigation. FBI directors would be appointed by the president with Senate approval. The most famous (and controversial) director was J. Edgar HOOVER, who was appointed to the position in 1924 and held it until his death in 1972. Soon after his appointment, Hoover overhauled the FBI and began building it according to his personal specifications, many of which have since come under fire. Hoover was a dictatorial director, and was consumed with issues of national security to the point where he collected data on thousands of prominent citizens, then often used that data to blackmail or manipulate situations to his own advantage. Hoover frequently resorted to illegal and unethical tactics to achieve his goals, but was also known for his stubborn (and often successful) fight against organized crime.

A fervent anticommunist, Hoover often used the FBI's resources to wage his own battles during the Cold War. He became particularly obsessed with the internal subversion that he felt was threatening national security, perhaps even more than external espionage. He focused his wrath on such leaders of the CIVIL RIGHTS MOVEMENT as Martin Luther KING, Jr., and targeted organizations such as the BLACK PANTHERS for investigation. In 1968, he launched COINTELPRO, a counterintelligence initiative aimed at destabilizing many radical organizations of the NEW LEFT.

After Hoover's death in 1972, a series of directors succeeded him. L. Patrick Gray III, appointed by Richard Nixon, was forced to resign following revelations of his participation in the WATERGATE cover-up. Subsequent FBI directors have included Clarence Kelley, George Bush, William Webster, William Sessions, and Louis J. Freeh. The bureau and its directors (who are allowed to serve no more than 10 years) are carefully monitored by a Congress wary of a repeat of Hoover's excesses.

feminism   See WOMEN'S MOVEMENT.

first strike

"First strike" is a strategy by which opponents in a war may gain an advantage by attacking the enemy's strategic forces or bases before a response can be prepared. The term has come to be applied exclusively to nuclear war, where the stakes are considerably higher; whichever side takes the first strike also puts the world at risk of nuclear annihilation. The implications of first strike capability were evident to President John F. KENNEDY and his advisers during the crucial resolution of the CUBAN MISSILE CRISIS. Intelligence showed that if the Soviet Union had succeeded in installing and deploying its missiles in Cuba, then initiated a first strike, only 15% of U.S. strategic forces would survive the attack, crippling the country's defenses. The crisis helped to accelerate the development of the American nuclear weapons program, resulting in the MX missile system and, later, President Ronald REAGAN's proposal for a STRATEGIC DEFENSE INITIATIVE. While these programs were, according to their creators, developed for defense purposes, critics were quick to point out their first strike capabilities.

flexible response

As the arms race between the United States and the Soviet Union heated up, many practical options were considered in formulating American policy in the event of nuclear war. One of these was the "flexible response"—the idea being that the country should be able to draw upon a number of different capabilities in order to prepare a variety of possible responses to foreign aggression. With flexible response, the country could have at the ready anything from conventional forces to short- and long-range missiles and bombers. As with any idea, this one had its supporters and foes. President Dwight EISENHOWER rejected it as being too expensive and ultimately unnecessary. President John F. KENNEDY supported it, feeling that it was highly preferable to the devastating effects of MASSIVE RETALIATION—a view endorsed by General Maxwell TAYLOR, who felt that flexibility would provide both a strong defense and a DETERRENCE to nuclear war. Nixon's secretary of state, Henry KISSINGER, firmly believing that new weapons technology should be developed along with the conventional as a safeguard for national security, was the strongest advocate of flexible response since Kennedy's time. Regardless of philosophy, the United States would continue to build its nuclear arsenal, eventually achieving superiority over the Soviets in the arms race and thus the capacity for a flexible response that proponents of the theory had envisioned.

flower children   See HIPPIES.

Fonda, Jane (1937–)

Jane Seymour Fonda, daughter of actor Henry Fonda, is an American film actress who became controversial with her political activism, especially during the 1970s and early 1980s. After graduating from high school, she enrolled in Vassar College, but left for New York City after two years to work as a model and to study under Lee Strasberg at his Actors Studio. Her acting career began in 1960 with appearances on Broadway (*There Was a Little Girl*) and in film (*Tall Story*). She went on to appear in numerous comic roles in the movies, including *Cat Ballou* (1965) and *Barefoot in the Park* (1967). In the late 1960s, she began turning to more substantial and socially conscious roles, and won Academy Awards for her roles in *Klute* (1971) and *Coming Home* (1978), a frankly partisan drama about veterans returning to the United States after service in the VIETNAM WAR. (The film lost the best picture Oscar to *The Deer Hunter,* another film relating to the war in Vietnam.) She also costarred with her father in *On Golden Pond* (1981).

Fonda became a left-wing political activist as a result of her opposition to the Vietnam War. In 1972, she traveled to Hanoi to denounce U.S. bombing campaigns there, inciting enormous negative comment at home and earning her the sobriquet of "Hanoi Jane." In later years, her public activism lessened and she focused on her acting career. She also devised a popular exercise program for women. She was married to and divorced from the French film director Roger Vadim as well as liberal American politician Tom Hayden before she married the wealthy media figure Ted Turner.

Ford, Gerald (1913–)

The 38th president of the United States was born Leslie Lynch King, Jr. While he was still an infant, his parents divorced, and his mother moved with him to Grand Rapids, Michigan. There she married Gerald Ford, Sr., who adopted her son and gave him his name. Young Gerald became a football star at the University of

Following Richard Nixon's resignation from the presidency as a result of Watergate, Vice President Gerald Ford is sworn in as president by Chief Justice Earl Warren. (FORD LIBRARY)

Michigan, then went on to obtain his law degree from Yale University in 1941.

In 1948, Ford, a Republican, was elected to the U.S. House of Representatives and was continually reelected thereafter, becoming House minority leader in 1965. After Spiro AGNEW resigned as vice president in October 1973, President Richard NIXON nominated Ford to fill the post. The first vice president to take office in the middle of an administration, Ford was sworn in on December 6, 1973. He was subsequently sworn in as president on August 9, 1974, after the WATERGATE scandal forced Nixon to resign. Ford thus holds the additional distinction of being the first president never to be elected as either president or vice president. One month after taking office, he granted a full pardon to Nixon "for all offenses against the United States" that he might have committed while in office. The pardon made it impossible for Nixon to be prosecuted for any crimes in connection with Watergate and caused a public outcry. To counter the negative reaction, Ford

appeared before a subcommittee of the House of Representatives on October 17, marking the first time an incumbent president had testified before a congressional committee. Ford went on to conduct an effective presidency, albeit one strained by poor relations with the Democratic majority in Congress.

By the time Ford took office, all U.S. forces had been withdrawn from Vietnam. He sought but could not win approval for greater U.S. aid for South Vietnam. It was under President Ford that South Vietnam fell to the North. In April 1975, he announced that the conflict was "finished as far as America was concerned." That same year, when Cambodia seized the American cargo ship *Mayaguez,* Ford declared the act to be piracy and sent the U.S. Marines to seize the ship in what became known as the MAYAGUEZ INCIDENT. Later that same year, he was subjected to two assassination attempts, both of which left him unharmed.

Although he was generally well-liked, Ford only narrowly defeated Ronald REAGAN for the Republican

President Gerald Ford at work (FORD LIBRARY)

nomination for president in 1976. That fall he became the first incumbent president to agree to public debates with the challenger. Ford's performance in the debates probably cost him the election; in one inexplicable (and endlessly replayed) blunder, he earnestly maintained that the Soviet Union exerted no military domination over Eastern Europe. Ford worked tirelessly and closed the "public opinion deficit" he had suffered from the beginning of the campaign, but in November 1976, he was narrowly defeated by Jimmy CARTER. Ford thereupon retired, becoming an elder statesman of American politics.

Forrestal, James (1892–1949)

James Vincent Forrestal was a distinguished government official who served as the first U.S. secretary of defense prior to his mysterious suicide in 1949. Although he attended both Dartmouth and Princeton Universities, Forrestal never graduated from college, but instead went directly into the business world, becoming a bond seller in upstate New York, then a broker for Reed and Co. on Wall Street. His financial career was put on hold during World War I, when he served as a naval aviator and subsequently as an administrator in Washington. Following the war, he returned to Wall Street, and by the age of 31 he had become a partner in Reed and Co. His early success brought him significant prestige, but also raised questions regarding his business ethics. In 1933, he was called before a congressional panel to answer questions about his business practices and the possibility that he may have been evading taxes; however, no charges resulted from the investigation.

After 20 years working on Wall Street, Forrestal decided to change careers. He was offered and accepted a position as undersecretary of the navy, and went to Washington in 1940, taking with him his younger colleague, Paul NITZE, who became his assistant (and also forged his own successful political career). He proved to be a highly able administrator, and met the demands of his job with such energy and efficiency that when Secretary of the Navy Frank Knox died suddenly in May 1944, there was no question that Forrestal would succeed him. Under his guidance, the navy's fleet continued to grow rapidly, reaching 50,000 warships and 3.4 million personnel by 1945 (from 1,100 ships and 161,000 personnel in 1940). He also achieved acclaim for his direct involvement in war affairs, to the point of flying to Iwo Jima and landing there under fire.

Despite his public accomplishments, Forrestal's private life was falling apart. He was obsessed with his work, and his wife was both an alcoholic and mentally unbalanced. He entered into a series of affairs that affected the level of respect with which he was regarded in the Washington community. Still, he continued to wield considerable political influence, even though he frequently found himself at odds with the new president, Harry TRUMAN, regarding defense goals and foreign policy. After the war's conclusion, Forrestal was among the first to perceive the threat that the Soviet Union posed to the United States, as well as the world at large. He lobbied vigorously against Truman's plans to reduce military forces and defense spending as well as his idea of unifying all branches of the military. Despite his opposition in these areas, however, he was Truman's choice to fill the newly created post of secretary of defense in 1947.

Initially successful in this capacity, Forrestal was a strong proponent of the policy of CONTAINMENT, and was greatly influential in Truman's decision to pursue containment in the early stages of the Cold War. However, he now found himself responsible for the unified military that he had opposed, and thus came into conflict with military leaders who resisted the changes. In particular, his onetime friend Secretary of the Navy Stuart SYMINGTON became highly antagonistic, and his public battles with Forrestal had an extremely negative effect on Forrestal's reputation, as well as his relationship with Truman. Matters were not helped by Drew PEARSON's highly critical radio broadcasts, which frequently attacked Forrestal and resurrected the tax evasion charges of the early 1930s, further damaging his image. Meanwhile, Forrestal continued to fight battles against efforts to reduce defense spending.

In January 1949, Truman advised Forrestal (who had secretly supported Thomas E. DEWEY in the 1948 presidential election) that he was to be replaced as defense secretary by Louis JOHNSON, an event that took place in March. Devastated, Forrestal plunged deeper into the depression that had already been plaguing him for some time. Eventually, friends arranged for him to be admitted to Bethesda Naval Hospital for treatment. It was there that, on May 22, 1949, Forrestal attempted to hang himself outside a window and died when he fell to a passageway roof 13 floors below. Just prior to his death, he had copied some verses from a Greek poem, "Chorus from Ajax"; historians are still uncertain what was meant by this cryptic suicide note. Yet despite this ignominious end, Forrestal's service to his country was honored with the naming of the U.S.S. *Forrestal,* the nation's first super aircraft carrier, as well as the James Forrestal Building in Washington, which serves as the headquarters for the Department of Energy. His book, *The Forrestal Diaries,* was published in 1951.

Free Speech movement   See ANTIWAR MOVEMENT.

"Freedom Now!"

Impatient with the slow gains being made in their struggle to achieve racial equality, civil rights leaders in the 1960s felt the need for a slogan that would define their goals and rally their audiences. Although the CIVIL RIGHTS MOVEMENT had succeeded in pushing through federal legislation that eliminated such symbols of white oppression as segregated schools and public facilities, there were still significant strides to be made in gaining white acceptance of black equality and participation in all arenas of American life. To signal the immediacy of the progress that still needed to be made, "Freedom Now!" was born.

freedom riders

As the CIVIL RIGHTS MOVEMENT gained momentum, one of its primary goals was ending segregation in the South. To that end, activists targeted hotels, restaurants, public facilities, and other places where black citizens were blatantly segregated from whites. After four black students were evicted from a lunch counter in Greensboro, North Carolina, the Congress of Racial Equality (CORE) acquired funding to sponsor a series of "freedom rides," which took place during the summer of 1961. In this experiment, groups of black and white riders boarded buses and traveled throughout the South (but mostly in Alabama) to test segregation of buses and of bathrooms in interstate bus terminals, as well as to test blacks' ability to eat alongside whites in public eating places. The reaction of Southern whites to the freedom rides was often extreme; riders were often subjected to harassment and sometimes to beatings. At one point, in Anniston, Alabama, a bus was burned. Following a riot in Montgomery, Alabama, during which the police protection that CORE had requested did not arrive until 22 freedom riders had been seriously injured, Attorney General Robert F. KENNEDY sent more than 600 deputy marshals to

Alabama. The remainder of the summer passed in relative quietness—and the freedom riders achieved their goal. In September 1961, the Interstate Commerce Commission desegregated the public facilities in all interstate bus terminals, and the Justice Department subsequently ordered an end to segregation in all public transportation. The results of the freedom rides were also seen in the CIVIL RIGHTS ACT of 1964.

French Indochina War

United States involvement in the French Indochina War would prove to be the action that triggered the long and controversial years of the VIETNAM WAR. Immediately following World War II, in 1946, France became the colonial administrator of Indochina, where a conflict soon arose between the French-run government and communist nationalists called the Vietminh. Consequently, three years later, the French granted nominal sovereignty to Cambodia, Laos, and Vietnam, naming them as associate states of the French Union while still retaining control of the area. In 1950, the United States officially recognized these three countries and began to provide economic aid by way of France. Military assistance was also provided, to the point that by 1954, the United States had become responsible for 78% of the war's costs. In the spring of that year, the French nearly crumbled under a communist-led siege at Dien Bien Phu, leading U.S. president Dwight D. EISENHOWER to consider sending in air and ground troops to provide support. Instead, a peace was negotiated, leading to the war's temporary end and what was intended to be a temporary division of Vietnam into northern and southern sections.

Fulbright, J. William (1905–1995)

A U.S. senator who became known for his articulate denunciation of U.S. involvement in Vietnam, James William Fulbright also created the international exchange program for students called the Fulbright Scholarship. A brilliant student, he graduated from the University of Arkansas, then went as a Rhodes Scholar to Oxford University, in England, where he earned two degrees. He subsequently received his law degree from George Washington University and went on to teach law at the University of Arkansas, where he later served as university president from 1939 to 1941.

In 1942, Fulbright turned his attention to politics, winning a seat as a Democrat from Arkansas in the House of Representatives. His most notable achievement

Senators William Fulbright and Eugene McCarthy (JOHNSON LIBRARY)

in that legislative body was the passing, in 1943, of the Fulbright resolution, which put the House on record as favoring U.S. participation in a postwar international organization—the UNITED NATIONS, established in 1945. Meanwhile, Fulbright ran successfully for the U.S. Senate in 1944 and was popularly reelected for four more terms after that. In 1945, he initiated the Fulbright Act, which established an educational exchange program between the United States and foreign countries. He subsequently threw his support behind the formation of the NORTH ATLANTIC TREATY ORGANIZATION (NATO). Although he voted against funding for Senator Joseph MCCARTHY's anticommunist investigations, Fulbright's popular reputation as a liberal was belied by his opposition to civil rights for blacks and efforts to integrate schools.

From 1959 to 1974, Fulbright chaired the Senate Foreign Relations Committee, of which he had been a member since 1949. In this capacity, he advised President John F. KENNEDY not to invade Cuba, and he strongly opposed President JOHNSON's 1965 intervention in the Dominican Republic. He initially supported the policy of CONTAINMENT, but with reservations, feeling that nuclear deterrence and the use of military power were perhaps inflexible tools in the everchanging modern world. Eventually, his views would change to the point where he became a strong opponent of the Vietnam War. In 1966, his committee held televised hearings on U.S. military involvement in Southeast Asia, from which he emerged as a leader in the calls to end U.S. bombing of North Vietnam and to commence peace talks to settle the conflict there.

Fulbright lost his Senate seat when he was defeated in the Arkansas Democratic primary contest in 1974; he retired later that year.

G

Galbraith, John Kenneth (1908–)

A popular economist and public servant, John Kenneth Galbraith is well known both for his liberal views and for the literary quality of his writings on public affairs, which has made his work on economics accessible to the general public. He was born in Canada and received his B.S. degree from the University of Toronto in 1931. He went on to the University of California at Berkeley, where he received his master's degree in economics, followed by a doctorate in 1934. It was at this time that he became a U.S. citizen. Between 1934 and 1942, he taught, first at Harvard, then at Princeton University. From 1943 to 1948, he worked as an editor for *Fortune* magazine.

Galbraith became involved in government service during World War II and the postwar period, when he held a variety of posts. In 1949, he resumed his academic career at Harvard, teaching there until 1975. He remained politically active, however, and served as a key adviser to President John F. KENNEDY, who appointed him ambassador to India in 1961. In this capacity, he served as a mediator during India's border war with China in 1962. Galbraith returned to Harvard in 1963, while continuing his involvement in public affairs. He served as national chairman of AMERICANS FOR DEMOCRATIC ACTION in 1967–68, and in 1972 he was president of the American Economic Association.

Among Galbraith's major works are: *The Affluent Society* (1958), in which he called for less emphasis on production and more on public service; *American Capitalism: The Concept of Countervailing Powers* (1951); *The Liberal Hour* (1960); *The New Industrial State* (1967); *A Life in Our Times: Memoirs* (1981); *the Anatomy of Power* (1983); and *Economics in Perspective. A Critical History* (1987).

generation gap

The "generation gap" was the ideological cleavage that formed between the free-thinking youth of the 1960s and their parents or any member of the older generation (also known as the ESTABLISHMENT). The children of the Cold War were among the first to rally against nuclear weapons and the VIETNAM WAR, especially during the 1960s, when student protest and the peace movement were at their height. The rift between the generations was in a sense defined by their upbringings; parents had endured the dark years of the Great Depression and World War II, while their children had enjoyed a postwar affluence that reached remarkable levels. The gap was often a wide one, with neither side quite able to understand the viewpoint of the other. The older generation was often perceived by the youth as reactionary and hypocritical, and the younger generation was seen as naïve and unappreciative of what their elders had gone through for their sake. The younger generation was impatient; they wanted to seize the reins of power to effect positive progress and change, while the older generation was reluctant to "pass the torch," as President Kennedy put it in his inaugural address to the nation. In the end, the generation gap symbolized the heady and divisive times that were the 1960s.

glasnost

Initiated by Mikhail Gorbachev in 1985, glasnost was a policy of open communication that paved the way to the eventual downfall of COMMUNISM in the Soviet Union. That downfall was perhaps already certain due to the Soviets' increasing struggle to keep up with the United States in the arms race, and the numerous internal problems that had been caused by the battle for nuclear superiority. Seeing that change was inevitable, Gorbachev put into motion a policy of *perestroika,* a program designed to reform the Soviet economic and political systems. One of the most revolutionary aspects of his program was the implementation of *glasnost,* which allowed freedom of speech and the press in a society previously known for its totalitarianism. Contrary to earlier Soviet thinking, Gorbachev declared: "Glasnost is an integral part of a socialist democracy. Wide, prompt and frank information is evidence of confidence in the people and respect for their intelligence and feelings, and for their ability to understand events for themselves." The openness of glasnost extended itself to the United States, providing for freer lines of communication that eased previous tensions experienced in arms control talks. Thus, the term entered the popular lexicon as a euphemism for improved relations between the United States and the USSR.

Inevitably, glasnost presented its own set of problems in a political system not previously known for its acceptance of free thought. The policy was often used against certain communist officials, who were forced to confess their mistakes and inform on others, thus causing a widespread "blame game." Glasnost and perestroika eventually caused such dissension among Soviet leaders that a struggle for power between the old and new orders ensued, leading finally to Gorbachev's ouster, as well as the dissolution of the USSR.

Goldwater, Barry (1909–1998)

A conservative icon in American politics, Barry Morris Goldwater was a college dropout who worked for many years in his family's Phoenix, Arizona, department store, Goldwater's. He was president of the store from 1937 to 1953. He had his first taste of politics in 1949, when he was elected to the Phoenix city council. In 1952, he narrowly won election to the U.S. Senate, representing the state of Arizona as a Republican. By 1958, he had become one of the most popular political figures in his state and easily won reelection. His conservative stance was marked by his strong opposition to arms control negotiations with the Soviet Union and calls for harsher diplomatic measures to stem the spread of COMMUNISM. He also charged the Democrats with creating a quasi-socialist state at home.

In 1964, Goldwater ran for the U.S. presidency, winning the Republican nomination on the first ballot and on the motto "Extremism in the defense of liberty is no vice." He fought a determined campaign against the incumbent president, Lyndon JOHNSON, but Johnson had three factors in his favor: the popular canonization of Johnson's predecessor, the murdered John F. KENNEDY; the prosperous economy at that time; and the widespread fear that Goldwater's extreme anticommunism might carry the country into a war with the USSR. During the campaign, Johnson skillfully exploited public doubts about Goldwater's hawkish position on Vietnam (see also DOVES AND HAWKS) and his ability to conduct foreign affairs in a complex world. In the end, Goldwater and his running mate, William E. Miller, were buried in a landslide victory for Johnson.

Goldwater was returned to the Senate in 1968 and was reelected thereafter until he retired in 1987. On August 7, 1974, he led the delegation of senior Republican politicians who persuaded President Richard NIXON to resign from office. In his later years, Goldwater became more moderate in his views and came to symbolize a high-minded brand of conservative Republicanism. He also published several books. By the time of his death, he had become a highly respected elder statesman of American politics.

Graham, Katharine (1917–   )

Once called "the most powerful woman in America," the owner and publisher of the *Washington Post, Newsweek,* and other American news publications was born Katharine Meyer, the daughter of stockbroker

Eugene Meyer and educator Agnes Meyer. Raised in Mount Kisco, New York, she attended Vassar College from 1934 to 1936, then went on to receive her B.A. degree from the University of Chicago in 1938. In 1933, her father bought the ailing *Washington Post* and proceeded to introduce innovations such as an advice column, women's pages, and an improved editorial page. His love for the newspaper was transmitted to his daughter. For about a year after receiving her degree, Katharine worked for the *San Francisco News,* then joined the editorial staff of the *Washington Post* in 1939. In 1940, she married Philip Graham, a law clerk who, after his service in World War II, joined the *Post* as an associate publisher in 1946. He subsequently became the *Post's* publisher. In 1948, Eugene Meyer sold the *Post* to the Grahams for a relatively small sum of money. The couple formed the Washington Post Company, and in 1961 they purchased *Newsweek.*

After Philip Graham committed suicide in 1963, his wife succeeded him as president of the Washington Post Company, a position she retained for the next 10 years. Under her leadership, the *Post* increased its circulation, becoming the most influential newspaper in the capital and one of the most powerful in the nation. In 1973, Graham became chairman of the board and chief executive officer of the Washington Post Company. She also owned a number of radio and television stations.

Two monumental stories pursued during her tenure established the *Post's* reputation for investigative journalism. In 1971, the *Post* joined with the *New York Times* in publishing the PENTAGON PAPERS, a hitherto secret history of decision-making in Vietnam. After a few installments, the federal government won injunctions barring further publication, marking the first instance of prior restraint on the press in U.S. history. The Supreme Court later decided against the government and for the newspapers.

In 1974, Graham personally approved the publication of the controversial stories on WATERGATE by *Post* reporters Carl Bernstein and Bob Woodward. President Richard NIXON's handling of the Watergate affair eventually led to his resignation in 1975.

Great Society

When Lyndon JOHNSON took office as U.S. president, he described his new administration as the provider of a "better deal" for Americans—an attempt not only to disassociate his administration from that of President John F. KENNEDY but also to capitalize on the "New Deal," "Fair Deal," and "Square Deal" initiatives of previous administrations. Failing to get a strong response to this, he cast about for a slogan that would capture the public imagination. He found it in the "Great Society," a term originally suggested by speechwriter Richard Goodwin that would forever be associated with the Johnson presidency. Johnson liked the slogan so well that he repeated it in innumerable speeches, and finally expanded on his theme in a graduation address at the University of Michigan: "The Great Society rests on abundance and liberty for all. It . . . is a place where every child can find knowledge to enrich his mind and to enlarge his talents . . . where the city of man serves not only the needs of the body and the demands of commerce but the desire for beauty and the hunger for community. . . . It is a challenge constantly renewed, beckoning us toward a destiny where the meaning of our lives matches the marvelous products of our labor."

Acting upon this theme, Johnson proceeded to develop numerous programs that changed the domestic landscape, enacting the most sweeping social reforms in welfare, civil rights, voting rights, and health care since the days of President Franklin Roosevelt's New Deal. The effects of the Great Society programs are still being felt today—negatively to some, who claim Johnson effectively turned the United States into a "welfare nation" ruled by a sense of entitlement, and placing an enormous burden on taxpayers in the process.

Grenada invasion

The first U.S. intervention in a Western Hemisphere country since the 1965 DOMINICAN CRISIS, the U.S. invasion of the small Caribbean nation of Grenada in 1983 proved to be a political triumph for President Ronald REAGAN. At one time a British colony, Grenada was a self-governing member of the West Indies Associated States until 1974, when it became an independent nation. In 1979, the Marxist-oriented People's Revolutionary Army led by Maurice Bishop seized control of the country and applied to Cuba and the Soviet Union for technical and economic assistance. In October 1983, Bishop was killed following a military coup led by his vice minister, Bernard Coard, who was even more pro-Soviet and apparently had plans to install a communist regime. As a result, the Organization of Eastern Caribbean States asked the United States for assistance in ousting Coard and restoring democracy on the island.

President Ronald Reagan and members of Congress meet to discuss the Grenada invasion. (REAGAN LIBRARY)

President Reagan was quick to comply, sending in 1,900 U.S. Marines on October 25, 1983; several hundred Caribbean troops accompanied the marines, who took only a week to overcome resistance from Grenadian and Cuban forces. The next year, free elections reestablished a democratic government on Grenada, enabling the foreign troops to withdraw in 1985. This action had the effect of reasserting American dominance in the Western Hemisphere, and Reagan also enjoyed the support and approval of many American citizens as a result.

Gulf of Tonkin   See TONKIN GULF INCIDENTS AND RESOLUTION.

Haig, Alexander (1924–)

Alexander Meigs Haig, Jr., is a former general who served as secretary of state under President Ronald Reagan. A 1947 graduate of the U.S. Military Academy at West Point, he went on to active duty in Japan (where he served for a short time as an aide to General Douglas MACARTHUR), Korea, and other countries before returning to the United States and obtaining his M.A. degree from Georgetown University in 1961. In 1962, having attained the rank of lieutenant colonel, he became a staff assistant at the Pentagon. He held a series of posts in the Department of Defense until 1965, including acting as a special assistant to Robert MCNAMARA, the secretary of defense. In 1966, he went to Vietnam as a battalion commander, and for his actions there was awarded the Distinguished Service Cross. When he returned to the United States, he was promoted to colonel and sent to West Point as a regimental commander and deputy commandant. He left West Point in 1969, when he was appointed military assistant to National Security Advisor Henry KISSINGER. In 1971, he became a deputy assistant in charge of national security affairs under President Richard NIXON, who sent him to Paris to participate in the Vietnam peace talks. Haig was promoted to four-star general in 1972, and in 1973 Nixon appointed him

army vice chief of staff. During the last year of the Nixon presidency (1973–74) Haig served as White House chief of staff. When Gerald FORD became president, Haig was appointed supreme allied commander of NATO, in which position he served from 1974 to 1979. After he resigned from that post, he retired from the army and became president of United Technologies Corporation.

In 1981, President Ronald REAGAN appointed Haig secretary of state, in which capacity he helped to fashion a policy opposing Soviet expansion in the world. He also worked to fight international terrorism and initiated attempts to normalize U.S. relations with the People's Republic of China. However, he frequently clashed with other members of Reagan's administration and found himself increasingly disillusioned with the administration's directions in foreign policy. He inadvertently created a negative backlash when, after an assassination attempt on Reagan, Haig appeared on camera to announce (on dubious constitutional authority), "I'm in charge here." After repeated disputes with others in the administration, he resigned in 1982 and subsequently founded Worldwide Associates, an international consulting firm. He campaigned unsuccessfully for the Republican presidential nomination in

President Gerald Ford meets with his chief of staff, Alexander Haig. (FORD LIBRARY)

1988. His memoir, *How America Changed the World*, appeared in 1992. An earlier book, *Caveat: Realism, Reagan, and Foreign Policy*, was published in 1984.

Haldeman, H. R. (1926–1993)

Harry Robbins Haldeman, known to friends and associates as Bob, was an advertising executive and campaign manager who served as White House chief of staff during the NIXON administration. He was also one of the leading figures in the WATERGATE scandal.

Haldeman graduated from the University of California at Los Angeles in 1948 with a degree in business administration. After working briefly for a prominent Los Angeles advertising agency, he joined a rival agency in 1949. He became an account executive and in 1959 he was promoted to vice president of the firm's Los Angeles office.

Early on, Haldeman had an interest in politics and proved himself to be one of Richard Nixon's most stal-

wart supporters. He managed Nixon's ill-fated attempt to become governor of California in 1962, but met greater success with his management of Nixon's second campaign for the presidency in 1968. During the president's first term, Haldeman served as chief of staff, earning the nickname "the Iron Chancellor." Along with John EHRLICHMAN, he formed a "palace guard" to protect Nixon, and determined who would and would not have access to the president.

Following the June 17, 1972, break-in at the Democratic Party National Headquarters in the Watergate complex, Haldeman participated in the White House cover-up of official involvement in that event as well as in other "DIRTY TRICKS" that had been employed during the 1972 reelection campaign. (Prominent among these was the burglary of the office of the psychiatrist of former federal official Daniel ELLSBERG, who had leaked the report known as the PENTAGON PAPERS to the MEDIA.)

Haldeman resigned in the spring of 1973, when White House involvement in the Watergate scandal was revealed to the public. He thereupon returned to his home state of California. In 1975, he was convicted of perjury, conspiracy, and obstruction of justice for his role in the scandal. He served 18 months at a federal minimum security facility. He was released in late 1978, and his autobiographical book, *The Ends of Power*, was published that same year. Haldeman subsequently engaged in real estate and restaurant ventures.

Hall, Gus (1910–)

A longtime communist leader in the United States, Gus Hall was born Arvo Kusta Halberg, the son of Finnish immigrants who were themselves charter members of the American Communist Party. He worked as a lumberjack and steelworker before going to Russia in 1931 to study at the Lenin Institute. After his return to the United States in 1934, he joined the Communist Party. From 1942 to 1946, he served in the U.S. Navy. Upon his release, he entered into party activities in earnest, serving as national secretary from 1950 to 1959, and as general secretary in 1959. As both a Communist leader and as a teacher, he advocated a violent overthrow of the American government. In 1951, he was tried and convicted on conspiracy charges; he was released in 1957. In 1972 and 1976, he ran for president of the United States as the Communist Party candidate. His numerous published books and pamphlets include *For a Radical Change: The Communist View* (1966) and *Fighting Racism* (1985).

Hammett, Dashiell (1894–1961)

Dashiell Samuel Hammett was an American writer who created the "hard-boiled" school of detective fiction. Hammett left school at the age of 13 and began working at a variety of low-paying jobs. In time, he became a detective for the Pinkerton agency and continued in that position for eight years. When the United States entered World War I, Hammett enlisted and served heroically, but eventually contracted tuberculosis, necessitating lengthy stays in army hospitals during the immediate postwar years. As a result, he turned to writing and began to publish short stories and novelettes in pulp magazines. Two novels, *Red Harvest* and *The Dain Curse*, appeared in 1929, one year before the publication in 1930 of the book that is generally considered to be his finest work, *The Maltese Falcon*. This book featured Hammett's now famous fictional detective, Sam Spade. Hammett also wrote *The Glass Key*

(1931) and *The Thin Man* (1932), the latter of which introduced his popular detective couple, Nick and Nora Charles. The character of Nora was based on Lillian HELLMAN, with whom he began an affair in 1930 that lasted until his death.

After 1934, Hammett devoted his time to left-wing political activities and to the defense of civil liberties. He again enlisted in the army during World War II. In 1951, he went to jail for six months because he refused to reveal the names of the contributors to the bail bond fund of the Civil Rights Congress, an organization for which he served as trustee. In 1953, he was blacklisted by the Hollywood establishment after his refusal to answer the questions put to him by the HOUSE UN-AMERICAN ACTIVITIES COMMITTEE (HUAC), headed by Senator Joseph MCCARTHY. His novels were also among those banned by the State Department in an effort to placate McCarthy. Hammett spent the last three years of his life with Lillian Hellman, a writer whose career he encouraged and influenced.

hard hats

Chief opposition to the peace movement of the 1960s and 1970s was usually represented by the "hard hats"—blue-collar workers and lower middle-class whites who supported the VIETNAM WAR and the U.S. government wholeheartedly. (They were so named in reference to the helmets worn in the construction trades.) Hard hats were fiercely patriotic, taking a "MY COUNTRY, RIGHT OR WRONG" attitude and openly deriding the "peaceniks" and "PINKOS" of the NEW LEFT whom they considered to be subversive elements of American society. Frequent clashes between hard hats and peace activists often provoked headlines and vividly delineated the wide gaps in ideology that marked the 1960s. Hard hats were probably the foremost promoters of the philosophy of "AMERICA, LOVE IT OR LEAVE IT."

Harriman, W. Averell (1891–1986)

A leading U.S. diplomat during the early years of the Cold War, William Averell Harriman was the son of railroad magnate E. H. Harriman. After graduating from Groton School, he enrolled in Yale University and obtained his A.B. degree there in 1913. He started his career as a vice president of the Union Pacific Railroad Company in 1915, eventually rising to become chairman of the board (1932–46). In 1920, he founded W. A. Harriman and Company. An active Democrat, Harriman

Two of President Lyndon Johnson's "Wise Men," Averil Harriman and Dean Acheson (JOHNSON LIBRARY)

was an officer of the National Recovery Administration under President Franklin D. Roosevelt (1934–35). He also served with the National Defense Advisory Committee and its successor agency, the Office of Production Management (1940–41). In 1941, he accompanied President Roosevelt to Great Britain for talks with Winston Churchill concerning the Atlantic defense (see ATLANTIC CHARTER). Roosevelt also sent Harriman on a special mission to the Soviet Union to expedite U.S. lend-lease assistance. He subsequently served as U.S. ambassador to the Soviet Union (1943–46), participating in all the major wartime conferences; as ambassador to Great Britain (April to October 1946); and as secretary of commerce (1947–48). From 1948 to 1950, he was named a special U.S. representative in Europe to supervise the administration of the European Recovery Program (see MARSHALL PLAN). In 1950, he was appointed special assistant to the president, then was made director of the Mutual Security Agency in 1951. He ran that agency until January 1953. Harriman tried

twice to win the Democratic nomination for president (1952 and 1956), but failed both times. In 1954, he was elected governor of New York State, but lost the next gubernatorial election to Nelson A. ROCKEFELLER in 1958. A classic Cold Warrior who favored a strong NATO and the popular policy of CONTAINMENT, he also opposed the LIBERATION ideas of John Foster DULLES, noting that they were not realistic under the circumstances.

From 1961 to 1963, Harriman served as President John F. KENNEDY's assistant secretary of state for Far Eastern affairs and for both Kennedy and his successor, Lyndon JOHNSON, as undersecretary of state for political affairs. During this period, he helped to negotiate the Partial Nuclear Test Ban Treaty and conducted negotiations to end the Laotian conflict. In time, he changed his views regarding containment, except as it applied to Southeast Asia.

Under President Johnson, Harriman served as ambassador-at-large and headed the U.S. delegation to the Paris peace talks between the United States and North Vietnam (1968–69). Harriman officially retired in 1969, although he remained active in foreign affairs in an unofficial capacity. The septuagenarian Harriman was replaced at the Paris peace talks by Henry Cabot LODGE. Subsequent to his retirement, he wrote several books, including *America and Russia in a Changing World* (1971). He also established the Harriman Institute at Columbia University for the purpose of studying the Soviet Union.

Harrington, Michael (1928–1989)

The most prominent American socialist of his time, Edward Michael Harrington was chairman and principal spokesman for the U.S. Socialist Party. A graduate of Holy Cross College and the University of Chicago, Harrington's original career plans were to become a poet, but after moving to New York he became involved in social activities that led him to political activism. He joined the Catholic Worker movement (see DAY, Dorothy) and the Young Socialist League during the 1950s, in addition to being a CONSCIENTIOUS OBJECTOR during the KOREAN WAR. An active participant in the CIVIL RIGHTS MOVEMENT and war protests of the 1960s, in 1973 Harrington founded the Democratic Socialist Organizing Committee as a way of bridging leftist radicalism with his concept of anticommunism. In 1981, this organization merged with the New American Movement to become the Democratic Socialists of America, a leftist coalition that seeks to work within the present political system to make the capitalist system more equitable and gain economic reforms.

From 1972 until his death in 1989, Harrington was a professor of political science at Queens College in New York. He was also a prolific writer; his many books include *The Other America: Poverty in the United States* (1962), widely thought to have inspired the antipoverty programs of the 1960s; *Toward a Democratic Left: A Radical Program for a New Majority* (1968) and *Socialism: Past and Future* (1989), a prospectus for a new, socialistic society. His autobiography, *The Long-Distance Runner,* was published in 1988.

Hawks   See DOVES AND HAWKS.

Hearst, Patricia (1954–   )

Patricia Campbell Hearst, an heir to the William Randolph Hearst newspaper empire, became a national figure overnight when she was kidnapped in 1974 by leftist radicals. The story took a sensational and unexpected turn when she was converted to the group's cause.

Hearst was the third of five daughters born to publishing magnate Randolph A. Hearst, son of William Randolph Hearst. She attended private schools in Los Angeles, San Mateo, Crystal Springs, and Monterey, California. Upon graduation from high school, she took classes at Menlo College and the University of California at Berkeley. On the night of February 4, 1974, three members of the self-proclaimed Symbionese Liberation Army (SLA) broke into the apartment she shared with her fiancé, Steven Weed, beat Weed, and abducted Hearst. She was confined in the closet of an apartment hideaway, brainwashed, and coerced into making public statements condemning her parents for their capitalistic "crimes." In an attempt to win her freedom, her father gave away $2 million in food to the poor. However, the SLA did not release Hearst, but managed to persuade her to join them in at least two robberies.

On May 17, 1974, most of the members of the SLA, including their leader, Donald DeFreeze, were killed in a police shoot-out and subsequent fire. Hearst remained at large, traveling across the country with her captors/confederates, William and Emily Harris and Wendy Yoshimura. On September 18, 1975, she and the others were captured in San Francisco. Hearst was tried and convicted in March 1976 for bank robbery and felonious use of firearms. She was sentenced to seven years but was released in February 1979 after serving two and a half years of her sentence. Shortly thereafter, she married her former bodyguard, Bernard Shaw. Hearst's own account of her ordeal, *Every Secret Thing,* was published in 1982.

"Hell, no, we won't go"

This was the chant that often rang out loudest in antiwar demonstrations. As opposition to the VIETNAM WAR grew, so did objections to the drafting of young men into the military to serve in what many believed to be a pointless and hypocritical war in a country of no perceived strategic value to the United States (Some, among them believers in the DOMINO THEORY, felt otherwise.) On numerous college campuses throughout the country, public draft card burnings symbolized the younger generation's refusal to participate in a war not of their making. Their discontent and rebellion was aptly represented with the angry declaration: "Hell, no, we won't go!"

Hellman, Lillian (1905–1984)

Lillian Hellman was a successful playwright and memoirist. She was raised in New York City and attended public schools there, as well as New York University and Columbia University. She married playwright Arthur Kober, but divorced him in 1932. By this time, she had begun an intimate relationship with novelist Dashiell HAMMETT, which would continue until his death 30 years later, in 1961. She began writing plays in the 1930s, after previously working as a book reviewer, press agent, play reader, and Hollywood screenwriter. In such dramas as *The Children's Hour* (1934) and *The Little Foxes* (1939), Hellman exposed the various forms that evil takes in daily life. With *The Watch on the Rhine* (1941), about the killing of a Nazi agent, Hellman earned her first New York Drama Critics' Circle Award. Although she was frequently criticized for creating impossible and impractical characters, Hellman was also praised for the realistic intensity of her plays, especially in the dialogue. In the 1950s she ventured into a subtler, Chekhovian style of drama with *The Autumn Garden* (1951) and also began translating and adapting the works of others. In this period, she edited Chekhov's *Selected Letters*.

When the Army-McCarthy hearings began in the 1950s, Hellman and her friends were subjected to intense security due to her longtime support of leftist cause. Hellman's stern refusal to cooperate during a 1952 appearance before the HOUSE UN-AMERICAN ACTIVITIES COMMITTEE led to a period where she could not work in Hollywood. (See also BLACKLISTING.)

Hellman returned to playwriting with such dramas as *Toys in the Attic* (1960), for which she won her second New York Drama Critics' Circle Award. In 1966, she published a collection of short stories and short novels by Dashiell Hammett that she had edited, *The Big Knockover.* Her reminiscences were published in 1969 under the title *An Unfinished Woman* and won the 1970 National Book Award in arts and letters. These memoirs were continued in *Pentimento* (1973), an account of her life with Hammett; *Scoundrel Time* (1976), a vivid record of the troubling McCarthy era; and *Maybe* (1980). Her final years were marred by a bitter feud with fellow writer Mary McCarthy.

Helms, Jesse (1921–   )

The first Republican elected senator from the state of North Carolina since 1895, Jesse Alexander Helms is best known for his outspoken conservative views. He began his career in the newspaper and broadcasting fields. In the late 1950s, he made his first foray into politics, serving on the Raleigh City Council from 1957 to 1961. He worked as an executive and commentator for the Capitol Broadcasting Company from 1960 to 1972. In 1972, he was elected for the first time to his Senate seat, which he has held ever since. His reputation for conservatism was sealed in 1981 with his introduction of a bill that would outlaw abortion at any time during a pregnancy. Over time, he has also sponsored bills allowing for school prayer, prohibiting busing to achieve integration of public schools, and requiring a federal balanced budget. He served as chairman of the Senate Committee on Agriculture, Nutrition, and Forestry from 1981 to 1987.

As a member of the Senate Foreign Relations Committee since 1981, Helms opposed the policy of DÉTENTE and various arms control agreements with the USSR. He also opposed the 1978 Panama Canal treaties. In 1995, with the Republicans in control of both houses of the Congress, he became chairman of the Senate Foreign Relations Committee.

Helms, Richard (1913–   )

Richard McGarrah Helms is best known for his conviction on charges of lying before a congressional committee in connection with his role as director of the CENTRAL INTELLIGENCE AGENCY (CIA) from 1966 to 1973. A 1935 graduate of Williams College, Helms worked as a newspaper reporter before enlisting in the U.S. Navy in 1942. Originally commissioned as a lieutenant, he was transferred to the OFFICE OF STRATEGIC SERVICES (OSS) in 1943. Later, he joined the CIA, the postwar intelligence successor to the OSS. He initially worked in covert operations, and during the 1950s supervised U.S. espionage activities inside the Soviet Union, as well as such illegal domestic activities as opening mail sent between the United States and Eastern Europe.

Throughout the 1950s and 1960s, Helms worked his way through the CIA ranks, until he was appointed director in June 1966. Beginning in 1967, Helms supervised the execution of Project Chaos, a secret initiative that aimed to trace the influence of foreign powers on U.S. political groups and individuals—a significant incursion into domestic political matters previously deemed off limits to the agency. Helms also oversaw a covert effort to undermine the legally elected president of Chile, Salvador Allende, fueling strike efforts that led to a military coup that cost Allende his life in 1973. That same year, he was fired as CIA director because of his refusal to involve the CIA in the WATERGATE cover-up. Nevertheless, President NIXON appointed Helms as ambassador to Iran. However, Helms' role as ambassador was compromised by investigations into CIA activities that required him to testify before several congressional investigating committees. His testimony revealed numerous conflicts and contradictions with investigation results. In defense against the charges that he had lied, he noted that, as head of the CIA, he was required to maintain a vow of secrecy. He finally pleaded guilty to two misdemeanors.

After Helms' conviction for perjury, he worked for a time as an international consultant and as president of the D.C.-based Safeer Company. With the election of President Ronald REAGAN, Helms was recruited to assist in preparing the United States for the possibility of nuclear war, and was appointed to serve on the Scowcroft Commission investigation into the MX mis-

sile system. In 1983, he was awarded the National Security Medal for "exceptional meritorious service."

Helsinki Accords

The Helsinki Accords (also called the Helsinki Treaties) were an outcome of the Helsinki Conference held from July 30 to August 1, 1975, in Helsinki, Finland. The agreements reached in this conference had been previously arranged through periodic meetings of the Conference on Security and Cooperation in Europe (CSCE) and were now ratified in Helsinki by means of a "statement of intent." Thirty-five nations signed the document, which outlined 10 principles relating to the security of Europe. These principles included pledges and guarantees covering such areas as human rights, economic cooperation, territorial integrity, and fulfillment of international obligations, among others. Human rights provided a key point for U.S. interest in the Helsinki Accords. DÉTENTE had changed the face of

President Gerald Ford signs the Helsinki agreement. (FORD LIBRARY)

the Cold War, and the United States was now approaching foreign policy, particularly in regard to the Soviet Union, from new directions. Thus, the Helsinki Accords provided a new weapon to use against the Soviet Union, which was notorious for its human rights violations. However, the accords' clear delineation of political spheres in Europe caused critics such as Ronald REAGAN to charge that President Gerald FORD had "placed the American seal of approval on the Soviet Empire in Eastern Europe."

Henderson, Loy (1892–1986)

Loy Wesley Henderson was a respected and sometimes controversial diplomat who became a fierce Cold Warrior in his opposition to COMMUNISM. He graduated from Northwestern University in 1915, and went on to get his law degree from the University of Denver Law School. He worked for the Red Cross during World War I, following which he was a member of the Interallied Commission to Germany. From 1919 to 1921, he returned to the Red Cross; then, in 1922, he joined the U.S. diplomatic service. He rose in the ranks via a series of diplomatic posts all over the world, including positions of increasing importance in Moscow, intermittently during the years 1934 to 1938. After a four-year posting as assistant chief in the Division of East European Affairs (1938–42), he went back to Moscow as a counselor in the U.S. embassy. He stayed in Moscow for the first part of World War II and was the U.S. representative at a meeting between Winston Churchill and Joseph Stalin in August 1942.

Henderson's experiences in Moscow created a firsthand familiarity with the Soviet communist system and its leaders, and contributed to his becoming a leading anticommunist. As the war progressed, he came into conflict repeatedly with his superiors at the embassy due to his cynical but strong belief that Stalin's cooperation with the Allies was merely temporary and that the Soviets were not to be trusted.

In 1943, Henderson was sent to Iraq, where, as minister, he coordinated diplomatic relations between the United States and several Middle Eastern countries. Following the conclusion of the war, in 1945, Henderson returned to the United States and was appointed chief of the Division of Near Eastern and African Affairs. In this capacity, he coordinated implementation of aid to Greece and Turkey according to the terms of the TRUMAN DOCTRINE, and also advised UNITED NATIONS ambassador Warren Austin on the U.S. position relating to the creation of Israel. In this latter regard, he was accused of being pro-Arab, due in large part to his concern that American support for the Zionists would alienate Arab oil-producing countries, thereby making them an easier target for Soviet conquest.

Between 1948 and 1955, Henderson held two ambassadorships, to India and to Iran. During this period, he worked to maintain India's neutrality during U.S. involvement in the KOREAN WAR. He was then appointed assistant secretary of state and subsequently undersecretary of state in 1955. Thanks to his experience in the Middle East, he was appointed a member of the Suez Commission and sent to the First and Second Suez Conferences in 1956. That same year, he was given the title of career ambassador, a singular honor.

Henderson retired from the State Department in 1961 and became a professor at American University, in Washington, D.C., and also directed the Washington Institute of Foreign Affairs.

hippies

Hippies, sometimes also called "flower children," were the younger members of the 1960s COUNTERCULTURE, who advocated love, peace, and individual freedom as a cure for societal ills. Considering themselves dropouts from the ESTABLISHMENT, most hippies originally came from the middle and upper classes of American society, against whose mores they rebelled. Hippies espoused lifestyles that went counter to accepted standards, and delighted in differing from the American norm both in appearance (long hair on men and women and unusual, colorful clothing) and behavior (blatant drug use and freewheeling sexual encounters). They rejected the educational and religious institutions commonly revered in U.S. culture and struck out against the federal, state, and local governments that they considered to be oppressive. Instead, they favored a socialist philosophy, as exemplified by the numerous hippie-founded communes around the country. Famous (sometimes infamous) hippie communities also grew in New York City's Lower East Side and in the Haight-Ashbury section of San Francisco.

Rock music and drug experimentation were hallmarks of the hippie movement. In addition, many hippies were strongly against the Vietnam War and were thus at the forefront of the peace movement. One of the most enduring photographic images of the 1960s shows a hippie placing a flower in the barrel of a gun being pointed at him by a member of the NATIONAL

GUARD. It was from this image that the term "flower children" was coined.

The hippie philosophy was also reflected in popular music of the time, which was written, sung, and played by a diversity of folk and rock artists, including Joan Baez, the Beatles, the Rolling Stones, Arlo Guthrie, Pete SEEGER, and, most notably, Bob DYLAN, whose song "Blowin' in the Wind" was considered by many to be the anthem of the hippie movement. In 1969, one of the most famous gatherings of hippies and musicians took place at the Woodstock music festival in a small town in New York. Woodstock was a three-day "love-in" marked by sex, drugs, and performances from Baez, Guthrie, Janis Joplin, Joe Cocker, Sly and the Family Stone, The Who, Crosby, Stills & Nash, Ravi Shankar, Canned Heat, the Grateful Dead, and Jimi Hendrix, whose psychedelic rock version of "The Star Spangled Banner" closed the festival and wowed the country. Hendrix and Joplin would later die of drug overdoses.

Many hippies eventually succumbed to the realities of the dominant culture, and some returned to the Establishment they had once rebelled against, settling down to jobs, families, and more conservative lifestyles. Nonetheless, pockets of hippie communities still remain.

Hiss, Alger (1904–1996)

Alger Hiss was a former U.S. State Department official who was convicted of perjury in relation to a sensational spy ring case in 1950. A Phi Beta Kappa graduate of Johns Hopkins University (A.B., 1926), Hiss went on to receive his law degree from Harvard University in 1929. For the next two years, he served as a law clerk to Supreme Court justice Oliver Wendell Holmes (1929–30). He entered government service in 1933 and served under President Roosevelt in the State Department, the Department of Agriculture, and the Department of Justice. In 1945, he was appointed director of the U.S. Office of Special Political Affairs and attended the YALTA CONFERENCE as an adviser to Roosevelt. He later served as temporary secretary-general in the San Francisco Conference of the UNITED NATIONS. From 1947 to 1949, he was president of the Carnegie Endowment for International Peace.

In 1948, Whittaker CHAMBERS, a self-confessed former member of the communist underground in Washington, D.C., accused Hiss of having been a member of the same espionage apparatus prior to World War II, and testified to this effect before the HOUSE UN-AMERI-

CAN ACTIVITIES COMMITTEE (HUAC). Hiss denied the charge, and sued Chambers for slander when he repeated it publicly. On December 6, 1948, the House committee, which included California representative Richard NIXON, released a copy of Chambers's sworn testimony. Hiss again denied the accusation that he had provided Chambers with classified State Department documents for transmission to a Soviet agent. A federal grand jury was convened to investigate the case, and both Chambers and Hiss were called to testify. Hiss again denied giving any documents to Chambers, and claimed he never talked to Chambers after January 1, 1937. On December 15, he was indicted on two counts of perjury, and pleaded not guilty to both. His first trial in 1949 ended in a hung jury, but he was found guilty in a second trial in 1950 and sentenced to five years in prison. He was released after three years in 1954, still publicly and privately claiming his innocence.

In 1992, when the Soviet Union archives were opened, Hiss asked Russian officials to check for information pertinent to his case. They did so, and an announcement was made that no evidence could be found of Hiss's involvement in a Soviet spy ring. However, in 1995, a file known as the Venona Project was released to the public, revealing information about American military interception and decoding of key Russian documents during World War II. This file, as well as subsequent information from the USSR archives, confirmed the existence of a KGB espionage ring, exactly as described by Chambers, and definitely named Hiss as an agent. Despite this, some of Hiss's supporters continue to defend him, and the question of his guilt or innocence remains a contentious and polarizing one.

Hoffa, James R. (1913–1975)

One of the most controversial labor leaders of this century, James Riddle Hoffa was the son of an Indiana coal driller who died when his son was seven years old. In 1924, Hoffa and his family moved to Detroit. He left school three years later at the age of 14, and spent several years working as a stockboy and warehouseman. By the 1930s, he had become involved in union activities and began organizing, starting as a business agent for Local 299 in Detroit. By 1940, he was chairman of the Central States Drivers Council. In 1942, he was made president of the Michigan Council of Teamsters. In 1952, he was elected an international vice president of the Teamsters and in 1957 he succeeded Dave Beck as international president after Beck went to prison for stealing union funds. At this point a U.S. Senate committee, with Robert F. KENNEDY as its chief counsel, began investigating Hoffa for his alleged ties to the underworld. Hoffa nevertheless went to work in revamping and centralizing the Teamster administration. He acquired a reputation as a tough bargainer, but was also respected for his knowledgeable handling of Teamster affairs. Largely through his efforts, the Teamsters became the largest labor union in the United States. Hoffa also played a key role in creating the first national freight-hauling agreement.

After a series of governmental prosecutions, Hoffa was convicted in 1967 of jury tampering, fraud, and conspiracy and sentenced to a federal facility in Lewisburg, Pennsylvania, for 13 years. Despite being in prison, he refused to resign as president of the Teamsters; in fact, he did not relinquish his position until June 1971. In December 1971, President Richard NIXON commuted Hoffa's sentence under the condition that he not engage in any union activity until 1980. However, Hoffa fought the restriction in court, and it was rumored that he was secretly continuing his efforts to regain control of the union. On July 30, 1975, he disappeared under mysterious circumstances from a suburban restaurant near Detroit. In 1982, he was declared "presumed dead." Hoffa's son and namesake went on to assume a leading role in Teamsters Union activities in the 1990s.

Hoffman, Abbie (1936–1989)

A political activist who loved the media, Abbott Hoffman, known as "Abbie," came to prominence as the founder of the Youth International Party, otherwise known as the YIPPIES. After receiving degrees in psychology from both Brandeis University (1959) and the University of California at Berkeley (1960), Hoffman became involved in the CIVIL RIGHTS MOVEMENT. In 1968, he concentrated his considerable energies on organizing the Yippies, a group dedicated to protesting the VIETNAM WAR and to exposing the injustices that it perceived in the American political system. Hoffman was a member of the so-called CHICAGO SEVEN, who were put on trial in 1969 on the charge of crossing state lines with intent to riot at the Democratic National Convention in Chicago in 1968. During the course of the trial, he gained considerable media attention with his courtroom antics, which were in keeping with the Yippie focus on "political theatre." His conviction was later overturned.

In 1973, Hoffman was arrested on charges of selling cocaine. To avoid serving time, he went underground, had plastic surgery, and assumed the alias of Barry Freed. As Freed, he worked as an environmental activist throughout the 1970s. He came out from hiding in 1980 and served a year in prison, after which he returned to his work for the environment. He wrote several books, including: *Revolution for the Hell of It* (1968); *Steal This Book* (1971); and his autobiography, *Soon to Be a Major Motion Picture* (1980). Hoffman, who apparently suffered from severe depression, died by his own hand in 1989.

Hollywood Ten

In September and October 1947, 43 people were called to testify before the HOUSE UN-AMERICAN ACTIVITIES COMMITTEE (HUAC) regarding their knowledge of supposed communist subversion in Hollywood. It was anticipated that a number of these witnesses would be "unfriendly" in their responses to the committee's questions, and in fact many refused to answer questions regarding their political affiliations or those of others. Negative public reaction to the hearings closed them down after only 10 of the "Unfriendly 19" had been subjected to intense grilling and a humiliating public examination. However, because of their refusal to cooperate with the committee, the "Hollywood Ten"—producers, directors, and scriptwriters—were sent to jail for contempt.

Consequently, the ten were subjected to BLACKLISTING in Hollywood, and they were no longer able to find work in their own industry. Writers, among them Dalton Trumbo, were able to get around the blacklist by using aliases or getting other writers to serve as "fronts" for their work. Others in the Hollywood Ten were not as successful in circumventing the blacklist's terrible effects; their careers were ruined as a result of HUAC's hounding.

The Hollywood Ten were: Alvah Bessie, Herbert Biberman, Lester Cole, Edward Dmytryk, Ring Lardner, Jr., John Howard Lawson, Albert Maltz, Samuel Ornitz, Adrian Scott, and Trumbo. In 1975, Trumbo received an Oscar for *The Brave One,* a movie he wrote during the blacklist era for which he had not previously received credit. In 1999, it was publicly acknowledged that he had written *Roman Holiday,* and that the credits on the film would be changed to reflect his authorship.

Hoover, J. Edgar (1895–1972)

John Edgar Hoover, director of the FEDERAL BUREAU OF INVESTIGATION (FBI) from 1924 to 1972, began preparing for his career by studying law at night at George Washington University. He received his bachelor of laws degree in 1916 and his master of laws degree one year later, at which point he went to work for the Department of Justice as a file reviewer. In 1919, he became special assistant to Attorney General A. Mitchell Palmer, and was given the assignment of overseeing the post–World War I deportations of suspected bolsheviks. In May 1924, he was named acting director of the Bureau of Investigation; seven months later, his full appointment as the bureau's director was confirmed. He took over an agency that had fallen into disarray with the scandals of the Harding administration. Hoover quickly set to work, reorganizing and rebuilding the Bureau and setting up rigorous methods of recruiting and training agents. He established what would become the world's largest fingerprint file, a scientific crime detection laboratory, and the FBI National Academy, a special training center for selected law enforcement officers recruited from all over the country.

Under Hoover's management, the FBI grew in size and responsibilities, and became famous for tracking down and capturing some of the country's most feared criminals. In the late 1930s, President Roosevelt assigned Hoover the job of investigating foreign espionage in the United States, as well as communist and fascist activities. This assignment became especially important to Hoover when the Cold War began in the late 1940s. He aggressively targeted radicals of every kind, in both the left and right spheres of political thinking, investigating white supremacy organizations such as the Ku Klux Klan and black activists such as Martin Luther KING, Jr. However, he steered clear of the Mafia, allowing it to operate nationwide without FBI interference.

Hoover's authoritarian control over the FBI was marked by frequent abuse of his powers. He used the agency's enormous capacities to conduct surveillance and collect data on politicians throughout the country. In this way, he secured his position as director by maintaining the power to leak potentially damaging information about any politician who might threaten him—including sitting presidents.

Throughout his career, Hoover remained a dedicated anticommunist. It was under his orders that the FBI launched the initiative known as COINTELPRO, whose purpose was the surveillance, destabilization,

FBI director J. Edgar Hoover (JOHNSON LIBRARY)

and "neutralizing" of various groups deemed by Hoover to be subversive, including many NEW LEFT organizations. By the early 1970s, Hoover had become the target of harsh public criticism for his persecution of those he regarded as radicals and subversives and the tactics he used to maintain his control of the FBI. Nevertheless, he retained his post to the time of his death, in 1972. He had been the FBI's chief for 48 years and had served under eight presidents and 18 attorneys general. His excesses notwithstanding, Hoover made many important contributions to the field of police technology. He also wrote a number of books, including *A Study of Communism* (1962).

Hope, Bob (1903–   )

Legendary entertainer Bob Hope started out in life as Leslie Townes Hope, the fifth of six sons born to a stonemason and a former Welsh concert singer. Born in England, Hope immigrated with his family to the United States when he was four years old, eventually ending up in Cleveland, Ohio. At the age of 10, he won a Charlie Chaplin imitation contest, the earliest indication of his future vocation. By the time he was in his 20s, he was working in vaudeville, and by 1927 he had appeared on Broadway in *The Sidewalks of New York*. He landed his first substantial role in the musical *Roberta* (1933). He also began doing radio monologues, and this led to a part in the film *The Big Broadcast of 1938*. It was this movie that introduced what was to become his trademark song, "Thanks for the Memories."

In 1940, Hope teamed up with Bing Crosby to make *The Road to Singapore*. The movie was a big hit, and

Hope and Crosby would go on to make six more pictures in the popular "Road" series. Hope's success extended into radio, with his program reaching the top of the ratings in 1944. He made his television debut in 1950, and would go on to appear in highly-rated TV specials throughout his career.

Hope is highly regarded for his longtime work with the United Service Organizations (USO), starting during World War II and continuing with more than 40 USO-sponsored Christmas tours to entertain U.S. troops stationed overseas. In the Vietnam era, Hope's USO shows for servicemen stationed in Southeast Asia boosted morale that often needed boosting during a complex, lengthy military engagement that grew more controversial with time. For his services, Hope has been given distinguished service awards from every branch of the armed forces, in addition to being made an honorary Commander of the Order of the British Empire. He received a People to People Award from President Dwight D. EISENHOWER, the Congressional Gold Medal from President John F. KENNEDY, and the Medal of Freedom from President Lyndon B. JOHNSON.

Hopkins, Harry (1890–1946)

Harry Lloyd Hopkins was a key figure of the Roosevelt administration who played a significant role in the development of American foreign policy before the Cold War swung into full gear. A social worker during the 1920s, in 1931 Hopkins was appointed executive director of the New York State Temporary Relief Administration that had been established by then-governor Franklin D. Roosevelt. (He later became chairman.) When Roosevelt became president in 1933, Hopkins accompanied him to Washington to serve as administrator of the Federal Emergency Relief Administration.

With the Democrats fully in control after the 1934 elections, Hopkins suggested major reforms to the president, including the introduction of the Works Progress (later Projects) Administration (WPA), which he directed with enormous zest and dedication. By 1938, Hopkins had spent more than $8.5 billion on unemployment relief, providing aid to over 15 million people. He also served on the President's Drought Committee, the Committee on Economic Security, the National Emergency Council, and the National Resources Planning Board, as well as heading the Federal Surplus Relief Board.

By the time of the 1936 election, Hopkins had become a valuable asset to President Roosevelt; he is often cited as FDR's most influential adviser. He had also acquired a deep interest in politics. A serious illness prevented him from pursuing his own political ambitions, but he continued to serve as an adviser so trusted by the president that he was invited to live at the White House.

Roosevelt appointed him secretary of commerce in 1938. Hopkins resigned his cabinet post in 1940, but as World War II progressed, he made several trips to London and Moscow to discuss military strategy and assistance on the president's behalf. In 1941, he was appointed to head the lend-lease program to aid the Allies; in this capacity, he went to Moscow to meet with Joseph Stalin. Hopkins also served as a member of the War Production Board and the Pacific War Council.

After Roosevelt's death in April 1945, Hopkins became an adviser to his successor, President Harry TRUMAN, and went to Moscow to support diplomatic efforts at the POTSDAM CONFERENCE. He also assisted the administration at the UNITED NATIONS conference in San Francisco, among other things helping to break the deadlock between the United States and the Soviet Union over the composition of the UN Security Council. Hopkins retired from public service in late 1945, just prior to his premature death in early 1946.

Hopper, Hedda (1890–1966)

Hedda Hopper, whose given name was Elda Furry, was an actress who became better known as a gossip columnist and rival to fellow journalist Louella Parsons. Raised in a strict Quaker family, she ran away from home at the age of 18 to pursue her love of the theater. She made her Broadway debut in *The Motor Girl* (1909) and her film debut in *Virtuous Wives* (1918). In 1913, she married musical comedy performer DeWolf Hopper, and shortly thereafter she changed her first name to Hedda. They were divorced in 1922, by which time Hopper had made dozens of films but had achieved no solid success. For several years she tried her hand in real estate and fashion commentary. Then, in 1936, she began a radio show in which she supplied the latest Hollywood gossip. In 1938, she started writing her own gossip column, first for the Esquire Syndicate, then for the syndicate belonging to the Des Moines (Iowa) *Register and Tribune*. In 1942, she moved to the *Chicago Tribune-New York Daily News* syndicate. Her familiarity with the celebrities and powerhouses of show business made her column highly popular, rivaling that of her competitor, Louella Parsons. The two columnists engaged in a feud that lasted for years as they wrote competing daily and Sunday syndicated columns. In addition to her writing career, she appeared in more than 100 films, including *The Women,* in which she played a gossip columnist.

Hopper was a woman of strong conservative and anticommunist opinions who was also suspicious of international movements. She described the 1945 UNITED NATIONS conference in San Francisco as "the greatest clambake in history." She was also one of the leading supporters of the effort to oust communists and communist sympathizers from the motion picture industry. She irreparably damaged the career of actor Larry Parks by writing that he had revealed "too little, too late" to the HOUSE COMMITTEE ON UN-AMERICAN ACTIVITIES. She was an enthusiastic supporter of the young Richard NIXON (many credit her with convincing Nixon to run for the Senate against Helen Gahagan DOUGLAS in 1950) and Joseph MCCARTHY. She used her column for repeated attacks on both Adlai STEVENSON and Eleanor ROOSEVELT, leading some editors to question whether Hopper's focus was on show business or politics.

Hopper's trademark was her unique variety of hats. She also gained a reputation for her snappy, ungrammatical use of language. Her autobiography, *From Under My Hat,* was published in 1952, with a follow-up memoir, *The Whole Truth and Nothing But,* published in 1963.

House Un-American Activities Committee (HUAC)

The House Un-American Activities Committee (HUAC) was established in 1938 by the House of Representatives as a special committee headed by Texas Democrat Martin Dies, Jr. The purpose of the Dies Committee at that time was to investigate extremist or subversive political organizations in the United States, including fascists and communists, in order to halt the spread of anti-American propaganda. Eventually, the committee shifted its focus to labor leaders, liberals, and intellectuals associated with the New Deal. The HUAC became a standing committee in 1945 and for the next 30 years investigated numerous liberal, left-wing, and communist organizations in the United States. As the Cold War got underway, the committee intensified its efforts, targeting individuals who were suspected of having communist affiliations. In 1947, 10 Hollywood directors, producers, and writers were called to testify before the

committee, but they refused to answer such questions as, "Are you now or have you ever been a member of the Communist Party?" This group, known as the HOLLYWOOD TEN, was subsequently jailed for failing to cooperate with the committee.

In 1948, the HUAC began to turn its attention to possible communist infiltration in the federal government, and particularly the State Department. It was during these hearings that the sensational case of Alger HISS came to light; Hiss, who vigorously denied the charges of espionage that had been lodged against him, was later convicted and imprisoned for perjury. A young committee member named Richard NIXON came to public attention as a result of this case.

By 1950, Senator Joseph MCCARTHY of Wisconsin had begun making sensational charges that over 200 members of the State Department were communists, setting in motion the "red scare" that would galvanize the nation. As a result of McCarthy's charges, the HUAC sponsored the INTERNAL SECURITY ACT (also known as the McCarran Act), which denied passports as well as federal and defense industry employment to U.S. communists, and also required them to register as foreign agents. The travel ban and registration provision would later be overturned by the courts.

The committee's work was soon overshadowed by McCarthy's own headline-grabbing investigations, although it continued to assist in the communist "WITCH HUNTS" of the 1950s. However, when public and governmental opinion began to turn against McCarthy and McCarthyism, the committee's power and influence declined along with the Wisconsin senator's. By 1969, the HUAC had been renamed the Internal Security Committee, and that body was formally disbanded in 1975, its functions transferred to the House Judiciary Committee.

Hull, Cordell (1871–1955)

U.S. secretary of state from 1933 to 1944 and winner of the 1945 Nobel Peace Prize, Cordell Hull started out as an attorney in his home state of Tennessee. He served in the U.S. House of Representatives for 22 years (1907–21, 1923–31) and also, more briefly, in the Senate (1931–33). As a congressman, he helped to create the federal income tax system (1913) and the federal inheritance tax (1916).

At the beginning of the New Deal, Hull was appointed secretary of state by President Franklin D. Roosevelt. In that capacity, Hull called for a reversal of high tariff barriers, among other proposals for expanding U.S. foreign trade. In March 1934, he persuaded Congress to pass the Reciprocal Trade Agreements Act, a forerunner to the General Agreement on Tariffs and Trade that would begin in 1948. Thus, his work in this area set in motion the mechanism for expanded world trade in the 20th century.

As secretary of state, Hull also implemented the "Good Neighbor Policy," which was designed to improve U.S. relations with Latin America. He attended several Pan-American Conferences and worked to forge harmony among nations in the Western Hemisphere. Thanks to the goodwill created by his efforts, Hull was able to successfully organize a united front of American republics against Axis aggression during World War II, and with the Japanese attack on Pearl Harbor in December 1941, the United States became fully committed to the war effort. Once this was the case, Hull and his State Department colleagues almost immediately began to plan an international peacekeeping body for the postwar era. At the Moscow Conference of Foreign Ministers in 1943, he obtained a pledge from four nations to continue the current spirit of cooperation after the war by means of an organization designed to maintain peace and security throughout the world. For this work, President Roosevelt described Hull as the "father of the UNITED NATIONS." He was subsequently awarded the Nobel Peace Prize, in 1945. Hull resigned his post after the 1944 presidential election. His book, *Memoirs of Cordell Hull,* was published in 1950.

Humphrey, Hubert (1911–1978)

The 38th vice president of the United States, and one of the country's most popular politicians, Hubert Horatio Humphrey was a liberal Democrat who started his career as a pharmacist at his family's drugstore. Atter working at a variety of jobs, he went on to earn degrees from the University of Minnesota (1945) and the University of Louisiana (1947). He found his niche in politics in 1944, when he became the Minnesota campaign manager for President Franklin D. Roosevelt. He also worked to merge the state's Democratic and Farmer-Labor parties. His own polltical career began in 1945 with his election as mayor of Minneapolis. Two years later, he cofounded the AMERICANS FOR DEMOCRATIC ACTION, whereupon he convinced the Democratic-Farmer-Labor Party to purge its ranks of communist members.

In 1948, Humphrey won election to the U.S. Senate, where he represented his state for the next 16 years. He

quickly developed a reputation for being a skilled leader and debater, and sponsored numerous progressive bills. His success in bringing together bipartisan support for the Partial Nuclear Test Ban Treaty of 1963 and the CIVIL RIGHTS ACT of 1964 won him high acclaim from his peers and from the American public. In 1961, he was named the assistant senate majority leader.

In 1964, Lyndon B. JOHNSON selected Humphrey as his running mate in the presidential race. As vice president, Humphrey's onetime "do-gooder" image was gradually supplanted by his emerging tendency to defend the status quo; he was widely viewed as an "ESTABLISHMENT" politician by many in the NEW LEFT. Among other things, he defended U.S. participation in the VIETNAM WAR from 1966 onward. However, he still retained many of his liberal interests, and he served as chairman of the National Advisory Council for the PEACE CORPS, coordinator for the Antipoverty Program, and chairman of the Civil Rights Council.

In 1968, Lyndon Johnson made the decision to withdraw from the presidential race, and from politics. Humphrey ran against the antiwar faction and became the Democratic candidate for president; however, his position that year was an unusually difficult one, given the tumultuous events of 1968 (which included the assassinations of Robert F. KENNEDY and Martin Luther KING, Jr.). He was also hampered by deep divisions within his party over the Vietnam War. Johnson tried to help Humphrey by launching new peace overtures, but his initiatives did not advance the peace process or secure enough support for Humphrey to win the election; he was narrowly defeated by Richard NIXON.

After leaving Washington, Humphrey began teaching at Macalester College in St. Paul, Minnesota, and at

Vice President Hubert Humphrey (JOHNSON LIBRARY)

the University of Minnesota in Minneapolis. In 1970, he was reelected to the U.S. Senate as the Democratic-Farmer-Labor Party candidate from Minnesota. In 1972, he failed in his bid for the Democratic nomination for president. Nevertheless, he remained in the Senate as an elder statesman and party sage. When he died, he was remembered not as the candidate of 1968 but as one of the giants in the history of the Senate.

hydrogen bomb

Following the creation and successful explosion of the ATOMIC BOMB in 1945, U.S. researchers began to explore further nuclear capabilities. Fearful of creating weapons that could cause even more massive destruction than that demonstrated by the atomic bomb, opponents of atomic research argued that there was no need for further research. But the advent of the Cold War and the developing arms race with the Soviet Union made further development of U.S. thermonuclear capabilities a necessity in the minds of President Harry TRUMAN and his advisers, who saw it as a means

of DETERRENCE. Thus, overriding the objections of J. Robert OPPENHEIMER and the ATOMIC ENERGY COMMISSION, Truman approved development of a hydrogen bomb; the first successful detonation took place on November 1, 1952, in the Eniwetok atoll of the Marshall Islands.

The hydrogen bomb differed from the atomic bomb in that its energy was derived from the formation of helium nuclei rather than from fission. In addition, the amount of radioactivity generated by a hydrogen bomb was more easily modified, making it technically possible to construct a "clean" bomb that would produce less radioactive damage. The development of the hydrogen bomb also provided new ways of boosting rockets, a great advantage to scientists engaged in devising the technology that would be used in the space race.

Within a few months after the United States exploded its first hydrogen bomb, the Soviet Union also successfully detonated a thermonuclear device. The British followed suit in 1957, the Chinese in 1967, and the French in 1968. See also TELLER, Edward.

I

"I shall go to Korea"

A famous statement by presidential candidate Dwight D. EISENHOWER, "I shall go to Korea" soon entered the American lexicon as a synonym for employing hands-on solutions to difficult problems. When the unpopular "POLICE ACTION" in Korea began to escalate and truce talks were delayed and postponed repeatedly, Eisenhower responded to a frustrated America by publicly promising to take action and go to Korea himself. He later made good on his promise, and an armistice was signed in July 1953. "I shall go to Korea" was later appropriated by other politicians as an assurance that a problem would be resolved, and cited by presidents such as Bill Clinton as an example of strong leadership.

Internal Security Act

The Internal Security Act, also called the McCarran Act after its primary sponsor, was passed in 1950 as a result of Senator Joseph MCCARTHY's charges that communists had infiltrated the U.S. State Department. Responding to public fears about the "red menace," Senator Patrick McCarran proposed a bill, subsequently passed by Congress over President Harry TRUMAN's veto, that would have a threefold purpose. First, a Subversive Activities Control Board was established as a means of investigating and countering suspected communist threats. The board conducted hearings on organizations and individuals that were suspected to be communist or communist-infiltrated, then submitted its findings to the Justice Department. Those organizations found to be communist were ordered to register with the Justice Department and to present data regarding their membership lists, finances, and activities. In addition, known communists were required to register as foreign agents and were denied both passports and employment in either the federal government or the defense industry. The travel ban restriction was later reversed on appeal, upon which some well-known communists, such as Paul ROBESON, left the United States.

Board actions could be appealed in the federal courts, and in 1961 the U.S. Supreme Court ruled that individual members of the Communist Party could not be compelled to register. As a result of this loophole, no communist-affiliated party or organization registered with the Subversive Activities Control Board thereafter, although the registration provision remained in effect until 1968, when the 1950 act was amended to eliminate the requirement.

Another provision of the McCarran Act made it a felony to contribute in any way to the establishment of a totalitarian dictatorship in the United States. Finally, the president was authorized to arrest and detain any individuals he suspected might engage in espionage or sabotage in an emergency situation such as invasion, war, or insurrection on behalf of a foreign enemy.

International Atomic Energy Agency (IAEA)

With a membership of 131 nations (as of 1999), the International Atomic Energy Agency (IAEA) is the largest organization dedicated to finding peaceful uses for atomic energy. Established in 1957 as a direct consequence of President Dwight D. EISENHOWER's ATOMS FOR PEACE program, first proposed in 1953, the stated goal of the IAEA is "to accelerate and enlarge the contribution of atomic energy to peace, health, and prosperity throughout the world. It shall ensure, so far as it is able, that assistance provided by it or at its request or under its supervision or control is not used in such a way as to further military purpose." In achieving this purpose, the IAEA retains close ties to the UNITED NATIONS.

Among the organization's many missions and activities has been the establishment of a control board and inspection system designed to ensure that cooperating nations do not use their atomic energy resources for military purposes. In addition, the IAEA coordinates worldwide atomic research, providing contracts and fellowships, funding for publications, organizing scientific meetings, and maintaining its own laboratories in Austria and Monaco. It also sponsors international symposiums and provides standards, guidance, and technical assistance to member states and developing areas in the development and maintenance of nuclear programs in industry, agriculture, and medicine.

Headquartered in Vienna, Austria, the IAEA has its own strict system of internal controls, with a 35-member revolving board of governors and an annual confer-

President Ronald Reagan and Senator Edmund Muskie listen as Senator John Tower (left) reports on his commission's investigation into the Iran-Contra affair. (REAGAN LIBRARY)

ence attended by all member nations. During the harsh years of the Cold War, the agency often stepped in to help mediate disputes and treaties, and to conduct inspections in both the Soviet Union and the United States, when necessary.

Iran-Contra affair

In 1986, a major scandal broke into the headlines that seriously affected the reputation of President Ronald REAGAN's administration. It began in 1981, when the CENTRAL INTELLIGENCE AGENCY (CIA) began a covert operation in Nicaragua to overthrow the ruling Sandinista government. To do this, they began training Contra rebels in special weapons and fighting tactics. (CONTRAS was the name given to former members of the Nicaraguan National Guard under Anastasio Somoza, Jr., and others who were opposed to the current regime.) As the Contra force grew to 30,000 troops, funding for their activities was obtained from private sources and also from the U.S. Congress. However, Congress suspended its aid as peace talks commenced between the Sandinistas and the Contras in 1988, leading the CIA to look for other ways to fund their continuing operations in Nicaragua.

Meanwhile, the administration was also facing the dilemma of how to secure the release of U.S. hostages being held in Iran. Early in 1985, Reagan's advisers received word from Israeli contacts that the hostages might be released if arms could be sold to certain Iranian moderates. The administration saw another advantage to the plan in that proceeds from the sale could be used to fund the Contras in Nicaragua, thus killing two birds with one stone.

The plan was put into effect under the direction of Colonel Oliver NORTH, an aide to National Security Advisor John POINDEXTER. Between the summer of 1985 and the fall of 1986, North supervised several shipments of arms to Iran by way of Israel. A large portion of the profits was then diverted to the Contras, starting in April 1986. The mission was conducted with a great deal of secrecy; apparently, not even President Reagan knew the full details of the transactions, and only scant information was provided to Congress. Thus, when the story broke as a result of revelations in a Lebanese publication in October 1986, a great public outcry followed. As a result, the president appointed a special commission to look into the affair and investigate any illegal activities on the part of the NATIONAL SECURITY COUNCIL (NSC). The commission was headed by former senator John

Tower of Texas, and as a result of its investigations, both the House of Representatives and the Senate conducted special hearings, during which North testified that his actions had been sanctioned by the NSC. Subsequently, Lawrence Walsh was appointed as special prosecutor, and proceeded to obtain indictments against Poindexter, North, and two others for their roles in the scandal. North and Poindexter were convicted on numerous counts and were sentenced to prison terms. Meanwhile, Reagan—whom many believed knew very little about what was going on—survived the scandal, his popularity with American citizens tarnished but otherwise intact. To date, no clear connection has been made regarding the extent of the CIA's role in the sale of arms to the Iranians, and in particular the involvement of director William CASEY, who presumably sanctioned the plan but died before he could testify to Congress about it.

iron curtain

The *iron curtain* was the name given to the infamous, invisible barrier that existed between the Union of Soviet Socialist Republics and the rest of the world during the darkest days of the Cold War. The term had been in use for decades in a variety of situations, most notably as a symbol of a country's political, social, or spiritual ISOLATIONISM. However, it was made famous by British prime minister Winston Churchill in a speech he gave on March 5, 1946, at Fulton, Missouri. Churchill had used the phrase previously, but now he gave it an indelible meaning when he said: "From Stettin in the Baltic to Trieste in the Adriatic, an iron curtain has descended across the continent. Behind that line lie all the capitals of the ancient states of central and eastern Europe. . . . The safety of the world, ladies and gentlemen, requires a new unity in Europe from which no nation should be permanently outcast." Churchill thus set the tone for future relations with the Soviet Union and its satellite countries by emphasizing the political, ideological, and communicative barriers that separated it from other nations.

The iron curtain held strong from Churchill's day through the 1960s. By the 1970s, however, it was showing signs of weakening, as President Richard NIXON and others worked to foster improved diplomatic relations with the Soviet Union and China, and many communist countries lifted travel restrictions and initiated cultural and economic exchanges with Western countries. Barriers came down entirely with the conclusion of the Cold War.

isolationism

Isolationism is the practice of abstaining from involvement in international affairs or forming alliances with other countries; it can also describe the factors that contribute to a nation's isolationist position. This was certainly the case for the United States from approximately 1800 to 1917, when it was geographically distant from events going on in Europe and Asia, and weak in both economic and military resources. However, as the country gradually grew stronger and the world grew smaller as a result of breakthroughs in transportation and communication, the difference of opinion arose between those who preferred the country's isolationist status and those who wanted to see the United States take its place as a world leader. Following World War I, the two viewpoints led to some sharp disputes and controversial decisions, such as the American refusal to join the League of Nations (precursor to the UNITED NATIONS). While isolationism did not prevent American leaders from involving the country in Latin American affairs, it did play a role in how the United States was slow to become involved in World War II—a decision that was made for the country's leaders when Japanese planes bombed Pearl Harbor in December 1941. Thereafter, the isolationists were outnumbered both by interventionists and the events that eventually dragged the United States into its position as a key combatant in the Cold War. The difference between the prewar and postwar United States was highlighted when the United States led the way in establishing the United Nations. However, an element of American society remains committed to the idea of a return to isolationism, feeling that the United States should attend to its own affairs first and not be called upon to serve as the world's caretaker.

J

Jackson, Henry (1912–1983)

Henry Martin Jackson, popularly known as "Scoop," was an important U.S. political leader with strong anticommunist leanings and a liberal social agenda. A resident of Everett, Washington, he returned there to set up a law practice after graduating from Stanford University in California and obtaining his law degree from the University of Washington. In time, he entered politics, and he was elected to the U.S. House of Representatives in 1941, where he served until 1953. In 1952, he was elected to the U.S. Senate from Washington, and was consistently reelected thereafter until his death.

Jackson was a vocal opponent of Senator Joseph MCCARTHY, going so far as to challenge McCarthy on national television during the Army-McCarthy hearings. He played a powerful role in legislation affecting the environment and the national defense through his chairmanship of the Committee on Energy and Natural Resources and as a member of the Armed Services Committee. Considered to be a liberal in domestic matters, Jackson was conservative when it came to foreign policy and took a strong anti-Soviet stance on many issues. He was critical of President Dwight EISENHOWER's defense policies, and advocated the MISSILE GAP theory, which postulated that the Soviet Union had more missiles than the United States He was a strong supporter of increases in defense spending, and was sometimes called "the senator from Boeing" due to Boeing Aircraft Company, a major contractor, being located in his home state of Washington.

Jackson opposed any normalization of relations with the Soviet Union, as well as any effort to regulate the arms race; this position included strong opposition to the Partial Nuclear Test Ban Treaty and, later, the STRATEGIC ARMS LIMITATION TREATY (SALT I). He supported Israel and the U.S. policy in Vietnam, blaming the failure of the U.S. military efforts on antiwar politics. In 1968, President-elect Richard NIXON asked him to be secretary of defense, but Jackson refused. He later became a vocal critic of the diplomacy of Henry KISSINGER, secretary of state under Nixon and his successor, Gerald FORD. In 1974, Jackson wielded his power to temporarily stop grain shipments to the Soviet Union under the U.S.-Soviet Grain Trade Agreement, which Jackson described as "the great grain robbery." That same year, the Jackson-Vanik Amendment was added to the East-West Trade Relations Act. It denied most-favored-nation trade status to the Soviet Union for as long as that country prohibited the emigration of its citizens.

Jackson ran for the Democratic presidential nomination in 1972 and 1976, but lost in the primaries both times. Despite his anticommunist views, he visited Communist China as a goodwill gesture shortly before his death in 1983.

Jackson, Jesse (1941–   )

A prominent civil rights advocate for black Americans, Jesse Louis Jackson was also the first African American to make a credible run for the U.S. presidency. Born into a poor family, he received a scholarship in 1959 to attend the University of Illinois. In 1960, he transferred to the Agricultural and Technical College of North Carolina in Greensboro, a predominantly black university, where he obtained his B.A. degree in sociology in 1964. In 1966, he moved to Chicago to pursue postgraduate work at the Chicago Theological Seminary. He was ordained as a Baptist minister in 1968.

Jackson became involved in the civil rights movement when he was still an undergraduate student. After he went to Selma, Alabama, in 1965 to march with Martin Luther KING, Jr., he joined and became a worker in King's Southern Christian Leadership Conference (SCLC). In 1966, he returned to Chicago to assist in setting up the Chicago branch of the SCLC's Operation Breadbasket, a program that addressed the economic problems of blacks in Northern cities. He subsequently served as Operation Breadbasket's national director from 1967 to 1971, and became the field director for the Congress of Racial Equality (CORE) in 1967. In 1971, he founded Operation PUSH (People to Save Humanity), a Chicago-based organization designed to pressure businesses into hiring and promoting more blacks, and to help achieve self-sufficiency for black Americans.

By the 1980s, Jackson had become an outspoken advocate for black Americans. In 1983, he conducted a voter registration drive that played a key role in the election of Chicago's first black mayor, Harold Washington. Jackson himself made two runs for the Democratic nomination for president, first in 1983–84 and again in 1987–88. In 1989, Jackson moved to Washington, D.C. He won his first elective office in 1990, when he ran for one of the district's newly created "shadow senator" seats meant to pressure Congress to grant statehood to the District of Columbia. Over the years, he has also attracted international respect and controversy by traveling widely in his attempts to mediate or call attention to numerous international

problems and disputes. Before the PERSIAN GULF WAR, Jackson worked to help bring about the release of a number of American hostages in Kuwait.

John Birch Society   See WELCH, Robert.

Johnson, Louis (1891–1966)

A onetime secretary of defense, Louis Arthur Johnson was an administrator whose attempts to restructure the American military met with failure. Johnson earned his law degree from the University of Virginia in 1912 and went on to set up his law practice in Clarksburg, West Virginia. In 1917, he won election to the West Virginia House of Representatives, but his service was interrupted when the United States entered World War I and he became an army colonel, serving in France. Upon his return, he threw himself into political work. From 1932 to 1933, he was the commander of the AMERICAN LEGION. Under President Franklin D. Roosevelt, he modernized the army in his capacity as assistant secretary of war (1937–40), a post in which he endorsed improved military preparedness. When Roosevelt did not appoint him secretary of war in 1940, Johnson resigned his position and returned to the law profession. However, he continued to work for Roosevelt, serving as the president's personal representative in India in 1942.

In reward for his work as finance chairman on President Harry TRUMAN's 1948 presidential campaign, Johnson was appointed secretary of defense in 1949. However, his plans to reconfigure and unify military forces (as per the NATIONAL SECURITY ACT of 1947), and his plan to reduce defense spending, aroused the ire of top officials within the administration. Navy admirals also revolted at Johnson's tendency to economize, and in time the navy and the air force were increasingly in conflict with each other because of the budget cuts. In 1949, Johnson was accused of corruption and conflict of interest; however, he was cleared of all charges. Later that year, he instituted a drastic series of budget cuts, focusing on the navy in particular—a move that caused such an outcry of protest that the House Armed Services Committee launched an investigation. Once again, Johnson came under attack, but the committee's conclusions supported his efforts to reduce spending and unify the services.

With the outbreak of war in Korea, Johnson's attempts to economize were cited as a contributing factor to the lack of U.S. military preparedness in dealing with the situation in Southeast Asia. As criticism and pressure mounted, he was finally compelled to resign his post, in September 1950. He subsequently returned to the practice of law, becoming a senior partner in the Washington firm of Steptoe and Johnson.

Johnson, Lyndon Baines (1908–1973)

Lyndon Baines Johnson, the 36th president of the United States, was a shrewd tactician and gifted politician. A moderate Democrat, Johnson was responsible for the most extensive civil rights legislation in the United States since Reconstruction, as well as the most fateful decisions regarding U.S. involvement in the VIETNAM WAR.

The eldest of five children, Johnson resisted college as a young man, preferring to hitchhike around the

President Lyndon Baines Johnson (JOHNSON LIBRARY)

country doing odd jobs. Eventually he enrolled at Southwest Texas State Teachers College in San Marcos, achieving his degree in only three years. One of his earliest teaching assignments was at Sam Houston High School in Houston, Texas, where he learned first-hand about problems faced by minorities, especially Mexican-Americans. He began working as a volunteer in state politics and then became a legislative assistant to Representative Richard M. Kleberg (for whom he had campaigned) in 1932. Johnson was soon befriended by the powerful Texas congressman (and eventual Speaker of the House) Sam Rayburn, and his political career blossomed rapidly. After two years as director of the National Youth Administration in Texas (1935–37), Johnson ran successfully for a seat in the U.S. House of Representatives. Johnson proved to be a classic New Deal Democrat whose career in politics was profoundly influenced by the leadership of President Franklin D. Roosevelt.

For 12 years, Johnson ably represented the 10th congressional district of Texas. His 1941 bid for a U.S. Senate seat ended in failure, but in 1948 he finally succeeded after a bitterly contested campaign that involved voting fraud on both sides in the all important Democratic primary. He served on the Senate's Armed Services Committee and was a strong advocate for defense spending and an early supporter of U.S. intervention in Korea. Johnson argued passionately for the formation of foreign policy objectives that could be supported by both parties in the face of Soviet aggression.

Johnson became Democratic whip in 1951 and senate majority leader in 1955. He gained a solid reputation for his ability to negotiate and achieve compromise, to the extent that he earned the honorific title "Master Legislator." A skilled and persuasive leader in the Senate, he was largely responsible for the passage of the civil rights bills of 1957 and 1960, the first such bills in the 20th century.

He surprised those who knew him by accepting the vice presidential slot on the Democratic ticket in the 1960 presidential election. Elected with President John F. KENNEDY, he quietly settled into the relative obscurity of his new office. In November 1963, Kennedy was assassinated, and Johnson ascended to the presidency. In his first few months in office, the new president succeeded in getting Congress to pass previously stalled but important legislation concerning civil rights, tax reduction, antipoverty measures, and conservation. Johnson also drew plans for a major military commitment in Vietnam. In November 1964, he won election in a landslide victory over Barry GOLDWATER, expertly

Lyndon Johnson takes the oath of office aboard Air Force One after President Kennedy's assassination. (JOHNSON LIBRARY)

exploiting doubts about Goldwater's extremism, especially as it might affect military policy in Vietnam. He viewed his electoral victory as a mandate to pursue his programs for domestic reform, which he called the "GREAT SOCIETY." Altogether, Johnson succeeded in pushing through the most impressive and progressive array of social legislation since the New Deal of the 1930s. Among his successes were the CIVIL RIGHTS ACT of 1964, the Voting Rights Act of 1965, and the Medicare bill of 1965. He also pursued initiatives in education, housing and urban development, transportation, environmental conservation, and immigration.

However, Johnson's stunning accomplishments on the domestic front were undermined by opposition to increasing U.S. military involvement in Vietnam. Although he had made a pledge during his campaign that hostilities in that area would not be expanded, he and his advisers, fearful that the communists would take over South Vietnam, steadily increased U.S. intervention. By 1967, bombing had been intensified, and 500,000 American troops had been sent to Indochina. Meanwhile, the ANTIWAR MOVEMENT had virtually taken over the left wing of the Democratic Party. With the promised end to the war proving elu-

Secretary of Defense Clark Clifford, Secretary of State Dean Rusk, Jerri Rudolph, President Lyndon Johnson, Assistant Press Secretary Tom Johnson, Walt Rostow, General Earle Wheeler, and CIA director Richard Helms meet in the Oval Office. (JOHNSON LIBRARY)

sive, support from middle America was rapidly eroding. Consequently, Johnson found his position battered by increasing antiwar demonstrations and public criticism of his administration's handling of the conflict. He realized that his presence in the 1968 presidential campaign would further polarize an already deeply divided nation, and serve as a public referendum on his Vietnam policy—a referendum he might well lose.

On March 31, 1968, Johnson stunned the nation with a televised address containing three crucial announcements. First, he had just ordered major reductions in the bombing of North Vietnam; second, he was requesting peace talks to bring about an end to the war; and third, he would neither seek nor accept his party's nomination to the presidency. In January 1969, after the election of Richard NIXON, Johnson returned home to his ranch near Johnson City, Texas. His memoirs, *The Vantage Point*, were published in 1971. In January 1973, Lyndon Johnson died of a heart attack at his home. Only a week later, an agreement to end the war in Vietnam was signed.

Kefauver, Estes (1903–1963)

Estes Carey Kefauver was the U.S. senator from Tennessee who gained national attention for his independent stands against economic monopolies and for his televised investigations of organized crime in the 1950s. Kefauver was a 1924 graduate of the University of Tennessee who earned his law degree at Yale University. Soon he set up a law practice in Chattanooga, Tennessee. He was first elected to the House of Representatives in 1939, and served for the next 10 years, establishing himself as a strong supporter of labor causes. Following the conclusion of World War II, he sponsored the GI Bill, which provided benefits to war veterans, and supported public power in the form of the Tennessee Valley Authority. Kefauver also opposed a 1946 bill proposing the creation of a "loyalty review board," which would investigate anyone whose loyalty was considered suspect and prosecute them when deemed appropriate. In 1947, as part of Kefauver's work for the Select Committee on Small Business, he chaired a subcommittee to investigate the growing power of monopolies in the American economy, and issued a report accusing the federal government of bypassing smaller companies for contracts in favor of the larger monopolies. To counteract this problem, he attempted to introduce legislation that would prevent corporations from taking over their competitors through acquisition of controlling interests of stock. His bill did not pass, but he established himself as a solid defender of the rights and protection of small business owners.

In 1948, Kefauver was elected to the Senate after waging a solid primary campaign against two conservative Democrats (one the incumbent). Both opponents had assailed his voting record, claiming it was marked by opposition to poll taxes, support for internal congressional reforms, vigorous enforcement of antitrust statutes, and "procommunist" leanings. Nevertheless, Kefauver represented Tennessee in the Senate until his death in 1963. He initially gained fame as a champion of civil rights, a position that aroused the ire of many fellow Southern politicians. In 1950, he voted against the INTERNAL SECURITY ACT (one of only seven senators to do so). That same year, the Kefauver-Celler Act was passed. It achieved Kefauver's goal of containing monopolies by closing a loophole in the Clayton Antitrust Act that allowed larger organizations to swallow up their competitors through purchase of stocks and other assets.

Kefauver achieved his greatest fame through his chairmanship of the Special Committee to Investigate

97

Organized Crime in Interstate Commerce. The public airing of the proceedings, which highlighted political and police corruption, came to be known as the "Kefauver Committee," and catapulted him to national attention. As a result of the committee's work, by 1957 the Justice Department had prosecuted and convicted hundreds of cases of criminal fraud. Kefauver's account of the investigation was published in 1951 as *Crime in America,* and became a best-seller.

In 1952, Kefauver—now a prominent national figure—made a bid for the Democratic presidential nomination, but lost to Adlai STEVENSON (despite obtaining the majority of the popular vote in the primaries). He tried again in 1956, once more losing to Stevenson, but was selected as the vice presidential candidate. The Stevenson-Kefauver ticket subsequently lost to Eisenhower and Nixon. From then on, Kefauver remained an effective member of the Senate, earning respect from his colleagues and the public as an expert critic of economic monopolies. In 1964, less than a year after his death, his career-long campaign to abolish the poll tax was achieved with the ratification of the 24th constitutional amendment.

Kennan, George (1904–)

A diplomat and historian, George Frost Kennan has become best known for his proposal of a postwar "CONTAINMENT policy" to counter potential Soviet expansion. He is also known as a hero of the antinuclear movement. He graduated from Princeton University in 1925, after which he joined the foreign service. He was immediately sent overseas to Geneva, and subsequently to other postings. Over the course of his many years with the foreign service, he would be posted to many such "listening posts" in Western Europe. In anticipation of the United States establishing diplomatic relations with the Soviet Union, he was sent to the University of Berlin in 1929 to study the Russian language and culture and become well-versed in Soviet thinking. He completed his studies in 1931. In 1933, following formal U.S. recognition of the USSR, Kennan accompanied newly appointed ambassador William C. BULLITT to Moscow. Kennan was transferred to Vienna in 1935, and subsequently went to posts in Prague and Berlin. He was in Berlin when World War II broke out and for a time he was interned by the Nazis. He was released in 1942 and went on to wartime work in Lisbon, London, and Moscow. Upon the conclusion of World War II, he was among those who opposed the division of Germany.

In February 1946, Kennan sent home a long cablegram from Moscow that analyzed U.S. policy toward the Soviet Union. Reaction to it was sensational, and it was passed around among top military and administration officials. He returned to the United States. later that year and worked briefly for the National War College before being appointed director of the State Department's policy-planning staff in 1947. He thereupon wrote an article for *Foreign Affairs* magazine entitled "The Sources of Soviet Conduct," signing it as "Mr. X." This famous article, which was to have great influence on the direction of U.S. foreign policy, analyzed Soviet strategic thinking in detail and questioned U.S. policy regarding diplomatic efforts with Moscow, which were more conciliatory than he felt was wise. He pointed out that Soviet expansion into surrounding countries was inevitable unless countermeasures were put into place that emphasized Western opposition to such expansion, and that these measures should include (but not be limited to) the preparedness of military force. (He felt that the Soviet threat was more political than it was military.) Kennan's logical arguments would eventually form the foundation for subsequent U.S. policy seeking the containment of Soviet communism and its allied movements. Kennan also laid the groundwork for a proposal for the postwar reconstruction of Europe. His suggestion and guidelines formed the basis for what became the MARSHALL PLAN.

In 1949, Kennan was appointed counselor to the State Department, but his work there was marred by frequent differences of opinion with the secretary of state, Dean ACHESON. He was increasingly convinced that military alliances such as the NORTH ATLANTIC TREATY ORGANIZATION (NATO) were ineffectual and in fact only aggravated the Cold War. In addition, he opposed the decision to order U.S. troops across the 38th parallel in Korea, as he felt this action would incite Communist China to enter into the war there.

Kennan resigned from the State Department in 1951 to go to the Institute for Advanced Study at Princeton. He was then named ambassador to Moscow (1952); however, after sharply criticizing the way American diplomats were treated in Moscow, he was declared persona non grata by the Soviets and he returned to the United States in 1953. He officially left the foreign service that year. In 1956, he became a professor of historical studies at the Institute for Advanced Study. He began to revise his views on containment in the late 1950s, and suggested instead a U.S. policy of "disengagement" from areas of conflict with the Soviets, particularly Central Europe. His idea was that the United States and the Soviet Union would agree to stay out of those areas and would maintain a "hands off" policy regarding all countries within them. Thus, Germany would be reunited, rearmed, and given non-aligned status. This proposal was opposed by Dean Acheson and John Foster DULLES, and eventually rejected as being too dangerous, as it would create a power vacuum in Central Europe that the Soviets were likely to co-opt. Disengagement was thus never put into practice.

Kennan was appointed U.S. ambassador to Yugoslavia in 1961, a post he held until 1963, by which time he had become distrustful of the KENNEDY administration's Cold War attitude. He subsequently returned once more to the Institute for Advanced Study. In his later years, Kennan argued against the institution of containment in such places as Vietnam and led the movement against nuclear weapons. His strong feelings against nuclear weapons were epitomized by the passion of his 1980 plea to the world's major powers to abolish weapons of mass destruction. His views frequently aroused public debate, and his prediction that the Soviet Union would collapse was later vindicated by history.

Kennan wrote a number of books and articles and won both the Pulitzer Prize and the National Book Award for *Russia Leaves the War* in 1956 and for *Memoirs, 1925–1950* in 1967. Other books include *Russia, the Atom, and the West* (1958); *Memoirs, 1950–1963* (1972); *A Cloud of Danger* (1977); *The Nuclear Delusion* (1982); and *At a Century's Ending: Reflections 1982–1995* (1996).

Kennedy, John F. (1917–1963)

John Fitzgerald Kennedy, the 35th president of the United States, was the nation's leader during a tumultuous period—a time when the Cold War precipitated a number of international crises, but also led to the Partial Nuclear Test Ban Treaty, the ALLIANCE FOR PROGRESS, and the PEACE CORPS. A Roman Catholic, he was the second of nine children born to Joseph Patrick Kennedy and his wife, the former Rose Fitzgerald. He graduated with a B.S. degree from Harvard University in 1940. That same year, he published his senior thesis. (It was later expanded into a best-selling book entitled *Why England Slept.*) He joined the U.S. Navy in the fall of 1941, and was sent to the South Pacific two years later. As the commander of a PT (motor

torpedo) boat, he became a hero when, after his boat was sunk behind enemy lines in the Solomon Islands, he managed to lead his men back to safety despite his own injuries. For his actions, he was awarded medals for heroism from the navy and the U.S. Marine Corps. At his own request, he was returned to active duty. As a result of this incident, Kennedy suffered medical problems the rest of his life that he would forever keep from public knowledge.

Although Kennedy had originally planned to become a journalist, his brother Joe's death during World War II caused him to become the heir apparent to their father's political ambitions. Upon his return to Massachusetts after the war, he began his quick rise in politics. In 1947, at the age of 29, he ran as a Democrat for a seat in the U.S. House of Representatives, which he won largely through the support and hard work of family, friends, and fellow navy officers rather than relying on the Democratic political machinery in

President John Fitzgerald Kennedy (KENNEDY LIBRARY)

Massachusetts. A "bread-and-butter liberal," he was also a supporter of U.S. foreign policy in the early days of the Cold War. He was reelected to the House in 1949 and 1951, then in 1953 won the U.S. Senate seat previously occupied by Henry Cabot LODGE, Jr.

In 1954, Kennedy—whose father, Joe, was a known admirer and supporter of Senator Joseph MCCARTHY—was absent on the day the Senate voted to condemn McCarthy's conduct during the communist "WITCH HUNTS" of the early 1950s. Originally suspected of pandering to McCarthy, he was in fact in the hospital, recovering from critical back surgery. During his subsequent recuperation period, he focused his efforts on the book *Profiles in Courage,* which was published in 1956 and received the Pulitzer Prize in 1957.

In the late 1950s, Kennedy, whose political views were becoming increasingly liberal, was named to the Senate Committee on Foreign Relations. As his stature increased among his fellow Democrats, he came close to being nominated for vice president in the 1956 race, a "near miss" that brought him to national prominence thanks to the new medium of television. In 1958, he won reelection to the Senate by the widest margin ever in Massachusetts politics. In January 1960, he formally announced his intention to run for president. He won the nomination on the first ballot at the Democratic convention, and chose Lyndon B. JOHNSON as his running mate. In the November elections, he won by a narrow margin over Richard M. NIXON, becoming the youngest man and the first Catholic ever to be elected president. One contributing factor to his win was thought to be his perceived successes in the televised debates with Nixon, which were attributed to his poise, charm, and good looks. Another factor was felt to be his role in obtaining the release of Martin Luther KING, Jr., from a prison in Atlanta, an action that gained him widespread support from the black community.

Kennedy began his presidency by initiating a liberal program he had already dubbed the "New Frontier." Although many of his bills failed to pass through Congress, he made some strides in achieving public school desegregation and began the process for civil rights legislation that was later passed after his death. His greater challenges came in the area of foreign affairs. In 1961, he accepted a recommendation by the Joint Chiefs of Staff to approve an invasion of Cuba by a force of CIA-trained anticommunist Cuban exiles. The subsequent invasion at the BAY OF PIGS proved disastrous, with every man on the force either captured or killed. Kennedy took full responsibility for the disaster,

President Kennedy was a media master who gave numerous press conferences. (KENNEDY LIBRARY)

although it had been planned prior to his presidency. He went head-to-head against his counterpart, Soviet premier Nikita Khrushchev, several times. The first occasion took place in Vienna, in June 1961. When Khrushchev ordered the erection of the BERLIN WALL and openly spoke of signing a separate peace treaty with East Germany, Kennedy activated the NATIONAL GUARD and reserve troops, forcing Khrushchev to back down. Their next confrontation occurred in October 1962, when it was discovered that the Soviets were storing and building up nuclear missiles in nearby Cuba. Kennedy ordered a blockade of the Cuban shores, preventing the arrival of further Soviet ships, and demanded that Khrushchev dismantle the missiles. After a 13-day standoff, during which the two countries seemed to be poised on the brink of a nuclear war, Khrushchev capitulated and announced that the weapons would be withdrawn from Cuba.

Having achieved acclaim for his handling of the CUBAN MISSILE CRISIS, Kennedy went on to further success by negotiating a Partial Nuclear Test Ban Treaty with the USSR and Great Britain. He also gained renown when he established the Peace Corps in the United States and the Alliance for Progress (Alianza) in Latin America.

On November 22, 1963, Kennedy was killed by a sniper's bullet as he was riding in a motorcade in Dallas, Texas. His accused assassin, Lee Harvey Oswald,

President Kennedy signs the Partial Nuclear Test Ban Treaty. (KENNEDY LIBRARY)

was subsequently shot by Jack Ruby on November 24. Although many people felt there was a conspiracy involved in the assassination, an investigation by the Warren Commission determined that Oswald had acted alone. The commission could not, however, explain certain irregularities in the details of the assassination. In 1977, the U.S. House of Representatives set up a special committee to reinvestigate the killing. After two years, this committee concluded that Oswald had not been the sole gunman and that he was part of a conspiracy that probably included organized crime.

In recent years, Kennedy's reputation has been tarnished by revelations of numerous sexual indiscretions both before and during his presidency. Nonetheless, he was an extremely popular president and a brilliant young leader whose potential for greatness was cut short by a bullet.

Kennedy, Joseph P.   (1888–1969)

A successful financier as well as the father of President John F. Kennedy and two U.S. senators, Joseph Patrick Kennedy was also an enterprising businessman and dabbler in politics who stirred up controversy during his tenure as ambassador to Great Britain. His grandfather was an immigrant from Ireland; his father was a politician. He graduated from Harvard University in 1912, and in 1914 he married Rose Fitzgerald, the daughter of Boston's mayor, John "Honey Fitz" Fitzgerald. Together, Joe and Rose would have four sons and five daughters, beginning a political dynasty that would make their family's name one of the best-known in the United States—and the world.

Kennedy was a man of many interests and abilities, as well as a staunch anticommunist. He became a bank president in 1914. By the time he was 30 years old, he was a millionaire. During World War I, he worked at a shipbuilding plant in Quincy, Massachusetts. From 1919 to 1924, he worked for Hayden, Stone, and Company as manager of the stock division. He became a master manipulator of the stock exchange, and enjoyed extraordinary success in his investments during the bull market of the 1920s. He also tried his hand in the motion picture industry. He was unaffected by the crash of 1929 due to his withdrawal from the market earlier that year, and continued to enjoy wealth and privilege throughout the Depression. He later helped to outlaw the very practices that had made him rich when he served as chairman of the Securities and Exchange Commission under President Franklin D. Roosevelt (1934–35). He also served as chairman of the United States Maritime Commission. In 1937, President Roosevelt appointed Kennedy U.S. ambassador to Great Britain—the first Irish-American to achieve that post. Kennedy was not a popular figure, due in part to his stated position that England would fall to the Nazis and that the United States should maintain an ISOLATIONIST stance. He resigned his post in November 1940.

By this time, his children were being raised as a tightly-knit, highly athletic, and competitive unit. They were also intellectually encouraged and expected to take part in family discussions of world and public affairs. The oldest son, Joseph P. Kennedy, Jr. (b. 1915), was being groomed for political office, as his father was determined to be the father of the first Catholic, Irish-American president. However, World War II intervened, claiming the life of Joe, Jr., in 1944. Kennedy then turned his attention to John (b. 1917), who had survived his own brush with death during the war. Although he had originally planned to be a journalist, John acceded to his father's desire for him to run for office. His campaign funded by his father's fortune, the young Kennedy served in the U.S. House of Representatives from 1947 to 1953, then as a U.S. senator from 1953 to 1960, when he realized his father's dream and was elected the 35th president of the United States. At their father's insistence, John's brother, Robert, became the attorney general.

Joseph Kennedy (who had been an important supporter of Senator Joseph MCCARTHY) remained heavily involved in his sons' political lives until he was incapacitated by the first of many strokes. John was assassinated in 1963. Robert, who became a U.S. senator from New York, was also killed, in 1968, just three months after announcing his candidacy for the presidential nomination. The patriarch's youngest son, Edward, took over John's Massachusetts seat in the Senate, where he has served ever since. A series of strokes continued to disable Joseph Kennedy, and in time he was secluded at the family compound in Hyannis Port, Massachusetts. He died there at the age of 81 in 1969. His wife, Rose, lived to the age of 104, dying in Hyannis Port on January 22, 1995.

Kennedy, Robert F. (1925–1968)

Robert Francis Kennedy was the third son of Joseph P. KENNEDY and brother to President John F. KENNEDY. Frequently overshadowed by his gregarious older brothers, Robert grew up rather shy, but was still equal to the demands of the athletic and intellectual atmosphere his family encouraged. He enrolled in Harvard University, but his studies were cut short when he enlisted in the U.S. Navy during World War II. He returned to Harvard after the war and graduated in 1948. He went on to the University of Virginia Law School and received his law degree in 1951. The next year, he managed John's successful campaign for the U.S. Senate. In early 1953, he was named as assistant counsel to the Senate Permanent Subcommittee on Investigations, headed by Senator Joseph MCCARTHY. Kennedy resigned from this position later that year, but returned in 1954 to serve as counsel to the Democratic minority. In 1957, he became chief counsel to another Senate committee, this time investigating labor racketeering. During the course of the hearings, he began his legendary and long-running feud with Teamsters Union president Jimmy HOFFA. He resigned from the committee in 1960 in order to manage John's run for the U.S. presidency, which resulted in a narrow victory in November of that year. John subsequently appointed Robert the U.S. attorney general.

Robert Kennedy quickly developed a reputation as a champion of civil rights and opponent of organized crime. In May 1961, he dispatched a troop of federal marshals to protect Martin Luther KING, Jr., and his supporters from angry opponents in Montgomery, Alabama. He subsequently worked with Southern law enforcement officials to devise ways of maintaining order during civil rights demonstrations. Robert Kennedy was one of President Kennedy's most important advisers in matters both foreign and domestic, and played a leading role in the CUBAN MISSILE CRISIS of 1962.

Initially criticized for his appointment as attorney general (critics felt he had benefited from nepotism), Kennedy soon came to be lauded for raising the standard of his office. After the president was assassinated in November 1963, Robert continued to serve as attorney general under President Lyndon B. JOHNSON, even though he was frequently overcome by grief for his murdered brother. He resigned in September 1964 in order to pursue his campaign for a U.S. Senate seat from New York. Elected in November 1964, he quickly established himself as a major political force and a spokesman for liberal Democrats. Despite his own significant role in major early decisions that led to an increased U.S. role in Vietnam, Kennedy became an outspoken critic of the war in Vietnam and of President Johnson, with whom he had a long history of mutual dislike and antagonism.

In March 1968, Kennedy announced his candidacy for the Democratic presidential nomination; in short

Robert F. Kennedy (JOHNSON LIBRARY)

order, he won three out of four primaries. On June 4, 1968, he won the California primary. That night, he went to the Ambassador Hotel in Los Angeles to speak to his supporters. Just after midnight on June 5, having concluded his speech, his left through a kitchen hallway, where a Palestinian immigrant, Sirhan Sirhan, approached and shot him. Kennedy died from his wounds and was buried near his brother in Arlington National Cemetery.

Kent State massacre

The infamous shooting of 13 students by NATIONAL GUARD troops galvanized citizens of the United States and turned an already negative public opinion even further against the VIETNAM WAR. The date was May 4, 1970, and on the campus of Kent State University in Ohio, approximately 600 students gathered for what was intended to be a peaceful demonstration protesting the unpopular war. Governor James A. Rhodes of Ohio had previously called in National Guard troops to maintain order on the Kent State campus in the wake of previous demonstrations. Now the guardsmen had been called in to break up this gathering before it got underway. Tensions ran high on both sides. Ordered to disperse, the students reacted with jeers and catcalls, prompting the military's commander, General Robert H. Canterbury, to order a tear gas attack. Still, students threw rocks and continued to taunt the troops. Finally one unknown guardsman fired a shot, starting a panic with a fusillade of gunfire. When the shooting stopped, nine students lay wounded and four were dead—including, ironically, several who had not been part of the demonstration and one who was a member of the Kent State RESERVE OFFICERS' TRAINING CORPS (ROTC). Photographs of the slaying taken immediately after the shooting were published in newspapers worldwide. In addition to shocking U.S. citizens, the pictures demonstrated that guardsmen had overreacted, and had not been in any danger from the students, as they had claimed in attempting to justify the shootings. Responding to the public outrage that followed, President Richard NIXON appointed former Pennsylvania governor William Scranton to head a commission investigating the massacre. The commission determined that the students' demonstration had been peaceful in nature, that the National Guard should not have ordered them to disperse, and that the shootings had been "unnecessary, unwarranted, and inexcusable." It further decried any acts of violence and noted that unwarranted American involvement in Vietnam had been a precipitating factor in the massacre. This finding bolstered the position of antiwar activists, who were now supported by the majority of the country's citizens. Despite overwhelming public opinion, however, none of the guardsmen involved in the shootings were indicted for the students' murders. Instead, Kent State would live on in the public consciousness as a symbol of some of the most turbulent times the country had ever seen.

King, Martin Luther, Jr. (1929–1968)

A preeminent civil rights leader and winner of the Nobel Peace Prize, Martin Luther King, Jr., was born to a Southern Baptist minister who was himself the son of a Baptist minister. In 1935, his father changed both their first names from Michael to Martin Luther in honor of the German religious leader.

A brilliant student, King was only 15 years old when he entered Morehouse College in Atlanta, where he received his B.A. degree in 1948. Although he had initially focused on a career in medicine or law, in his senior year his father convinced him to enter the ministry. He subsequently received his bachelor of divinity degree in 1951 from Crozer Theological Seminary in Chester, Pennsylvania, and went on to earn his doctorate from Boston University in 1955. During his years in school, he learned about the philosophy of nonviolent resistance as practiced by Mahatma Gandhi, and also formed his own ideas about the relationship of man to God. These ideas provided a foundation for his future career in civil rights.

King met Coretta Scott during his stay in Boston; they married in 1953 and later had four children

Rev. Dr. Martin Luther King, Jr. (NARA STILL PHOTOS DIVISION)

together. They returned to her native Alabama that same year, where he became pastor of the Dexter Avenue Baptist Church in Montgomery. On December 1, 1955, Rosa Parks was arrested for refusing to surrender her seat to a white passenger on a Montgomery city bus. To protest this action, black activists formed the Montgomery Improvement Association and chose King to be their leader. The group decided to initiate a boycott of the public transit system in Montgomery. Without black passengers, ridership on city buses plummeted, seriously affecting the city coffers. King's life and his family were threatened numerous times, and his home was bombed, but he continued to lead the boycott until the group achieved its goal of total desegregation of Montgomery's buses a little over a year later. With this success under his belt, King proceeded to organize the Southern Christian Leadership Conference (SCLC). He began to lecture throughout the country and became a well-known advocate for the civil rights of blacks. After meeting in 1959 with Prime Minister Jawaharlal Nehru of India, he became convinced that the principle of resistance through NONVIOLENCE, as practiced by Gandhi and his followers, was the best way to achieve freedom from white oppression in the United States.

In 1960, King moved his family back to Atlanta, where he became copastor, with his father, of the Ebenezer Baptist Church. However, King had now become fully focused on the goals of the SCLC. He was arrested in October 1960, when he took part in a protest at a segregated lunch counter in an Atlanta department store. He was unjustly sent to a prison farm on a trumped-up charge in connection with a minor traffic offense, and only the intervention of Democratic presidential candidate and senator John F. KENNEDY succeeded in obtaining his release. After this, King devoted himself to a series of marches and SIT-INS designed to protest injustices to blacks throughout the country.

In the spring of 1963, King was arrested in Birmingham, Alabama, where he and other demonstrators had been protesting segregation at lunch counters, as well as in hiring practices. Lacking support from both black and white clergy, he wrote his now famous letter from the Birmingham jail in which he detailed his philosophy of nonviolent resistance to effect change for the common good. After his release, he met with other leaders of the civil rights movement and helped to organize a MARCH ON WASHINGTON. This historic, interracial event took place on August 28, 1963, and, if only for a few hours, realized King's hope that someday all men, regardless of their color, would be broth-

Martin Luther King, Jr., delivers his "I Have A Dream" speech at the March on Washington, August 1963. (NARA STILL PHOTOS DIVISION)

ers. This hope was epitomized in his famous "I have a dream" speech, delivered to more than 200,000 gathered by the Lincoln Memorial.

In 1965, a campaign to achieve voting rights for blacks in Alabama revealed some erosion in support for King's methods. When a march from Selma to Montgomery was foiled by state troopers wielding nightsticks and tear gas, King decided to lead a second march. However, just outside of Selma, he and 1,500 marchers were met by a barricade of troopers. Instead of going on, King led his followers in prayer, then turned back—a move that provoked considerable criticism from younger, more radical blacks. Although the publicity generated enough support for the passage of the 1965 Voting Rights Act, there was a growing lack of patience among those blacks who wanted to see more substantial change achieved more quickly and with more militant methods than King's. In 1966, his campaign against racial discrimination in Chicago resulted in an essentially ineffective agreement between the city government and a coalition consisting of blacks, liberals, and labor organizations. Failing to attain great strides in the unfamiliar North, King was also forced to contend with increasing opposition from blacks in the South. He decided to broaden his goals beyond combating racism, and turned his attention to matters of poverty and unemployment affecting all races, but most especially blacks. However, the methods he used in bringing down segregation laws in the South were not as effective in tackling the more complex social and economic issues he was now addressing, and his attempts to form an interracial coalition of the poor failed to gain him the additional support he sought. Meanwhile, he openly opposed the war in Vietnam.

King had begun planning a Poor People's March to Washington in the spring of 1968, when he went to Memphis, Tennessee, to lend his support to a strike by the city's sanitation workers. On April 4, 1968, he was shot and killed by a sniper as he was standing on the balcony of his motel room. When news of the assassination spread, rioting broke out in a number of major American cities. A hunt for the assassin led to the arrest of James Earl Ray, who pleaded guilty on March 10, 1969, and was sentenced to 99 years in prison. (Claims that a conspiracy existed to murder King have been common. In 2000, a Memphis jury concluded, without offering specific findings, that this had been the case.)

King, who had been target of governmental wiretapping and surveillance efforts for years, was eventually accorded the status of a cultural hero. In 1985, the U.S. Congress voted to observe a national holiday in his honor, on the third Monday in January.

Kirkpatrick, Jeane (1926–)

Born Jeane Jordan, the United States' first female ambassador to the UNITED NATIONS has been a longtime government official and political scientist. A graduate of Barnard College, where she obtained her A.B. degree in 1948, and Columbia University, where she earned her M.A. in 1950, she married Evron M. Kirkpatrick in 1955. In her early career, Kirkpatrick worked as researcher, first for the State Department and subsequently for George Washington University and the Fund for the Republic. She started working as a teacher in 1962, first at Trinity College, and later at George Washington University.

In 1967, Kirkpatrick received her doctorate from Columbia University. From 1967 to 1981, she taught at George Washington University, where she returned to teach whenever she was not called for public service. In 1974, she published her first book, *Political Women*. Originally a Democrat, she switched parties primarily because of her opposition to President Jimmy CARTER's foreign policies. A 1979 article she wrote and published in *Commentary* magazine, "Dictatorships and Double Standards," attracted the attention of Ronald REAGAN. Subsequently, President Reagan appointed her to serve as U.S. ambassador to the United Nations, and made her a member of his cabinet. In her four years as ambassador, Kirkpatrick frequently attacked COMMUNISM and communist governments, and played a key role in the formulation of foreign policy in the Reagan administration. Her presentation at the United Nations following the Soviet downing of a Korean civilian jet airliner in 1983 was particularly effective. However, she also developed a reputation among her colleagues for being closed-minded and didactic.

Despite her staunch conservatism, and notwithstanding her influence over Central American affairs, Kirkpatrick was frequently passed over for promotions within the Reagan administration. Consequently, she resigned her post in 1985 and returned to teaching. She is currently the Leavy Professor at Georgetown University, and also serves as a senior fellow at the American Enterprise Institute. She is a recipient of the Medal of Freedom and has received many other awards for her work, both nationally and internationally. In addition to *Political Women,* other Kirkpatrick books include *Dismantling the Parties* (1978) and *The Reagan Phenomenon* (1982).

Kissinger, Henry (1923–)

A political scientist and government official, Henry Alfred Kissinger was to play a major role in the shaping of foreign policy during the administrations of Presidents Richard NIXON and Gerald FORD. The Kissinger family immigrated to the United States in 1938 to escape Nazi persecution in their native Germany. In 1943, Henry Kissinger became a naturalized U.S. citizen; he entered the U.S. military and fought against the Axis during World War II. At the conclusion of the war, he participated in the U.S. military government of Germany. He then returned to the United States and resumed his interrupted college studies, receiving his doctorate from Harvard in 1954.

Following his graduation, Kissinger became an instructor at Harvard, where he wrote *Nuclear Weapons and Foreign Policy* (1957), a book that gained him national recognition as an authority on U.S. foreign policy. A subsequent book, *The Necessity for Choice,* was published in 1960. Kissinger advocated what he termed a FLEXIBLE RESPONSE to a Soviet nuclear threat, an approach in which new weapons technology was developed along with the use of conventional means to promote national security.

From 1955 to 1968, Kissinger was frequently called upon as a consultant for matters of foreign security; he acted as an adviser to Presidents Dwight EISENHOWER, John F. KENNEDY, and Lyndon JOHNSON before being appointed in December 1968 by President-elect Richard NIXON as an assistant for national security affairs. He was executive secretary of the NATIONAL SECURITY COUNCIL from 1969 to 1971, then was chosen by President Nixon to serve as secretary of state, a post in which he continued to serve under President Gerald Ford until 1976. During these years, Kissinger acted as the chief adviser to Presidents Nixon and Ford on all matters pertaining to foreign and security affairs. He promoted DÉTENTE with the Soviet Union and China, and worked as a peace negotiator between Israel and its Arab enemies. His efforts to normalize relations with the Soviets were met with opposition from various domestic corners, but also produced the STRATEGIC ARMS LIMITATIONS TALKS (SALT) of 1969 and the SALT I arms agreement of 1972.

Although a HAWK regarding Vietnam, Kissinger negotiated the withdrawal of U.S. troops from that country and oversaw the signing of a cease-fire agreement in Paris on January 27, 1973. (However, his announcement that "Peace is at hand" a few weeks before the presidential election led many Americans to expect a more immediate breakthrough; in fact, Nixon intensified bombing a month and a half after winning his landslide victory.) In 1973, Kissinger was awarded the Nobel Peace Prize, along with Le Duc Tho, the North Vietnamese negotiator. Later it would be revealed that he had played a major role in the U.S. bombing of Cambodia during 1969 and 1970, as well as in secret CIA operations in Chile and elsewhere.

After the Arab-Israeli war in 1973, Kissinger resorted increasingly to the use of SHUTTLE DIPLOMACY to negotiate peaceful settlements between warring countries and factions. Following Gerald Ford's loss to Jimmy CARTER in the 1976 presidential elections, Kissinger became a lecturer and international consultant, and also published several more books, including *The White House*

Secretary of State Henry Kissinger (FORD LIBRARY)

Years (1979), *For the Record* (1981), and *Diplomacy* (1994). In 1983, he was appointed by President Ronald REAGAN to head a bipartisan committee on Central America. He has made numerous television appearances as a political commentator in recent years.

Korean War

The conflict that became known as the Korean War had its beginnings in the late stages of World War II. Prior to that time, Korea had belonged (unwillingly) to Japan. However, at a 1943 conference in Cairo, Egypt, three nations—the United States, Great Britain, and China—came to an agreement that Korea would be granted independence following the war, an arrangement to which the Soviet Union later agreed. As the war in the Pacific came to a conclusion in 1945, the Korean question again arose for the United States, which proposed to the Soviets that until such time as an independent government could be established, the two superpowers would share occupation of the country, with the Soviet Union overseeing the portion north of the 38th parallel and the United States overseeing the southern portion—essentially bisecting the country. Once again, the Soviets agreed. However, once inside the country, the Soviet fortified the 38th parallel line, cutting off all communications and transportation between North and South Korea. They then established a communist regime in the north, led by Kim Il Sung. In South Korea, the Americans set up an administration led by an anticommunist named Syngman Rhee.

Korea's infamous 38th parallel crossing (NARA STILL PHOTOS DIVISION)

The Soviets did not cooperate with U.S. efforts to arrange general elections for a unified Korea. They showed no sign of giving up their occupation of the north, and communists in the south were provoking numerous incidents designed to upset the stability in the south. By late 1947, it seemed certain that no elections would take place and that Korea would remain divided as long as the Soviet Union remained in control in the north. Although mindful of the DOMINO THEORY, the administration of President Harry TRUMAN did not consider Korea to be of great strategic importance. On the advice of the Joint Chiefs of Staff, the administration prepared to withdraw U.S. troops from the south. It also arranged through the UNITED NATIONS (UN) to set up an electoral commission that would supervise elections in South Korea (after a UN resolution failed to achieve elections for a unified Korea). The election took place in the spring of 1948, and the Republic of Korea (ROK) was established with Syngman Rhee as the new president. The ROK claimed jurisdiction over the entire country, although it was understood from the start that its authority would not extend beyond the 38th parallel. Three weeks after the ROK was established, North Korea also set up a new government, this one led by Kim Il Sung and called the Democratic People's Republic of Korea (DPRK). This government also claimed dominion over the whole peninsula. Subsequently, both U.S. and Soviet troops began to withdraw from the country.

Despite Syngman Rhee's pleas to the United States to continue to provide military support as his government took shape, American troops were withdrawn from South Korea by June 29, 1949; only 500 U.S. military advisers remained to assist Rhee and to provide instruction and guidance to his military leaders. The United States supplied a steady stream of weapons and other equipment to the South Koreans, but it became increasingly clear that the Rhee government was weak and would probably not be able to survive an invasion from the north. Communist guerrillas had already been inciting disruptions throughout the southern portion of the peninsula. Inevitably, on June 25, 1950, DPRK forces crossed the 38th parallel into South Korea, and the conflict known as the Korean War officially began.

On June 27, two days after the invasion, the United States submitted a resolution to the United Nations Security Council asking that UN troops be sent to South Korea to assist in defending the country against the invaders. As the Soviet Union was then boycotting the Security Council and could therefore not exercise its veto power, the resolution was passed. President Harry Truman thereupon ordered the immediate deployment of American air and naval troops to South Korea; they were followed by army ground troops several days later. The UN Security Council subsequently recommended that the United States head up a unified command of combined military forces from the United States and 20 other participating member nations. President Truman named General Douglas MACARTHUR to lead this command.

The initial weeks of the war were difficult, with the UN-bolstered South Korean troops suffering repeated defeats. But by August, the northern offensive had been halted along the Pusan perimeter, near the southeastern tip of the peninsula. At that point, MacArthur planned and carried out a marine landing at Inchon, 20 miles west of Seoul, while UN forces pushed through the Pusan perimeter to repel the invaders. Both moves were so successful that soon the North Koreans retreated beyond the 38th parallel.

UN soldiers in Korea fought in all kinds of weather. (NARA STILL PHOTOS DIVISION)

MacArthur and others wanted to follow the enemy and thereby invade North Korea. That possibility provoked a warning from China that it would not "supinely tolerate the destruction of its neighbors by the imperialistic powers." Believing this statement to be just a bluff, the UN General Assembly sanctioned the move into North Korea. In the meantime, Chinese forces advanced into North Korea and prepared to launch a counteroffensive that American leaders believed would not take place. On November 21, UN battalions reached the Yalu River, where the Chinese were waiting. On the evening of November 25, the Chinese struck with such force that the UN troops were compelled to retreat.

At this point, MacArthur wanted to launch an air strike to destroy key Chinese bases and depots in Manchuria to neutralize the Chinese threat. However, officials in Washington dismissed the idea, fearful that such an action would launch a major war outside the confines of Korea. Still, the general persisted in asking for expansion of the war effort into China and publicly criticized the Truman administration's foreign policy decisions, angering the president, who directed him to make no more statements to the press.

By March 1951, UN forces had once again succeeded in pushing communist troops back across the 38th parallel. This time, however, they elected to go no farther, much to MacArthur's disgust. In direct violation of the president's orders, General MacArthur, determined to expel the communists from North Korea, issued a statement on March 24, 1951, to the effect that the Chinese should remove themselves from North Korea or face devastating consequences. He subsequently wrote to Representative Joseph W. Martin that "There is no substitute for victory." Truman, who had been about to announce a peace initiative, angrily fired MacArthur from his command and appointed Lieutenant General Matthew B. Ridgway to take his place. MacArthur's firing outraged the American public at first, but upon learning the details of the Korean campaign and the rationale for keeping UN troops below the 38th parallel, they ultimately supported Truman's decision.

Peace negotiations began in July 1951, but were repeatedly stalemated over the next several months, while fighting continued. Eventually, the only issue delaying a settlement was that of repatriation. When the UN learned that over 50,000 communist prisoners of war did not want to return home, they insisted that repatriation be voluntary, a condition the communists refused to accept. Thus, the war dragged on, and Americans became increasingly disheartened. During the presidential campaign, Korea became a central issue; candidate Dwight D. EISENHOWER promised, "I shall go to Korea," and upon his election, he made good on his promise. A month after taking office, Eisenhower quietly advised the communists that massive (i.e., nuclear) force would be used if necessary to bring about a conclusion to the war, and that such force would extend beyond the Korean borders, also if necessary. These threats, along with the death of Soviet leader Joseph Stalin on March 5, 1953, apparently had an effect; by April 1953, the communists had reversed their position on repatriation. Syngman Rhee, meanwhile, wanted to continue an offensive to expel the communists from all of Korea, but he was advised that the UN and the United States would not support such an effort, and would simply provide economic and military support for security's sake. Peace negotiations proceeded smoothly after that, resulting in an armistice that was signed on July 27, 1953.

For the most part, Americans supported the war in Korea, until it reached a point where it seemed that too many U.S. servicemen were being lost (54,246 by the war's end) in a cause that was dragging on far too long. They little knew that they would experience even greater frustration and devastation in the forthcoming VIETNAM WAR. See also POLICE ACTION.

Repatriated prisoners of war at Panmunjon, Korea (NARA STILL PHOTOS DIVISION)

Korff, Baruch (1914–1995)

Rabbi Baruch Korff was a noted Jewish leader who came to be known as "Nixon's rabbi." He was the son of Grand Rabbi Jacob Korff, and became the 73rd generation in an unbroken line of rabbis that dated back to the 11th century and included the founder of the Chassidic movement. In 1919, his mother was killed during a pogrom in the Ukraine, and his father, who had been charged with treason, was smuggled out of Russia. Young Baruch was sent to Kozec, Poland, then journeyed to United States in 1926 for his bar mitzvah under his father's instruction. He subsequently returned to Poland to further his education. It was at this time that he became a proponent of revisionist Zionism. Following courses of study at yeshivas in Kozec and Warsaw, he pursued further studies in New York City, and was finally ordained as a rabbi in 1934 at Yeshiva Ohr Torah. In 1935, he received advanced degrees in the Talmud and the law from Yeshiva Beth Mordechai in Jerusalem. He went on to serve as headmaster of a yeshiva in Brooklyn (1936–37) and rabbi of a congregation in New York City (1938–40).

During World War II and subsequent to the war, Korff became an adviser to the Union of Orthodox Rabbis of the United States and Canada, director of the Emergency Committee to Save the Jewish People of Europe, and executive vice president and UNITED NATIONS observer of the Political Action Committee for Palestine. Throughout the war, he was untiring in his efforts to secure the rescue of Jews being persecuted by the Germans, badgering countless U.S. and European officials and heads of state and even conducting negotiations with representatives of high-ranking Nazi official Heinrich Himmler to purchase Jews from the Nazis at the price of $26 a head. In 1944, he established a reception center for Holocaust refugees at Oswego, New York. He also gave newspaper columnist Drew PEARSON damning evidence against the U.S. government, demonstrating a lack of action regarding victims of the Holocaust, and he demanded that railroad lines to the Auschwitz death camp be bombed. He subsequently helped to organize a march on Washington of 1,000 rabbis to demand that 100,000 Jewish refugees in Europe be allowed to move to Palestine, and presented a petition to this end carrying over 500,000 signatures. After the British refused to allow the exodus, Korff was arrested for an alleged terrorist plot to bomb Buckingham Palace. He was found innocent, but years later admitted his guilt in the plot. During Israel's war for independence, he worked in Menachem Begin's underground movement.

After 1949, Korff remained active but less militant. He served as rabbi of Temple Israel in Portsmouth, New Hampshire, from 1950 to 1953; as rabbi of the Congregation Agudath Achim in Taunton, Massachusetts, from 1954 to 1971; and as a chaplain with the Massachusetts Department of Health from 1954 to 1974. He also made numerous trips to the Middle East to pursue the interests and political agenda of the Jewish community.

Korff became friends with President Richard NIXON during the 1968 presidential campaign, and he exerted a strong influence on the Nixon administration's support for Israel and for the emigration of Soviet Jews. In 1973, as Nixon became embroiled in the WATERGATE affair, Korff founded the National Citizens Committee for Fairness to the Presidency, and, in 1974, the President Nixon Justice Fund and the United States Citizens Congress. Korff was among the most passionate and energetic defenders of President Nixon during this period. After Nixon resigned in 1975, Korff became one of the few people to regularly visit the former president. He even encouraged Nixon's later return to the public spotlight. In 1983, Korff moved to Providence, Rhode Island, to act as a consultant to Brown University, which had established the Rabbi Baruch Korff Archives, containing more than 50,000 documents and memorabilia from Korff's long career.

Prior to his death in 1995, Korff made a public announcement that television reporter Diane Sawyer, a onetime aide to President Nixon, had been the anonymous source known as "Deep Throat" during the Watergate era. The claim was refuted by both Sawyer and Bob Woodward, the *Washington Post* reporter whose meetings with "Deep Throat" helped to break the Watergate story. Korff was the author of many books, including one about his friendship with Richard Nixon, *The President and I* (1995).

Kunstler, William (1919–1995)

William Moses Kunstler, the "flaming crusader," was a lawyer and social activist who rose to prominence during the 1960s when he defended a number of radical clients in controversial trials. He graduated from Yale University in 1941, then enlisted in the U.S. Army and served in the Pacific during World War II. He was

awarded a Bronze Star for his heroism. After the war, he returned to his studies and received his law degree in 1948 from the Columbia University School of Law. Subsequently, he entered into private practice with his brother, taking cases involving marriage, estate, and business law throughout the 1950s. More significant was his work for the AMERICAN CIVIL LIBERTIES UNION; after handling some cases for that organization, he began rethinking his purpose for being in law. In 1961, he went to Mississippi to help defend the FREEDOM RIDERS for the Congress of Racial Equality. This proved to be a transforming experience for him, as it started him on the road to his reputation as a defender of the underdogs and less popular elements of society. Thereafter he became a special counsel for Martin Luther KING, Jr., and acted as a legal adviser for the Southern Christian Leadership Conference, the Council of Federated Organizations, and others.

Becoming increasingly liberal over time, Kunstler began to do more civil rights work, eventually entering the movement itself. He also gained more controversial clients, including Stokely Carmichael and Bobby SEALE of the BLACK PANTHERS, and militant antiwar activists Daniel and Philip BERRIGAN. Kunstler became particularly notable during the trial of the CHICAGO SEVEN. The defendants in that trial were accused of conspiring to incite riots during the antiwar demonstrations that erupted during the 1968 Democratic convention in Chicago. The courtroom was disrupted daily by the defendants and by their lawyer, who was frequently cited for contempt, and was eventually sentenced to four years and 13 days of imprisonment. However, he did not serve any time, and most of the charges against him were dropped.

In later years, Kunstler continued to draw fire for choosing to defend such clients as the inmates accused of rioting at the state prison in Attica, New York; Mafia figure John Gotti; flag burners, and terrorists suspected of masterminding the 1993 World Trade Center bombing in New York. However, as a man proud of his own outspokenness, he resolutely continued to defend those he determined needed justice in a prejudicial court system. He also continued to teach at the New York University Law School throughout his career. He published 11 books, including *Beyond a Reasonable Doubt* in 1961, *The Case for Courage* in 1962, and *Deep in My Heart* in 1966.

Lattimore, Owen (1900–1989)

A scholar and adviser to the U.S. government on the Orient, Owen Lattimore came to public attention in the 1950s, when he was accused of being a Soviet agent by Senator Joseph MCCARTHY. Although born in the United States, Lattimore was raised in China and sent to schools in Switzerland and England before returning to China in 1919. By this time he had become fluent in Chinese, Russian, and Mongol. He used his knowledge and abilities to engage in a successful business career while also studying anthropology. After touring regions of Sinkiang and Mongolia in 1926 and 1927, Lattimore went to live in Peking. His expertise on China, particularly in the areas of Mongolia, Manchuria, and Sinkiang, soon gained him the notice of government officials in both the United States and China. In 1938, he was named director of the Walter Hines Page School of International Relations at Johns Hopkins University. During the initial years of World War II, he acted as an adviser to Chiang Kai-shek, and subsequently served in the U.S. Office of War Information. In 1944, he and Vice President Henry Wallace visited a village in Siberia, not knowing that it was actually a concentration camp whose inmates had been replaced by KGB agents for the purpose of their visit. Lattimore's approv-

ing report inadvertently helped to mask the true conditions existing in the Soviet Union at that time.

Lattimore opposed the corruption he saw within the regime of Chiang Kai-shek, and so became a target of the U.S. CHINA LOBBY that sought to continue supporting Chiang. After the victory of communist forces in China, Lattimore was assailed as a key figure responsible for the West's having "lost" China. This charge resulted in a loss of confidence in all China experts within the State Department, so that over the next 20 years there was a serious lack of knowledgeable advice regarding Chinese matters.

In 1950, Lattimore appeared before a Senate subcommittee investigating Senator Joseph McCarthy's charge that he had been the "chief Soviet espionage agent in the United States." Lattimore in turn accused McCarthy of "telling the kind of lies about the United States that Russian propagandists could not invent." Lattimore went on to create a sensation during the hearings by delivering a stinging diatribe against his accuser, noting that "He has invited disrespect to himself and his high office by refusing to live up to his word. Twice on the floor of the Senate he stated that any charges he made under the cloak of immunity, he would repeat in another place so that their falseness could be tested in a court of the United States. He said if he should fail to do this he would resign. He has been called to repeat his charges so that they could be tested in a court of action. He has failed to do so. And he has not resigned."

The allegations of disloyalty against Lattimore were subsequently found to have no basis in fact, and he was cleared (although McCarthy continued to hammer away at him with repeated public accusations). Lattimore described his experience in *Ordeal by Slander,* published that same year. He went on to work for the UNITED NATIONS, and also toured as a lecturer. The experience returned to haunt him, however, when he was indicted in 1952 on charges that he had committed perjury before an Internal Security subcommittee headed by Senator Pat McCarran. Those charges were dropped in 1955. From 1963 to 1970, Lattimore taught at Leeds University in England, where he was director of Chinese studies. In addition to his memoir, he published numerous books about Asian culture, peoples, and politics.

LeMay, Curtis (1906–1990)

Curtis Emerson LeMay was an aviator and onetime candidate for U.S. vice president who was lauded for his longtime military service. He attended Ohio State University, where he studied engineering. After his graduation, he received his commission in 1928 from the RESERVE OFFICERS' TRAINING CORPS (ROTC). He went on to become an outstanding pilot during the 1930s, and assisted in both the technical and tactical aspects of bomber plane development. He served during World War II, and in 1942 he was promoted to brigadier general and put in charge of the 305th Bombardment Group. With his unit, he helped to develop daylight precision bombing. Due to the many successful bombing missions that he oversaw, he was promoted to major general in March 1944, and transferred to the area encompassing China, Burma, and India. There he commanded the 20th Bomber Command and developed new and revolutionary tactics for low-level bombing. He went on to head the 21st Bomber Command and the 20th Air Force, headquartered in Guam. From there, he helped to plan and direct the atomic bomb missions against Hiroshima and Nagasaki in 1945. By then he held the post of chief of staff for the U.S. Army Strategic Air Forces.

After his return to the United States in October 1945, LeMay took charge of the Air Technical Service Command in Dayton, Ohio. In 1948, he directed the airlift of supplies from the United States to Berlin. That same year, he was given the leadership of the Strategic Air Command, which he proceeded to build into a force for nuclear DETERRENCE. As an advocate of an arms buildup, he testified before a Senate subcommittee in 1956 that with the present state of planning, the United States would be outstripped in strategic striking power sometime between 1958 and 1960.

LeMay was promoted to general in 1951, became vice chief of staff of the air force in 1957, and served as air force chief of staff from 1961 to 1965. He became known in the 1960s for his unapologetic support for an aggressive U.S. military role in Vietnam. In 1968, he ran for vice president on the American Independent Party (AIP) ticket headed by George Wallace. The pair advocated strong action in Vietnam and respect for states' rights. They won nine million votes and five states. The presence of the AIP ticket pointed to deep divisions in the Democratic Party's historic base of support—divisions that almost certainly played a part in why Hubert HUMPHREY, the Democratic candidate, lost the election to Richard NIXON.

Lennon, John (1940–1980)

John Winston Lennon (later John Ono Lennon) was a member of the influential rock band the Beatles, and generally considered to be the group's leader and resident intellectual. He was born and raised in Liverpool, England, where his early interest in music was represented by the styles of American rock-and-roll artists such as Chuck Berry, Elvis Presley, and Jerry Lee Lewis. In 1955, Lennon, a guitarist, formed his own group. He was joined in 1956 by Paul McCartney, another guitarist, and in 1957 by George Harrison, who also played guitar. The group, which became known as the Quarrymen, was also supplemented by Lennon's friend, bassist Stu Sutcliffe (who left the band for a career as an artist and died in 1962), and by drummer Pete Best. They adopted the name "Beatles" in 1960.

The Beatles initially played in cellar clubs in Liverpool and Hamburg, West Germany, until they were discovered by manager Brian Epstein, who ousted Pete Best and recruited Ringo Starr to do the drumming. In 1962, the Beatles released their first singles and rocketed to the top of the charts, quickly becoming the most popular group in England. They soon achieved the same status in the United States after they appeared on the *Ed Sullivan Show* in February 1964. The international frenzy they set off became known as "Beatlemania."

Throughout the 1960s, the Beatles exerted a powerful influence on youth culture, and received public attention not only for their increasingly sophisticated music but also for their experimentation with drugs and with Indian mysticism. They ceased to perform publicly in 1966, devoting themselves instead to studio work, and achieved their zenith with the release of *Sgt. Pepper's Lonely Hearts Club Band* in 1967. As they matured and developed separate interests, the members of the group increasingly found themselves at odds with each other; the Beatles finally disbanded in 1970.

A thoughtful and intelligent man, Lennon poured a great deal of social consciousness into his later songs. In 1969, he married Yoko Ono, an avant-garde artist; they later had a son, Sean. Ono and Lennon became prominent social activists, protesting the war in Vietnam and espousing the cause of peace through such MEDIA-attended events as "bed-ins" (impromtu hotel-room press conferences) after their wedding. Elements within the administration of President NIXON fought to keep Lennon from assuming permanent residence in the United States. Theoretically, the government's opposition to Lennon's living in the United States arose from a marijuana conviction in the United Kingdom; in actuality, Lennon's vocal and unyielding opposition to the VIETNAM WAR that began in the late 1960s was the more important obstacle. Lennon finally resolved his immigration problems in the mid-1970s. (The song *Free as a Bird*, eventually released in 1995 as a "reunion" single by McCartney, Lennon, and Starr, was said to have been composed as Lennon's reaction to his new status as a long-term legal resident of the United States)

On December 8, 1980, Lennon was approached outside his New York City apartment building and shot to death by Mark David Chapman, a Beatles fan and former mental patient.

Lewis, Fulton, Jr. (1903–1966)

Fulton Lewis, Jr., was a well-known news commentator who gained attention for his virulent anticommunism and his support of Senator Joseph MCCARTHY. A graduate of the University of Virginia, he worked as a reporter and editor for the *Washington Herald* from 1924 to 1928 before becoming a reporter for Universal News Service and International News Service from 1928 to 1937. In 1937, he became a radio news commentator for the Mutual Broadcasting System. Lewis was openly critical of President Roosevelt, whose for-

eign policy he excoriated, and he supported a strong national defense. In 1939, following the outbreak of war in Europe, he invited Charles Lindbergh to speak on his radio program regarding Lindbergh's isolationist views; this program created a brief storm of controversy, which was renewed the following year when Lewis derided news coverage of the Battle of Britain. (See ISOLATIONISM.)

Following World War II, Lewis became an outspoken anticommunist, using his program to attack such prominent figures as Harry HOPKINS and David LILIENTHAL. He also provided strong support to Joseph McCarthy during the anticommunist "WITCH HUNTS" of the 1950s.

liberation

In the early 1950s, as Republican leaders searched for alternatives to the then-popular policy of CONTAINMENT against Soviet aggression, they came up with the concept of "liberation." The phrase was first used by John Foster DULLES in 1952 to describe a foreign policy that would supposedly enable the independence of Soviet-dominated nations in Eastern Europe and Asia; it proved successful enough to be included in the Republican Party platform and in EISENHOWER administration policy. The means of achieving this so-called liberation would be such measures as nuclear DETERRENCE and MASSIVE RETALIATION; Dulles was quick to emphasize that the policy was intended to be peaceful. A high-minded concept, it failed to meet expectations, if there were any for it at all, for it was never really put into practice. The prime example of liberation's failure occurred during the Hungarian revolt of 1956. In this instance, some form of liberating intervention on the part of the United States should have been expected according to its policy. However, the Americans made no move to assist the rebels, thus putting the lie to the policy of liberation.

Liddy, G. Gordon (1930–   )

George Gordon Battle Liddy was one of the most notorious figures involved in the WATERGATE scandal of the 1970s, and served a longer prison sentence than any other conspirator. A sickly boy burdened by a chronic respiratory complaint, Liddy determined at an early age to change himself into a "strong, fearless man," and set his sights on becoming a soldier. (His unique determination led him to devise unusual and sometimes frightening ways of demonstrating his inner strength, such as deliberately burning the flesh of his left hand and helping a butcher to kill chickens.) However, his military aspirations were lost when World War II ended before he graduated from St. Benedict's Prep School in Newark, New Jersey (1948). Liddy then went on to Fordham University, and graduated in 1952. Hoping for a chance to eventually go to war against the Soviet Union, he joined the army reserve, but he went no further than an antiaircraft radar unit in Brooklyn, New York. He returned to Fordham and earned his law degree in 1957, then joined the FEDERAL BUREAU OF INVESTIGATION (FBI), becoming an agent working in several U.S. cities, and culminating in his tenure as a bureau supervisor at the Crime Records Division in Washington.

Liddy left the FBI in September 1962, and went to work in his father's law firm, specializing in patent law. Four years later, he joined the district attorney's office in Dutchess County, New York, where he gained attention for his role in a raid on "LSD guru" Timothy Leary's office in March 1966. In 1968, concerned about what he called "the tide of national disorder and weakness," he decided to enter politics, and made an unsuccessful bid for the Republican nomination as a New York congressman in the 28th district. He was then asked to oversee the Nixon/Agnew campaign in New York's mid-Hudson Valley region, a job he handled with such success that he was given the job of special assistant to the secretary of the treasury for organized crime, and subsequently appointed legislative counsel on enforcement. His work was so impressive that he was recommended to Attorney General John MITCHELL, who transferred Liddy to the White House under the supervision of John EHRLICHMAN. Here he was assigned to a small and special investigations group whose goal was to fix "leaks" of information. The group became known as the "PLUMBERS." Along with fellow chief plumber E. Howard Hunt, Liddy burglarized the office of the psychiatrist of Daniel ELLSBERG, the man responsible for leaking the PENTAGON PAPERS to the *New York Times,* in an effort to find evidence to discredit Ellsberg.

Liddy then joined the Committee for the Re-election of the President (CREEP). As part of his duties, he created an elaborate plan for gathering intelligence and sabotaging the Democratic campaign, and also volunteered to assassinate columnist Jack ANDERSON (who had revealed the name of an overseas intelligence source in print). Liddy's plan was pared down, and the result was two break-ins at the Democratic National Headquarters in the Watergate apartment complex in Washington. The purpose of the break-ins had been to plant electronic surveillance equipment throughout the headquarters and to photograph documents. It was the second break-in, on June 17, 1972, that created a national sensation when the Cuban operatives hired by Liddy and Hunt were discovered and arrested, along with James McCord, CREEP's security coordinator. Liddy and Hunt were also arrested later and indicted in September 1972. Hunt and the Cubans received light sentences, but because Liddy refused to cooperate he was given a sentence of 21 years and a $40,000 fine. (He would later also be fined for the Ellsberg case and would also be disbarred as a lawyer.) His sentence was commuted by President Jimmy CARTER in April 1977.

As a means of getting out of debt, Liddy began writing novels, and also published an autobiography entitled *Will.* In recent years, he has been a talk radio host.

Lilienthal, David (1899–1981)

David Eli Lilienthal was a lawyer and government official who played a major role in the development of the U.S. atomic weapons program. He was a graduate of Depauw University in Indiana, and received his law degree in 1923 from Harvard Law School. He focused his law practice on cases involving labor and public utilities. In 1931, after winning a highly publicized telephone-rate case, he was appointed by the governor of Wisconsin to serve on the Wisconsin Public Service Commission. His successful work in rewriting the state's public utility statutes brought him to the attention of President Franklin D. Roosevelt, who named him as one of the three codirectors of the Tennessee Valley Authority (TVA) power program in 1933. Lilienthal fought hard to keep the TVA focused on its main goals of effective flood control and the provision of cheap electricity, in addition to ensuring that conservation efforts were respected. In 1941, Lilienthal became the program's chairman, and in 1947 he was named the first chairman of the ATOMIC ENERGY COMMISSION (AEC). In this capacity, he assumed responsibility for the development of the U.S. nuclear program (which had previously been overseen by the army). He devoted himself to the improvement and expansion of nuclear power plants, stockpiling atomic bombs, and increased development of nuclear weapons.

In 1950, Lilienthal resigned from the AEC, and subsequently became chairman and chief executive officer of the Development and Research Corporation, which he founded in 1953 for the purpose of providing technical assistance to underdeveloped countries. Here his efforts centered on a program for developing resources such as dams, power for electricity, and flood control. He wrote several books, including *Big Business, a New Era* (1953); *Change, Hope and the Bomb* (1963); and *Atomic Energy, a New Start* (1980).

Lippmann, Walter (1889–1974)

Essayist, journalist, and editor, Walter Lippmann was also a political philosopher who gained a reputation for his farsighted and insightful analysis of foreign policy, as well as for making the phrase "cold war" a part of the modern lexicon. Lippmann graduated with honors in 1910 from Harvard University, where he had met such well-known intellectuals and philosophers as George Santayana and William James. During his time at Harvard, he also served as president of the Socialist Club, engaging in debates wherein he defended the rights of workers against exploitation and advocated voting rights for women. However, by 1912, after serving as an aide to a socialist mayor, he had come to the conclusion that socialism was sterile, and he steered away from politics into a career as an editor.

In 1914, after publishing his first book, *A Preface to Politics,* Lippmann helped to found the *New Republic,* a progressive magazine. He also worked there as an editor. He left in 1917 to join the war effort, during which time he served in numerous capacities: he was assistant to Secretary of War Newton D. Baker and a captain in U.S. Military Intelligence, working on propaganda aimed at forcing a German surrender. He also helped President Woodrow Wilson to prepare the Fourteen Points that would form a foundation for a peace settlement.

Lippmann returned to the *New Republic* at the conclusion of World War I. In 1921, he became a journalist when he joined the staff of the *New York World,* becoming its editor in 1929 and serving in that capacity until its demise in 1931, when he became a columnist for the *New York Herald Tribune.* His column, "Today and Tomorrow," became widely syndicated, and was published from 1931 until his retirement in 1967. He moved his base of operations to the *Washington Post* in 1962, the same year he won his second Pulitzer Prize for international reporting; the first was awarded in 1958 for his insightful analysis of national and international affairs in such books as *U.S. War Aims* (1944), *Isolation and Alliance* (1952), and *The Public Philosophy* (1955).

Lippmann published a number of books over the years that reflected his changing political views, from the liberal socialism of his youth to the moderate conservatism of his later years. Although he was an early supporter of the New Deal, Lippmann eventually turned against collectivism, condemning it in his 1937 book, *The Good Society.* In his writings, he urged those who would be public servants to base their decisions within a framework of statesmanship rather than politics. Even more than his books, Lippmann's newspaper column, which came to be printed in more than 200 newspapers, was highly respected by and influential on the politicians, diplomats, public officials, and even foreign dignitaries who read and consulted it for 36 years.

Lodge, Henry Cabot, Jr. (1902–1985)

A U.S. senator and diplomat, Henry Cabot Lodge was born into a political family that included six senators and a Massachusetts governor. He was the grandson of Henry Cabot Lodge, Sr. (1850–1924), the Republican senator from Massachusetts who led the opposition that defeated the U.S. entry into the League of Nations following World War I. The younger Lodge, who graduated from Harvard in 1924, started out as a journalist, then entered into the "family business" in 1933 when he became a Republican representative in the Massachusetts legislature. He served for two terms, then was elected to the U.S. Senate, serving two terms (1937–44 and 1947–52; the interim period was spent in military service). In 1952, he lost his reelection bid to John F. KENNEDY. In 1953, President Dwight D. EISENHOWER, whose candidacy Lodge had actively supported, appointed him as a permanent U.S. representative to the United Nations. In this role, Lodge represented the administration in debates and disagreements with the Soviet Union over disarmament and espionage issues, and also intervened in such major issues as the Suez crisis and the U.S. presence in Lebanon. During the infamous U-2 AFFAIR, Lodge was able to defuse public criticism of the United States by providing photographic evidence of Soviet ESPIONAGE.

Lodge ran for vice president in 1960 on the unsuccessful ticket headed by Richard M. NIXON. He created controversy during the campaign with his promise to include a black person in Nixon's cabinet—a promise that effectively weakened the Republican campaign in the South. The following year, Lodge was named director general of the Atlantic Institute, an organization of

Ambassador Henry Cabot Lodge, Jr. (JOHNSON LIBRARY)

American and European government officials and business leaders working to economically unite Europe, Canada, and the United States—a goal the group ultimately failed to achieve.

In 1963, President John F. KENNEDY appointed Lodge U.S. ambassador to South Vietnam. From the beginning, Lodge was a key player in the formation of U.S. policy and a crucial figure in the government's complex on-again, off-again relationship with the popular and corrupt South Vietnamese president, Ngo Dinh Diem, as well as the military leaders who sought to—and eventually did—launch a coup. Lodge was an especially important figure in South Vietnam in the months following the coup, during which time he lobbied for reforms and sought to stabilize the country. In May of 1964, he resigned his post and returned to the United States. in an unsuccessful attempt to keep Senator Barry GOLDWATER of Arizona from becoming the GOP presidential candidate. The following year, he returned to his role of ambassador to South Vietnam and served in that capacity until 1967. During this period, he worked to draw the North Vietnamese into peace negotiations. Lodge then became ambassador to West Germany, where he stayed for less than a year, 1968–69. In January 1969, he was sent to Paris as the chief U.S. negotiator in the peace talks to end the war in Vietnam, and served in that role until June 1970.

During the 1970s, Lodge was special envoy to the Vatican. Over the years he wrote many books, including *Cult of Weakness* (1932), *The Storm Has Many Eyes* (1973), and *As It Was* (1976).

Los Alamos　See ATOMIC BOMB: OPPENHEIMER, J. Robert; TELLER, Edward.

Lowenstein, Allard K. (1929–1980)

Allard Kenneth Lowenstein was a lawyer and political activist who played a prominent role in the civil rights and antiwar protests of the 1950s and 1960s. His father, an immigrant from Lithuania, held a Ph.D. degree but abandoned his science career to support his family in the restaurant business. Lowenstein graduated from the University of North Carolina at Chapel Hill in 1949, and received his law degree from Yale Law School in 1954. He subsequently pursued different career paths, never settling in any one occupation. He held a variety of university jobs and was appointed to several short-term government posts, in addition to running the campaign for Reform Democrat William Fitts Ryan of Manhattan in the 1960 congressional race. Lowenstein himself ran for elected office often, but served only one term as a congressman—1969–71, in Nassau County, New York. Nevertheless, as he grew older, he developed a following among younger people who were attracted to him for his charismatic personality and liberal politics. (He advocated a liberal, anticommunist Democratic Party.) As a lawyer, he frequently assisted (at no charge) civil rights workers who were jailed in the South during the early 1960s.

After a trip to South Vietnam in 1967, during which time he was a civilian observer of elections held there, Lowenstein formed the Conference of Concerned Democrats and the Coalition for a Democratic Alternative. Both organizations were vigorously opposed to President Lyndon JOHNSON's war policies and worked to block his nomination as the Democratic candidate for president. Thus was born the "Dump Johnson" movement of 1967 and 1968, which played a major role in Johnson's decision not to run for reelection. During the 1968 Democratic National Convention in Chicago, Lowenstein led the opposition against Hubert HUMPHREY's nomination for president and tried unsuccessfully to insert a peace plank into the party platform. He subsequently supported Humphrey's presidential campaign, after the Johnson administration ceased bombing in North Vietnam.

After being defeated for reelection to Congress in 1970, Lowenstein returned to teaching at the Yale University School of Urban Studies. He continued his activism throughout the 1970s. In 1971, he started a nonpartisan voter registration drive for young people, with the aim of preventing President Richard NIXON's reelection in 1972. From 1971 to 1973, he was the national chairman of AMERICANS FOR DEMOCRATIC ACTION. He also served as the U.S. representative to the UNITED NATIONS Commission on Human Rights. In 1980, not long after his 51st birthday, Lowenstein was murdered by one of his young followers, a former protegé.

Luce, Clare Boothe (1903–1987)

Clare Boothe Luce, born Ann Clare Boothe, was a playwright and U.S. congresswoman who played a prominent role in American politics of the 1940s, 1950s, and 1960s. She was educated privately in Garden City, New York, and Tarrytown, New York. From 1930 to 1934, she was associate editor and managing editor of *Vanity Fair* magazine. In 1931, she published a selection of articles written for *Vanity Fair* in a book entitled *Stuffed Shirts*. Divorced from her first husband, George Tuttle Brokaw, she married magazine publisher Henry R. LUCE in 1935. In 1936, after a previous failed attempt at playwriting, she wrote *The Women*, a comedy that ran for 657 performances on Broadway and was subsequently made into a movie. This was followed by *Kiss the Boys Goodbye* in 1938 and *Margin for Error* in 1939, both also adapted for the movies.

Long interested in politics, Luce ran for Congress as a Republican in 1943 and won, representing Connecticut in the House until 1947. She was a vocal critic of both President Roosevelt and President TRUMAN, blaming those administrations for not providing enough financial and military support to Eastern Europe or to Chiang Kaishek's campaign against the communists in China. She introduced a bill in 1945 that cited U.S. responsibility for yielding Poland to the Soviet Union during the YALTA negotiations. The following year, she anticipated the MARSHALL PLAN by introducing a bill to provide assistance to war-ravaged Europe. On the domestic front, Luce was primarily a conservative; however, she was a supporter of civil rights and women's rights.

After leaving Congress, Luce returned to playwriting. In 1953, she was appointed ambassador to Italy by President Dwight D. EISENHOWER, a position in which she served until 1956, when she was forced to resign due to ill health. As ambassador, she worked vigorously to hold the power of the Italy's Communist Party in check. In 1959, Eisenhower appointed Luce ambassador to Brazil, but she declined the post after Senator Wayne MORSE of Oregon, in an attempt to block her confirmation, publicly criticized her involvement in Italian politics.

Throughout the 1950s and early 1960s, health concerns prevented Luce from taking an active role in Republican politics, but she remained influential. After 1964 (a year in which she offered outspoken support for presidential candidate Barry GOLDWATER), Luce quietly withdrew from the political scene. She lived in Phoenix, Arizona, with her husband until his death in 1967, and thereafter in Honolulu, Hawaii. In 1981, she was appointed by President Ronald REAGAN to the Foreign Intelligence Advisory Board. In 1983, she was awarded the Presidential Medal of Freedom.

Luce, Henry R. (1898–1967)

Henry Robinson Luce was a publishing magnate who, with his ownership of *Time, Fortune,* and *Life* magazines, exerted a powerful and lasting influence on American journalism and culture. Luce was born to Presbyterian missionaries in China, where he spent the first 10 years of his life, with his three siblings. At the age of 10, he was sent to a British boarding school in the north of China, and from there to England. He subsequently went to preparatory school in the United States In 1916, he arrived at Yale University, where he quickly earned a reputation for brilliance. In addition to editing the school newspaper, he was a Phi Beta Kappa student. He graduated in 1920 and became a reporter for the *Chicago Daily News* and, subsequently, the *Baltimore News.*

It was at Yale that Luce met Briton Hadden, with whom, in 1923, he scraped together $86,000 and launched *Time* magazine. With its unusual presentation and emphasis on personalities of the era, *Time* quickly became popular on the newsstands, and by 1927, it was easily making a profit. Hadden died in 1929, the same year that Luce produced *Fortune,* a business magazine that succeeded in spite of the Depression. He launched a radio series entitled *The March of Time* in 1931, and four years later produced theater newsreels with the same name. He added to his empire with the acquisition of *Architectural Digest* in 1932. In 1936, he brought out the first issue of *Life,* which ushered in the novel journalistic technique of the photo essay. The advent of photojournalism marked a new era in news reporting, and *Life* immediately became one of the most popular magazines of all time.

Other Luce-owned publications under the Time, Inc. banner included *House & Home* (begun in 1952 and later sold to McGraw-Hill Publishing Company) and *Sports Illustrated* (1954). In addition, Luce's empire included a magazine export business, radio stations, real estate, and a successful mail-order bookselling business, Time-Life Books.

From 1929 until 1964, Luce was the editor-in-chief of all Time, Inc. publications; for the last three years of his life, he served as editorial chairman. In 1935, he married playwright Clare Boothe, who later became a U.S. representative from Connecticut. Both Luce and his wife were conservative in their political thinking and exerted a strong influence on Republican politics, as well as on national affairs. Luce once described himself as "in favor of God, the Republican Party, and free enterprise." Luce was an outspoken critic of President Harry TRUMAN, whom he blamed for not taking a hard enough line against Soviet and Chinese communists. This view was evident in *Time's* coverage of the president and in Luce's membership in the CHINA LOBBY. Luce's magazines often reflected his conservative views, as well as his strong support of the nationalist Chinese leader, Chiang Kai-shek, who was featured on *Time's* cover seven times. When Chiang and his followers were forced to flee mainland China in 1949, Luce held Secretary of State DEAN ACHESON to be primarily responsible.

Luce campaigned for Republican presidential candidate Thomas DEWEY during the 1948 elections, believing that the economic and military support of a Republican administration would enable Chiang to defeat the communists in China. Despite his strong anticommunist stance and conservative views, Luce did not endorse Senator Joseph MCCARTHY's activities during the 1950s and was a staunch supporter of civil rights until his death.

M

MacArthur, Douglas (1880–1964)

U.S. Army general Douglas MacArthur, known both for his military brilliance and his personal flamboyance, was one of the most notable military men of the 20th century, figuring prominently in American foreign policy in the Far East. He was the third son of a senior army officer and Civil War hero, Arthur MacArthur, and his wife, Mary Hardy MacArthur.

The young MacArthur graduated from the U.S. Military Academy at West Point, New York at the top of his class in 1903, and immediately took on several posts as he slowly worked his way up through the ranks. In 1914, he conducted himself valiantly during a secret mission in Veracruz, Mexico. When the United States entered World War I, he served on the 42nd Division staff, becoming in turn chief of staff, brigade commander, and divisional commander, a rank he retained during the Rhine occupation that followed the war. Upon his return to the United States, he became superintendent at West Point (1919–22), where he implemented several reforms, then went on to two commands in the Philippines, in addition to heading the 1928 U.S. Olympic Committee. Having been promoted from brigadier general to major general in 1925, in 1930 he was selected as the army chief of staff and given the rank of general. As the youngest man ever appointed chief of staff, he inherited an army substantially weakened as a result of the Depression. MacArthur was roundly criticized when, in 1932, he ordered army troops to force the exit of the so-called Bonus Army veterans from Washington, and called the veterans, who were demonstrating for money the government had promised them, "communists."

From 1935 to 1941, he served as military and field adviser to the Philippines, and tried in vain to build a Filipino defense force. In 1937, MacArthur married his second wife, Jean Faircloth; that same year, in December, he retired from the U.S. Army. However, with the start of World War II in Europe and concurrent U.S. diplomatic efforts to contain Japan yielding no positive results, he was recalled to active duty in July 1941. From late 1941 to early 1942, he conducted the defense of the Philippines against Japanese forces. He then became commander of the Southwest Pacific area from 1942 to 1945, during which time he conducted a brilliant series of military maneuvers that forced the Japanese out of New Guinea and from strategic islands in the Pacific. In October 1944, he made good on an earlier promise to return when U.S. forces made their way back to the Philippines. In December 1944, MacArthur was promoted to general of the army, and four months later was made supreme commander of all U.S. Army forces in the Pacific. He presided over the

General Douglas MacArthur (right) with Lieutenant General Matthew Ridgeway and Major General Doyle Hickey near the 38th parallel in Korea. (NARA STILL PHOTOS DIVISION)

Malcolm X (1925–1965)

A militant black leader of the 1960s who eloquently represented the goals of the Nation of Islam, Malcolm X was born Malcolm Little, and later took the Muslim name of El-Hajj Malik El-Shabazz. He grew up in dire circumstances in Lansing, Michigan, enduring the burning of his home by the Ku Klux Klan, the murder of his father two years later, and the subsequent removal of his mother to a mental institution. Young Malcolm lived in various detention homes before moving to his sister's home in Boston when he was in his early teens. Frequently in trouble with the law, he was in prison for burglary in 1946 when he was converted to the Black Muslim faith. After his release from prison in 1952, he traveled to Chicago, where he met Elijah Muhammad and was welcomed into the Nation of Islam. Following a tradition among Nation of Islam members, who renounce the names given to their ancestors by white slaveholders, he changed his last name to "X."

Malcolm quickly discovered a gift for oratory and was sent on speaking tours throughout the country, greatly increasing the Nation of Islam's membership through his abilities as a speaker and an organizer. A 1959 television documentary that portrayed him as a threat to whites brought him to national attention. In 1961, he started what became the official organ of the Nation of Islam, a publication entitled *Muhammad Speaks.* Having founded many new mosques for the movement, he was eventually awarded the ministry of a key mosque in the Harlem area of New York City. In the meantime, he came to be widely known for his provocative speeches embracing black separatism and black pride. A critic of the mainstream, nonviolent civil rights movement, he was himself criticized for advocating the use of violence, which he claimed was for purposes of self-protection.

By November 1963, Malcolm had incited the jealousy of others within the leadership of the Nation of Islam. He was suspended from the movement by Elijah Muhammad after he said the assassination of President John F. KENNEDY was an example of the kind of violence whites had always used against blacks, and that it was therefore a case of "chickens coming home to roost." Malcolm responded to his suspension by leaving the Nation of Islam in March 1964, and forming his own religious sect called the Muslim Mosque. In April 1964, he made a pilgrimage to Mecca, and in his travels observed a virtual lack of racial discrimination in the Muslim countries he visited. When he returned, he had modified his views regarding black separatism and was now willing to concede that brotherhood among whites and blacks was possible. By October 1964, he had become a firm convert to

Japanese surrender on September 2, 1945, and subsequently became military governor of Japan (1945–50). During this period, he demobilized Japanese military forces and worked to create a state of democracy in Japan. He also headed the army's Far East command.

In July 1950, the KOREAN WAR broke out, and MacArthur became commander of the United Nations forces in that country. He enjoyed initial success in his direction of the Inchon offensive, pushing back the invasion of the North Koreans and advancing his troops into North Korea by October 1950. However, the following month China entered the war and forced the retreat of MacArthur's army from above the 38th parallel to south of Seoul. MacArthur thereupon returned to the offensive, once again driving his troops into North Korea, and strongly advocated extending the war into China. This suggestion led to conflict with President Harry TRUMAN, who wanted to keep the conflict localized. Eventually fed up with MacArthur's insubordination, Truman relieved him of his command in April 1951—an act that infuriated many of the popular general's supporters. MacArthur returned to the United States and received a hero's welcome. In a speech before Congress, he cited the axiom "Old soldiers never die, they just fade away."

MacArthur considered running for political office, but it was generally considered that he was a better soldier than a politician, especially after the details of a Senate investigation into his dismissal became public knowledge. For several years, he served as chairman of the board for Remington Rand, Inc., after which he retired to life as an honored war hero.

orthodox Islam and had formed the Organization of Afro-American Unity in the hope of creating a cooperative effort against discrimination with progressive white groups. Meanwhile, the tensions between different factions of the Black Muslims had escalated into threats against Malcolm's life. On February 21, 1965, while at a rally of his followers at the Audubon Ballroom in Harlem, he was shot to death by three members of the Nation of Islam. After Malcolm's assassination, Alex Haley published *The Autobiography of Malcolm X,* a book based on a series of interviews conducted prior to the attack. A best-seller at the time, it is now considered a classic of black nonfiction writing.

Manhattan Project   See ATOMIC BOMB

Manila Pact

Formally called the Southeast Asia Collective Defense Treaty, the Manila Pact is an agreement negotiated and signed in September 1954 that provides joint protection of countries in the South Pacific, with the exception of Taiwan and Hong Kong. It was ratified by the U.S. Senate in February 1955. The basic idea behind the pact is that, in the event of attack on one country, the others would unite in its defense. The pact also covers assistance in dealing with subversion from outside powers, as well as economic and social cooperation among all participating members. The pact was formulated after the Geneva Accords of 1954 and fears increased about the spread of COMMUNISM throughout Southeast Asia. In keeping with the favored policy of CONTAINMENT through a creation of alliances, Secretary of State John Foster DULLES led the U.S. team in negotiations. He is considered to be its primary designer. The treaty is administered by the SOUTHEAST ASIA TREATY ORGANIZATION (SEATO), which also offers umbrella protection of Cambodia, Laos, and Vietnam.

Mansfield, Mike (1903–   )

Michael Joseph Mansfield is a former U.S. senator and Senate majority leader who also served as U.S. ambassador to Japan for 11 years. A native of Montana, he dropped out of school at age 14 to enlist in the U.S. Navy for World War I service. When his age was discovered, he was discharged, but he subsequently enlisted with both the army and the marine corps, serving until 1922. Upon his return to civilian life, he married and went to work in the copper mines in Montana. Eventu-

ally he was persuaded by his wife to resume his schooling, and in 1933 he simultaneously received both his high school diploma and an A.B. degree from the University of Montana. He followed these degrees with a master's degree in 1934, and later became a professor at the University of Montana, specializing in Far Eastern and Latin American history, as well as political science.

Mansfield entered politics in 1940, when he made an unsuccessful run for elective office. He was elected to the House of Representatives as a Democrat in 1942. He was a committed liberal who fully supported President Franklin D. Roosevelt's domestic programs. As a member of the House Foreign Affairs Committee, he also became an adviser to Presidents Roosevelt and TRUMAN regarding foreign policy in China and Japan. In that regard, he undertook a special mission to China in 1944 for the purpose of investigating the political situation there.

In the early 1950s, Mansfield was accused by Senator Joseph MCCARTHY of being "too accommodating" to communism. Despite these charges, Mansfield was elected to the U.S. Senate, where he served on the Senate Foreign Relations Committee. He also attended the Sixth United Nations General Assembly in Paris in 1951–52, as well as the Manila Conference of 1954. In 1957, he was elected majority whip; he subsequently became the majority leader in 1961, after Lyndon JOHNSON became U.S. vice president. During the 1964 elections, he refused Johnson's request that he run for vice president.

The March on Washington, 1964 (NARA STILL PHOTOS DIVISION)

In 1971, Mansfield, who had become a vocal opponent of the war in Vietnam, sponsored an unsuccessful bill calling for a cease-fire and the gradual withdrawal of American troops from that country. He subsequently supported the war powers bill of 1973, which restricted the president's authority to involve the country in foreign military actions. Mansfield retired from the Senate in 1976, but was recalled to government service a few months later when he was asked to take part in a com-

mission investigating the fate of U.S. servicemen still missing in Indochina. In 1977, President Jimmy Carter appointed him U.S. ambassador to Japan. Mansfield retired in 1988.

March on Washington

One of the highlights of the CIVIL RIGHTS MOVEMENT, the March on Washington in August 1963 would

Leaders of the March on Washington meet with President Kennedy at the White House, August 23, 1963. (KENNEDY LIBRARY)

prove to be one of the largest mass demonstrations in U.S. history and a key event during some of the most emotional years of the Cold War. The march was originally conceived by A. Philip Randolph, a black labor leader who, upset with discrimination against blacks in wartime America, had originally proposed his idea to President Franklin D. Roosevelt in 1943. That march never took place, but 20 years later the civil rights leader Bayard Rustin set plans in motion to realize Randolph's vision of a march that would register "a great moral protest against racial bias." Enlisting the help of other African-American leaders, including Reverend Martin Luther KING, Jr., Rustin appealed to President John F. KENNEDY for support, which was ultimately given with some misgivings, and only after the original idea of a massive march through Washington, ending at the Capitol, was changed to a demonstration at the Lincoln Memorial. One of Kennedy's fears was that the march, which had already received an enormous amount of publicity in the MEDIA, might, if anything went wrong, jeopardize the civil rights legislation on which he was then working (it would become the CIVIL RIGHTS ACT of 1964).

As it turned out, he had nothing to worry about. With the media recording its every move, the demonstration went smoothly and peacefully. It began in the morning with a racially mixed crowd of over 200,000 (including a proud Randolph) gathering at the Washington Monument, where they listened to a number of performers, including Joan Baez, Bob DYLAN, Odetta, and others. Before the noon hour, the demonstrators began marching up Independence and Constitution Avenues, arriving quietly at the Lincoln Memorial, ahead of march leaders who had been lobbying that morning on Capitol Hill. There began a long afternoon of songs and speeches. The most famous was King's resounding "I have a dream" speech, the final speech of the day. As his thrilled audience cheered him on, King capped the day's events by invoking the words of an old Negro spiritual: "Free at last! Free at last!! Thank God Almighty, we are free at last!"

After closing their demonstration with the anthem of the civil rights movement, "We Shall Overcome," the crowd quickly and quietly dispersed to return to their homes. The march had been a huge success, and President Kennedy declared it to be a proud moment in the nation's history. Others did not share his view, with some radical black leaders viewing it as (in Stokely Carmichael's words) "only a sanitized, middle-class ver-

Protesters sing during the March on Washington. (NARA STILL PHOTOS DIVISION)

sion of the real black movement." MALCOLM X contemptuously referred to the march as the "Farce on Washington." Nevertheless, many felt that it was one of the most moving demonstrations ever, and to this day images from the March on Washington are reproduced in countless books, magazines, and documentaries, keeping it forever etched in the national memory.

Marshall, George C. (1880–1959)

George Catlett Marshall, Jr., was a career soldier and a winner of the Nobel Peace Prize who achieved fame for the MARSHALL PLAN, his proposal to aid Europe's recovery after World War II. He was born in 1880, the son of a coke and coal merchant from Virginia. In 1897, the young Marshall entered the Virginia Military Institute. He got off to a poor start, but by the time he graduated, in 1901, he had become first captain of the cadet corps. He was commissioned as a second lieutenant in the infantry in February 1902, and was posted to the Philippines for the next 18 months. An outstanding and respected officer, he rose quickly through the ranks.

With the outbreak of World War I, Marshall was sent to France as chief of operations for the First Infantry Division, then for the First Army. His military maneuvers and conduct brought him to the attention of General John Pershing, who made Marshall his personal aide in 1919. In 1924, Marshall left this assignment to go to China for three years. He returned to the United States to work with the Civilian Conservation Corps, and later became assistant commandant in charge of instruction at the infantry school at Fort Benning, Georgia (1927–33). He subsequently became chief of the army's war plans division and deputy chief of staff (1938–39). By this time he had acquired a reputation for both self-confidence and political adeptness, as well as for superior organizational and administrative abilities. On the day that Germany invaded Poland and began World War II (September 1, 1939), Marshall was appointed chief of staff of the U.S. Army. In this capacity he organized the training of the army's rapidly increasing forces (from fewer than 200,000 officers and troops in 1939 to a force of 8,300,000 by 1943); drew up strategic plans; arranged the equipment of the largest ground and air force in U.S. history; and made key military appointments, including his selection of Dwight D. EISENHOWER to command operations in North Africa and Sicily. He also worked to achieve a diplomatic balance of competing plans amongst the political and military leaders of the Allied powers. By 1944, he had become general of the army and was also named chief of staff, in which capacity he attended the YALTA Conference and POTSDAM Conference in 1945. At the conclusion of the war, Churchill heralded him as "the true organizer of victory."

From late November 1945 to 1947, Marshall returned to China in what proved to be a failed attempt to mediate the civil war there and to form a coalition

government. In 1947, he was appointed secretary of state under President Harry TRUMAN. In this regard, he began implementation of the historic Marshall Plan, also known as the European Recovery Plan, to assist a war-ravaged Europe in getting back on its feet. He also oversaw the provision of aid to Greece and Turkey (a key early CONTAINMENT decision meant to forestall the advance of communism), the recognition of Israel as an independent country, and the initiation of negotiations that ultimately resulted in the formation of the NORTH ATLANTIC TREATY ORGANIZATION (NATO). Marshall served as secretary of state until early 1949, then resigned due to ill health. From 1949 to 1950, he headed the American Red Cross, but returned to government service with the outbreak of the war in Korea, becoming secretary of defense for one year, 1950–51.

Although Marshall advocated military preparedness and maintained a tough attitude toward the Soviet Union, he was nonetheless accused by Senator Joseph MCCARTHY of being "SOFT ON COMMUNISM" for his efforts to mediate peace in China in 1946 and for failing to provide major military assistance to Chiang Kaishek (a circumstance that many felt contributed to the victory of Mao Zedong and the communists). However, Marshall was stoutly defended by others and nothing came of McCarthy's charges. In 1953, he became the only professional soldier to be awarded the Nobel Peace Prize, in recognition of his efforts to bring peace and order to the postwar world and for his contributions to Europe's economic resurgence. He remained on the active duty list until his death in 1959, and was one of the most influential, respected, and admired military leaders of this century.

Marshall Plan

Officially known as the European Recovery Plan, the Marshall Plan was an ambitious and highly successful scheme devised by Secretary of State George C. MARSHALL and others for the purpose of helping the ravaged nations of Europe recover economically and industrially from the devastating aftereffects of World War II. The plan was first proposed publicly by Marshall in a speech at Harvard University's commencement on June 5, 1947. However, in many respects, the groundwork had already been laid when, prior to the war's conclusion, Paul NITZE suggested that an economic program be formulated to assist European countries following the war; George KENNAN subsequently began laying the foundations of a proposal for such a

General George C. Marshall is sworn in as secretary of state; President Truman looks on. (TRUMAN LIBRARY)

program. In 1946, Congresswoman Clare Boothe LUCE introduced a bill to provide financial assistance to wartorn Europe; subsequent loans and grants totaled over $5 billion, which was quickly used up by emergencies, many of them occurring during the extremely severe winter of 1946–47. Ultimately, though, it was Marshall who perceived the need for a long-term plan of reconstruction, noting in his Harvard speech that Europe "must have substantial additional help or face economic, social, and political deterioration of very grave character."

The United States had another reason for wanting to assist its European allies. Although Marshall made no mention of it in his speech, there was every reason to fear that a Europe weakened by lack of food, housing, and employment opportunities would be susceptible to communist influences, perhaps even a takeover by the Soviet Union. The communist parties in France and Italy were then on the rise, communist guerrillas were creating innumerable problems in the Greek civil war, and Turkey was considered to be extremely vulnerable to the Soviet threat. The TRUMAN DOCTRINE had already been passed by Congress as a means of providing economic aid to Greece and Turkey to keep them stable and to hold the subversive elements at bay. The Marshall Plan would turn its attention to the stability of the entire European continent.

As an attempt to preserve the peace, Marshall deliberately included the Soviet Union in the initial planning sessions held in Paris in mid-1947. However, the Soviet delegation balked at certain conditions that were being imposed in exchange for U.S. aid, and subsequently they and other countries in the Soviet bloc refused to participate. The remaining European countries—with the exception of Finland, which chose to be neutral, and Spain, which was considered to be fascist—set up the Committee for European Economic Cooperation, which put together a report detailing what aid was needed for each country over the next four years. Areas of need covered by the report included food, raw materials, and technical assistance.

Meanwhile, Congress had already authorized aid in the amount of $597 million to Austria, France, and Italy while it considered the plan. In April 1948, the Economic Cooperation Act was passed and a system set up whereby the aid would be administered over the next four years (through the auspices of the Economic Cooperation Administration, acting upon requests from the Organization for European Eco-

nomic Cooperation). The vast majority of financial aid supplied to a total of 16 European nations was in the form of grants; only one-eighth would represent loans. All in all, the United States provided assistance of $13.15 billion between 1948 and 1952. Gratifyingly, results were as hoped for; industrial and agricultural production in the participating countries rose dramatically, and the gross national product experienced an average 25% rise over the four years that the Marshall Plan was in effect.

For many, more important was that the plan succeeded in containing Soviet influences in Europe. The communist guerrillas in Greece were finally defeated, and communists were expelled from the Italian and French governments. On the other hand, the plan was criticized for adding to Cold War tensions by obligating the Europeans to military alliances with the United States. This objection aside, it was generally agreed that Europe's astounding economic recovery was due primarily to the great success of George C. Marshall's plan.

massive retaliation

The threat of "massive retaliation" was often used by diplomats in the 1950s as a means of letting the Soviet Union (and other nations) know that the United States was not afraid to meet force with even greater force. Secretary of State John Foster DULLES first popularized the phrase, using it in speeches and negotiations. In essence, massive retaliation is the ability to respond to a military attack with nuclear forces that could devastate the enemy. It was considered to be an important defense strategy and was strongly supported by President Dwight EISENHOWER as a means of achieving nuclear DETERRENCE by putting the United States in a position of strength. It was also an important reason for the development of the HYDROGEN BOMB and other weapons of mass destruction; similarly, the STRATEGIC DEFENSE INITIATIVE proposed over thirty years later by President Ronald REAGAN grew out of this reasoning. Objections to this strategy were often strenuous; General Maxwell TAYLOR, furious over reductions in army troops in favor of a buildup of nuclear arms, resigned his commission and later referred to massive retaliation as "a great fallacy." President John F. KENNEDY agreed, and endorsed Taylor's preferred option of a "flexible response." Other critics of massive retaliation noted that it put the United States in an "all or nothing" position of having to choose

President Ford meets with his National Security Council to discuss the Mayaguez situation, May 13, 1975. (FORD LIBRARY)

between using nuclear force as promised, or avoiding the possibility of a nuclear holocaust by choosing inaction, thus defeating the purpose of the strategy.

Mayaguez incident

On May 12, 1975—less than one month after the communist Khmer Rouge regime had taken power in Cambodia—the U.S. merchant ship S.S. *Mayaguez* was seized by Cambodian patrol boats. The ship, which had been transporting goods from Hong Kong to Thailand, was captured in the Gulf of Siam, 60 miles off the Cambodian mainland, and taken to nearby Tang Island. The 39-man crew was taken hostage. An angered U.S. government at first attempted to retrieve the ship and its crew through diplomatic means. When diplomacy failed, President Gerald FORD ordered the use of military force and dispatched warships and aircraft to the area. In the battles that followed, an airbase and a

petroleum depot on the Cambodian mainland were destroyed. Meanwhile, 300 marines landed on Tang Island, sank three Cambodian gunboats, recaptured the ship, and rescued the hostages. The incident brought a gain in prestige for Ford, who won the approval of the American public for his decisive actions, despite some military mishaps that resulted in the loss of 18 marines in combat and an additional 23 in a plane crash.

McCarran Act   See INTERNAL SECURITY ACT.

McCarthy, Eugene (1916–)

Eugene Joseph McCarthy was a U.S. senator from Minnesota whose run for the Democratic presidential nomination in 1968 played a key role in Lyndon JOHNSON's decision to drop out of the race. McCarthy received his bachelor's degree in 1935 from St. John's University in

Collegeville, Minnesota, and went on to study for his master's degree at the University of Minnesota while working as a high school teacher. In 1940, he became a professor at St. John's, working there until 1943 when he left to serve in the military intelligence division of the War Department. After the war, he returned to teaching, joining the faculty of the College of St. Thomas in St. Paul, Minnesota.

In 1948, McCarthy made a successful bid for a seat in the U.S. House of Representatives, running on the Minnesota Democratic-Farmer-Labor Party ticket. A dedicated liberal, he remained in the House for the next 10 years, then was elected as a senator in 1958. He served on the Senate Finance and the Foreign Relations Committees, but was largely unknown until he announced his candidacy for the U.S. presidency on November 30, 1967, challenging the Democratic incumbent, Lyndon B. Johnson. By this time, the dovish McCarthy had become one of Johnson's sharpest critics for the president's conduct of the war in Vietnam. He won voters over with his charm and a witty manner of speaking, with the result that in March 1968, he surprised his fellow Democrats by winning 42% of the vote in the New Hampshire primary. At this point, Johnson stunned the nation with a televised announcement that he would not seek reelection.

McCarthy went on to sweep the next three primaries, but soon lost ground to Senator Robert F. KENNEDY, who won four out of five primaries before he was assassinated on June 4, 1968. At the Democratic convention in Chicago, however, McCarthy lost the nomination to Hubert HUMPHREY, who had not run in any of the primaries, and who subsequently lost the presidential election to Richard NIXON, the Republican nominee. In 1970, McCarthy declined to run for reelection to the U.S. Senate; his vacant seat was won by Hubert Humphrey. Thereafter, he became a writer and lecturer, but remained active in politics, conducting two more unsuccessful bids for the presidency—in 1972 as a Democrat (losing the nomination to George MCGOVERN), and in 1976 as an independent. McCarthy surprised the liberal establishment twice in the 1980s, first by endorsing Ronald REAGAN for president in 1980, then by an attempt (unsuccessful) to regain his Senate seat in 1982.

McCarthy, Joseph (1908–1957)

Joseph Raymond McCarthy was a U.S. senator from Wisconsin who, in the 1950s, conducted highly-publi-cized investigations of Americans he believed to be communists. He also gained notoriety for his vehement, yet unproved charges of widespread communist subversion in the government. McCarthy received his law degree from Marquette University in 1935. After graduation, he worked as an attorney for four years, then as a Wisconsin circuit judge (1939–42) before enlisting in the marines during World War II. He served as an intelligence officer and voluntarily flew on several combat missions, a fact he would later trumpet for campaign purposes when he gave himself the nickname of "Tail Gunner Joe." McCarthy first ran for the Senate in 1944, while he was still in service, disregarding Marine Corps regulations against political activities; he came in second in a field of four. Two years later, he defeated Wisconsin senator Robert F. La Follette, Jr., in the Republican primaries by attacking the latter's ties to organized labor and exaggerating his own wartime record. He won the fall election easily.

Although a pushy, pedantic, and fiercely anticommunist member of the Senate from the start, McCarthy was relatively unknown nationally until February 1950, when he made the first of his sensational charges to the effect that over 200 communists had infiltrated the State Department. His talk on February 9 in Wheeling, West Virginia (which was read in the Senate on February 20) followed the Republican National Committee's recent decision to focus congressional elections around the theme of "Liberty Against Socialism." In part, McCarthy noted that "While I cannot take the time to name all the men in the State Department who have been named as members of the Communist Party and members of a spy ring, I have here in my hand a list of 205 that were known to the secretary of state as being members of the Communist Party and are still working and shaping the policy of the State Department." The public furor that followed this announcement led to an investigation by the Senate Foreign Relations Committee. Called to testify, McCarthy was unable to prove his allegations with any names or hard evidence; he could not even find the list he had referred to in his speech. Despite this, he took advantage of the current American atmosphere of fear and suspicion concerning the KOREAN WAR and communist takeovers in China and eastern Europe, and pressed forward with his own investigations against suspected communists in the United States.

Although many people were appalled by the undermining of civil liberties that was part and parcel of McCarthy's crusade, he initially had widespread support for his efforts from both the public and from the Republican leadership. However, in June 1950, seven Republican senators, led by Margaret Chase Smith of Maine, issued a DECLARATION OF CONSCIENCE, which condemned what McCarthy was doing without ever mentioning him by name. After McCarthy's reelection to the Senate in 1952, he became chairman of the Government Committee on Operations of the Senate, giving him control over its permanent subcommittee on investigations. He thus remained in the headlines for the next two years as he investigated supposed communist plots in various branches of the government and pursued and badgered anybody he even remotely suspected of communist connections. His carefully worded accusations and methods of presenting his cases resulted in the destruction of numerous careers, yet McCarthy was unable to prove a single charge, even as other government agencies succeeded in identifying and dealing with real communist infiltrators.

As time passed, McCarthy and his counsel, Roy COHN, became increasingly reckless in their charges and attacked Democratic and Republican leaders, as well as President Dwight D. EISENHOWER. It seemed, in fact, that no American—not even one as widely respected as George C. MARSHALL, whom McCarthy denounced in June 1951—could be deemed safe from the senator's attacks. He deftly improvised his way through one headline-grabbing personal assault after another, but overestimated his abilities when he spoke out against the U.S. Army. After McCarthy brought charges of subversion against army officers and civilian officials in 1954, the subsequent hearings were televised, revealing his brutal methods of interrogation as well as the lack of substantiation for his accusations. As scrutiny of his tactics increased, a turning point occurred when, on March 9, 1954, Edward R. MURROW's *See It Now* television program focused on McCarthy's subcommittee and the threat to civil liberties provoked by its investigations. Finally, between April and June 1954, McCarthy himself came under investigation. Subjected to incisive questioning by Joseph N. Welch, a special U.S. Army counsel, McCarthy retaliated by impugning the reputation of a young lawyer in Welch's Boston law firm named Frederick G. Fisher. With Fisher's career hanging in the balance, and the nation looking on, a shocked Welch asked McCarthy, "Have you no sense of decency, sir, at last?" With this, public opinion turned irrevocably against McCarthy.

In November 1954, McCarthy was replaced as chairman of the investigating committee when the Republi-

cans lost control of the Senate in the midterm elections. Subsequently, the Senate cast a vote of 67 to 22 to formally censure him for "conduct contrary to Senate traditions." Thereafter he was ignored by both his fellow senators and by the MEDIA. He died in 1957 of an alcohol-related illness. His only lasting legacy was the term "MCCARTHYISM," which now denotes the use of unfair and unsubstantiated accusations and bullying investigation practices to create fear and distrust, violate individual rights, and enforce political conformity.

McCarthyism   See MCCARTHY, Joseph.

McCone, John (1902–1991)

John Alex McCone was a businessman and government official who served as director of the CENTRAL INTELLIGENCE AGENCY (CIA) under President John F. KENNEDY. After graduating from the University of California in 1922, McCone began his career as an engineer at the Llewellyn Iron Works, eventually becoming an executive. From 1933 to 1937, he was executive vice president of Consolidated Steel. In 1937 he left that company to form an international engineering firm with Stephen Bechtel; they named the company Bechtel-McCone. Two years later, McCone joined a firm that built planes and ships for use in the European theater of World War II, which resulted in criticism against him for war profiteering.

In 1947, McCone joined the Air Policy Commission under President Harry TRUMAN. The following year, he was appointed as a deputy to Secretary of Defense James FORRESTAL. In this capacity, he helped to create the CIA. He became an undersecretary of the air force in 1950, but served only one year, leaving government service in 1951. He returned in 1958, when he was named chairman of the ATOMIC ENERGY COMMISSION. In 1961, President John F. Kennedy appointed McCone director of the CIA. Although he was initially thought to be unsuited for the job, McCone quickly proved to be a strong administrator who did not let his conservative inclinations influence his decisions or his public attitudes; for instance, he publicly supported the Kennedy administration on the Partial Nuclear Test Ban Treaty, although he privately opposed it.

It was McCone who reported to the administration on the secret cache of Soviet missiles in Cuba, leading to the CUBAN MISSILE CRISIS between the United States and the Soviet Union in October 1962. He became one of President Kennedy's closest advisers during this period. He was among those who advocated air strikes against the missile sites, but Kennedy chose instead to quarantine Cuba. After the successful resolution of the Cuban Missile Crisis, McCone devoted himself to the increasing U.S. involvement in Vietnam, among other things advising against direct intervention in a military coup against the regime of President Ngo Dinh Diem.

Nearly 10 years later, it would be revealed that during McCone's tenure as director of the CIA, it had conducted illegal surveillance of more than 10,000 U.S. citizens and had also attempted to assassinate certain foreign leaders, including Fidel Castro. McCone's possible knowledge of these covert activities could not be established during a Senate investigation in 1974 and 1975.

Unsupportive of President Lyndon JOHNSON's decision to send U.S. troops to South Vietnam, McCone left the CIA in 1965 to become the head of International Telephone and Telegraph, where he worked until his retirement in 1973. He also became an expert on urban violence, testifying before several congressional committees and serving on the panel that investigated the riots in Watts. He died in 1991.

McGovern, George (1922–)

George Stanley McGovern is a former U.S. senator known primarily for his liberalism and his unsuccessful run for the U.S. presidency in 1972. The son of a Methodist minister, McGovern was a good student who early on showed a talent for debate. In 1940, he enrolled in Dakota Wesleyan University, which he attended on scholarship until 1943, when he was inducted into the U.S. Army Air Forces. He served heroically during World War II, flying 35 missions as a B-24 pilot and earning the Distinguished Flying Cross. Upon his return to the United States, he entered a seminary, but later enrolled in Northwestern University, where he taught history and earned his Ph.D. He subsequently returned to Dakota Wesleyan, becoming an American history teacher there from 1952 to 1953, then left to take the post of executive secretary of the South Dakota Democratic Party. In 1956, he was elected to the U.S. House of Representatives, but was defeated in his bid for a seat in the U.S. Senate in 1960. In 1961, he was appointed by President John F. KENNEDY as director of the Food for Peace Program, and served in this capacity until 1962, when he won his second try for a U.S. Senate seat representing South Dakota.

Although he voted (with considerable reluctance) for the TONKIN GULF RESOLUTION, giving President Lyndon B. JOHNSON authority to pursue military efforts in Indochina, McGovern soon became openly critical of increased defense spending and the expansion of U.S. troops in Vietnam, and in time found himself at the forefront of the ANTIWAR MOVEMENT. In the late 1960s, he also devoted himself to legislation aimed at eliminating hunger and malnutrition in the United States. In 1969, he became chairman of the Democratic Reform Commission, in which role he ensured the increased participation of minorities at the 1972 Democratic National Convention. After winning the Democratic presidential nomination that year as an outspoken antiwar candidate, McGovern's campaign started poorly when he was forced to replace his vice-presidential running mate, Thomas Eagleton, with Sargent Shriver after it was revealed that Eagleton had been treated for depression. In addition, McGovern's support of a recommended annual income that would be guaranteed for every American family was seen by many as a handout to nonworking Americans. Labeled by the Republicans as the candidate of "acid, amnesty, and abortion," McGovern was effectively, but inaccurately, portrayed as a radical whose views were well outside the political mainstream. During the campaign, McGovern also called for the "immediate and complete withdrawal of U.S. troops from Vietnam." In the final weeks of the campaign, Secretary of State Henry KISSINGER suggested that American involvement in the Vietnam war would conclude in a matter of weeks. Voters had never really warmed to McGovern, but the announcement blunted his campaign's message. He lost the election to Richard NIXON, with McGovern winning only 38% of the popular vote and losing 49 states.

In 1974, McGovern was reelected to the Senate, but then lost in 1980 to a Republican, James Abdnor. He thereupon became a traveling lecturer in foreign policy. He ran again for president in 1984, but withdrew from the race after failing to win a single primary. He has published several books, including *War Against Want* (1964); *A Time of War, A Time of Peace* (1968); and *The Great Coalfield War* (1973). His autobiography, *Grassroots*, was published in 1978.

McNamara, Robert (1916–)

As secretary of defense from 1961 to 1968, Robert Strange McNamara played a key role in the U.S. military escalation in Vietnam. He graduated from the

University of California at Berkeley in 1937, and went on to earn a graduate degree from Harvard Business School in 1939, after which he became a member of Harvard's faculty. Poor vision prevented him from enlisting in the military during World War II, but he served the country by creating logistical and statistical systems for monitoring troops, supplies, and bomber raids. After the war, he joined the Ford Motor Company. He enjoyed considerable success in revitalizing the company, and by 1960 had become its president. One month later, newly elected president John F. KENNEDY asked him to become secretary of defense, and he left the Ford Motor Company to take up his new duties. Using the cost-efficiency methods that had worked so well for him in private industry, he quickly began to make major changes in Pentagon operations and the bloated military bureaucracy, in addition to restructuring the defense budget and cutting back on spending for what he considered to be unnecessary weapons systems. He also encouraged a change in military strategy from the EISENHOWER administration's policy of MASSIVE RETALIATION to a more FLEXIBLE RESPONSE to counter possible attack from communist forces.

McNamara supported U.S. military involvement in Vietnam, and was optimistic that the South Vietnamese government would prevail against the attempts of the North Vietnamese to overthrow them. He made several trips to South Vietnam in the 1960s and represented President Lyndon JOHNSON in making key military decisions. However, by 1967, realizing that many of the assumptions he had made about Indochina were erroneous, he began attempts to bring about negotiations for a peace settlement. When the decision was made to bomb North Vietnam, McNamara's opposition weakened his position in the Johnson administration. In February 1968, he stepped down as secretary of defense to become president of the World Bank, where he would work for the next 13 years to serve the needs of THIRD WORLD countries. After his retirement, he continued to serve in various capacities for numerous organizations in such areas as foreign policy and the fight against world hunger. In 1986, he published an analysis of nuclear war entitled *Blundering Into Disaster: Surviving the First Century in a Nuclear Age.* His 1995 memoir, *In Retrospect: The Tragedy and Lessons of Vietnam,* examines the political climate of the 1950s and 1960s, and the mistaken assumptions and misjudgments—his own and those of the government he served—that led to the failure of the war in Vietnam.

Meany, George (1894–1980)

A labor organizer and leader, George Meany became known as the first president of the merged unions of the American Federation of Labor and the Congress of Industrial Organizations (AFL-CIO), a position he held for 24 years. The son of a plumber, Meany started out as a plumber himself, joining the United Association of Plumbers and Steam Fitters (United States and Canada) in 1915. In 1922, he was elected business agent of a New York local, and in 1932, he became vice president of the New York State Federation of Labor. He was elected the federation's president in 1934, and served in that capacity until 1939, when he was elected secretary-treasurer of the American Federation of Labor (AFL), then headed by William Green. After Green's death in 1952, Meany became the AFL's president, whereupon he set about effecting a merger between the AFL and the Congress of Industrial Organizations (CIO), which was organized according to industry where the AFL was organized by crafts. After the completion of the merger in 1955, Meany's election as president made him one of the most powerful representatives for labor in the country. Under his leadership, the organization became less radical and more conservative, which brought him into conflict with the leaders of some of the member unions. In 1957, he expelled the Teamsters Union and its leader, Jimmy HOFFA. In 1967, the United Auto Workers, led by Walter REUTHER, also left the AFL-CIO after a dispute with Meany. Meanwhile, although initially slow in creating

Defense Secretary Robert McNamara points to a map of Vietnam during a press conference. (NARA STILL PHOTOS DIVISION)

equal opportunities for jobs, the program Meany eventually created was used as the foundation for the CIVIL RIGHTS ACT of 1964.

A lifelong Democrat and anticommunist, Meany was a strong supporter of the GREAT SOCIETY programs of President Lyndon JOHNSON. He maintained cool relations with Richard NIXON, whose economic policies Meany frequently attacked. Meany opposed George McGovern's candidacy for the presidency in 1972, his preference being the hawkish senator Henry JACKSON of Washington, who, like Meany, opposed DÉTENTE with the Soviet Union. When McGovern won the Democratic nomination, the AFL-CIO refused to endorse any candidate in the general election, although some of its affiliates later threw their support to McGovern. After Nixon was reelected, Meany joined the administration as a member of the Productivity Commission and was influential in Nixon's decision to negate a number of wage-price controls. However, he was soon at odds again with the Republican administration, even after Nixon's resignation. He later gave lukewarm support to Jimmy Carter in the 1976 elections and his relations with the Carter White House were no better than they had been during the Nixon administration. However, in 1977, he played a major role in the U.S. withdrawal from the International Labor Organization after it refused to condemn repressive policies in communist countries. Thereafter, Meany lived quietly until his death in 1980.

media

Few words can inspire such mixed reactions as "the media," a phrase that variously conveys communication, information, disinformation, and intrusion into privacy. Technically, *media* refers to the instruments of mass communication that are a large part of today's society, including newspapers, magazines, television, radio, the cinema, and, most recently, the Internet. But modern media also encompasses the individuals who dispense information to the public through these instruments: news reporters and photographers, columnists, commentators, talk show hosts, filmmakers, advertisers, and so on. No longer just a means of obtaining and conveying the news, the media often creates the news and affects, if not exploits, public reaction to current affairs.

While history has many examples of newspapers influencing national and international events and popular opinion with intentionally biased or distorted

Walter Cronkite and a CBS News crew interview an army officer in Vietnam. (NARA STILL PHOTOS DIVISION)

reporting, it was during the Cold War years that the media acquired its current dubious reputation as a master manipulator. This was due in no small part to the emergence of television in the 1950s and 1960s, not just as a form of entertainment but also as a way of bringing information into American homes with previously unparalleled speed. As a result, citizens became more directly involved in events at nearly the very moment they occurred. This fact was brought home by the reporting of the VIETNAM WAR, which became known as the "living room war," as images from the other side of the world were broadcast directly into U.S. homes. Those images were so often horrifying and heartbreaking that they effectively helped swell the peace movement. Years later, Americans witnessing the PERSIAN GULF WAR on their television sets could actually follow the path of a missile from launch pad to target, providing an almost gruesome intimacy with the ongoing battles.

As the Cold War intensified, the media became more involved, more influential, and, according to many, more powerful. During the televised Army-McCarthy hearings in the 1950s, American citizens could see for themselves the deleterious effects of Senator Joseph MCCARTHY's increasingly bizarre campaign to root out suspected communists in the government. Richard NIXON initially used television to solicit sympathy in his famous "Checkers" speech; that medium would later work against him when his haggard appearance was up against the youthful (and made-up) John F. KENNEDY in the first of their televised debates. Many felt that Nixon's poor showing actually cost him the 1960 election. Nixon and many others had a mixed relationship with the press, who were often perceived to be the enemy, due to what were thought to be their frequent distortions or inaccuracies—sometimes intentional—that could depict a politician or celebrity in an inaccurate light. In fact, when two *Washington Post* reporters published certain revelations about the WATERGATE scandal, they set in motion the train of events that resulted in Nixon's resignation.

The media can also be used by those who wish to tap into its powers to provide access to public opinion and perceptions. Abbie HOFFMAN and John LENNON were just two of many who organized "media events" to bring widespread attention to a favorite cause, or even to themselves. On the other hand, many people, such as members of the Kennedy family, are subjected to intense scrutiny and denied their right to privacy, ostensibly because the public has a right to know and the media is the chosen means of access to knowledge. In recent years, another phrase has been added to the American lexicon: "media hype" denotes that sense of overkill felt when media coverage of a particular personality or event becomes especially strident or unrelenting.

The media has become such a pervasive part of life in today's world that for some there is a fearful possibility of its taking on a "Big Brother" role, monitoring and controlling a population to such an extent that individual freedoms are lost. While this totalitarian scenario has been a popular theme in the movies, there has been no support for it in real-life events other than complaints of media intrusions into private lives that often seem to be the inevitable outcome of major news stories.

military-industrial complex

The term *military-industrial complex* describes the association of the armed forces with the private industries that supply them with weapons, ships, aircraft, and so on. It has been posited that the military-industrial complex, if left unchecked, could abuse power and

President Ford faces the media in a press conference. (FORD LIBRARY)

resources—essentially, take over the U.S. economy—and direct foreign policy to disastrous results. It was President Dwight D. EISENHOWER who first warned the public of this danger in his farewell address to the nation on January 17, 1961, when he said "In the councils of government, we must guard against the acquisition of unwarranted influence, whether sought or unsought, by the military-industrial complex. The potential for the disastrous rise of misplaced power exists and will persist."

While concerns about military takeovers of government have always existed, the complications posed by the arms race and the battle for nuclear superiority during the Cold War made it more of a grim possibility for the United States, many of whose industries courted the large defense contracts offered by the Pentagon. It seemed logical to fear that generals in disagreement with presidential or congressional foreign policy decisions would join forces with industry leaders to create a power base that would take control of the government out of the hands of the politicians. Eisenhower' s words were therefore taken seriously, although no major crisis ever actually took place.

miscalculation

One of President John F. KENNEDY's favorite words, *miscalculation* referred to the possibility of war due to one side's underestimating or mistaking the other's military capacities or political intent. Miscalculation usually occurs as a result of the political "games" that world leaders and diplomats inevitably play in negotiations and confrontations. For instance, during the KOREAN WAR, the Chinese erred in assuming that, if South Korea were invaded from the north, there would be no response from either the United States or the UNITED NATIONS. Conversely, when the United States received warnings in 1951 that the Chinese would retaliate if General Douglas MACARTHUR and his troops crossed the 38th parallel, the decision to proceed anyway resulted in stalled peace negotiations and a prolonged war. Similar risks would be taken later, in the VIETNAM WAR, when each side tried to second-guess the other's intentions, and the United States in particular seriously miscalculated the guerrilla capabilities of the Vietcong. Kennedy himself had direct experience with miscalculation as a result of his standoff with Nikita Khrushchev during the CUBAN MISSILE CRISIS, when the Soviet premier clearly underestimated the young American president's ability to take decisive

action. Saddam Hussein made a similar mistake in assuming that President George BUSH and the United States would not take action following his invasion of Kuwait; Operation Desert Storm, which drove Iraqi troops out of Kuwait, proved him wrong.

missile gap

The "missile gap" was an outgrowth of the arms race between the United States and the Soviet Union. The term was originally used by presidential candidate John F. KENNEDY to warn voters that the United States was seriously lagging behind the Soviets in production of missiles. This information was a result both of Soviet propaganda and of a poll conducted by the UNITED STATES INFORMATION AGENCY showing that Europeans believed the Soviets to be leading the United States in the race for nuclear arms. However, the missile gap later proved to be an exaggeration—in fact, U.S. missile production was ahead of the USSR, whose only real advantage in the late 1950s and early 1960s was its lead in the space race, prompting the EISENHOWER administration to step up American efforts on all nuclear fronts. When, after Kennedy's election, it was revealed that no real danger of a missile gap actually existed, he and his administration found themselves embarrassed by a "credibility gap." Several years later, in 1966, information leaked from the Pentagon indicated that the missile gap had become a strong possibility by that time. However, with the memory of Kennedy's so-called missile gap still fresh in their minds, many members of the press and the public refused to put much faith in the rumor, believing that it was probably based on false or mistaken intelligence.

Mitchell, John (1913–1988)

John Newton Mitchell was the U.S. attorney general during the NIXON administration and a major player in the WATERGATE scandal, for which he served 19 months in prison. A graduate of Fordham University and Fordham Law School, he worked as an investment lawyer in New York City before becoming a torpedo boat commander for the U.S. Navy during World War II. After the war, he returned to his law practice and became an expert in state and municipal bonds. When his law firm merged with Richard Nixon's in 1967, he became friendly with Nixon and soon became a political adviser. In 1968, he served as manager of Nixon's successful campaign for the U.S. presidency. He was rewarded with an appointment as attorney general. During his time in that office, he came under sharp attack for numerous transgressions, including the use of illegal wiretaps against radicals and activists. Mitchell actively prosecuted antiwar protesters, and attempted unsuccessfully to block the publication of the PENTAGON PAPERS.

In March 1972, Mitchell resigned from the Justice Department to direct the Committee for the Re-election of the President (CREEP), but left the organization in July after the break-in at Democratic National Committee headquarters in the Watergate apartment complex became public knowledge. In 1974, he was indicted on charges of conspiracy with regard to the break-in, and was also accused of obstruction of justice and perjury in connection with the administration's attempt to cover up the affair. He was convicted in 1975, entered prison in 1977, and paroled in 1979.

Mondale, Walter (1928–)

A liberal Democrat in the Hubert HUMPHREY tradition, Walter Frederick Mondale is a former U.S. senator and vice president who ran unsuccessfully for president in 1984. Mondale received his B.A. degree from Macalester College in 1951, then earned his law degree from the University of Minnesota Law School in 1956. Between degrees, he served two years (1951–53) in the U.S. Army, stationed at Fort Knox, Kentucky.

Mondale became involved in politics quite early, first in 1947 as a member of the "Diaper Brigade," a group of student volunteers supporting the campaign by Humphrey and others to keep ultra-left elements out of the Democratic-Farmer-Labor Party. He went on to work in Humphrey's successful senatorial campaign of 1948, serving as campaign manager in the Second Congressional District. In 1949, he accompanied Humphrey to Washington, where he worked for a year as executive secretary of Students for Democratic Action (a branch of AMERICANS FOR DEMOCRATIC ACTION). Before joining the army, in the early 1950s, Mondale managed the unsuccessful campaign of Orville Freeman for Minnesota attorney general—a post Mondale later won, in 1960, after four years of private law practice.

When Hubert Humphrey became U.S. vice president in 1964, Mondale was appointed to fill Humphrey's Senate seat. He was subsequently elected to the seat in 1966 and won reelection in 1972. During his years in the Senate, he was a member of Senate

Committees for Budget and Finance, and also served on the Committee on Labor and Public Welfare. Mondale was a fierce supporter of President Lyndon JOHNSON's GREAT SOCIETY programs, as well as an important advocate for civil rights legislation (he was instrumental in the Senate's passage of the CIVIL RIGHTS ACT of 1968). He also opposed the allocation of additional funds for missiles, Supersonic transports, and Skylab, and frequently pointed out the need to concentrate on such domestic issues as the rights of migrant workers and abused children. Mondale was a supporter of the war in Vietnam until 1968, when he reconsidered his position, became an active opponent, and spoke out in favor of increased arms control. He also supported DÉTENTE and advocated increased trade with the Soviet Union, with whom he felt it was possible to take on shared responsibility for Third and Fourth World development.

In 1976, Mondale was chosen as Jimmy CARTER's running mate in his successful campaign for the presidency and subsequently served for four years as vice president. Mondale was an influential and respected member of the Carter decision-making team. However, he and Carter were defeated for reelection in 1980 by Ronald REAGAN and George BUSH. In 1984, Mondale won the Democratic nomination for president and made history by selecting a woman, Geraldine A. Ferraro, as his running mate. After suffering another resounding defeat at the hands of Ronald Reagan, Mondale went into private law practice. During the Clinton administration, he was named ambassador to Japan.

Morgenthau, Henry Jr. (1891–1967)

Henry Morgenthau, Jr., was a longtime secretary of the treasury and creator of the MORGENTHAU PLAN whose career in public service was cut short by the death of his friend and mentor, Franklin D. Roosevelt. He was born into a prosperous Jewish family; his father, a real estate investor, had been ambassador to Turkey during World War I. After attending a number of private schools, Morgenthau went to Cornell University, but left after three semesters, choosing instead to become a farmer on a large tract of land in East Fishkill, New York. From 1922 to 1933, he published a farm weekly entitled *American Agriculturalist*.

While living in East Fishkill, Morgenthau and his wife met their neighbors, Franklin and Eleanor ROOSEVELT. The two men became friends, and when Roosevelt was governor of New York, he appointed Morgenthau to serve as chairman of the Agricultural Advisory Committee (1928) and subsequently as commissioner of conservation (1930). Upon Roosevelt's election to the presidency, he named Morgenthau to head the Farm Credit Administration (1933). As an administrator, Morgenthau was handicapped by his lack of education or experience in finance and law, but made up for it by enlisting able and trustworthy experts to assist him.

Roosevelt also trusted Morgenthau's sound instincts, and in 1933 he tapped his friend to aid in negotiations for the recognition of the Soviet Union. As head of the Farm Credit Administration, Morgenthau helped farmers during the Great Depression by instituting ways to ease their debt and increase their loans. He also created a program to raise commodity prices by buying gold, and began making large purchases and sales of grain in line with Roosevelt's desire to squeeze out speculators. His successful efforts were rewarded when Roosevelt named him, in order, undersecretary, acting secretary, and finally secretary of the treasury (1934), a position he would hold for the next 11 and a half years. As secretary, he worked to stabilize and strengthen the dollar and to put the United States back on sound economic footing as the Great Depression waned. His policies frequently brought him into conflict with other members of the administration who resented his closeness to Roosevelt, who in turn put increasing trust and responsibility into Morgenthau's hands.

Such responsibilities included crucial and confidential matters relating to international affairs. In 1941, Morgenthau supervised the drafting of the Lend-Lease Act and, later, arranged for aid to the Soviet Union during World War II. At the Bretton Woods conference in 1944, he achieved a career high point when he negotiated the agreements that established the World Bank and the International Monetary Fund.

The Morgenthau Plan developed as a result of Morgenthau's belief that postwar Germany would continue to threaten international stability unless certain measures were taken. He wanted to demilitarize and deindustrialize Germany and turn it into a peaceful, rural country, with an emphasis on an agricultural economy. Both Roosevelt and Winston Churchill endorsed his plan initially, but other U.S. administration officials were vigorously opposed, including Secretary of State Cordell HULL and Secretary of War Henry L. STIMSON. Eventually public opinion held against the plan, and Roosevelt dropped his support of it. The plan contin-

ued to be discussed even after Roosevelt's death, and it influenced postwar policy in the occupation period, until Secretary of State James F. BYRNES killed it once and for all in a September 1946 speech that set the tone for the future U.S. attitude as the Cold War got under way.

Upon leaving government service in July 1945, Morgenthau returned to his farm in New York. For some time, he raised money for the United Jewish Appeal and Bonds for Israel. In his later years he became devoted to philanthropic work.

Morgenthau Plan   See MORGENTHAU, Henry.

Morse, Wayne (1900–1974)

A noted liberal, Wayne Lyman Morse was a U.S. senator for 24 years who was an early and outspoken opponent of U.S. military involvement in Vietnam. Morse graduated from the University of Wisconsin in 1923, and went on to earn law degrees at both the University of Minnesota and Columbia University. In 1929, he began teaching law at the University of Oregon, becoming dean of its law school in 1937. He also became a nationally-known labor mediator.

Morse ran successfully for the Senate as a Republican in 1944 and was reelected in 1950. However, as his political views became increasingly liberal, he often found himself at odds with the Republican Party. In 1950, he was one of seven Republican senators who signed a DECLARATION OF CONSCIENCE assailing the tactics of Senator Joseph MCCARTHY (although the document did not single out McCarthy by name). By this time, Morse had acquired a reputation as a champion of human rights and education and a supporter of environmentalism and progressive farm policies. He supported Democratic hopeful Adlai STEVENSON's bid for the presidency in 1952, then resigned from the Republican Party and became an independent in 1953. He joined the Democratic Party in 1955 and a year later was reelected as senator from Oregon. He completed another reelection bid in 1962. He also chaired a Senate subcommittee on Latin America that had an impact on President John F. KENNEDY's decision to create the ALLIANCE FOR PROGRESS.

During the course of the 1960s, Morse emerged as one of the most vocal critics of American military involvement in Vietnam. He was one of only two senators who, in 1964, voted against the TONKIN GULF RES-

OLUTION (which effectively approved President JOHN-SON's decision to launch raids on North Vietnamese targets and gave him authority for further military action, leading to ESCALATION of the war). The other dissenting senator was Ernest Gruening of Alaska, a Democrat. Both were vindicated in 1971 when the publication of the PENTAGON PAPERS recalled that President Johnson had drafted the main text of the resolution months before the incident in the Gulf of Tonkin. In addition, questions about the specifics of the Tonkin incident cast serious doubts on the administration's version of events.

Morse's unyielding opposition to U.S. involvement in Vietnam led to his defeat for reelection in 1968. He ran again for his old seat in 1974 and won the Democratic nomination, but died prior to the general election.

Murrow, Edward R. (1908–1965)

Born Egbert Roscoe, the journalist Edward R. Murrow would live to become one of the most highly respected and influential pioneers of broadcast journalism in both radio and television. He grew up in the state of Washington and worked in logging camps while he attended Washington State College in Pullman. From 1929 to 1931, he was president of the National Student Association. He was assistant director of the Institute of International Education from 1932 to 1935, during which time he worked to bring German scholars to the United States after the rise of Nazism made it impossible for them to study in their own country. In 1935, he joined the Columbia Broadcasting System (CBS). Two years later he went to London to head the CBS European Bureau. He soon became famous for his vivid, eyewitness accounts of the German takeovers in Austria (1938) and Czechoslovakia (1939), as well as the Munich Conference of 1938. He made radio history with his live broadcasts from the rooftops of London during the German bombing raids. His signature line, "Good night, and good luck," became a watchword to his listeners in the United States.

After the war, Murrow returned to New York, where he became a vice president at CBS and served as director of public affairs from 1946 to 1947. He resumed newscasting on radio in 1947, then joined forces with Fred W. Friendly to create a weekly news digest entitled *Hear It Now* (1950–51). In 1951, he moved the series to television as *See It Now*; the program ran for the next seven years. The March 9, 1954 episode focused on the anticommunist investigations then being conducted by

Senator Joseph MCCARTHY and helped to expose McCarthy's tactics to the nation. Murrow's broadcast was a major turning point in the McCarthy period; within months, McCarthy had been censured by the U.S. Senate. Many credit Murrow's decision to tackle McCarthy and his methods as one of the high points in the history of American journalism.

Murrow also launched another television series, *Person to Person*, which aired from 1953 to 1959. On it, he interviewed notable public figures and celebrities of the day. In 1961, President John F. KENNEDY appointed him director of the UNITED STATES INFORMATION AGENCY. Murrow resigned in 1964 due to ill health and died of cancer a year later.

Muskie, Edmund (1914–1996)

Governor of Maine, U.S. senator, secretary of state, and both a presidential and vice presidential nominee, Edmund Sixtus Muskie was one of the most prominent U.S. public figures of the post-World War II period. His father was a Polish tailor named Marciziewski who immigrated to the United States in 1903, at which time the family name was changed to Muskie. Edmund graduated Phi Beta Kappa from Bates College in 1936 and from Cornell University Law School in 1939. He worked as an attorney in Waterville, Maine, prior to the outbreak of World War II, during which he served as a naval officer. After the war, he entered politics, running as a Democrat for the U.S. House of Representatives in 1946 in a heavily Republican state. He won and was subsequently reelected in 1948 and 1950, becoming minority leader of the House in the process.

In 1954, Muskie was elected as Maine's first Democratic governor since the 1930s, and was then reelected in 1956. He succeeded in implementing reforms to the Maine economy. Working effectively with a Republican legislature he succeeded in implementing reforms to Maine's economy. After leaving the governor's office in 1959, he became the first Democrat in Maine's history to be elected to the U.S. Senate, where he served with distinction for the next 20 years and also became an authority on air and water pollution. In addition to serving on the Foreign Relations Committee and the Budget Committee (as chairman), Muskie was the assistant majority whip from 1966 to 1980.

Muskie became Hubert HUMPHREY's running mate in the 1968 elections, after which he became a vocal critic of the war in Vietnam. He was a front-runner for the Democratic presidential nomination in 1972, but withdrew from the race after an overly cautious primary campaign that was undermined by a series of "DIRTY TRICKS" engineered by aides to President NIXON. (Cameras had recorded Muskie losing his composure in the aftermath of one of these dirty tricks.) As chairman of the newly established Senate Budget Committee in 1975, he fought hard to reduce government spending. In 1980–81, he served as secretary of state during the final months of President Jimmy CARTER's administration, when the Iranian hostage crisis occupied almost all his attention. He then returned to his private law practice. In 1986, he served as a member of the Tower Commission to investigate the IRAN-CONTRA affair.

Muste, A. J. (1885–1967)

Abraham Johannes Muste was a clergyman and social activist who exerted an important influence on the career of Martin Luther KING, Jr. Muste's father was a Dutch coachman who brought his family to the United States in 1891 and settled in Michigan. The young Muste, who came to be known as A. J., grew up with a solid religious foundation, and by 1909 was a minister in the Dutch Reformed Church. He became the minister of a church in New York City, where he became aware of many social problems and encountered such people as Norman Thomas and Eugene Debs, important theorists in the socialist movement. In 1915, he was appointed minister of a Congregational church in Newtonville, Massachusetts, but was forced to resign in 1917 due to his outspoken opposition to World War I. A committed pacifist, he became a Quaker during the war, and subsequently helped to found the AMERICAN CIVIL LIBERTIES UNION. He went on to become involved with a number of groups promoting various causes, among them PACIFISM and socialism, and also played a key role in the militant labor movement of the 1920s and 1930s. For a time he was a disciple of Leon Trotsky, even helping to found a Marxist workers party in 1933. However, in 1936, he returned to Christianity as his philosophical base, and thereafter worked with the Fellowship of Reconciliation, a pacifist group sponsored by the Quakers. Muste also helped to found the Congress of Racial Equality.

During World War II, Muste worked with the government to find ways for CONSCIENTIOUS OBJECTORS to serve the country without engaging in combat. At the conclusion of the war, he began a series of nonviolent protests against the buildup of nuclear arms. His 1940 book, *Nonviolence in an Aggressive World,* promoted pacifism as a solution to the world's problems. In 1949, he gave a talk at Crozer Theological Seminary in Chester, Pennsylvania, that made a lasting impression on a young Martin Luther King, Jr. Throughout the 1950s, Muste continued his campaign of nonviolent resistance to military buildups, serving a jail sentence of nine days in 1959 for climbing over a fence at a missile site. Out of principle, he also refused to pay income taxes from 1948 until his death.

During the 1960s, Muste worked in the CIVIL RIGHTS MOVEMENT and founded *Liberation,* a radical and influential journal of the NEW LEFT. Later he became a leading protester against the VIETNAM WAR, among other things organizing "Walks for Peace." In a move that won both admiration and amazement from many quarters, he attempted to negotiate a peace with Ho Chi Minh just weeks before his death in 1967. A. J. Muste is generally recognized as having set the stage for the later work of the civil rights movement, a fact appreciated by Martin Luther King, Jr., who had written to Muste to express his appreciation and later lauded him as "America's Gandhi."

"My country, right or wrong"

This phrase was one of the favorite responses of the NEW RIGHT to ANTIWAR MOVEMENT demonstrators during the 1960s and early 1970s. Despite the constitutional provision for free speech, many conservatives, including such factions as the HARD HATS, believed that any criticism of the government was unpatriotic. As a retort to the chants of "HELL, NO, WE WON'T GO," these conservatives proudly declared, "My country, right or wrong" as proof that they were loyal American citizens whose love of their country and support of the current administration, no matter what its political affiliation, was undeniable and unequivocal.

My Lai   See CALLEY, William.

National Guard

The National Guard is an organization consisting of reserve forces from the United States Army and U.S. Air Force who serve under the command of state and territorial governors, unless called by the president or Congress for active duty in times of national emergency (i.e., war). Unlike reserve forces directly attached to the national military, volunteers in the National Guard enlist for duty within their states on a reserve basis for eight years. The guard serves federal and state domestic military needs in times of peace; in war, its members are assimilated into the regular militia.

The idea of a National Guard, in which citizens serve as soldiers for brief periods according to necessity, has been in practice since colonial days. Members of the guard may be called upon at any time to maintain order during times of civil unrest—for example, to quell riots or regulate potentially violent public demonstrations. It is this function that has frequently brought it into the public spotlight, especially during the turbulent years of the Cold War, when National Guard presence at civil rights and antiwar demonstrations frequently led to controversial and sometimes violent confrontations between the guard and the public.

One such incident occurred in Arkansas, in September 1957, when Governor Orval Faubus, in an effort to prevent the integration of Little Rock Central High School, called in National Guard troops to surround the school and keep out nine black students who had been scheduled to enroll there. After a two-week-long standoff, President Dwight EISENHOWER federalized the units and used them to force Faubus to allow the school's integration. A similar event took place six years later, when President John F. KENNEDY used National Guard troops to ensure the integration of the University of Alabama despite Governor George WALLACE's stiff opposition.

The National Guard was frequently called in during controversial civil rights demonstrations and peace rallies. Sometimes, this resulted in disaster, as was the case with the KENT STATE MASSACRE in May 1970. This event outraged the nation to such an extent that there were calls to disband the National Guard. However, today the Army National Guard has more than 3,000 units in 2,600 locations throughout the United States and its territories, while the Air National Guard maintains in excess of 90 flying units and 500 mission support units.

National Organization for Women See
WOMEN'S MOVEMENT.

National Security Act

Of paramount concern to any country is its safety and stability in times of both war and peace, and the ability of its citizens to live freely and without fear of attack from outside threats. To this end, national security is a perpetual burden for the government. This became especially true after World War II, when the United States had become a major player in the Cold War. In 1944, concerned about maintaining a strong defense in the event of future wars, the U.S. Congress began to consider options for a postwar policy that would unify the armed services, making for interrelated and therefore more controlled military operations. This idea was endorsed by army generals Dwight EISENHOWER, George MARSHALL, and Douglas MACARTHUR, but opposed by navy leaders. The Eberstadt Report, released in 1945, subsequently recommended that the services become federated rather than unified and also suggested the creation of a council to advise the president on issues and policies regarding national security, an agency to gather and process intelligence data, and a board to coordinate military resources.

The National Security Act, passed by Congress in 1947, responded to the report's recommendations by establishing an independent air force that was coequal with the army and the navy, in addition to creating safeguards for the Marine Corps and the Navy Air Corps. The act also originated a new cabinet position, that of secretary of defense, who would draft policies and coordinate programs of the newly created national military establishment. This new position eliminated the cabinet participation of the secretaries of the army, navy, and air force, who would continue in executive positions. Finally, several boards and agencies were set up under the act, according to suggestions made in the Eberstadt Report: the NATIONAL SECURITY COUNCIL, the CENTRAL INTELLIGENCE AGENCY, the National Security Resources Board (which was subsequently abolished), the Joint Chiefs of Staff (already in existence, but now legally recognized), the Joint Staff, the Munitions Board, the Research and Development Board, and the War Council, to be renamed the Armed Forces Policy Council. The National Security Act was amended in 1949, changing the National Military Establishment into the Department of Defense, and making it an executive government office, a move that

further reduced the power of the secretaries of the three military branches. Other amendments appointed a chairman to head the Joint Chiefs of Staff and provided budgetary allowances for operating and organizational expenses.

National Security Agency (NSA)

The National Security Agency (NSA) was created under the direction of President Harry TRUMAN in 1952 as a secret intelligence-gathering unit that worked to intercept communications and break codes of other (enemy) countries, in addition to protecting those of the United States. Arising from the signal intelligence duties of the Armed Forces Security Agency, which served the military, the NSA's assigned mission was to serve all branches of government. From its headquarters at Fort Meade, Maryland, the agency scans millions of communications, electronic and otherwise, on a daily basis, looking (for example) for key words that may prompt it to investigate anything that is perceived to present some threat to national security. In addition, the NSA monitors the communications of over 2,000 stations worldwide.

The NSA was at one time so secret that most U.S. citizens were unaware of its existence. It came to public attention in the early 1970s, when it was revealed that the NSA had been conducting covert surveillance of certain targeted Americans, including many who were opposed to the VIETNAM WAR. This gave the agency an ominous aspect that outraged the public.

National Security Council (NSC)

Established by the NATIONAL SECURITY ACT of 1947, the National Security Council (NSC) is a means of providing information and counsel to the president on issues of national defense and security and assisting in formulating foreign policies that address those issues. The council members consist of the president, vice president, secretary of state, secretary of defense, and director of the Office of Emergency Planning, while advisers include the director of the CENTRAL INTELLIGENCE AGENCY (CIA) and the chairman of the Joint Chiefs of Staff. The NSC staff, which investigates events and current developments that affect national security and makes recommendations to the council, is headed by the president's national security advisor and the deputy assistant to the president for national security affairs.

President Lyndon Johnson meets with his National Security Council; Robert McNamara is to his left. (JOHNSON LIBRARY)

One of the council's best-known recommendations was the 1950 document known as NSC-68. It emphasized the political and ideological divisions between the United States and the Soviet Union and asserted a need for taking measures to protect noncommunist countries threatened by Soviet expansion, even if it meant using military force. The report described the council's perceptions of the Soviet quest for world domination and its capabilities for achieving its goals. It advised against diplomatic negotiations in favor of strengthening military forces and developing and amassing nuclear arms, including the hydrogen bomb. In addition, the report recommended the creation of military alliances and the use of propaganda to promote anticommunism and pro-Americanism among citizens of the United States and the Soviet Union. Following the publication of NSC-68, war broke out in Korea, giving credibility to the report's conclusions and resulting in significant increases in defense spending.

NSC-68 was one of the few instances in the council's history when its recommendations had a clear impact on foreign policy. The idea for a National Security Council was first proposed by Secretary of the Navy James FORRESTAL, who perceived a need for a strong advisory board that would guide the president,

First meeting of President Richard Nixon's National Security Council (NIXON LIBRARY)

especially a weak one, in making foreign policy and domestic security decisions. In the years since its creation, the NSC has only partially fulfilled its original designated functions, and in many cases has gone beyond them, depending on the president in power; some would consult the council for advice regularly, while others, such as Lyndon JOHNSON and Ronald REAGAN, did not consider it to be a particularly useful or even necessary tool for the development of foreign policy. On the other hand, Richard NIXON and his secretary of state, Henry KISSINGER, developed the NSC's role to such an extent that it became the Nixon administration's primary body for the creation of foreign policy, effectively circumventing the State Department. Indeed, the NSC's role so overlaps that of the State Department that there have been frequent and sometimes rancorous rivalries between the incumbent national security advisor and the secretary of state. Serious questions were raised about the NSC's involvement in the IRAN-CONTRA AFFAIR, which provoked

suggestions that its role as a government agency be reviewed and overhauled to guide it back to its original agenda.

New Left

The New Left was a group of young intellectual liberals who, late in the 1950s, rejected the philosophy of the then-current liberal ESTABLISHMENT and struck out in more radical directions that scorned bureaucracy and embraced free thinking, as well as endorsing a socialist (not communist) standard of living. The movement began in England and soon spread to the United States, where it flowered within the movements for peace and civil rights and was embraced by members of the COUNTERCULTURE. The New Left had no discernible agenda, nor were there any clear leaders of the movement; those identified with the faction simply and unequivocally opposed the Establishment. New Left liberals asked questions—but did not necessarily pro-

President George Bush meets with his National Security Council to discuss Iraq's invasion of Kuwait, an event that led to the Persian Gulf War. (BUSH LIBRARY)

vide answers—to the problems and inconsistencies in the society they disparaged. Perhaps because of this, they had little mainstream political support. However, the New Left did leave an imprint on society, most notably in how they fostered public debate on such controversial issues as the VIETNAM WAR, feminism, violence as a means of protest, presidential foreign policy decisions, and black militancy.

New Right

Just as the New Left could be considered the radical edge of liberalism, so could the New Right be called the extremist edge of conservatism. The New Right developed during the 1960s out of conservative disgust with such liberal activities as the ANTIWAR MOVEMENT and the passing of legislation that, in their minds, was turning the country over to whiners and "PINKOS." The core of the New Right at this time consisted of "HARD HATS" and self-described patriots, such as members of the JOHN BIRCH SOCIETY, and other right-wing radical groups such as the Minutemen and the American Nazi Party. These groups decried the passage of civil rights and affirmative action legislation, as well as numerous Supreme Court rulings, and frequently clashed with peace demonstrators. The "battle cry" of the New Right in the 1960s was "AMERICA, LOVE IT OR LEAVE IT!"

Another New Right movement emerged during the 1970s and came to real prominence in the 1980s. This group consisted of a group of politicians, business leaders, conservation organizations and committees, and evangelical Christians who were previously supportive of the Republican Party's agenda, but who had become increasingly impatient with the party's trend toward moderation, especially during the administration of President Gerald FORD. This New Right movement therefore began calling for stronger, more decisive leadership that would cement the United States's position as the world's most powerful and influential nation.

Unlike the New Left, the New Right had a clear agenda and powerful leaders around whom adherents could rally. These included evangelists such as Jerry Falwell and organizations such as the Christian Coalition. Those leaders and others contributed to a public perception of the New Right as a group composed largely of religious zealots. The New Right often worked on a grassroots basis to create political support for its social and legislative goals, which included a return to what members saw as basic moral values and the imposition of restrictions on government interven-

tion in American society. Many attracted to the New Right's message (usually white Protestants) were those who had become unhappy with the government's perceived loss of control to the liberal and socialist elements that were, in their view, tearing apart the fabric of American society and weakening the structures that had made the country great. The New Right grew into a powerful and influential movement that continues to this day, lobbying Congress and making its presence as self-appointed moral arbiter felt throughout the nation.

Newton, Huey P. (1942–1989)

Huey Percy Newton was a prominent political activist of the 1960s and cofounder of the BLACK PANTHER party. Illiterate when he graduated from high school, Newton taught himself to read, enabling him to graduate from Merritt College in Oakland, California, and the San Francisco School of Law. It was in San Francisco that he met Bobby Seale, with whom he would create the Black Panther Party for Self-Defense, in 1966. They created the Black Panthers in response to several incidents of police brutality in Oakland, and as an extension of their militant desire to fight racism and promote self-reliance for blacks. By the late 1960s, the party had attracted over 2,000 members, many forming affiliated chapters in various cities around the country.

In 1967, Newton was arrested, tried, and convicted in the death of a police officer. He was released from prison in 1969, after his conviction was overturned. He then attempted to create a nonviolent credo for the Black Panthers, and in 1971 announced that the party would thereafter be dedicated to providing social services to the black community. (Opposition to this approach was publicly voiced by Eldridge CLEAVER, who continued to advocate violent revolution.) When Newton was charged with another murder in 1974, he fled the country to escape trial.

Newton lived in Cuba for three years, then returned to the United States. The two trials that followed resulted in hung juries. Newton thereupon continued his education, and in 1980 he was awarded a doctorate in social philosophy from the University of California at Santa Cruz after writing a dissertation entitled *War Against the Panthers*. By 1982, the Black Panther party had crumbled due to internal factionalism and outside pressures, especially from the government. (The organization had been targeted by the FBI's COINTELPRO operation for destabilization.) In March 1989, Newton was again arrested, this time for misappropriating public funds that had been intended for an Oakland school founded by the Black Panthers. In August 1989, he was gunned down on a street in Oakland.

Nitze, Paul (1907–   )

Paul Henry Nitze was a public official who proved to be highly influential in the design of U.S. foreign policy during the early years of the Cold War. A professor's son, the young Nitze went to Hotchkiss before graduating cum laude from Harvard University in 1928, after which he joined the New York investment banking firm of Dillon, Read & Co. His supervisor at that company was James Forrestal, who, in 1940, sent him a telegram instructing him to come to Washington immediately. Nitze went, and was put to work on a draft of the United States' first peacetime selective service act.

With the outbreak of World War II, Nitze served the government in a variety of capacities, including that of vice chairman of the Strategic Bombing Survey toward the end of the war. After the war, he was put to work on economic issues, and he was the first to suggest that the United States implement a program to aid war-ravaged Europe. (The initiative later took shape as the MARSHALL PLAN.) In 1949, Nitze became the deputy to George KENNAN on the Policy Planning Staff, eventually succeeding Kennan as director. In this capacity, he worked closely with Secretary of State Dean ACHESON to create a blueprint for the Truman administration's policy regarding the Cold War. The document that Nitze produced became known as NSC-68. In it, he advocated a build-up of U.S. military forces and urged a strategy of increased U.S. expenditures to counter the threat of military action by the Soviet Union. He also recommended the development of a hydrogen bomb.

Nitze left the Policy Planning Staff in 1953 to become president of the Foreign Service Education Foundation, but he continued to be involved in government service and Cold War policy planning. Under President John F. KENNEDY, Nitze served as assistant secretary of defense for international security affairs. He subsequently served as secretary of the navy (1963–67) and deputy secretary of defense (1967–69) under President Lyndon B. JOHNSON. He later served as a member of the U.S. delegation to the STRATEGIC ARMS LIMITATION TALKS (SALT, 1969–73) and also as chairman of the U.S. team to negotiate an arms control agreement (1981–84). From 1973 to 1976, he was the assistant secretary of defense for internal affairs. He oversaw the Intermediate-Range Nuclear Forces Treaty (INF) and was frequently called in to advise the government on matters of foreign policy. In the 1970s, Nitze publicly opposed the SALT II treaty, and warned against the possible consequence of DÉTENTE with the Soviets, whom he mistrusted. He also took part in the formation of the COMMITTEE ON THE PRESENT DANGER.

Nixon, Richard M. (1913–1994)

The 37th president of the United States, Richard Milhous Nixon was one of the most controversial and influential chief executives in U.S. history, and the first to resign the office. In 1934, Nixon graduated from Whittier College in Whittier, California, and went on to receive his law degree in 1937 from Duke University in Durham, North Carolina. He then returned to Whittier, where he entered into private law practice. Just prior to the outbreak of World War II, he went to Washington to work in the Office of Price Administration (OPA), and was left with a sense of disillusion-

President Richard M. Nixon (NIXON LIBRARY)

ment about government bureaucracy that would endure for decades to come. He left OPA to enlist in the navy, where, based in the Pacific region, he served as a noncombat aviation ground officer during the war.

On the suggestion of a friend, Nixon declared himself a candidate for the 1946 Republican nomination for Congress, and subsequently defeated the Democratic incumbent, Jerry VOORHIS. Key to Nixon's victory was his exploitation of public dissatisfaction with the shortages of meat and housing, as well as his ability to raise doubts in voters' minds about the patriotism of his opponent. (During the campaign, Nixon made the most of the fact that Voorhis had been endorsed by the Congress of Industrial Organizations' Political Action Committee, a group that had been charged with links to COMMUNISM.) Nixon was reelected to his House seat in 1948.

He attained national prominence as a member of the HOUSE COMMITTEE ON UN-AMERICAN ACTIVITIES, where he played a leading role in the investigation of former State Department official Alger HISS, who was eventually imprisoned for perjury. The Hiss case raised Nixon's national profile and established him as a fervent anticommunist. He was elected to the Senate in 1950 after a rugged campaign in which he accused his opponent, Helen Gahagan DOUGLAS, of harboring communist sympathies. During his first year in office, Nixon accused the TRUMAN administration of "barefaced appeasement" in Korea.

When he was 39, Senator Nixon was selected by Dwight D. EISENHOWER as his running mate for the 1952 presidential election; the move was meant to shore up support among younger voters as well as members of the party "old guard" who would react positively to Nixon's vigorous anticommunist stance. The young senator survived a scandal about political funds, thanks to an impressive televised speech (the so-called Checkers speech), and the Eisenhower/Nixon ticket was victorious in both 1952 and 1956.

Nixon was a highly visible and controversial vice president. He became famous for his handling of anti-U.S. demonstrations in South America in 1958, and for the impromptu "kitchen debate" he conducted in 1959 with Soviet leader Nikita Khrushchev at an exhibit of American-made home appliances in Moscow. In 1960, Nixon ran for president, but lost by an extremely narrow margin to John F. KENNEDY. He then returned to California, where he lost a 1962 bid for the governorship—and, during his concession speech, his poise. (His bitter speech, in which he said, "You won't have

Nixon to kick around anymore" was only the most obvious early sign of a poor relationship with members of the MEDIA—a problem that would follow him for much of his career.)

After the loss, Nixon announced his retirement from public service and moved to New York City to practice law. He then made a halfhearted attempt to secure the 1964 Republican nomination. After Barry GOLDWATER's drubbing at the hands of Lyndon JOHNSON in 1964, Nixon took advantage of an organizational vacuum within the Republican Party to lay the groundwork for his successful quest for the 1968 nomination. Unveiling a "new Nixon," the former vice president formed an alliance with two important forces: advertising and media management professionals who helped him to appeal to an American voting public reeling from the many social upheavals of 1968, and Southern Republicans who sought Nixon's assurance that he would endorse greater military spending and make Supreme Court appointments favorable to their social agenda.

Nixon's announcement that he had a "secret plan" to conclude the VIETNAM WAR honorably, and his emphasis on law and order issues during a year of violence, chaos, and division, led him to a narrow victory over Hubert HUMPHREY in the 1968 election. (Humphrey's Democratic Party was badly divided over the Vietnam War, and independent candidate George WALLACE had siphoned off many Southern votes, winning five states.) As he celebrated the victory, Nixon pledged to "bring the American people together."

Although he had promised a quick end to the war in Vietnam, Nixon could not keep his promise until 1973, when U.S. troops were gradually withdrawn and replaced by South Vietnamese soldiers who nonetheless required air support and economic aid from the United States. This policy of reducing the presence of American forces on foreign soil by providing a combination of military and economic assistance came to be known as the NIXON DOCTRINE.

At home in the United States, Nixon had difficulties dealing with the increasing level of social unrest, as well as with the high level of inflation. Despite his attempts to reduce government expenses, his annual budget mushroomed, becoming the largest in history. However, he achieved major foreign policy successes and vastly improved U.S. relations with both the USSR and China. He was lauded for signing an arms limitation treaty with the Soviets (SALT I) as well as an accord for bilateral trade and the initiation of an agreement to conduct joint scientific ventures on Earth and in space. He was also acclaimed for a visit to China in 1972 that paved the way for a new diplomatic relationship with that country. He was reelected in 1972, defeating George S. MCGOVERN in a landslide. His place in history as a statesman seemed to be secure, until revelations of the break-in at WATERGATE led to further revelations of various misdeeds and "DIRTY TRICKS" conducted by those working on his behalf. As successive members of his administration were indicted on criminal charges and public support eroded, Nixon found himself faced with certain impeachment. He resigned his office on August 8, 1974, and was succeeded by his vice president, Gerald FORD, on August 9. In September, Ford pardoned him for his role in the Watergate affair.

After Nixon's resignation, he retired to his estate in San Clemente, California, where he devoted himself to writing and publishing a number of books on political affairs. Although disbarred in New York

State, enmity against him faded enough over time to allow him to resume public appearances, to act as a foreign affairs consultant to sitting U.S. presidents, and to campaign for both the economic and political support of Russia and other former republics of the Soviet Union. By the time of his death in 1994, he had regained a certain respectability as an elder statesman of American politics.

Nixon Doctrine

Originally called the Guam Doctrine because it was delivered to reporters on Guam, the Nixon Doctrine was a pledge of continued U.S. nuclear and military support for countries in southeast Asia, including Japan, but with the caveat that those countries' own troops would fight any land wars. President Richard NIXON revealed the doctrine in July 1969, during a tour of the Far East, and noted that it would become effective after the VIETNAM WAR had reached its con-

Richard Nixon, elder statesman, poses with Presidents Reagan, Ford, and Carter at the funeral of Egyptian leader Anwar Sadat, 1981.
(REAGAN LIBRARY)

clusion. The policy did not nullify any existing treaties or pacts in the region, such as SEATO; it simply reaffirmed U.S. involvement in world affairs but eased the burden put on the United States by requiring foreign nations to supply their own conventional defense forces. In November 1969, Nixon made a public announcement of the doctrine and its principal conditions: "First, the United States will keep all of its treaty commitments. Second, we shall provide a shield if a nuclear power threatens the freedom of a nation allied with us or of a nation whose survival we consider vital to our security. Third, in cases involving other types of aggression, we shall furnish military and economic assistance when requested in accordance with our treaty commitments. But we shall look to the nation directly threatened to assume the primary responsibility of providing the manpower for its defense." The Nixon Doctrine was subsequently applied to justify military and economic aid to Iran.

nonviolence

Nonviolence was a commonly used tactic during the CIVIL RIGHTS MOVEMENT and ANTIWAR MOVEMENT in the 1960s; Martin Luther KING, Jr., was its chief proponent. Also called passive resistance (the form of protest favored by Mohandas Gandhi, whom King admired), nonviolence drew on principles of PACIFISM and the biblical instruction to "turn the other cheek" when marches and demonstrations were met with violent opposition. The use of nonviolence often had a dramatic impact, as it brought about desired, significant social change through peaceful means. This was especially true in the early 1960s, when King and his followers took pride in the black response to white violence against the civil rights movement. However, as the decade progressed and tensions rose, King's hopes of maintaining a policy of nonviolence were dashed in the wake of frightening confrontations between blacks and whites in the South, and impatience on the part of many African Americans that the movement was not bringing about change fast enough. This impatience resulted in the emergence of the BLACK PANTHERS and other black extremists who believed that only violent measures would result in an end to white oppression.

North, Oliver (1943–)

Oliver Laurence North, Jr., a key player in the IRAN-CONTRA AFFAIR, was a 1968 graduate of the U.S. Naval Academy who subsequently joined the Marine Corps and served a tour of duty in Vietnam. In 1981, he became a staff member of the NATIONAL SECURITY COUNCIL (NSC), eventually rising to the position of deputy director of political affairs. Under the instructions of the NSC's director, Robert McFarlane, and later his successor, Admiral John POINDEXTER, North initiated a plan to sell arms to the government of Iran, then use part of the profits to provide covert support to the Contra guerrillas in Nicaragua. (This was done as a way of circumventing a congressional ban on U.S. aid to the CONTRAS.) With the apparent approval of CENTRAL INTELLIGENCE AGENCY (CIA) director William CASEY, North began to create a larger operation designed to conceal illegal CIA activities.

When the Iran-Contra plan was discovered in 1986, North was dismissed from the NSC. In 1987, he testified before a congressional committee that his actions had been authorized by his superiors at the NSC, in particular William Casey. However, by this time Casey had died, and other North superiors denied his version of the events or confessed no knowledge of his actions. North was indicted by a federal grand jury in March 1988, on charges of conspiracy to defraud the government. On May 4 of that year, he was convicted on three counts, including those of obstructing Congress and destroying documents. A year later, in July 1989, he was sentenced to a three-year prison term that was suspended, a probationary period of two years, and 1,200 hours of community service, in addition to a fine of $150,000. In July 1990, the U.S. Court of Appeals in Washington, D.C., overturned one of North's convictions and suspended the other two, a decision that the U.S. Supreme Court eventually decided to let stand. All charges against North were subsequently dropped, in September 1991.

Considered by some to have been a "fall guy" in the Iran-Contra affair, North recovered sufficiently from his experience to achieve a certain public respectability. In 1994, he ran in Virginia as a Republican for the U.S. Senate, but failed to win the election.

North Atlantic Treaty Organization (NATO)

The North Atlantic Treaty Organization (NATO) was one of the most important organizations formed as a result of Cold War tensions. An outgrowth of the North Atlantic Treaty, NATO came into being in August 1949 as the first major postwar alliance to be approved by the U.S. Congress. Its original signatories were: Belgium, Canada, Denmark, France, Iceland, Italy, Luxembourg, the

Netherlands, Norway, Portugal, the United Kingdom, and the United States. Additional members since 1949 include West Germany (now Gerrnany), Greece, Turkey, and Spain. The treaty's basic precept was to provide security for Western European countries against the threat of Soviet expansion, thus making NATO an endorsement of the then-favored policy of CONTAINMENT.

NATO is administered by the North Atlantic Council, which oversees a military force of combined troops from participating nations. This force serves under the Supreme Allied Commander for Europe, who operates out of the Supreme Headquarters of the Allied Powers in Europe; the first commander, appointed in 1950, was Dwight D. EISENHOWER. In 1952, as a result of the newly established European Defense Community (later to become the West European Union), German troops were added to NATO's forces, creating a lively controversy for a time. By 1954, however, NATO was having problems recruiting troops, and so began acquiring nuclear weapons to give it some tactical protection. The organization was also influenced by the idea (favored by Eisenhower) of MASSIVE RETALIATION. Originally headquartered in Paris, NATO moved to Brussels in 1966, at which time French president Charles de Gaulle removed French troops from the organization in a quest to become more politically independent.

The United States remains a key participant in NATO and maintains close to 300,000 troops in the organization. Since its inception, problems have existed regarding how to share the financial burden posed by NATO's programs and obligations, an issue that reached a crisis point in the late 1980s, when member nations were also concerned about the U.S. commitment to the organization's goals in view of the Cold War's approaching end.

NSC-68   See NATIONAL SECURITY COUNCIL.

Nuclear Regulatory Commission (NRC)

The Nuclear Regulatory Commission (NRC), formerly the ATOMIC ENERGY COMMISSION, is an independent agency established in October 1974, at the direction of President Gerald FORD. The NRC's primary responsibilities are the licensing and regulation of the use of nuclear energy for civilian purposes, as well as ensuring public health and environmental safety. Additionally, the NRC oversees the possession and disposal of nuclear materials. Most of the commission's duties revolve around nuclear power as it is used to generate electricity. The NRC is headquartered in Bethesda, Maryland, and maintains five regional offices throughout the United States. Although independent of the U.S. government, the NRC's commissioners are appointed by the president.

nuclear trigger

A nuclear trigger is any means by which a nuclear war may be launched suddenly. The phrase was used by Ted SORENSEN in reference to President John KENNEDY's status as "the custodian of the trigger." Its antecedents, however, are found in the early days of the Cold War, when public fears and debate over the possible outbreak of nuclear war led many to wonder whose finger was on "the button," which, if pressed, would lead to annihilation. President Dwight EISENHOWER had publicly commented on the strains placed on the person responsible for the nuclear trigger, noting that emotions and stress can result in regrettable actions. As a result, presidential candidates have often had to prove that they are sensible and responsible guardians of the nuclear trigger. Barry GOLDWATER, a war HAWK, was generally regarded as "trigger-happy" during his 1964 campaign for president, a fact that his opponent, Lyndon JOHNSON, exploited to chilling effect in a famous ad depicting a nuclear countdown as a little girl pulled petals off a daisy. (He subsequently defeated Goldwater in a landslide.) Jimmy CARTER later tried to use the same charge against Ronald REAGAN, but Reagan convinced voters that he would take care not to push the nuclear button (even as he built up U.S. nuclear arms, including the controversial STRATEGIC DEFENSE INITIATIVE).

Office of Strategic Services (OSS)

The Office of Strategic Services (OSS) was an intelligence-gathering agency that operated during World War II; it is considered to be the precursor of today's CENTRAL INTELLIGENCE AGENCY (CIA). Major General William J. Donovan headed the OSS, which provided information about conditions behind enemy lines, in addition to providing contact with and support for anti-Axis resistance movements. Although it was chiefly concerned with wartime intelligence, the OSS anticipated the Cold War in its reports regarding not just U.S. enemies, but also its allies, chief among them the Soviet Union. In 1945, President Harry TRUMAN received a report warning that "Russia will emerge from the present conflict as by far the strongest nation in Europe and Asia, strong enough to dominate Europe and at the same time establish her hegemony over Asia." The report went on to note that Russia might exceed the United States in military strength, a point of real concern to top officials in the administration and backed up by such experts as Averell HARRIMAN. The OSS was disbanded on October 1, 1945, but the necessity of continuing its functions became readily apparent to administration officials. In 1947, the CIA came into being, its core formed by operatives and intelligence experts from the OSS.

Operation Phoenix   See COLBY, William.

Oppenheimer, J. Robert (1904–1967)

Renowned physicist and science administrator Julius Robert Oppenheimer, known popularly as the father of the ATOMIC BOMB, gained notoriety when he was stripped of his security clearance as a government

J. Robert Oppenheimer (NARA STILL PHOTOS DIVISION)

adviser and suffered accusations questioning his loyalty. Oppenheimer was the son of a wealthy German-immigrant textile importer. An outstanding student who spent part of his youth in a boarding school in Los Alamos, New Mexico, Oppenheimer attended Harvard University, where he shone in the sciences as well as in languages, literature, and Oriental philosophy. He graduated in 1925 and went to Europe to pursue graduate studies, first at the University of Cambridge Cavendish Laboratory (England), then at Göttingen University in Germany. It was here that he met physicists Niels Bohr and Paul Dirac and collaborated with Max Born on a molecular quantum theory, the "Born-Oppenheimer Method" (1926). He received his Ph.D. from Göttingen in 1927, made short scientific visits to laboratories in Leiden and Zurich, then returned to the United States, where he became a teacher of theoretical physics at both the University of California at Berkeley and California Institute of Technology. He also conducted his own research into atomic structure, particularly quantum theory and the processes of electrons, positrons, and cosmic rays.

In the mid-1930s, Oppenheimer became interested in politics. His support of the republic during the Spanish Civil War of 1936 introduced him to COMMUNISM, which he later renounced after learning of Stalin's persecution of Russian scientists. Meanwhile, his father's death in 1937 provided a large inheritance that he used to support antifascist organizations. When Germany invaded Poland in 1939, fears (prompted by warnings from Albert Einstein, among others) began to arise within the U.S. government that the Nazis were developing an atomic bomb. In August 1942, the U.S. Army was given supervision of a project to develop an atomic bomb for military purposes, using the combined resources of American and British scientists; it became known as the "Manhattan Project." As an expert in atomic structure and research who had begun to find a way to separate uranium-235 from natural uranium, Oppenheimer was given the task of heading the scientific aspects of the project. He established a laboratory for this purpose in Los Alamos, New Mexico, in 1943. Two years later, after intensive work by a brilliant team of scientists, the first nuclear bomb was tested at Alamogordo, New Mexico on July 16, 1945. Later that year, a few months after the bombing of Hiroshima and Nagasaki, Oppenheimer resigned from his post.

In 1947, Oppenheimer became the head of the Institute for Advanced Study at Princeton University.

That same year, he was also appointed to chair the General Advisory Committee of the ATOMIC ENERGY COMMISSION (AEC). In this capacity, he worked to establish international nuclear power regulations in order to ensure peace and stability in the postwar world. In 1949, his committee voted against the development of the HYDROGEN BOMB. He stepped down as chairman in 1952, but remained as an adviser to the AEC.

Late in 1953, Oppenheimer was made aware of a military security report that accused him of associating with communists and delaying the naming of Soviet agents in 1942 (an incident that resulted in the dismissal of a friend from the faculty of the University of California). The report also noted his opposition to the hydrogen bomb. He was subjected to a security hearing in which he was cleared of treason charges, but declared a security risk who should be denied access to military secrets. The resulting furor in the scientific world set off a debate on the relationship between science and society, as well as the moral and political difficulties presented by profound scientific achievements. Oppenheimer was defended vigorously by the Federation of American Scientists, and many felt he had been victimized by the WITCH HUNTS of the McCarthy era. Oppenheimer returned to his duties at Princeton, retiring just a year before his death. With the decline of the Cold War in the 1960s, President Lyndon B. JOHNSON restored Oppenheimer to governmental favor by presenting him with the Enrico Fermi Award of the AEC. Oppenheimer is credited with having trained and influenced an entire generation of outstanding American physicists.

Organization of American States (OAS)

The Organization of American States (OAS) is an alliance of Western Hemisphere countries, collectively dedicated to preserving peace and security on the American continents. The organization was founded in 1948, with its principles and plans for inter-American defense incorporated into the UNITED NATIONS charter. Since that time, the OAS has worked to resolve numerous disputes among its member nations, playing a role in the settlement of the 1965 DOMINICAN CRISIS and in the resolution of the 1982 Falkland Islands War. The OAS has 31 active members (not including Cuba, which was suspended from the organization in 1962) and 20 members whose status is "permanent observer." There are numerous economic, social, and cultural agencies that act under OAS auspices, and the organization also sponsors the Inter-American Conference, which meets every five years.

The United States participates in the OAS as part of its declared "good neighbor" policy of nonintervention unless U.S. interests or safety are threatened. Nevertheless, strained relations have often existed between the organization and the world superpower, as exemplified in the U.S. invasion of Grenada.

Oswald, Lee Harvey (1939–1963)

The accused assassin of President John F. KENNEDY, Lee Harvey Oswald was himself shot by Jack Ruby two days after the president's murder. Oswald's troubled youth was marked by numerous stepfathers and repeated moves around the country. He dropped out of high school in October 1956 and enrolled in the Marine Corps, where he became a sharpshooter. An indifferent soldier, Oswald requested his release from the marines in September 1959, pleading hardship. Nine days after his discharge, he renounced his U.S. citizenship and immigrated to the Soviet Union, where he unsuccessfully applied for citizenship but was assigned to work in Minsk. There he met and married his wife, Marina, with whom he had a daughter.

In June 1962, Oswald and his family returned to the United States, moving to Dallas, Texas. Several months later, in early 1963, he bought via mail order a .38-caliber revolver and a rifle with a telescopic sight. After allegedly shooting at former U.S. Army general Edwin A. Walker in April, he went to New Orleans, where he passed out pro-Castro leaflets on the city streets and established the Fair Play for Cuba Committee. (Oswald was the committee's sole member.) He subsequently traveled to Mexico City in a failed attempt to gain permission to return to the Soviet Union and to obtain a visa for travel to Cuba. In October 1963, he returned to his family in Dallas and got a job working at the Texas School Book Depository. It was from the sixth floor of this building on November 22, 1963, that Oswald used his rifle to shoot and kill President Kennedy, who was riding in an open car in a motorcade. His shots also wounded Governor John B. Connally of Texas. Forty-five minutes later, Oswald was stopped by a Dallas policeman, J. D. Tippitt, whom Oswald killed with his revolver. Half an hour after that, he was spotted in the Texas Theater, where he was arrested and taken into custody. In the early morning hours of November 23, he was formally arraigned for Kennedy's assassination. The next morning, as he was being transferred from a jail cell, he was approached and shot by Jack Ruby, a Dallas nightclub owner, who presumably acted out of anguish over the president's death.

Late in November 1963, a special President's Commission on the Assassination of President John F. Kennedy was established to investigate the murder and determine whether Oswald had acted alone. Led by Chief Justice Earl Warren, the team concluded its investigations in September 1964, and determined that Oswald had indeed been the lone assassin. However, a committee of the U.S. House of Representatives determined in January 1979 that there may have been a conspiracy and that a second assassin may have been present on the scene in Dallas. Whatever the truth may be, the fact remains that Oswald altered the course of history by assassinating a young and popular president who may have led the country to a different outcome in the Cold War.

pacification

Pacification is a word of double meaning. On the one hand, it conveys a sense of peace; those who seek pacification are looking to bring about agreement or entente; those who advocate APPEASEMENT are pacifiers. On the other hand, pacification conveys a sense of force; peace is achieved by ridding an area of guerrillas or terrorists, using either military or psychological measures to bring about the desired change. In the context of the Cold War, pacification usually denotes the latter. Pacification is, in essence, a system of persuasion that enables political leaders to impose a policy on a nation or region that ensures their own concept of peace and stability. This policy was applied especially during the VIETNAM WAR, in an effort to justify U.S. military intervention to root out and, hopefully, banish the guerrilla troops of the Vietcong. In later years, another euphemism, "peacekeeping," was substituted for pacification.

pacifism

Equivalent to the philosophy of NONVIOLENCE, pacifism is the practice of peaceful opposition to war or violence and the refusal to participate in military activities due to moral objections. Most CONSCIENTIOUS OBJECTORS are pacifists due to their religious upbringing or finely honed personal beliefs. In the 20th century, the concept of pacifism has grown from that practiced by individuals to encompass movements for social justice, such as the programs of passive resistance espoused by Mohandas Gandhi and Martin Luther KING, Jr. In recent years, many pacifists have centered their attention on nuclear weapons and the desire to eliminate all instruments of mass destruction.

Patton, George S. (1885–1945)

George Smith Patton was a flamboyant and frequently controversial general of the U.S. Army whose reputation for discipline and outstanding military strategic abilities earned him the nickname "Old Blood-and-Guts." Patton came from a Virginia family with strong military roots; in keeping with the family tradition, he attended the U.S. Military Academy at West Point, from which he graduated in 1909. Among the many accomplishments of his impressive career, he took part in the 1912 Olympic Games, placing fifth in the military pentathlon.

General George S. Patton stands at attention, flanked by General Dwight D. Eisenhower and President Harry S. Truman. (TRUMAN LIBRARY)

In 1916, Patton served as an aide to General John Pershing in Mexico, then accompanied Pershing to France in 1917, when the United States entered World War I. There he fought with the U.S. Tank Corps, an experience that, in combination with his profound knowledge of U.S. Civil War history, provided him with an appreciation of and support for the concept of a highly mobile force capable of making bold strikes against the enemy. After experiencing success in commanding a tank brigade, he became convinced that tanks were the military weapons of the future. He put his theories to good use during World War II, starting as commander of the Second Armored Division and subsequently becoming commanding general of the I Armored Corps. He directed the North African campaign of 1942, then led the Seventh Army in a successful drive across Sicily, resulting in the capture of Palermo in 1943. In the summer of 1944, he boldly disregarded conventional rules of military warfare and pushed the Third Army through northern France, capturing numerous cities and playing a key role in the Battle of the Bulge (December 1944). His

forces penetrated the German frontier in January 1945, and proceeded to sweep through the northern region of Germany, forcing the surrender of thousands of enemy soldiers. Meanwhile, his often unorthodox military strategies, combined with the harsh discipline he enforced within his troops, often brought him under personal attack. In August 1943, he verbally abused two hospitalized soldiers, one of whom (a sufferer of combat fatigue) he slapped. He later apologized publicly for the incident, but it nearly cost him his career.

Considered to be the most successful field commander of all time, Patton did not demonstrate a similar adeptness in the political world. At the war's conclusion, he promoted a strong anticommunist stance, and suggested that high-ranking Nazis be kept in administrative posts to enable a military alliance of the Allies and Germany against the Soviet Union. This unpopular position resulted in his being removed from the command of the Third Army in October 1945. In December 1945, he was struck by a car; he died shortly thereafter in a hospital in Heidelberg. His memoirs, *War As I Knew It,* were published in 1947.

Pauling, Linus (1901–1994)

A renowned chemist, pacifist, and activist for the control of nuclear testing, Linus Carl Pauling distinguished himself by earning two Nobel Prizes, one for his scientific achievements and one for his efforts in promoting peace. Pauling was born in Oregon and attended what was then called the Oregon State Agricultural College in Corvallis (now Oregon State University), where he received his B.S. degree in chemical engineering in 1922. He went on to graduate work at the California Institute of Technology (Caltech), obtaining his doctorate from that institution in 1925. From there Pauling pursued postdoctoral studies in Europe, working with some of the preeminent scientists of the time, including Niels Bohr.

In 1927, Pauling returned to Caltech to teach chemistry, rising from assistant professor to full professor in just four years. Over time, he expanded his scientific research into the field of biochemistry. In 1936, he was appointed director of the Gates and Crellin Laboratories of Chemistry, a position he held until 1958. During World War II, he worked (as a civilian) with the Office of Scientific Research and Development. In 1954, he received the first of his Nobel prizes, awarded for his achievements in chemistry and particularly for his groundbreaking work in applying the principles of quantum mechanics to the structure of molecules. His introduction of the concept of "resonance hybrids" came under sharp attack from communist scientists in the Soviet Union, who viewed the idea as illogical. However, Pauling's theory prevailed.

Throughout his career, Pauling applied a conjectural method to his work, combining an exhaustive knowledge of chemistry with an intuitive approach that led to a number of scientific breakthroughs with other leading investigators. With the increasing development of atomic weapons in the United States and Russia, Pauling began to fret about the consequences of nuclear testing, particularly human exposure to the radiation it produced and the possible genetic damage it could cause. In 1952, he was denied a passport after Senator Joseph MCCARTHY denounced him for being procommunist. Nevertheless, Pauling continued his work against nuclear proliferation. In 1957, he circulated a petition among fellow scientists around the world to urge an end to the testing of nuclear weapons. It was presented to the United Nations in January 1958, with 11,021 signatures. That same year, he published *No More War!* In the early 1960s, Pauling worked on behalf of the Partial Nuclear Test Ban Treaty, for which he was awarded the 1962 Nobel Prize for peace; he received the award on October 10, 1963, the day that treaty provisions banning U.S. and Soviet nuclear testing were put into effect.

Pauling left the California Institute of Technology in 1963 to work at the Center for the Study of Democratic Institutions in Santa Barbara, California. There he applied himself to studying the problems inherent in both war and peace. In 1967, he joined the faculty of the University of California at San Diego, but resigned two years later in protest against the educational policies of Ronald REAGAN, then governor of California. Pauling subsequently went to Stanford University as a professor in chemistry, becoming professor emeritus in 1974. By this time he had also become interested in the effect of massive doses of vitamins and minerals, particularly vitamin C, in the prevention and treatment of illness. He wrote several books about vitamin C and its use in nutrition therapy, which caused a stir in medical and scientific circles for his unorthodox and sometimes controversial views. Following his retirement from Stanford, he created the Linus Pauling Institute of Science and Medicine, where he was a professor until his death.

Peace Corps

The Peace Corps was one of the most famous programs to come out of the administration of President John F. KENNEDY. Emphasizing the more idealistic aims of the NEW LEFT to bring about change in the world through peaceful rather than militaristic efforts, the Peace Corps grew from an idea to provide government-sponsored technical assistance to THIRD WORLD countries. Hubert H. HUMPHREY originally conceived the idea and proposed it to Kennedy, who subsequently tested it with audiences during his presidential campaign and, receiving a positive reaction, made it one of the goals of his new administration. However, General James Gavin is given credit for formulating many of the program's basic tenets and laying the actual groundwork for its implementation. The plan was based on religious principles of helping one's neighbors; volunteers were (and still are) sent to developing countries to perform works of social and economic assistance, helping communities primarily in the areas of education, nutrition, health, and agriculture, and secondarily in such fields as construction, trade, banking, and tourism. The Peace Corps assistance involves hands-on training, rather than material assistance. It is for this reason that the corps relies on skilled volunteers willing to share their expertise.

The Peace Corps was established by executive order on March 1, 1961. In September 1961, Congress provided authorization and funding for the program with its passage of the Peace Corps Act. Kennedy's brother-in-law, Sargent Shriver, was appointed first director of the Peace Corps, and an initial force of 900 volunteers was recruited to serve in 16 countries. By the early 1990s, the corps had over 6,200 volunteers situated in 94 countries around the world. The only requirement for becoming a Peace Corps volunteer is a minimum age of 18; otherwise, anybody of any age, sex, race, or religion can enlist for service. The normal tour of duty is two years. Since its creation, the Peace Corps has remained faithful to its original intention and has provided the United States with a positive image of genuine altruism as opposed to one of selfish interventionism. Many former volunteers have gone on to a life in public service, and many more continue to perform volunteer work within the United States. The Peace Corps proved to be so successful that many other nations went on to establish similar programs.

President Kennedy greets Peace Corps volunteers. (KENNEDY LIBRARY)

peace movement   See ANTIWAR MOVEMENT.

peaceful coexistence

The definition of "peaceful coexistence" varies, depending on who defines it. The catchphrase emerged first in the Soviet Union during the 1920s, when Vladimir Lenin used it to describe desired Soviet relations with the rest of the world. At first, it conveyed the idea of a state of peace; over time, however, the meaning shifted to signify the triumph of COMMUNISM over capitalism, a concept that was emphasized by Soviet premier Nikita Khrushchev in the late 1950s when he described it as "a form of intense economic, political, and ideological struggle of the proletariat against the aggressive forces of imperialism in the international arena." This conflicted with a 1961 statement from the Communist Party program that declared, "War cannot and must not serve as a means of settling international disputes . . . The policy of peaceful coexistence is in accord with the vital interests of all mankind, except the big monopolymagnates and the militarists." Because of this seeming contradiction, many U.S. politicians wondered just what the Soviet Union really meant at any given time by "peaceful coexistence," and, distrusting it for the public relations ploy it probably was, rarely used the phrase. Some even attempted to debunk it; George KENNAN, for example, was a prominent critic who cited numerous instances of Soviet actions that he felt declared a quest for world domination rather than a true, literal peaceful coexistence. Nevertheless, the phrase continued to have its defenders in the United States, among them Adlai STEVENSON, who felt that the ideal of peaceful coexistence was far preferable to the grim possibility of "coextinction." However, most critics stressed that it could be no more than an ideal; for peaceful coexistence to succeed, all countries must be willing to adapt and compromise, an unrealistic hope when two or more political ideologies are at stake.

Pearson, Drew (1897–1969)

Andrew Russell Pearson was a muckraking journalist who eventually became one of the most well-known columnists in modern U.S. history. Pearson's father was a Quaker and onetime governor of the U.S. Virgin Islands who sent his son to the prestigious Phillips Exeter Academy in New Hampshire. In 1919, Pearson graduated Phi Beta Kappa from Swarthmore College in Pennsylvania. He traveled through Europe, where he became involved in postwar relief activities, serving with the American Friends Service Committee in the Balkans, and subsequently with the British Red Cross. Upon his return to the United States, he settled down to a position teaching industrial geography at the University of Pennsylvania, but quit after three years in order to become a journalist.

As an interviewer of top personalities of the time and reporter of major events, Pearson covered a wide area, including the 1925 strikes against foreigners in China and the 1927 Naval Conference in Geneva. From 1926 to 1933, he wrote for the *United States Daily,* also going to work for the *Baltimore Sun* in 1929. In 1931, a book entitled *Washington Merry-Go-Round* was published anonymously. A gossip-filled exposé of life and politics in the District of Columbia, it created a sensation. When Pearson and fellow reporter Robert S. Allen were revealed to be the book's authors, they were fired from the *Sun.* However, they received an immediate invitation to write a syndicated column together. "Washington Merry-Go-Round" first appeared in 1932, and it paved the way for subsequent similar columns. Ten years later, in 1942, the two collaborators parted company when Allen enlisted in the war effort; Pearson retained sole control of their column. He also conducted a popular radio show.

After the publication of John F. KENNEDY's book *Profiles in Courage,* Pearson charged that the Pulitzer Prize-winning volume had been ghostwritten by Kennedy aide and counsel Theodore SORENSEN. However, it was later proven that Sorensen had done only

the biographical research on the book, and that Kennedy had in fact done the writing himself. Pearson finally withdrew his charges. With this exception, he remained an influential reporter, who achieved distinction for his interviews of world leaders and landed a major scoop in his talks with Soviet premier Nikita Khrushchev. Pearson later wrote a book entitled *Will Khrushchev Bury Us?* (1962).

In 1947, Pearson hired Jack ANDERSON as a reporter, making the younger man his partner in 1965. After Pearson's death in 1969, Anderson inherited "Washington Merry-Go-Round." In 1974, *Drew Pearson's Diaries: 1949–1959* was published.

Pentagon Papers

The publication of the Pentagon Papers was one of the most notorious events connected with the movement against the war in Vietnam. In the late 1960s, a Defense Department analyst, Daniel J. ELLSBERG (who had previously done intelligence work in Vietnam), was assigned to work on a study entitled "A History of the Decision-Making Process on Vietnam Policy." The resulting 47-volume report was sensational, detailing innumerable lies that had been told to the American public and to Congress in order to generate continued support for the war, and citing officials in the JOHNSON administration and the Pentagon as the primary prevaricators. The Pentagon wasted no time in classifying the report as top secret. By this time, however, Ellsberg had become disgusted with American policy in Vietnam and aligned himself firmly on the side of antiwar protesters. Covertly, he released copies of the report to the *New York Times,* which began to publish them as the "Pentagon Papers" on June 13, 1971. The *Washington Post* soon followed suit, and also began to publish sections of the classified documents. Consequently, United States Attorney General John MITCHELL resorted to legal steps to prevent further publication. Injunctions were at first successful; however, the U.S. Supreme Court eventually ruled that the American public had a right to know, and allowed newspapers to continue printing the Pentagon Papers.

President Richard NIXON, fearing that the Pentagon Papers' publication had seriously damaged his reelection chances (despite the fact that the worst of its revelations related to previous administrations), ordered wiretaps and investigations to find out who was responsible for the leak. Ellsberg soon stepped forward voluntarily. Subsequently, he was indicted under the

Espionage Act for theft, violation, and conspiracy, among other charges, all of which were dropped in 1973 when details of the WATERGATE scandal began to emerge in the press and it was revealed that Ellsberg had been secretly targeted by White House officials for prosecution.

Among the many scandalous disclosures to come out of the Pentagon Papers was the information that the Tonkin Gulf Resolution had been drafted months before the 1964 incident that had presumably provoked it. However, the papers' most lasting legacy was that it ignited the events that led directly to Watergate and to Nixon's downfall as president. See also TONKIN GULF INCIDENTS AND RESOLUTION.

perestroika   See GLASNOST.

Persian Gulf War   See BUSH, George.

Philbrick, Herbert (1915–1993)

Herbert Arthur Philbrick was an agent of the Federal Bureau of Investigation (FBI) specializing in counterintelligence who conducted a nine-year espionage campaign against the U.S. Communist Party during the 1940s. Philbrick attended the Lincoln Technical Institute of Northeastern University in Boston, where he studied engineering. He subsequently began his career as an advertising salesman. It was in this capacity that he first encountered the Massachusetts Youth Council. He became sufficiently interested in the council's work to assist in the establishment of a subsidiary organization, the Cambridge Youth Council, in Cambridge; he subsequently became the nominal leader of that organization. However, he began to realize over time that the organization was actually a cover for the Communist Party. After reporting his suspicions to the FBI, Philbrick was asked to go undercover to compile evidence against the communists. He complied with this request, and began his work in 1940.

The Cambridge Youth Council, a pacifist organization, collapsed after with Hitler's attack on Russia in June 1941, as did other pacifist communist organizations. However, Philbrick's communist connections asked him to join the Young Communist League, which he did. After a period of indoctrination, he went to work for the communists, and when he moved to Wakefield, Massachusetts, he was ordered to build up the communist cell in that town. He gradually moved up in the communist organization, and by 1944 he had joined the Communist Party. Philbrick was recruited to act as a counterspy to detect traitors in the organization, a job he performed with such lukewarm results that the responsibility was eventually taken away from him.

Over the course of nine years, Philbrick observed and wrote about numerous misdeeds and violations of U.S. law perpetrated by his associates in the Communist Party and the Professional Group of the Communist Party. Finally, in 1949, 11 communist leaders were arrested and indicted on charges of conspiracy against the U.S. government. In April of that year, Philbrick created a sensation when he testified against the communist leaders. Although the defense tried to discredit him, Philbrick could not be shaken, and his testimony avowing the revolutionary intent of the communists in the United States was hugely instrumental in convicting the communist leaders.

After the trial was over, Philbrick returned to the work he had always maintained in sales and advertising. In 1951, he wrote a series of articles about his experiences that eventually became the 1952 bestseller, *I Led Three Lives*.

"Ping-Pong" diplomacy

In the early 1970s, relations between the United States and the People's Republic of China began to show signs of easing. The potential for establishing diplomatic relations became more of a reality in April 1971, when an American table tennis (Ping-Pong) team was unexpectedly invited to play and tour in China. This paved the way for President Richard NIXON's historic visit to the communist country in February 1972; the negotiations that led up to Nixon's trip came to be known as "Ping-Pong diplomacy," in tribute to the event that had initiated the proceedings. Although U.S.-China relations improved markedly, it would be many years later before Chinese-American interactions could be called "normalized."

pinko

Pinko was a label attached to anybody whose political views were extremely leftist; most often it was used against suspected communists, but it could be applied to any liberal in a disparaging manner by conservatives on the attack. The term was especially prevalent during the MCCARTHY era of the 1950s, when one's reputation could be ruined simply by being called a pinko. Pejorative use of the word has continued in the 1990s, but with the end of the Cold War, it carries less weight and is most likely to be used by members of the NEW RIGHT.

Plowshares movement

The Plowshares movement consists of a group of antiwar and antinuclear activists, most notably Daniel and Philip BERRIGAN, that takes its name from a biblical passage (Isaiah 2:4): ". . . and they shall beat their swords into plowshares, and their spears into pruning hooks; nations shall not lift up sword against nation, neither shall they learn war anymore." Plowshares members are primarily nuns, priests, teachers, and other professionals, mostly Catholics, who have frequently gone to extraordinary measures to register their message for peace in the American conscience and protest the activities of defense contractors. In September 1980, eight members of the Plowshares movement, including the Berrigan brothers, entered a room at the General Electric plant in King of Prussia, Pennsylvania, where they pounded on warhead nose cones with hammers, shredded blueprint plans, and poured vials of blood all over the room. They were quickly arrested, tried, and found guilty for their actions. In recent years, the Plowshares movement has focused on the battle to eliminate nuclear arms and to point out American governmental culpability in the buildup of destructive nuclear forces, despite its presumed commitment to arms reductions.

plumbers

After the release of the PENTAGON PAPERS in 1971, officials in the NIXON White House saw a need to plug the holes that were leaking secret information to the American public. From this need emerged the select group of men who became known as the "plumbers." Finding ways to prevent or plug leaks has been a concern of every presidential administration, but Nixon's group was to acquire a reputation for both insidiousness and bungling that would make the term "plumbers" a familiar part of the American political lexicon in the wake of the WATERGATE revelations. The plumbers operated under the auspices of the Special Investigations Unit headed by Egil Krogh, Jr., and David Young. The chief plumbers, however, were E. Howard Hunt

and G. Gordon LIDDY, whose initial goal was to investigate and discredit Daniel ELLSBERG, the man responsible for leaking the Pentagon Papers to the news MEDIA. In addition to using illegal wiretaps, the two broke into the office of Dr. Lewis J. Fielding, Ellsberg's psychiatrist, hoping to find information that could be used against Ellsberg. Their activities eventually expanded to include surveillance of Democratic presidential candidates. However, their lack of success was evident in their bungled hiring of Cuban operatives (who had previously participated in the BAY OF PIGS INVASION) to place wiretaps in the Democratic Party campaign headquarters located at the Watergate apartment complex in Washington. This operation was discovered accidentally and subsequently reported in the papers, setting off a chain of events that led to Nixon's resignation from the presidency.

Podhoretz, Norman (1930–)

Author, editor, and literary critic, Norman Podhoretz has been acclaimed for his direction of *Commentary*, an intellectual journal for modern Jewish opinion. Born in New York City, he attended the Jewish Theological Seminary and Columbia College simultaneously, receiving his B.H.L. and B.A. degrees in 1950. While at Columbia, he became a student of Lionel Trilling, who influenced him to such a degree that he began his career as a literary critic and promoted the idea of a post-Marxist radicalism. He went on to Cambridge University, where he earned a B.A. degree in 1952 and an M.A. degree in 1957. In 1955, he was hired as an assistant editor at *Commentary*. When he became editor in chief in 1960, he shifted the journal's editorial focus to the left, espousing many liberal causes of the New York Jewish intellectual world. However, he later came to distrust the power exerted by intellectuals on the social, political, and moral fabric of the country, and expressed his doubts in two autobiographies—*Making It* (1968) and *Breaking Ranks* (1979). By the late 1970s, he had abandoned Trilling's ideas entirely and broken away from democratic socialism to become firmly entrenched in the neoconservative movement of the right. *Commentary's* editorial policy followed suit, and the journal was used freely to strike out against his former friends and allies of the NEW LEFT, including his former mentor, Trilling.

Podhoretz continued to take part in American political debate with the publication of such books as *With the Present Danger* (1980) and *The Bloody Crossroads:*

Where Literature and Politics Meet (1986). He was a strong supporter of President Ronald REAGAN's military build-up and drive against communism. In later years, he became critical of the peace process in Israel. In January 1995, after more than three decades at the helm, he retired as *Commentary's* editor in chief, but continued to write. He is currently at work on the third volume of his autobiography.

Poindexter, John (1936–)

John Marlan Poindexter is a former vice admiral and national security advisor (under President Ronald REAGAN) who became embroiled in controversy as a result of his role in the IRAN-CONTRA AFFAIR. After high school, he enrolled in the U.S. Naval Academy and graduated in 1958 at the top of his class. He later obtained a Ph.D. degree in nuclear physics from the California Institute of Technology. Throughout his years in the navy, he was posted to several overseas locations, where he engaged in active duty. In 1971, he became an aide to the secretary of the navy and subsequently to the chief of naval operations. From 1978 to 1981, he was the deputy chief who oversaw education and training in the navy. He was appointed to the NATIONAL SECURITY COUNCIL in 1981, serving as National Security Advisor Richard ALLEN's assistant. In this capacity, he played an important role in the 1983 U.S. invasion of the Caribbean island of GRENADA, which was conducted ostensibly to protect U.S. citizens there after a coup by pro-Cuban marxists. (The operation not only overthrew the leftist government, it also restored President Reagan to public favor after a downward slide in the polls.)

In December 1985, after some promotion through the ranks, Poindexter was selected to be Robert Mac-Farlane's successor as national security advisor. In this role, he was a strong proponent of using military force to achieve diplomatic objectives. He was therefore in favor of a secret plan to sell U.S. weaponry to the government of Iran as part of the negotiations to release American hostages then being held by Iranian terrorists, and using the profits from the arms sales to support the CONTRAS, guerrilla insurgents in Nicaragua. When news of this covert operation became public knowledge, Poindexter resigned his position on November 25, 1986. The following July, he testified before investigating committees in the Senate and U.S. House of Representatives that he had approved the diversion of funds to the Contras but had not informed President Reagan that he had done so.

Upon leaving the White House, Poindexter was demoted from vice admiral to rear admiral. Publicly and privately, he defended his actions during the Iran-Contra Affair and declared that he had no regrets about what he had done. In March 1990, he was indicted for conspiracy and obstruction of Congress, among other charges. He was tried and found guilty on all counts the next month, and sentenced to six months in prison. In November 1991, a federal appeals court panel overturned his conviction.

Point Four program

Point Four, also known as the Technical Cooperation Administration, was a U.S.-designed program designed to provide industrial, economic, educational, health, and agricultural assistance to countries in Latin America; the name was derived from the fourth point in President Harry TRUMAN's inaugural address of 1949. The program itself was enacted on June 5, 1950, by means of the International Development Act, and administered by a unit of the State Department. Truman's original hope was to effect a multilateral plan in partnership with private businesses that would provide investment capital and share American skills and know-how with developing nations. The end result would be mutually beneficial relations with the added benefit of ensuring peace and stability through means other than military power. Point Four started out successfully, and within the next 10 years, 58 countries benefited from the assistance of over 6,000 U.S. technicians. Nevertheless, the program never quite achieved the ambition of its original goals, and under President Dwight D. EISENHOWER, it was absorbed into other foreign aid programs.

police action

When is a war not a war? When it is a "police action," as was the case in the KOREAN WAR. In diplomatic terms, *police action* refers to a military conflict regulated by the United Nations. The United States was able to intervene in Korea by means of a UNITED NATIONS Security Council resolution that allowed combined UN military forces (including American troops) to enter the country for the purpose of suppressing what President Harry TRUMAN referred to as a "bandit raid." As this was the announced purpose of the intervention, no declaration of war was ever made, nor was it ever admitted that military forces were in fact engaged in an act of war. Reporters picked up on the phrase *police action,* and thereafter it was used

At the opening session of the Potsdam Conference, U.S. president Harry Truman (foreground) meets with Soviet prime minister Joseph Stalin (right) and British prime minister Winston Churchill (upper left). (TRUMAN LIBRARY)

as an ironic comment on any open conflict that was not, technically, a war.

Potsdam Conference (1945)

The Potsdam Conference was the last major meeting of the leaders of the three major World War II Allies: the United States, represented by President Harry TRUMAN and Secretary of State James F. BYRNES the Soviet Union, represented by Premier Joseph Stalin and Foreign Minister V. M. Molotov; and Great Britain, represented initially by Prime Minister Winston Churchill and Foreign Secretary Anthony Eden, who were then replaced by newly elected prime minister Clement Attlee and his foreign secretary Ernest Bevin. The meeting took place from July 17 to August 2, 1945, and primarily dealt with political

and economic issues rising from the end of the war in Europe and the occupation of Germany. During the course of the conference, it became clear that both the United States and the Soviet Union were seeking to establish their influence in key portions of Eastern Europe. In this regard, Truman's confidence at the conference was bolstered by the recent successful testing of the ATOMIC BOMB, which gave the United States a temporary monopoly that supplied some key leverage against the Soviet Union (and effectively signaled the start of the arms race between the two superpowers; it was during the Potsdam Conference that Truman secretly conferred with Churchill and made the decision to drop the bomb on Japan by August 10). Nevertheless, the Soviets came away from the conference with key concessions made in their favor—most notably, an agreement to the Russian occupation of eastern Poland as well as the portion of Germany east of the Oder River. Truman saw in this the Soviet intention to invade Turkey and thus extend its influence even further, and felt the time had come to stop "babying" the Soviets and make the U.S. position on foreign affairs, as well as its strength, abundantly clear. From this resolve sprang the TRUMAN DOCTRINE, as well as the idea of CONTAINMENT of Soviet expansion.

Powers, Francis Gary (1929–1977)

Francis Gary Powers was a U.S. pilot who achieved notoriety when his plane was shot down over the Soviet Union in 1960 and was later revealed to be on an espionage mission. In what came to be known as the U-2 AFFAIR, Powers was on a reconnaissance flight to photograph Soviet missile installations and was over the city of Sverdlovsk when Russian antiaircraft artillery brought him down. He was captured on May 1, 1960, and later was brought to trial for espionage. Found guilty, he was sentenced to 10 years in prison. However, in 1962 Powers was released from prison in exchange for Soviet spy Rudolf Abel. Upon his return to the United States, Powers testified about his flight before a Senate investigating committee. He wrote about his experiences in his 1970 book *Operation Overflight*. In the 1970s, he became a helicopter reporter for Los Angeles television station KNBC. While on an assignment in 1977, his helicopter ran out of fuel over Balboa Park in San Diego, and he died in the ensuing crash.

Project Chaos   See HELMS, Richard.

Pueblo incident

The USS *Pueblo* was an American naval intelligence ship seized by North Korean forces in January 1968, setting off an international incident that became a major embarrassment for the United States and a long ordeal for its crew. On January 23, the *Pueblo*, disguised as oceanographic research vessel, was presumably in international waters when it was surrounded by four North Korean patrol boats and ordered to surrender. Commander Lloyd Bucher protested that the *Pueblo* was well outside the 12-mile restricted zone; nevertheless, he and his crew could offer little resistance and were forced to surrender to the North Koreans. A scuffle ensued when U.S. crewmen were caught burning classified documents on Bucher's orders, and in the resulting exchange of gunfire, four Americans were wounded; one subsequently died. Meanwhile, the North Koreans managed to obtain 10 bags of secret documents.

Bucher and 82 other officers and crewmen were taken prisoner and brought to Wonsan, North Korea. Outraged, the United States demanded their release, but the North Koreans refused, insisting that the *Pueblo* had been caught in their waters and therefore the seizure was legal. As a result, President Lyndon JOHNSON called for more U.S. troops to be brought into the area. The North Koreans subsequently broadcast a purported confession by Bucher to the effect that the *Pueblo* had indeed invaded Korean waters in an act of espionage, then sent a letter to President Johnson declaring that the prisoners would be released only if the United States admitted that they had violated North Korean territorial waters and promised that it would never occur again; the letter was presumably signed by the 82 officers and crewmen. Johnson was tempted to react with a military strike, but due to the complications posed by the VIETNAM WAR and the need to bring about the safe return of Bucher and his crew, he chose a more diplomatic route.

After nearly a year of negotiations between the North Koreans and U.S. diplomats in Panmunjom, the conditions of the letter were met and the United States issued a formal statement "confessing" to being in North Korean waters illegally and apologizing for its actions. However, in an unusual move, before reading the statement, the chief U.S. negotiator, Major General Gilbert Woodward, read an additional statement repudiating the declaration of guilt, which he said was issued simply to bring about the crew's release from captivity. Subsequently, Bucher and his crew, along with the body of the killed crewman, were allowed to return to the United States, on December 22, 1968— after nearly a year of brutal treatment at the hands of their captors. The North Koreans retained the ship.

Bucher had another ordeal to face, this one before a naval court of inquiry in 1969, where he was forced to defend his decision to surrender the *Pueblo*. His contention that there was no way to defend the ship or burn the documents that were on board quickly enough was backed up by other high-ranking officers. He also described the beatings to which he and his crew had been subjected as well as the confessions they had been forced to sign. Nevertheless, the court recommended that he and another officer be court-martialed, but this decision was overturned by Navy Secretary John Chaffee.

Pumpkin Papers   See CHAMBERS, Whittaker.

Quayle, Dan (1947–)

James Danforth Quayle, known as Dan, is a former senator and vice president of the United States under George BUSH. He was born into a wealthy and influential family whose business was newspaper publishing. His parents were members of the John Birch Society, endorsing extreme right-wing political views that would have a major influence on their son. The young Quayle had his first venture into politics in 1964, when he handed out leaflets for Republican presidential candidate Barry GOLDWATER at the Arizona State Fair.

In 1969, Quayle earned his bachelor's degree from DePauw University in Greencastle, Indiana. After receiving his law degree from Indiana University in 1974, he went to work in the family business, serving as associate publisher of the *Huntington Herald-Press* until 1976. That year, he won his first election as a Republican, to the U.S. House of Representatives. He was reelected in 1978. In 1980, Quayle was elected to the U.S. Senate, then reelected six years later. A dedicated conservative, he was selected by George Bush to be his running mate in the 1988 presidential election. He drew fire from the press during the campaign when it was suggested that he had joined the NATIONAL GUARD in 1969 as a means of evading the draft and

Newly elected President George Bush and Vice President Dan Quayle (BUSH LIBRARY)

avoiding military service in Vietnam. His youth and relative inexperience also came under attack, with many suggesting that Quayle would be the least qualified vice president in the history of the office. Nevertheless, the Bush/Quayle team won the election.

Quayle's four years as vice president were spent traveling around the United States and the world on a number of political and goodwill missions. He became infamous for embarrassing gaffes that some felt exposed his immaturity and lack of intelligence. However, he remains popular with the conservative right, especially for his staunch defense of "family values."

Reagan, Ronald (1911–)

Fortieth president of the United States, Ronald Wilson Reagan is credited by many with having ended the Cold War with his determined buildup of U.S. defenses against potential communist aggression in the face of stiff congressional opposition. Reagan grew up in Illinois and attended Eureka College, from which he graduated in 1932. After graduation, he went to Iowa, where he became a radio sports announcer, a career he pursued in several midwestern states. He turned to acting in 1937 after his discovery by a Hollywood talent agent. He went on to make over 50 films, most notably *Brother Rat* (1938); *Knute Rockne—All American* (1940); and *Kings Row* (1941). From 1954 to 1962, with his movie career on a decline, he worked for the General Electric Company and served as host of television's *General Electric Theater.* Meanwhile, his political philosophy had undergone a change, from the liberal Democratic viewpoint he espoused in his early years to the conservative Republicanism that emerged in the 1950s. He served as president of the Screen Actors Guild from 1947 to 1952, during which time he assisted in the government's probe into supposed communist infiltration into the motion picture industry. He was SAG's president for a second time in 1959–60.

President Ronald W. Reagan (REAGAN LIBRARY)

By 1964, Reagan had become a Goldwater Republican and was fully entrenched in a political career, due in part to the ease with which he communicated with voters. In 1966, he ran a successful campaign for governor of California. Just one year later, he made a brief stab at the Republican nomination for president. He went on to serve two undistinguished terms as governor, from 1967 to 1974. In 1976, he made another, more serious try for the presidency, but failed to wrest the nomination away from the incumbent, Gerald FORD. In 1980, however, Reagan succeeded in winning both the nomination and the election, enjoying an easy victory over President Jimmy CARTER. He won another landslide over Walter MONDALE in his reelection bid in 1984.

Two months after being sworn in as president, in March 1981, Reagan was shot by John W. Hinckley, Jr., in an assassination attempt. He recovered quickly and went on to become a president who inspired both public approval and controversy. He set about instituting a policy of "supply-side" economics that built up military spending while reducing other spending. He also implemented the tax cuts he had promised during his campaign. Congress approved most of his proposals in 1981, and after a recession in 1982, the country enjoyed several years of economic growth and a drop in the inflation rate. However, the tax cuts resulted in budget deficits that doubled the national debt between 1981 and 1986.

Reagan's greatest accomplishments during his presidency centered around his crusade against COMMUNISM. He ensured that U.S. power was felt throughout the world. In the Middle East, efforts to contain communist expansion in that area resulted in an anti-Soviet alliance forged with both Arabs and Israelis (although this alliance would become uneasy due to terrorist attacks against the U.S. military in Beirut, Lebanon). Meanwhile, the Reagan administration began working to destabilize the pro-Marxist Sandinista government in Nicaragua, and supported the government of El Sal-

Premier Mikhail Gorbachev and President Ronald Reagan sign the INF Treaty, 1988.

vador in its fight against leftist insurgents. In 1983, Reagan enjoyed military success and renewed popular support when U.S. forces invaded GRENADA, a small island in the Caribbean, ostensibly to rescue U.S. citizens (mostly students), but primarily to remove the island's marxist government.

Reagan's die-hard resolve to build up American military strength as well as his public denunciations of the Soviet leadership resulted in such strained relations between the two superpowers that the early years of his administration were often referred to as "Cold War II." Nevertheless, Reagan entered cautiously into arms control negotiations with the SOVIET UNION even as he continued the arms buildup, reasoning that a solidly prepared military would put the United States in a position to obtain concessions more favorable to the West. His devotion to defense spending included a proposal called the STRATEGIC DEFENSE INITIATIVE (SDI), also known as "Star Wars." Despite strong opposition to the program from a Democratic Congress, Reagan's determined advocacy of the SDI gave him the leverage he wanted with the Soviet Union, which was economically unable to support a comparable program. Thus, in 1988, Reagan participated in a summit meeting with Mikhail Gorbachev that concluded with the signing of the Intermediate Range Nuclear Forces (INF) Treaty.

Throughout the years of his administration, Reagan continued to press Congress to approve increases in defense spending, despite approving legislation to make cuts in government spending and opposing tax increases to cover deficits. Reagan's ironclad determination to maintain strong military defenses and counter communist initiatives throughout the world has been credited by many with contributing to the subsequent collapse of communism in the Soviet Union.

Late in 1986, the details of the IRAN-CONTRA AFFAIR were revealed to the public, resulting in a weakening of support for Reagan in the final two years of his administration. Nevertheless, he has remained one of the most popular presidents ever, in addition to being the oldest person ever to hold the office and the overseer of the largest peacetime military expansion in U.S. history.

Reagan Doctrine

The Reagan Doctrine evolved as a result of President Ronald REAGAN's determination to provide support to any foreign forces engaged in resisting communist or Soviet-backed regimes in their countries. Although not backed up by a clearly defined published statement, the doctrine, which encompassed guerrillas and opposition forces in Latin America, Asia, and Africa, was understood to support any effort to bring about democracy in previously marxist regions. President Reagan came closest to making a public declaration of his doctrine in a State of the Union address delivered just before Mikhail Gorbachev took the reins of power in the USSR, saying: "We must not break faith with those who are risking their lives on every continent from Afghanistan to Nicaragua to defy Soviet-supported aggression and secure rights that have been ours since birth. . . . Support for freedom fighters is self-defense."

This doctrine lay behind the Reagan administration's backing of the CONTRA rebels in Nicaragua (*see* IRAN-CONTRA AFFAIR), as well as his invasion of GRENADA—two moves that some critics considered overly interventionist but that were in keeping with the president's anticommunist stance. The doctrine did not entail only covert or military involvement, however; many times intervention took the form of financial aid, approved by Congress, to assist in funding revolutionary efforts in any given country. Thus, the administration's support could be found in resistance movements in Afghanistan, Chad, Poland, Cambodia, and in numerous countries in Latin America, Asia, Africa, and the Middle East. The Reagan Doctrine would establish the tone for the Reagan administration—in essence, a commitment to win back what had been lost to the communists in the past and to contain any further Soviet expansion.

realpolitik

Realpolitik is the term given to the pursuit of national security by building up military strength. This philosophy has its roots in the primal traits of the human animal, who is assumed to be greedy and self-serving, and therefore in need of protection from enemies who are equally greedy and self-serving. The best defense, therefore, is a well organized military that can deter enemy forces from invasion or domination. In addition, the need to have an adequate supply of arms—during the Cold War in particular, nuclear arms—is a prerequisite to national security. However, this presents a conundrum: As one nation builds up forces and arms, other nations begin to feel insecure and threatened, and thus begin their own nuclear build-up, thus presenting a threat to still other countries. The end result is an arms race that can threaten the security of the entire world, not just single nations, with no quarter given to those who advocate other means of achieving national security. An internationally used word, realpolitik is also known in the United States as "power politics."

Reserve Officers' Training Corps (ROTC)

The Reserve Officers' Training Corps (ROTC) is a U.S. Defense Department program designed to train and subsequently commission high school and college students for service in any one of the branches of the military. The program was established by the National Defense Act of 1916, and was based in part on a similar British system. Students who enroll in ROTC attend regular academic courses, but they also get a supplemental education in military subjects. The ROTC program is divided into two levels: junior, for high school students and senior, for college students. The senior program is also divided into two levels; those who complete the first level after two years and have shown themselves to have officer potential are able, if desired, to take the more advanced (and difficult) courses of study. Scholarships are available to help ROTC students meet their college expenses. Upon successfully completing the ROTC course, graduates receive commissions as second lieutenants. Those who enter the army are likely to serve on active duty for two to four years, then are placed on reserve lists. Those who enter the air force will serve four years on active duty and two years on reserve. Navy graduates become either ensigns in the U.S. Navy or second lieutenants in the Marine Corps.

Attention was often focused on the ROTC during the civil rights and peace movements of the 1960s and early 1970s. Many activists called for an abolishment of the program, emphasizing as it did the militarization of the country's youth, which was anathema to antiwar protesters and others. However, tradition won out and the ROTC persevered. ROTC buildings were frequently targeted by campus activists; some were even burned to the ground. More tragically, an ROTC student was mistakenly killed during the 1970 KENT STATE MASSACRE.

Reuther, Walter (1907–1970)

Walter Philip Reuther was a labor leader who, as president of the United Automobile Workers (UAW) and the Congress of Industrial Organizations (CIO), succeeded in obtaining long-term improvements in wages and benefits for union members. The son of a socialist who was also a union activist, Reuther began working as a tool-and-die craftsman at the age of 15, but later finished high school and three years of higher education at Wayne State University in Detroit. He went on to work for five years at a Ford Motor Company plant, but was fired for trying to organize a union. In 1932, he and his brother, Victor, went on a three-year tour of Europe, which included a visit to the Soviet Union, where they labored in the Gorki Auto plant. It was this experience that turned Reuther against the communist system and later caused him to fight communist influences in the UAW and the CIO.

Upon Reuther's return to the United States in 1935, he went to work for General Motors and became president of his local union in Detroit. There he helped to lead a sit-down strike that led to the formation of the United Auto Workers. He became director of the UAW's General Motors Department in 1939. With war an imminent possibility, Reuther suggested a plan to mass-produce aircraft in automobile plants. As a result, he was appointed during the war to serve on the War Manpower Commission and the War Production Board, and played a major role in improving production in almost 5,000 defense plants.

In 1945–46, Reuther organized a strike against General Motors, then was elected president of the UAW in 1946. His power and influence as president resulted in numerous gains on behalf of the labor force he represented, including higher wages, fringe benefits, long-term contracts, and unemployment benefits, among other things. In 1952, Reuther was elected president of the CIO, in which capacity he helped to bring about that union's merger with the AFL in 1955. Thereafter he served as both a vice president of the AFL-CIO (second only to George MEANY) and president of its Industrial Union Department. He also became vice president of the International Confederation of Trade Unions, created to counteract the communistic World Federation of Trade Unions.

Reuther advocated many social programs such as health insurance, urban renewal, and low-cost housing, and became impatient with what he saw as the AFL-CIO's inattention to these matters. In 1968, after repeated disputes with George Meany, Reuther took the UAW out of the AFL-CIO and joined forces with the Teamsters Union to form the Alliance for Labor Action. He and his wife were killed in a plane crash in 1970. At the time of his death, he was still president of the UAW, and had held the position for 24 years.

Reykjavik Summit

By the mid-1980s, talks between President Ronald REA-GAN and Soviet premier Mikhail Gorbachev were creating great strides in the improvement of relations between the United States and the Soviet Union. On October 11 and 12, 1986, they met for their second summit conference in Reykjavik, Iceland, to talk primarily about the terms of the STRATEGIC ARMS REDUCTION TALKS (START). The meeting provoked some controversy, chiefly because of Reagan's firm stand on the STRATEGIC DEFENSE INITIATIVE (SDI); he made no promises to Gorbachev beyond agreeing that there would be no deployment of SDI missiles for at least 10 years. There was also a misunderstanding regarding the elimination of nuclear weapons, which was to take place within a decade. Gorbachev believed that it referred to *all* nuclear weapons, whereas what Reagan meant to agree to was all nuclear *ballistic* weapons; he later reluctantly conceded that the agreement was as Gorbachev remembered it. Gorbachev and Reagan also agreed to reduce strategic offensive weapons by half within five years.

Richardson, Elliot (1920–   )

Elliot Lee Richardson is a longtime government official, the only one to have served in four different cabinet positions. He graduated from Harvard University in 1941 and became an army lieutenant during World War II. After the war, Richardson returned to Harvard, where he received his law degree in 1947. He then worked as a law clerk under Judge Learned Hand and U.S. Supreme Court justice Felix Frankfurter. He was admitted to the Massachusetts bar in 1949 and went into private law practice, but felt the call to public service more keenly than the law. In 1957, President Dwight H. EISENHOWER appointed Richardson assistant secretary for legislation in the Department of Health, Education and Welfare. Two years later, he was appointed U.S. attorney for Massachusetts, and in

Soviet premier Mikhail Gorbachev and U.S. president Ronald Reagan meet in Reykjavik, Iceland. (REAGAN LIBRARY)

1965–67 he was elected lieutenant governor of Massachusetts. In 1969, he was named an undersecretary in the U.S. Department of State.

A moderate Republican, Richardson became an important member of the NIXON administration, working closely on matters of foreign policy with Henry KISSINGER and, over time, taking on several positions: secretary of health, education and welfare (1970–72); secretary of defense (January 1973–May 1973); and attorney general (May 1973–October 1973). In the latter role, he attempted to restore public confidence in the Justice Department after the WATERGATE affair, and appointed Archibald Cox as a special prosecutor to investigate the scandal. When Cox tried to obtain evidence from Nixon, the president ordered Richardson to fire him. Instead, Richardson resigned, in October 1973.

After Nixon's resignation, Richardson returned to government service under President Gerald FORD, first as ambassador to Great Britain (1975–76), then as secretary of commerce (1976–77). As ambassador, he worked on such matters as NATO strategy and relations between the United States and the European Economic Community and between the United States and the WARSAW PACT nations. Following the end of the Ford administration, Richardson was appointed by President Jimmy CARTER as ambassador-at-large as well as chief delegate to the Law of the Sea Conference (1977–80). Richardson has practiced law in Washington since 1980, but has often been called upon for diplomatic missions or advice. In 1989, he was appointed as a special UNITED NATIONS observer in the Nicaraguan elections. In 1990, President George BUSH, seeking help with certain initiatives, made him a special representative to the Philippines. Richardson is now retired from government service. His published books include *The Creative Balance* (1976) and *The Uses and Limitations of Law* (1982).

Robeson, Paul (1898–1976)

Paul Bustill Robeson was a celebrated singer who achieved notoriety and ostracism for his communist views. Born to a preacher who had once been a slave, Robeson graduated Phi Beta Kappa from Rutgers University and was valedictorian of his class. An All-American football player, he rejected the opportunity to play professionally. Instead, he enrolled in Columbia University Law School and obtained his law degree in 1923. However, given the scarcity at that time of job opportunities for blacks in the legal profession, he began to make his living by acting, first in London, then moving on to a New York theater group called the Provincetown Players. He appeared in Eugene O'Neill's *All God's Chillun Got Wings* in 1924, then received great acclaim for his starring turn in *The Emperor Jones* in 1925, a role he repeated in the 1933 film version. Also in 1925, he put on the first of many recitals of Negro spirituals that showed off his extraordinary singing voice. Robeson achieved international fame in the musical *Show Boat* for his role as Joe and his rendition of "Ol' Man River." In 1930, he played the title role in *Othello* on the London stage, repeating the role on Broadway in 1943 and setting a record run for a Shakespearean play in that venue.

Over the years, Robeson continued to put on concerts and make numerous recordings and theatrical appearances. He also made many films, including *Show Boat* (1936), *Song of Freedom* (1936), and *The Proud Valley* (1940). However, he also became increasingly known for his left-wing political views, especially after he made a much-publicized visit to the Soviet Union in 1934. In time he became extremely outspoken on the issue of racial justice and international peace. In 1950, when he refused to sign an affidavit to disclaim his membership in the Communist Party, his passport was revoked by the U.S. Department of State. He subsequently came under mounting attack for his procommunist leanings. In 1958, he published his autobiography, *Here I Stand.* That same year, the U.S. Supreme Court overturned the affidavit restriction, and Robeson departed from the United States for travel and concerts in Europe and the Soviet bloc. In 1963, suffering from poor health, Robeson returned to the United States, where he lived quietly and died in 1976. He remains for many a symbol of the 20th century's black protest movement in its earliest days, his creative achievements outweighed by his unpopular sympathy for COMMUNISM.

Rockefeller, Nelson (1908–1979)

Nelson Aldrich Rockefeller was a longtime political leader and former governor of New York State who failed to achieve the U.S. presidency despite three attempts. Born into a business dynasty as the grandson of John D. Rockefeller, Sr., he attended Dartmouth College in Hanover, New Hampshire, graduating with a degree in economics in 1930. Over the next 10 years, he joined the family businesses at

Vice President Nelson A. Rockefeller (FORD LIBRARY)

Chase National Bank (later Chase Manhattan Bank), Rockefeller Center, and Creole Petroleum. As a result of Rockefeller's work as director of Creole Petroleum (1935–40), he developed a strong interest in Latin American affairs. This led to his appointment in 1940 as coordinator of inter-American affairs at the U.S. Department of State. Although he was a moderate Republican, he became assistant secretary of state for the American republics in 1944 during the Roosevelt administration.

Rockefeller left government service in 1945 to become a founder of a private, nonprofit group dedicated to assisting developing countries in Latin America. In 1950, he was appointed by President Harry TRUMAN to head the International Development Advisory Board. Two years later, President-elect Dwight D. EISENHOWER named him to chair an advisory committee on government organization. With the resulting formation of the Department of Health, Education and Welfare, Rockefeller was appointed as an undersecretary for that department, and served from 1953 to 1955. During that time, he also headed a group of experts who put together a plan under which designated agents would carry out regular air reconnaissance missions of the major powers to ensure that each was adhering to agreed-upon arms limits. President Eisenhower liked this "open skies" inspection plan, and proposed it during the July 1955 meeting in Geneva of the principal Western and Soviet leaders. However, no measures were taken to follow through on it after the meeting.

Rockefeller subsequently withdrew from government service for the second time in order to run for an elective office. In 1958, a heavily Democratic year, he unseated Averell HARRIMAN from the governor's office in New York State. He considered running for the presidential nomination in 1960, but withdrew from the race in favor of Richard NIXON after it was determined by party elders that Rockefeller was too liberal. He subsequently was elected governor of New York for three more terms, and in that period he oversaw a tremendous expansion in the state university system as well as in the bureaucracy and budget. In 1964, he ran for the Republican nomination for president, but was narrowly defeated by the ultraconservative Barry GOLDWATER. He again lost the nomination in 1968, this time to Richard Nixon. After his fourth election as governor, in 1970, he aroused controversy by refusing to go to the state prison at Attica, New York, where prisoner riots were taking place, and instead ordering an attack by the New York State Police that resulted in the deaths of 43 prisoners and guards.

In 1973, Rockefeller stepped down as governor in order to give his full attention to the National Commission on Critical Choices for America and the Commission on Water Quality. However, just a year later, he was asked by President Gerald FORD to become his vice president. Rockefeller was approved by Congress and sworn in to the position on December 19, 1974. He served until the conclusion of Ford's administration in January 1977.

Roosevelt, Eleanor (1884–1962)

As the wife of President Franklin D. Roosevelt and an exemplary social activist, Anna Eleanor Roosevelt became one of the most admired American women of the 20th century. Born into a prominent New York family (her uncle was President Theodore Roosevelt), she received a traditional "lady's education" at a school in England. After returning to the United States, she was married to Franklin, who was a distant cousin, and with whom she had five children. In 1921, Franklin was stricken by polio. On his physician's recommendation, to renew her dispirited husband's interest in politics, she began to become more involved in public work, joining the Women's Trade Union League, among other organizations. She also increased her activities with the New York State Democratic Party; from 1924 to 1928, she was financial chairman of the women's division.

Eleanor Roosevelt at the United Nations (ROOSEVELT LIBRARY)

Eleanor Roosevelt displays a Spanish translation of the UN Declaration of Human Rights. (ROOSEVELT LIBRARY)

After her husband was elected president in 1932, Roosevelt became even more active, espousing a large number of liberal—often controversial—causes. She also continued to help her husband by touring the country and reporting back to him on what she had seen and heard, providing him with valuable insight into current public opinion, as well as supporting New Deal initiatives for humanitarian purposes. In 1936, she began writing a daily newspaper column called "My Day." After World War II broke out, she continued to travel extensively to theaters of operation in order to provide morale boosts to the troops. She also served as assistant director in the Office of Civilian Defense. She was generally regarded as one of the best assets of her husband's administration.

Subsequent to the president's death in April 1945, Roosevelt continued her humanitarian and political work. She was appointed to serve as a delegate to the UNITED NATIONS (UN) by President Harry TRUMAN in 1945 and 1949–52, and by President John F. KENNEDY in 1961. During her years at the UN, she worked for a number of liberal causes. Among other things, she favored the partition of Palestine into Jewish and Arab states, and also opposed the 1948 arms embargo to Israel. From 1946 to 1951, Roosevelt served as chairman of the UN Commission on Human Rights, in which capacity she was a major player in the creation of the 1948 "Universal Declaration of Human Rights." She favored recognition of the People's Republic of China and also opposed nuclear testing, arguing instead for a negotiated end to the Cold War. Additionally, in 1947 she helped to found the AMERICANS FOR DEMOCRATIC ACTION.

Over time, Roosevelt became an American icon, highly respected and influential on both the social and the political scene. When Alger HISS was brought to trial on charges of perjury and then convicted, Roosevelt was one of the prominent liberals who defended him, seeing Hiss as a scapegoat for Republican failures. She later deplored the advent of McCarthyism, noting that "McCarthy's methods, to me, look like Hitler's." She was a strong supporter of Adlai STEVENSON, campaigning for him in 1956 and leading a movement to draft him at the Democratic National Convention in 1960.

Roosevelt published her autobiography in two parts: *This Is My Story* in 1937 and *On My Own* in 1958. Her best known book was *This I Remember*, published in 1949. Throughout her final years, she continued to travel widely, meeting with national leaders the world over. No other first lady, before or since, has had as distinguished a public career as Roosevelt.

Roosevelt-Litvinov Agreements

Prior to 1933, no diplomatic relations existed between the United States and the Soviet Union. Following the Russian Revolution in 1917, the United States, believing that the communist regime could not possibly last, chose to wait until Russia's experiment with communism was past. By 1933, however, it had become clear that the Union of Soviet Socialist Republics was here to stay. Consequently, several advantages, economic and diplomatic, could be seen in normalizing relations with the Soviet Union. Thus, Soviet foreign minister Maxim Litvinov paid a visit to Washington, and after a series of meetings with President Franklin Roosevelt, the Roosevelt-Litvinov agreement, which established full diplomatic relations between the two countries, was signed. As part of the agreement, the Soviets pledged to recognize and protect the religious freedom of Americans living in Russia and to support no organizations dedicated to overthrowing the American government. Although the agreement did effectively normalize diplomatic relations between the two countries, it soon became apparent that the Soviet Union was not keeping its promises, and some critics called for an end to diplomatic relations. Roosevelt would not sanction such a move.

Rosenberg, Julius (1918–1953) and Ethel (1915–1953)

Julius and Ethel Rosenberg were the first civilians in the United States to be charged, convicted, and executed for espionage. Both established members of the Communist Party, they were married in June 1939. That same year, Julius Rosenberg graduated from college with a degree in electrical engineering. In 1940, he became a civilian engineer with the U.S. Army Signal Corps. Almost immediately, he and Ethel began acquiring military secrets that they tried to turn over to the USSR. The information they gathered came not only through Julius's work with the Signal Corps, but also via Ethel's brother, Sergeant David Greenglass, who had been working as a machinist on the atomic bomb project in Los Alamos, New Mexico, since 1943. It was Greenglass who passed crucial data on U.S. nuclear weapons over to the Rosenbergs, who then transmitted it to a courier, Harry Gold. The data was then passed to Anatoly A. Yakovlev, the Soviet vice consul in New York City.

In 1945, Julius Rosenberg was fired from the army for lying about his Communist Party membership.

Five years later, a British physicist, Klaus Fuchs, was convicted by the British courts of selling atomic secrets. Fuchs pointed the FEDERAL BUREAU OF INVESTIGATION (FBI) toward Gold and Greenglass. On May 23, 1950, Gold was arrested in connection with the Fuchs case. He soon revealed the culpability of Greenglass and the Rosenbergs, as well as another conspirator, Morton Sobell. The Rosenbergs and Greenglass were quickly arrested, while Sobell escaped to Mexico City. He was detained there, and was later extradited to stand trial in the United States Greenglass received a prison sentence of 15 years in exchange for testifying against the Rosenbergs as the chief witness for the prosecution, while Gold and Sobell were sentenced to 30 years imprisonment. Meanwhile, the Rosenbergs, who loudly protested their innocence, were put on trial and found guilty of espionage, for which they were sentenced to death. A campaign for leniency soon followed, and the Rosenbergs made several appeals, receiving a certain

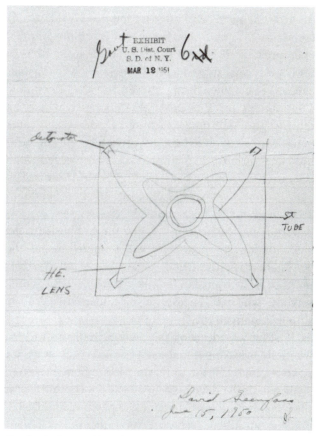

Sketch of a lens mold used as evidence in the case against Julius and Ethel Rosenberg (NARA NORTHEAST REGION)

amount of public support for their case, particularly from opponents of the death penalty, who lodged major protests against the execution. Nine out of a total of 16 appeals reached the U.S. Supreme Court; all met in failure, and the Rosenbergs were executed on June 19, 1953, at Sing Sing Prison, the first such sentence ever carried out in peacetime. To many who believed in their innocence and even to others who doubted it, the trial and execution of the Rosenbergs was unjust—a case of both anti-Semitism and of McCarthyism carried to an extreme. In the early 1990s, formerly secret files of the Soviet Union came to light that revealed that the Rosenbergs had indeed been employed by the KGB.

Rostow, Eugene V. (1913–)

Eugene Victor Debs Rostow is a lawyer and economist who has served in numerous government posts under several different presidents. He obtained his law degree from Yale University in 1937, and a year later joined the law school faculty there, where he continued to teach until 1961. From 1942 to 1944, he served as an assistant general counsel for the World War II lend-lease program, then became director of economic operations in the North African theater from 1944 to 1945. He was subsequently appointed an assistant executive secretary of the UNITED NATIONS Economic Commission for Europe (1949–50), after which he returned to full-time teaching. During this same period, he also served as executive vice chairman of the North African Economic Board and worked as an executive assistant to Secretary of State Dean ACHESON. Rostow was made dean of the Yale Law School in 1955, and made numerous changes in the school's direction and curriculum, putting the emphasis on the study of law in relation to other operations of the world, both political and social. As he put it, "Our purpose is to train lawyers, law teachers, and public servants who will be capable of constructive leadership in American life."

Rostow was dean of Yale Law School until 1966, when he was appointed undersecretary of state for political affairs. Prior to that, in 1961, he was elected chairman of the development assistance committee for the Organization for Economic Cooperation and Development, an alliance of Western countries. As undersecretary of state, in addition to supervising economic programs involving assistance to other countries (par-

ticularly India), Rostow also became involved in formulating potential peaceful solutions to the conflict in Vietnam, which was now raging out of control. He was a believer in CONTAINMENT, and felt the solution lay in strong political and economic alliances with European and Asian countries outside the communist sphere of influence.

In 1969, Rostow left the State Department to return to Oxford University to teach for one year, then went back to Yale, where he taught at various intervals from 1970 to 1984. He also taught at the National Defense University and served as president of the Atlantic Treaty Association. In 1981, President Ronald REAGAN appointed him as director of the Arms Control and Disarmament Agency; he continued in this post until 1983.

Now an emeritus professor at Yale University, Rostow has written several books, including *Planning for Freedom* (1959); *Law, Power, and the Pursuit of Peace* (1968); and *Peace in the Balance* (1972).

Rostow, Walt Whitman (1916–)

Walt Whitman Rostow is an economist and former national security advisor (under President Lyndon B. JOHNSON) who, in 1961, cowrote a controversial report in support of increased U.S. involvement in Vietnam. The son of Jewish emigrants from Russia, and younger brother to Eugene V. ROSTOW, he was born and raised in New York City, then attended Yale University, from which he graduated in 1936. He went on to study at Oxford University as a Rhodes scholar, then earned his Ph.D. degree from Yale in 1940.

After World War II broke out, Rostow joined the OFFICE OF STRATEGIC SERVICES (OSS), where he became a planner in strategic bombing (1942–45). Following the war, he spent two years teaching at Oxford University, then spent another two years working for the Economic Commission for Europe before returning to the United States and becoming a writer and a professor of economic history at the Massachusetts Institute of Technology (MIT). He stayed at MIT for the next 10 years, during which time he also served as a staff member for the Center of International Relations and became both a friend and an adviser to John F. KENNEDY. After Kennedy was elected president in 1960, he brought Rostow to Washington as a deputy to the new national security advisor, McGeorge BUNDY, and as chairman of the Policy Planning Council in the State Department. Rostow soon became renowned within the administration for the number and length of the memorandums he churned out, with Kennedy noting that he could write faster than he could think. During this time, Rostow also assisted in the formation of the ALLIANCE FOR PROGRESS.

In 1961, Rostow and General Maxwell TAYLOR went on a fact-finding trip to Indochina. Upon their return, they wrote a report advocating, among other things, that a "logistic task force" of 8,000 men be sent to South Vietnam in order to maintain what Taylor called a "FLEXIBLE RESPONSE" to the communists' ability to generate crises. In explaining it, Rostow wrote: "We must seek . . . to expand our arsenal of . . . countermeasures if we are in fact to make crisis-mongering, deeply built into communist ideology and working habits, an unprofitable occupation." The core group subsequently sent to Vietnam would grow to a force of 20,000 "advisers" and U.S. military troops by the time of Kennedy's assassination in 1963.

A leading proponent of the DOMINO THEORY, Rostow succeeded Bundy as national security advisor in 1966, remaining in that position until the end of Lyndon B. JOHNSON's presidency. He strongly believed in the policy of CONTAINMENT, so much so that he drew criticism for his supposed inflexibility and what some saw as his inability to deal effectively with changing world conditions.

In 1969, Rostow became a professor of economics and history at the University of Texas. He has written several books, including *The Stages of Economic Growth* (1960); *The United States in the World Arena* (1960); *The World Economy* (1978); and *Eisenhower, Kennedy, and Foreign Aid* (1985).

Rubin, Jerry (1938–1994)

Jerry Rubin was a well-known political agitator during the 1960s who achieved notoriety for his antics during the trial of the "CHICAGO SEVEN" in 1969. The son of a union organizer, Rubin briefly attended Oberlin College in Ohio before graduating from the University of Cincinnati, and subsequently studied at Hebrew University in Jerusalem and the University of California at Berkeley. He started his career as a journalist, reporting for the *Cincinnati Post and Star-Times* from 1956 to 1961.

With the buildup of military involvement in Vietnam during the 1960s, Rubin became an active antiwar protester. He moved to Berkeley, California, where, in 1965, he cochaired the Vietnam Day Committee. In 1966, he ran for mayor of Berkeley, and lost. That same year, he testified before the HOUSE COMMITTEE ON UN-AMERICAN ACTIVITIES (HUAC), the first ever to do so in costume. In 1967, he cofounded the Youth International Party (otherwise known as the YIPPIES) with Abbie HOFFMAN and Paul Krassner, and acted as one of the leaders of an antiwar march on the Pentagon. He ran for vice president on the Peace and Freedom Party ticket in 1968, the same year he and several of his Yippie compatriots caused an uproar at the Democratic National Convention in Chicago. They were put on trial for conspiracy to incite a riot, becoming known in the process as the "Chicago Seven." The trial itself was marked by outbursts and outrageous behavior on the part of the defendants and their lawyers. Five of the seven were convicted, but the verdicts were later overturned.

Rubin continued his work as an activist until 1972, when he became a spokesman for holistic and other alternative therapies then in vogue. In the late 1970s, he became a businessman and stockbroker. He moved to New York City, and in 1982, he started Jerry Rubin's Business Networking Salon. In 1985 and 1986, he again joined forces with Abbie Hoffman to put on approximately 40 Yippie (Hoffman) versus Yuppie (Rubin) debates throughout the country. During the early 1990s, he marketed and sold a nutritional drink containing ginseng, kelp, and bee pollen. In November 1994, Rubin was hit by a car while jaywalking in Los Angeles; he died of a heart attack two weeks later.

Rusk, Dean (1909–1994)

David Dean Rusk, secretary of state under Presidents John F. KENNEDY and Lyndon B. JOHNSON, was one of the most consistent defenders of U.S. policy in Vietnam. Rusk graduated from Davidson College in 1931, and went on to attend St. John's College in Oxford, England, as a Rhodes scholar. After earning his master's degree in 1934, he returned to the United States to teach political science at Mills College, in Oakland, California, where he became faculty dean in 1938.

A member of the military reserves, Rusk was called to active duty in December 1940. For most of World

War II, he served under General Joseph W. Stilwell as deputy chief of staff for the China-Burma-India theater of operations. He continued his government work after the war, holding positions in both the State Department and the War Department. It was Rusk who first suggested that the 38th parallel be used as a dividing line between North and South KOREA. After his appointment as assistant secretary of state for far eastern affairs in 1950, Rusk took an active role in policy and planning regarding the war in Korea, which he supported. However, he was firmly against expanding the war into China, as advocated by General Douglas MACARTHUR.

In 1952, Rusk became president of the Rockefeller Foundation, and worked in that role until John F. Kennedy's election as president in 1960. In 1961,

Kennedy appointed him secretary of state, a crucial position in the ensuing years due to the growth of the Cold War and situations arising in Vietnam, Cuba, and Berlin. Rusk developed a reputation for cool, level-headed thinking and strong negotiating abilities. He advised the president not to engage in the BAY OF PIGS operation, for reasons that later proved to be correct. He was also among the president's closest advisers during the CUBAN MISSILE CRISIS, advocating a surprise air attack against Cuba to neutralize the missiles discovered there before they became active. (Kennedy ordered a naval quarantine of Cuba instead, playing a game of "chicken" with Nikita Khrushchev, which was ultimately successful.)

After Kennedy's assassination, Rusk remained secretary of state under Lyndon B. Johnson. Rusk was inflex-

Secretary of Defense Clark Clifford and Secretary of State Dean Rusk (JOHNSON LIBRARY)

ible in his hawkish support of U.S. military involvement in Vietnam and opposition to diplomatic recognition of China, a position that made him a prime target for antiwar protesters and other critics of the Johnson administration. Fully occupied with the war and the containment of communism, Rusk paid little attention to other diplomatic concerns of his department, especially those of the THIRD WORLD.

Rusk left government service in January 1969, and became a professor in international law at the University of Georgia. He retired in 1984 and passed away 10 years later.

S

SALT I/SALT II **SALT I/SALT II**   See STRATEGIC ARMS LIMITATION TALKS.

Schlafly, Phyllis (1924–   )

Phyllis Schlafly (née Stewart) is a conservative activist best known for her successful opposition to the Equal Rights Amendment (ERA). Schlafly received her B.A. degree from Washington University in 1944 and her master's degree in political science from Radcliffe College in 1945; years later, she went on to earn her law degree at Washington University, in 1978. After receiving her master's degree, Schlafly began working as a researcher for several congressmen in Washington, and was also an aide in the campaign of Claude Bakewell, a Republican, for Congress in 1946. For the next three years, she was a librarian and researcher for a bank in St. Louis, Missouri, during which time she met and married John Fred Schlafly, Jr., with whom she had six children. After her marriage, she devoted her work to numerous volunteer activities and Republican politics.

In the early 1950s, Schlafly conducted research for Senator Joseph MCCARTHY and began to generate anticommunist propaganda, an activity she would continue into the 1960s. With her husband, she founded the Cardinal Mindszenty Foundation in 1958; the primary goal of this organization was to alert the world to the dangers of communism. Schlafly also produced two reading lists of right-wing materials: *Reading List for Americans* in 1954 and *Inside the Communist Conspiracy* in 1959; these lists included books by Joseph McCarthy and Robert H. WELCH, Jr., founder of the John Birch Society. In 1962, she aired her conservative views on a weekly radio program sponsored by her husband's right-wing organization, "America Wake Up." An enthusiastic supporter of presidential candidate Barry M. GOLDWATER, Schlafly published her first book in 1964. The book, *A Choice Not An Echo,* was an unabashed promotion of Goldwater's candidacy that became a best-seller. The book's success led the publisher, Père Marquette Press, to produce a series of books on national defense cowritten by Schlafly with retired U.S. Navy rear admiral Chester Ward (*The Gravediggers* in 1964; *Strike From Space* in 1965; and *The Betrayers* in 1968). Taking a vigorous anticommunist stance, Schlafly and Ward sharply criticized the U.S. government and its leaders, going so far as to accuse them of taking a "no-win" attitude in Vietnam and adopting policies that left the United States open to attack from the Soviet Union. Without Ward,

Schlafly also wrote *Safe—Not Sorry*, in which she holds the communists responsible for the widespread rioting in 1967 in many of the nation's urban ghettos.

In addition to campaigning for other conservatives, Schlafly herself ran for Congress, first in 1952, then in 1960 and 1970; she failed to be elected on all three occasions. From 1960 to 1964, she served as president of the Illinois Federation of Republican Women. In 1964, she became first vice president of the National Federation of Republican Women, putting her in line to succeed to the presidency of that organization. However, she lost the 1967 election to a more liberal candidate. At this point she established an organization called "The Eagles Are Flying" and set up the Eagle Trust Fund to support conservative candidates for public office. She also began publishing the *Phyllis Schlafly Report*. In the February 1972 issue, her first attacks on the ERA appeared in print. By that time, Schlafly had become a leading opponent of the women's liberation movement; she founded "Stop-ERA" in the belief that passage of the ERA would bring about the end of the American family unit, in addition to forcing women into military service. As national chairman of her cause, Schlafly launched a massive publicity campaign and lobbying organization that resulted in the congressional defeat of the amendment in 1982.

In 1975, Schlafly founded another group to promote the traditional view of women as housewives and mothers, naming her new movement the Eagle Forum. Her books in later years include *The Power of the Positive Woman* (1977); *Who Will Rock the Cradle* (1989); and *Meddlesome Mandate: Rethinking Family Leave* (1991).

Schlesinger, Arthur M., Jr. (1917–   )

Arthur Meier Schlesinger, Jr., is a well-known historian and Pulitzer Prize winner who was an influential liberal spokesman during the administration of President KENNEDY. He graduated from Harvard University in 1938, and went on to a year's study at Cambridge University, in England. In 1939, Schlesinger published a biography, *Orestes A. Brownson: A Pilgrim's Progress*. He served in the Office of War Information (1942–43) and the OFFICE OF STRATEGIC SERVICES (1943–45) during World War II, then returned to Harvard to teach history (1946–61). In 1945, he published his seminal work, *The Age of Jackson*, for which he was awarded the Pulitzer Prize in 1946. He subsequently wrote and published a major biography and examination of Franklin D. Roosevelt, *The Age of Roosevelt*, which was published in three volumes: *The Crisis of the Old Order,*

1919–1933 (1957); *The Coming of the New Deal* (1958); and *The Politics of Upheaval* (1960). In addition, his 1951 book, *The General and the President and the Future of American Policy*, examined the effects on the nation of President Harry TRUMAN's recall from Korea of General Douglas MACARTHUR.

A lifelong liberal, Schlesinger became involved in politics during the 1950s, when he founded AMERICANS FOR DEMOCRATIC ACTION (ADA) and became a speechwriter for Adlai STEVENSON's presidential campaign. An adviser to both Stevenson and John F. KENNEDY (with whom he shared the view that politics should be rational, practical, and unsentimental), Schlesinger left the ADA in 1961 to become a special assistant for Latin American affairs under President Kennedy. Concurrently, he served as a liaison with Stevenson, the newly appointed ambassador to the United Nations. When the decision was made to launch the ill-advised BAY OF PIGS operation, Schlesinger was among its strongest opponents.

Schlesinger left the White House two months after Kennedy's assassination, explaining that there was no longer any exhilaration to working there. However, he continued to comment on U.S. politics, and focused a great deal of intellectual attention on the war in Vietnam, which he believed was becoming unwinnable. He suggested a cautious approach of de-escalation and negotiation, but his suggestion fell on deaf ears. In *The Bitter Heritage: Vietnam and American Democracy, 1941–1966* (1966), Schlesinger wrote that "Vietnam is the triumph of the politics of inadvertence," and opined that it was not to be blamed on specific government policies or individuals.

Schlesinger won a Pulitzer Prize in 1966 for his 1965 book, *A Thousand Days: John F. Kennedy in the White House*. Since 1966, he has taught history at the City University of New York, holding the position of Schweitzer Professor of Humanities. He has remained active in his writings and political commentary and frequently provides historical perspectives to the MEDIA in relation to current events in the United States. Other books he has written include *The Imperial Presidency* (1973) and *The Cycles of American History* (1986). He won a National Book Award for his 1978 biography *Robert Kennedy and His Time*.

Schlesinger, James (1929–   )

James Rodney Schlesinger was a public official who served during the Nixon and Ford administrations and came under fire for his resistance to DÉTENTE policies. Schlesinger received his bachelor's, master's, and doctorate degrees from Harvard University. He started his career as a teacher of economics at the University of Virginia, then took a position at the Rand Corporation as a specialist in strategic analysis, with a focus on nuclear weapons. He began in public service in 1969 as an assistant director of the Budget Bureau for the NIXON administration, helping to create an energy policy. In 1971, Schlesinger was appointed chairman of the ATOMIC ENERGY COMMISSION (AEC), a position he held for the next two years. In this role, he aimed to make the AEC more of a guardian for the public interest than it had been in the past.

In 1973, Schlesinger was appointed director of the CENTRAL INTELLIGENCE AGENCY (CIA) by President Nixon. As he had done in the AEC, he set about making changes. He fired many CIA agents who had engaged in covert schemes, and changed the agency's focus to gathering and analyzing information. He had served just a few months when he was appointed secretary of defense. As secretary, he focused his efforts on building the defense budget and achieving parity in U.S.-Soviet military power by building up arms and ensuring "first strike capability" for the United States. Although initially in agreement with the defense policies of the FORD administration, Schlesinger later found himself at odds with the president over détente with the Soviet Union. In 1975, Ford dismissed him from his post.

With the election of Jimmy CARTER to the presidency, Schlesinger once again returned to public service as an adviser to the Carter administration on energy policy. He became the first secretary of energy, serving in that post from 1977 to 1979. However, he was unable to help Carter put his energy initiatives through Congress. After leaving the Carter administration, Schlesinger became a member of the Center for Strategic and International Studies at Georgetown University.

Scowcroft, Brent (1925–   )

General Brent Scowcroft is a former air force officer best known for his role as national security advisor under President George BUSH and for the commission he headed to investigate the MX missile system and issues of arms control. Scowcroft received his B.S. degree from the U.S. Military Academy at West Point, New York in 1947. He subsequently became a fighter pilot in the U.S. Air Force, but had to give that up when he suffered major injuries in a plane crash.

Between 1948 and 1953, he held a number of different staff positions in the air force. He also continued his higher education over the years, obtaining his M.A. degree in 1953 and his Ph.D. degree in 1967, both from Columbia University. In the process, he became an excellent linguist, specializing in Slavic languages.

In 1953, Scowcroft started teaching, first at West Point and subsequently at Georgetown University. For a time, he was posted to the U.S. embassy in Belgrade. Upon his return in 1962, he took a teaching post at the Air Force Academy in Colorado Springs, and soon became head of the political science department. In 1964, he was sent to work at air force headquarters in Washington, D.C. After earning his doctorate in 1967, he returned to teaching, now at the National War College. However, a year later, he began working in the first of many posts in the Department of Defense, with an emphasis on issues of national security.

By late 1971, Scowcroft had become a colonel in the air force, as well as a military aide to President Richard NIXON, whom he accompanied on a historic trip to China. He was soon promoted to brigadier general and appointed to be part of the advance team that went to the Soviet Union prior to Nixon's 1972 visit there. Henry KISSINGER then chose him to replace Alexander HAIG as deputy assistant (subsequently assistant) for national security affairs. In 1975, Scowcroft—by this time a lieutenant general—succeeded Kissinger as head of the NATIONAL SECURITY COUNCIL, at which point he resigned his commission in the air force. Although he was often publicly criticized as being nothing more than an "errand boy" for Kissinger, Scowcroft in fact proved himself to be a skillful and diplomatic officer who earned high praise and respect from his colleagues. He also played a major if quiet role in the development of the interim SALT II pact signed by President FORD in 1974, and coordinated the evacuation of U.S. personnel from Saigon, South Vietnam, in 1975. That same year, when Cambodia seized the American freighter S.S. *Mayaguez,* Scowcroft helped to prepare the U.S. response. (*See MAYAGUEZ INCIDENT.*)

With Jimmy CARTER's election to the presidency, Scowcroft resigned from the National Security Council, but he continued in government service throughout the administrations of Presidents Carter, REAGAN, and Bush, participating in a number of committees and commissions, usually related to matters of national security, weapons development, and arms control. In 1983, President Reagan appointed Scowcroft to head the bipartisan Commission on Strategic Forces, whose

Vice President Nelson Rockefeller, Deputy Assistant of National Security Affairs Brent Scowcroft, and CIA director William Colby discuss the situation in Vietnam, 1975. (FORD LIBRARY)

goal was to evaluate and recommend ways to utilize the MX missile system for future strategic purposes. This panel, consisting of many high-ranking personnel and former government officials, came to be known as the Scowcroft Commission. Remarkably, the group reached a consensus within three months, an achievement attributed to Scowcroft's leadership and diplomatic skills. The commission's report recommended that 100 multi-warhead MX missiles be deployed in existing Minuteman silos, that the total number of warheads be limited, and that a number of small, mobile, single-warhead intercontinental ballistic missiles be developed to arrest the trend toward multiple-warhead weapons. The report further stated that the United States should create a missile program that would effectively "confound, complicate, and frustrate the efforts of Soviet strategic war planners." Although the Scowcroft Commission's recommendations met

with significant opposition, they nevertheless paved the way toward eventual congressional approval of funding for the MX missile system. In 1984, the commission issued a final report urging President Reagan to move forward on arms control negotiations using "extreme caution," while at the same time disputing the idea of a nuclear freeze, which would hamper the nation's stability.

Scowcroft continued to advise the Reagan administration on national security. In 1986, he was appointed to the three-member President's Special Review Board headed by Senator John G. Tower to investigate the National Security Council's role in the IRAN-CONTRA AFFAIR. The commission's report, issued in February 1987, found little to criticize in the overall setup and conduct of the council, but much to target in the behavior of numerous officials of the Reagan administration, which was subjected to enormous public embarrassment as a result of the Tower Commission's investigations.

In 1989, President George Bush appointed Scowcroft national security advisor, a position he held throughout the Bush administration. He later became president of the Scowcroft Group, as well as the Forum for International Policy. In February 1997, President Bill Clinton reappointed Scowcroft as a member of the Board of Visitors to the United States Air Force Academy.

Scowcroft Commission   See SCOWCROFT, Brent.

Seale, Bobby (1936–)

A cofounder (with Huey NEWTON) of the BLACK PANTHER Party, Robert George Seale became one of the best-known political activists during the 1960s. A high-school dropout, his military career ended abruptly when he was discharged from the U.S. Air Force for disobeying a superior officer. Seale met Huey Newton in 1962, when they were students at Merritt Community College in Oakland, California. Together, they formed a black separatist student group and became increasingly involved in the political and social unrest then brewing.

In 1966, Seale and Newton founded the Black Panther Party for Self-Defense, initially for the purpose of providing services to the community and patrolling ghettos to protect residents from police brutality. However, the group gradually became more marxist in nature and drew public criticism for its militant efforts to "police the police," especially after several shootouts occurred in various cities and Newton was imprisoned for the murder of a police officer. In 1968, Seale was among a large group of agitators that disrupted the Democratic National Convention in Chicago. Arrested along with seven others, his wildly disruptive behavior in court brought him to national attention; at one point, the trial judge ordered him gagged and manacled. Seale's case was finally separated from the others. He was subsequently found guilty of contempt of court and sentenced to four years in prison.

In 1971, Seale was again put on trial, this time for his possible role in the kidnapping and murder of a former Black Panther who allegedly had been an informant for the police. However, the charges against him were dropped after a mistrial. In the next few years, his political views became more moderate, and he conducted an unsuccessful run for mayor of Oakland in 1973. He resigned as chairman of the Black Panther Party in 1974. In the 1980s, he became an associate in the African-American history department at Temple University as well as an advocate for gun control. He has published several books, including *Seize the Time: The Story of the Black Panther Party and Huey P. Newton* (1970) and his autobiography, *A Lonely Rage* (1980). In 1987, he wrote a cookbook entitled *Barbeque'n with Bobby*, the proceeds of which are contributed to grassroots political organizations.

Seeger, Pete (1919–)

Peter Seeger is a nationally known folksinger, songwriter, and social activist who, with his group, the Weavers, became controversial during the 1950s for his left-wing activities. The son of musicologist Charles Seeger and stepson of composer Ruth Crawford-Seeger, he was raised in a tradition of American folk music that led him to leave Harvard in 1938 (after two years of study in sociology) for travel around the country, gathering songs that represented wide aspects of the native culture. A virtuoso banjo player, he formed a quartet called the Almanac Singers in 1940 with Woody Guthrie. The group had a populist focus and played primarily in union halls and at farm meetings. They disbanded after the end of World War II.

In 1948, Seeger formed another group with Lee Hays, Ronnie Gilbert, and Fred Hellerman; they called themselves the Weavers. Their initial success with both concerts and recordings was cut short when Seeger came under fire for his previous political activities and the group was blacklisted within the entertainment industry. Unable to keep going, they broke up in 1952, but reunited for a Christmas concert at Carnegie Hall in 1955. The acclaim for this concert brought about a resurgence in the group's concerts and recording contracts.

Seeger left the Weavers in 1958, after which he generally worked solo or with members of his family. He nevertheless continued to be victimized by BLACKLISTING. In 1955, he refused to answer questions put to him by the HOUSE UN-AMERICAN ACTIVITIES COMMITTEE, resulting in his 1961 conviction for contempt of Congress. His conviction was overturned in 1962, but for several years afterward he was denied the opportunity to appear on television. In time, negative opinion of Seeger's politics waned, and network executives softened, especially given his role in promoting American folk music. In the 1970s and 1980s, he focused his attention on efforts to curb water pollution and also engaged in antinuclear and environmental demonstrations.

A relaxed and informal performer, Seeger is credited with the popularization of the hootenanny, in which musicians play and sing for each other in front of an audience and often encourage audience participation. The hundreds of songs he has written (alone and with others) have become an important part of American musical culture. In 1972, he published *The Incompleat Folksinger,* a collection of writings on the history of folk songs and performers and their role in the CIVIL RIGHTS MOVEMENT. He rejoined the Weavers for two reunion concerts in 1980.

segregation

A key target of the CIVIL RIGHTS MOVEMENT, segregation in the United States was the practice of separating the races on economic, social, and educational levels to maintain white superiority. In the United States, the chief victims of segregation in the 20th century were African Americans, primarily those living in the South. However, segregation was not limited to this region; in fact, some believed that the overt racial separation enforced in the South was more "honest" than the subtle forms often practiced in the North (i.e., "quiet" discrimination against blacks in housing, education, and employment opportunities).

The original justification behind segregation was bolstered by the Supreme Court ruling in *Plessy v. Ferguson* (1896), which upheld a Louisiana law mandating separate railroad cars for blacks and whites, as long as the cars were "equal." The ruling stated in part: "Laws permitting, and even requiring, their separation in places where they are liable to be brought into contact do not necessarily imply the inferiority of one race over another . . ." Seizing on the word "separation," white Southern lawmakers used the Supreme Court decision to set up a system in which blacks presumably had "separate but equal" status. Thus came into being segregated schools, segregated housing, segregated restaurants, even segregated public facilities such as rest rooms. Southern blacks were forced to take second place to whites in every arena, and even their right to vote was suppressed by segregationist laws (known as "black codes" or "Jim Crow laws").

The passing of legislation to enforce separation of the races was known as de jure segregation; this practice has virtually disappeared as a result of subsequent

Supreme Court rulings such as *Brown v. Board of Education* (1954), a unanimous decision that struck down racial segregation in public schools on the grounds that it denied equal educational rights to minority groups. In addition, the CIVIL RIGHTS ACTS passed by Congress in the 1950s and 1960s (particularly the 1964 act) effectively eliminated any last vestiges of de jure segregation, making black codes and Jim Crow laws illegal and ensuring full equal rights to blacks in the eyes of the law. In this regard, the civil rights movement achieved rousing success.

However, "de facto" segregation continues to exist within the United States, involving both overt and covert attempts by members of one group to keep other groups separated, particularly in the areas of housing and employment. To combat this practice, Congress has passed affirmative action laws that require employers and property owners to demonstrate their compliance with the principles of full integration of the races. In addition, many schools throughout the country have disproportionate numbers of black versus white students, depending on the region, creating a continued de facto segregation of the educational system.

Selective Service   See DRAFT RESISTANCE.

Service, John Stewart (1909–   )

The son of missionaries, John Stewart (spelled Stuart in some sources) Service was a foreign service officer who was assailed in the Cold War era for his leftist political views. During his years working for the U.S. foreign service in China (1933–45), he promoted (to no avail) the recognition of the communist regime. In 1945, he was dismissed for allegedly passing secret government documents to *Amerasia,* a journal with a procommunist bent. He was eventually cleared of the charges and the U.S. Supreme Court overturned his dismissal, enabling him to be reinstated to active service.

Service came to public attention in 1950, when he was placed prominently among those accused by Senator Joseph MCCARTHY of being communist spies, primarily because of the *Amerasia* affair. Subsequent investigations uncovered no proof to support the allegations; however, many retained doubts about Service's character. In 1962, he left government service and went to teach at the University of California. A few years later, Service testified before the Senate Foreign

Relations Committee with regard to President Richard NIXON's plan to normalize U.S. relations with Communist China, which he supported, and which he informed the committee was well overdue.

Sheen, Fulton J. (1895–1979)

Archbishop Fulton John Sheen was a Roman Catholic priest who achieved renown through his use of television and radio to popularize religion. He graduated from St. Victor College in Bourbonnais, Illinois, in 1917, after which he went to study at St. Paul's Seminary in St. Paul, Minnesota. Sheen was ordained as a priest on September 20, 1919. He continued his studies at Catholic University of America (graduate degree in philosophy, 1920); University of Louvain, Belgium (degree in philosophy, 1923); and the Collegio Angelico, Rome (degree in theology, 1924).

In 1925, Sheen became a member of the faculty at Saint Edmond's College in Ware, England. The following year, he accepted a position teaching the philosophy of religion at the Catholic University of America. In 1950, he resigned from the Catholic University to take on a new role as national director of the Society for the Propagation of the Faith. The following year, he was named titular bishop of Caesariana and auxiliary bishop of New York.

Sheen became a nationally recognized personality through his radio program, *The Catholic Hour* (1930–52) and his television program, *Life Is Worth Living* (1952–65). He often used his programs to conduct a vigorous campaign against COMMUNISM. He was named the bishop of Rochester, New York in 1966, then titular archbishop of Newport, Wales, in 1969. He retired in 1969 with the title of archbishop, whereupon he turned to writing and making public appearances. Over the course of his career, Sheen published hundreds of articles and more than 50 books, including *Life Is Worth Living* (1953); *Walk With God* (1965); and *The Moral Universe* (1967).

Shultz, George (1920–)

George Pratt Shultz is an economist and government official who served in the administrations of Presidents Richard NIXON and Ronald REAGAN. After graduating from Princeton University in 1942, Shultz enlisted in the U.S. Marine Corps, serving to the conclusion of World War II. He then resumed his education and earned his Ph.D. degree from the Massachusetts Insti-

tute of Technology (MIT) in 1949. In 1948, he became a professor of economics at MIT, working in that capacity until 1957, when he became a professor of industrial relations at the University of Chicago. He subsequently became dean of the university's business school, in 1962. Over the next few years, in addition to his teaching duties, he served on various employment task forces and acquired a reputation as an outstanding labor negotiator.

In 1969, President Nixon named Shultz to be secretary of labor, in which role he worked to stave off a national rail strike before assuming his next appointment, as director of the newly-created Office of Management and Budget (1970–72). He then served as secretary of the treasury from 1972 to 1974, after which he left government service to become an executive vice president of the Bechtel Corporation, an international construction firm, and to teach management and public policy at Stanford University.

In 1981, Shultz agreed to become chairman of President Reagan's Economic Policy Advisory Board. Reagan then designated him secretary of state in 1982. During his time in this office, Shultz won praise for his calm and rational conduct of foreign policy, overseeing vast changes in U.S. relations with the Soviet Union that resulted in major reductions in nuclear weapons for both nations, but not before the United States had built up its armed forces with the goal of circumventing the spread of communism as well as deterring possible Soviet aggression. Shultz also worked to create a loose-knit alliance of the United States with Arabs and Israelis in an effort to prevent Soviet expansion into the Middle East. (At one point, defending the presence of U.S. troops in Lebanon, he firmly stated, "It's important to show the world that we have resolve.") Later, as diplomatic relations with the Soviet Union took a more positive turn, Shultz responded to charges that the Soviets could not be trusted by noting, "We do not need to trust the Soviets; we need to make agreements that are trustworthy because both sides have incentives to keep them."

When administration officials began planning the negotiations that would later become known as the IRAN-CONTRA AFFAIR, Shultz objected vigorously, noting that such a plan would not only violate established U.S. policy, but also make the country appear hypocritical in its flouting of the rules imposed on other countries. He failed in his attempts to convince Reagan not to pursue the affair, but continued to serve as secretary of state until the end of the Reagan administration. In 1987, he successfully negotiated the Intermediate

Nuclear Force Treaty. Shultz left government service in 1989. In 1993, he published his memoirs, *Turmoil and Triumph*.

shuttle diplomacy

Chiefly practiced by Henry KISSINGER, shuttle diplomacy is a means of achieving quick, "hands-on" results in the attainment of diplomatic goals. The term came into use after the 1973 Arab-Israeli war, when Kissinger made numerous trips to the Middle East, where he shuttled by jet plane from one capital to another in an attempt to negotiate a mutually satisfactory solution for peace. He subsequently used shuttle diplomacy to resolve other crises, and the term entered the modern lexicon. Although chiefly associated with Kissinger, the practice has been used by other diplomats since his time.

Silent Majority

Cited by President Richard NIXON as "the forgotten Americans," the Silent Majority was comprised of those citizens who did not take part in antiwar or civil rights demonstrations, nor expressed outrage or discontent with the government or its justice systems, but simply and quietly lived according to the laws of the land. It was this core of "silent" Americans and their collective opinion that Nixon felt supplied the country's backbone. He noted as much in a presidential campaign speech when he said that "We must remember that all the center is not silent, and all who are silent are not center. But a great many 'quiet Americans' have become committed to answers to social problems that preserve personal freedom."

After Nixon's election in 1968, antiwar demonstrations died down, but late in 1969 they resumed with a fervor that disturbed the president. Seeking to rouse action against the demonstrations, Nixon broadcast a speech to the nation on November 3, 1969, in which he said (in part): "If a vocal minority, however fervent its cause, prevails over reason and the will of the majority, this nation has no future as a free society. Let historians not record that when America was the most powerful nation in the world we passed on the other side of the road and allowed the last hopes for peace and freedom of millions of people to be suffocated by the forces of totalitarianism. And so tonight—to you, the great silent majority of my fellow Americans—I ask for your support." It should be noted that although the

phrase had been used many times before in many variants by other politicians, it was Nixon who placed it firmly in popular usage with this speech and with whom it would be associated from then on. The phrase continues to be used today in reference to the majority of Americans who support government laws and policies.

sit-ins

Sit-ins were a popular tactic used by civil rights and antiwar demonstrators during the 1960s and 1970s. Sit-ins have, in fact, been used in protest movements for decades, but they became an especially popular ploy during the Cold War years, when protesters sought to make an effective statement without resorting to violence; paradoxically, their passively resistant actions sometimes resulted in violence being used against them. During the CIVIL RIGHTS MOVEMENT, sit-ins were frequently used to challenge SEGREGATION laws. An example of this occurred on February 1, 1960, when four black students in Greensboro, North Carolina, sat down at a Woolworth's lunch counter and stayed there the rest of the day, waiting for service that never came. They returned the next day with 16 more black students and received the same lack of service. The following day the group had grown to 50, including several sympathetic whites. Before long, their numbers reached into the hundreds and their peaceful demonstration had extended to another store in Greensboro. This action yielded widespread MEDIA attention and consequently resulted in the extensive use of sit-ins throughout the country. Sit-ins were employed to register protests against unfair laws, discriminatory practices in a number of arenas, the VIETNAM WAR, the draft, and ESTABLISHMENT organizations. On occasion, attempts to break up sit-ins resulted in notorious incidents in which police officers used excessive force and sometimes beatings, leading to charges of police brutality. But for the most part, sit-ins have been and continue to be marked by the principle of NONVIOLENCE as a means of achieving social change.

Smith, Walter Bedell (1895–1961)

Walter Bedell Smith, known as "Beetle" Smith, was a career soldier who performed distinguished diplomatic service to the United States during the early years of the Cold War. As a teenager still in school, Smith enrolled in the Indiana NATIONAL GUARD, there receiving training that he continued after high school, when he was unable to go on to college. (He pursued a private, independent education on his own over the years.) By November 1917, he had received a commission as a second lieutenant in the U.S. Army. He went to fight in France in April 1918, then returned to the United States the following September and entered service in the Bureau of Military Intelligence. Over the ensuing years, he was assigned to a number of different positions and locations, and rose in rank and importance. He also continued his military education and training, graduating from the Army War College in June 1937. He then went to teach at the Fort Benning Infantry School.

Late in 1939, Smith was recalled to Washington and assigned to the General Staff, becoming secretary in 1941. By 1942, he had been promoted to brigadier general and assigned as chief of staff for U.S. forces in the European theater of operations. He played such key roles in major battle campaigns, including the invasions of North Africa and Normandy, that Dwight D. EISENHOWER referred to Smith as "the general manager of the war" as well as "a godsend," while Winston Churchill, who admired Smith's tenacity, nicknamed him "Bulldog." Smith signed the Italian surrender document for Eisenhower, for whom he had become a deputy. By the end of the war, he had been promoted to the rank of major general and had also received the Distinguished Service Medal.

In 1946, President Harry TRUMAN appointed Smith U.S. ambassador to Moscow and also sent him to numerous peace conferences, including the Paris Peace Conference of 1946. Smith's diplomatic duties included attempts to ease the tension caused by the Soviet presence in northern Iran and intercession in the BERLIN BLOCKADE by way of negotiations with Joseph Stalin and Soviet foreign minister V. M. Molotov. Smith continued as ambassador until 1949, when he was given command of the U.S. First Army, but just a year later he took over as director of the CENTRAL INTELLIGENCE AGENCY (CIA). He held this position until 1953, when President Eisenhower appointed him undersecretary of state, in which role he led the U.S. delegation to the 1954 peace conference in Geneva and also headed the Psychological Strategy Board, the aim of which was to evaluate U.S. foreign policy and its impact on other nations. He also served as acting secretary of state in the absence of John Foster DULLES. Meanwhile, Smith was promoted to four-star general in 1951.

Although he continued to act as an adviser to the State Department on occasion, Smith officially retired from government service in 1954 and went into private business, serving as vice chairman of American Machine and Foundry Company. His books include *My Three Years in Moscow* (1950) and *Eisenhower's Six Great Decisions* (1956).

Smith Act

Also called the Alien Registration Act, the Smith Act was a 1940 law named for its chief sponsor, Representative Howard W. Smith of Virginia. Passed just prior to U.S. entry into World War II, the law was a response to growing fears of fascism, COMMUNISM, and subversion within the United States. In essence, the Smith Act made it a crime to teach or advocate the overthrow of a U.S. government, or to be a member of any organization that follows such principles. The law also required aliens to be fingerprinted and registered.

Critics of the Smith Act objected to a "guilt by association" provision and thought it to be unconstitutional with regard to First Amendment rights of free speech. Nevertheless, the controversial law was upheld in 1951, when the U.S. Supreme Court refused to overturn the convictions of 11 U.S. Communist Party leaders (*Dennis v. United States*). However, six years later, in *Yates v. United States,* the Court ruled that advocating the violent overthrow of the government without actually inciting others into such action did not violate the Smith Act.

Snow, Edgar (1905–1972)

Edgar Parks Snow was an author and journalist who provided riveting eyewitness accounts of the early years of COMMUNISM in China. Snow attended the University of Missouri and then graduated from the Columbia School of Journalism in 1927, whereupon he became a reporter for the *Kansas City Star.* He went to China in 1928 and stayed there for the next 12 years while he dispatched reports to the United States on happenings in the East Asia region, particularly Chinese affairs. In 1936, Snow broke through a nationalist blockade and made his way to the communists' base camp in Yenan province, where he spent several months talking to and observing Mao Zedong and other leaders. He then returned to file reports with major U.S. newspapers and magazines, providing the West with its first concrete accounts of the communist movement in China. Snow's news reports from Yenan also frequently portrayed the communist revolutionaries as dedicated workers for reform in China, as well as defenders of the country against Japanese aggression, and not as the "Red Bandits" the nationalists claimed them to be. Snow's reports from the Far East were collected into a book entitled *Red Star Over China,* which was published in 1937 and remains a valuable resource for information on the Chinese communist movement.

In 1941, Snow returned to the United States and became a reporter for the *Saturday Evening Post,* covering the Soviet Union and other countries during World War II. Eventually he dedicated himself to writing and lecturing. He moved to Switzerland in 1959. He went back to China in 1960 to examine what had occurred within the country after the communists had been in power for 11 years, and published his findings in his 1962 book, *The Other Side of the River: Red China Today.* Subsequent trips to China, during which he was treated as a valued friend by Mao Zedong and Zhou Enlai, brought about other books, including *The Long Revolution* in 1972.

Snow's friendship with Mao and Zhou played an important role in the normalization of relations with China. In 1971, following an invitation for Americans to participate in a table tennis tournament, Mao informed Snow that he "would be happy to talk [to President NIXON] either as a tourist or as a president." This led to Henry KISSINGER conducting secret negotiations and, subsequently, to Nixon's historic trip to China in February 1972.

"Soft on communism"

This was a charge frequently leveled at DOVES and others, especially during the era of Senator Joseph MCCARTHY in the 1950s, when fears of communist subversion in the U.S. government often led to unsubstantiated charges against those who were felt to be "soft on communism"—i.e., unwilling to take a hard line with regard to the Soviet Union and failing to provide adequate support to a U.S. buildup of nuclear arms as protection against potential Soviet weaponry. Right-wing conservatives were most likely to attack others with the phrase, and at one point the entire Democratic Party developed a reputation for being soft on communism, which the Republicans often used to their benefit. Although this particular phrase is no longer in use, the word "soft" continues to be employed in a derogatory fashion, whenever political leaders want to attack others who criticize or will not support a military action (i.e., "Soft on Saddam").

Sorensen, Theodore (1928–   )

Theodore Chalkin Sorensen was a lawyer, speechwriter, and government official who served during the administration of President John F. KENNEDY. He received his undergraduate degree from the University of Nebraska in 1949 and then enrolled in the university's college of law. While pursuing his studies, he also worked as a lobbyist in the Nebraska state legislature on behalf of groups favoring the Fair Employment Practices Committee law against racial discrimination. After receiving his law degree in 1951, Sorensen went to work in the legal department at the Federal Security Agency (later the Department of Health, Education and Welfare). His work for a congressional subcommittee on the issue of railroad retirement made an impression on Senator Paul Douglas of Illinois, who recommended Sorensen for a job as an administrative assistant with the new senator from Massachusetts, John F. Kennedy. The two men struck an instant rapport, and Sorensen went to work doing research, studying bills, and drafting memoranda for Kennedy.

In 1955, Sorensen conducted such extensive research for Kennedy's book, *Profiles in Courage* (which won a Pulitzer Prize), that journalist Drew PEARSON later claimed that Sorensen had ghostwritten the book. However, evidence later showed that Kennedy had in fact written it himself, and Pearson finally retracted his allegations.

Sorensen became an indispensable member of Kennedy's team and completely devoted himself to his friend's best interests. In 1956, he wrote a memorandum advocating the inclusion of a Roman Catholic on the presidential ticket, as a result of which Kennedy nearly won the nomination for vice president. During the presidential campaign of 1960, Sorensen worked for Kennedy as a chief strategist and speech writer. After Kennedy's election, he served as special counsel to the president from 1961 to 1963. In this capacity, he helped in the writing of many of the president's major speeches. He was so close to Kennedy that he was considered by many to be (in the words of Barry GOLDWATER) "the man behind [Kennedy's trademark] rocking chair." He came under fire for being a CONSCIENTIOUS OBJECTOR and evading military service in Korea, but it was later shown that there were no irregularities in his military classifications.

In 1966, Sorensen went into private law practice as well as writing. A devoted caretaker of Kennedy's memory, he published *The Kennedy Legacy* in 1969 and edited *Let the Word Go Forth* in 1985.

Southeast Asia Collective Defense Treaty   See MANILA PACT

Southeast Asia Treaty Organization (SEATO)

In keeping with the U.S. policy of forming alliances with other nations as a way to contain communist expansion, the Southeast Asia Treaty Organization (SEATO) was formed in 1954 as a result of the MANILA PACT, which it administered. Similar to the NORTHEAST ATLANTIC TREATY ORGANIZATION (NATO) and the CENTRAL TREATY ORGANIZATION (CENTO), SEATO's purpose was to form a mutually beneficial defense mechanism for the participating nations, in this case in the South Pacific. However, unlike NATO, SEATO had no provisions for an allied military force in the event of emergencies in the region. It did, however, provide for consultation with other member nations, which included Australia, France, Great Britain, New Zealand, Pakistan, the Philippines, Thailand, and the United States. Oddly, the organization did not include India, Burma, and Indonesia. This fact created geopolitical problems, especially because of the conflict between India and Pakistan and because so many of the member nations were located outside the area the organization was supposed to protect. It was in the role of a "consultant" that the United States first became involved in the VIETNAM WAR, using its commitment to SEATO as a major reason. Over time, SEATO ceased to function effectively and in 1977 it was formally dissolved.

"Star Wars"   See STRATEGIC DEFENSE INITIATIVE

Stassen, Harold (1907–   )

Harold Edward Stassen was a Republican governor of Minnesota who became best known for his repeated but never successful campaigns for the U.S. presidency. He put himself through college, earning both his bachelor and law degrees at the University of Minnesota (in 1927 and 1929, respectively). From 1930 to 1938, he practiced law in St. Paul, Minnesota, and also became a leader of the Minnesota Young Republican League. He then became Minnesota's youngest governor when he was elected in 1938 as a reform-minded Republican. He resigned during his third term as governor, in 1943, in order to enlist in the war effort. Joining the navy, he served first as a lieutenant commander and subsequently as an aide to Admiral William Halsey. During

this time, he put out his first feelers for the presidential nomination, letting it be known that he was available during the 1944 race.

At the war's conclusion, Stassen became a U.S. delegate at the founding meeting of the UNITED NATIONS, during which he tried without success to block the veto provision in the Security Council. In 1948, he pursued his most strenuous national campaign for the office of president, but lost the Republican nomination to Thomas E. DEWEY by a narrow margin. Stassen then became president of the University of Pennsylvania, serving from 1948 to 1953.

After another failed bid for the U.S. presidency in 1952, Stassen joined the administration of President Dwight D. EISENHOWER in 1953, starting as director of the Mutual Security Agency and going on to serve as director of the Foreign Operations Administration, then as an assistant to the president directing disarmament studies. In 1958, he ran for governor of Pennsylvania, but lost, suffering the same fate in his bid for mayor of Philadelphia in 1959. He thereupon went back to private law practice, but resurfaced to run for president in the races from 1964 through 1980, always without success.

Steinem, Gloria (1934–   )

A well-known feminist and political activist, Gloria Steinem is also a writer and editor who has provided some of the most articulate and passionate rationales for the cause of women's liberation. After graduating from Smith College in 1956, she went to India to study while also working as a freelance writer and writing a guidebook. She later returned to the United States to pursue a career as a writer and journalist. From 1958 to 1960, she worked for the Independent Research Service, which was later discovered to be covertly subsidized by the CENTRAL INTELLIGENCE AGENCY (CIA). One of Steinem's many responsibilities was to recruit American students to attend communist youth festivals in Europe. This was later used against her by opponents, who accused her of being a CIA agent. She vehemently denied the charges, but they resurfaced during the late 1970s, for a time sending the WOMEN'S MOVEMENT into discord.

After settling in New York City, Steinem began to actively pursue work as a freelance journalist, coming to national attention with the publication of her article, "I Was a Playboy Bunny," an exposé of Playboy Clubs that turned her into a celebrity. Toward the end of the

1960s, she became interested and then involved in the growing women's movement and in political activism. In 1968, she began writing a column entitled "The City Politic" for the newly-created *New York* magazine, in addition to publishing a strong article, "After BLACK POWER, Women's Liberation." This was also the year she became involved with the Redstockings, a radical women's group; accompanied Latino labor activist César Chávez on a Poor People's March in California; and served as treasurer for the Committee for the Legal Defense of Angela DAVIS. In the presidential race that year, she initially supported Eugene MCCARTHY, but later shifted her support to Robert F. KENNEDY.

In 1971, Steinem became one of the founders of the National Women's Political Caucus, a group dedicated to putting more women into political office. The following year, she helped to found *Ms.* magazine (she served as its editor until 1987). Throughout the 1970s and 1980s, Steinem founded or became associated with various women's political organizations, while frequently coming under attack from some feminists for being "too glamorous" for such a serious cause. Nevertheless, she continued writing, lecturing, and organizing. In 1986, she published *Marilyn,* a biography of Marilyn Monroe presented from a feminist viewpoint. She has also written numerous other books, including *Revolution from Within: A Book of Self-Esteem* (1992).

Stevenson, Adlai (1900–1965)

Adlai Ewing Stevenson II was a Democratic leader and consummate diplomat who helped to found the United Nations and also conducted two unsuccessful runs for the U.S. presidency. Stevenson entered Princeton University in 1918, pursuing studies in history and literature and graduating in 1922. He went on to attend Northwestern University Law School while also working at the Bloomington (Illinois) *Daily Pentagraph.*

After earning his law degree, Stevenson joined the Chicago law firm of Cutting, Moore and Sidley in 1927. From 1933 to 1935, he served as special counsel for the Agricultural Adjustment Administration. Over time, he became increasingly devoted to public service, in such roles as head of the Civil Rights Committee of the Chicago Bar Association, president of the Chicago Council of Foreign Relations, and chairman of the Chicago chapter of the Committee to Defend America by Aiding the Allies. During World War II, he became a special assistant to Secretary of the Navy Frank Knox (1941–44), and was also appointed in 1943 to lead a Foreign Economic Administration mission to Italy, with the intent of developing a relief program.

In 1945, Stevenson was appointed a special assistant to Secretary of State Edward Stettinius, Jr., in which role he was an adviser to the U.S. delegation attending the founding of the UNITED NATIONS at the San Francisco Conference in 1945. He subsequently became senior adviser to the U.S. delegation at the UN's first meeting of the General Assembly in London (1946), and served as a delegate during 1946 and 1947.

In 1948, Stevenson ran for governor of Illinois and was elected by the largest margin ever recorded in the state's history. He proceeded to implement widespread reforms in many areas, among them the state police system, hospital care for mental patients, education, and civil service. In 1952, he was drafted by the Democrats to run against Dwight D. EISENHOWER for the U.S. presidency; he lost the election despite immense public respect for his eloquence and principles. It was during this race that Senator Joseph MCCARTHY, a strong supporter of the Eisenhower-Nixon ticket, gave a famous speech in which he deliberately referred to Stevenson as "Alger—I mean Adlai," insidiously referring to Soviet agent and former State Department official Alger HISS. Stevenson ran for president again in 1956, and again lost. In 1957, he founded the Democratic Advisory Council and then returned to his law practice in Chicago.

Initially a rival and then a supporter of John F. KENNEDY in the 1960 presidential race, Stevenson became the U.S. ambassador to the United Nations under President Kennedy in 1961, and was given cabinet status. Nonetheless, his advice during the planning for the BAY OF PIGS fiasco was ignored. During the CUBAN MISSILE CRISIS, he suggested attempting to achieve a diplomatic solution by working out an exchange between the United States and the Soviet Union, but this advice was also rejected. Nevertheless, he later played a major role in easing many of the world tensions brought on by the Cold War and representing U.S. policy during the VIETNAM WAR and the DOMINICAN CRISIS. In 1963, he was a member of the delegation that signed the U.S.-Soviet Partial Nuclear Test Ban Treaty. Under President Lyndon JOHNSON, Stevenson attempted to initiate peace discussions with Hanoi, but the president halted his efforts. In 1965, still the U.S. ambassador to the UN, he died of a heart attack on a London street. Stevenson's many books include *Call to Greatness* (1954), *What I Think* (1956), and *Looking Outward: Years of Crisis at the United Nations* (1963).

President Harry Truman and Assistant Secretary of State Adlai Stevenson (TRUMAN LIBRARY)

Stimson, Henry L. (1867–1950)

Henry Lewis Stimson was a lawyer and statesman who served in various capacities under five U.S. presidents and played a major role in U.S. foreign policy during the 1930s and 1940s. After graduating from Yale and Harvard, Stimson was admitted to the New York bar in 1891. Two years later, he joined Elihu Root's law firm. From 1906 to 1909, he was appointed by President Theodore Roosevelt to be U.S. attorney for the southern district of the state of New York. He made an unsuccessful run for governor of New York in 1910, then served as secretary of war under President William Howard Taft from 1911 to 1913, after which he returned to private law practice. For a short period during World War I, Stimson fought as a field artillery officer in France. He was recalled to public service in 1927 by President Calvin Coolidge to

mediate a civil dispute in Nicaragua, a mission he completed successfully. He then went to the Philippines to serve as governor general from 1927 to 1929, returning to the United States in 1929 to become secretary of state under President Herbert Hoover. In January 1932, following the 1931 Japanese invasion and occupation of Manchuria, he wrote to the governments of Japan and China that the United States would not recognize Japanese rule in Manchuria, nor would it recognize any treaty or agreement that impaired U.S. treaty rights. This declaration subsequently became known as the "Stimson Doctrine," and made him the target of harsh criticism from some international quarters. He stepped down as secretary of state in 1933.

A Republican as well as a leader on the Committee to Defend America by Aiding the Allies, Stimson was nonetheless tapped in 1940 to become secretary of war under President Franklin D. Roosevelt, a Democrat. With the entry of the United States into World War II, Stimson oversaw the expansion, mobilization, and training of military forces. He also served as a chief adviser on atomic policies to both President Roosevelt and President Harry TRUMAN. As the war in the Pacific drew to a close, Stimson justified his recommendation to Truman that the ATOMIC BOMB be dropped on strategically important Japanese cities by noting that the action saved more lives than would have been lost if the war continued, as it hastened Japan's surrender.

After Truman became president, Stimson strongly encouraged a cautious, more diplomatic approach to relations with the Soviet Union. He left his cabinet post in September 1945, and in 1948 published an autobiography (cowritten with McGeorge BUNDY) entitled *On Active Service in Peace and War.* Upon the formation of the UNITED NATIONS, Stimson voiced the opinion that such an organization would work only if the major powers agreed to work out their differences first.

Stone, I. F. (1907–1989)

Born Isidor Feinstein, I. F. Stone was a journalist who created a nationally acclaimed newsletter that provided a witty, incisive, and liberal view of modern politics. Making his career choice at an early age, Stone started out as a high school newspaper reporter and subsequently joined the Socialist Party during the 1920s. After three years at the University of Pennsylvania (1924–27), he went to work for the *Philadelphia Inquirer* and subsequently for the *New York Post,* the *Philadelphia Record,* and *The Nation* during the period from 1933 to 1946. Following this, he worked as a reporter for several different New York newspapers, as well as a liberal daily entitled *PM,* which folded in 1948.

In 1937, Feinstein had changed his name to I. F. Stone, and in 1953, he launched his own weekly publication, *I. F. Stone's Weekly.* Among the earliest subscribers to *I. F. Stone's Weekly* were Albert Einstein, Bertrand Russell, and Eleanor ROOSEVELT. It gained a reputation very quickly for the quality of its research and journalism, as well as for the wit and erudition of its writer and editor. Stone was assisted in the production of his newsletter only by his wife.

A lifelong liberal, Stone frequently championed causes such as CIVIL RIGHTS well before they became popular. He vigorously opposed the Cold War policies established by President Harry TRUMAN as well as the MCCARTHYISM that pervaded the country in the early 1950s, feeling that the country had become obsessed with anticommunist panic. He was also a vocal opponent of the VIETNAM WAR from its earliest stages. In columns, he frequently printed statements from government sources that directly contradicted each other. In 1967, his weekly newsletter became *I. F. Stone's Bi-Weekly,* until it folded in 1971. Over the years, Stone also wrote many books examining U.S. policies and procedures. In 1946, he published an account of his own involvement in the attempts by Jewish refugees to attain a homeland, entitled *Underground to Palestine.* His columns have been collected and published in 1963, 1967, 1971, and 1989.

Strategic Arms Limitation Talks (SALT)

As arms control talks between the United States and the Soviet Union intensified during the late 1960s, specific areas began to be targeted for discussion. Among these was the mutual desire to put constraints on the development and use of strategic weapons systems. Thus began the Strategic Arms Limitation Talks (SALT), to be followed eventually by the Strategic Arms Reduction Talks (START). The specified aim of these talks was to limit and, finally, reduce the U.S. and Soviet nuclear arsenals.

The first round of talks, known as SALT I, got under way in 1969, with Henry KISSINGER overseeing the delicate negotiations. SALT I resulted in several agreements: the 1972 signing of the Anti-Ballistic Missile Treaty, the Accident Measures Agreement (a revision of a previous "hotline" agreement), and an Interim Agreement regarding strategic weapons. President Richard NIXON and Soviet premier Leonid Brezhnev represented their countries at the signing in Moscow. Later that year, in November 1972, SALT II was launched. Its initial goals focused on meeting the terms specified in the Interim Agreement. By 1974, both the United States and the Soviets agreed that the five-year time limit placed on limiting strategic offensive weapons was not feasible. However, a tentative agreement outlining the SALT II goals was signed by Brezhnev and President Gerald FORD in November 1974; this became known as the Vladivostok Agreement.

The talks continued over the next few years, and in late 1977, more tentative agreements had been reached. Finally, under the stewardship of President Jimmy CARTER, SALT II was signed in July 1979. This new agreement placed specified limits on the numbers of certain offensive weapons each side could have, but this did not affect Soviet intercontinental ballistic missiles. SALT II was never ratified by the Senate, due in large part to Carter's failure to achieve domestic support for it, but also because of the Soviet invasion of Afghanistan in December 1979. Despite this, both the United States and the Soviet Union adhered to SALT II terms throughout the 1980s, all the while continuing talks regarding an Intermediate Nuclear Force Treaty and initiating START. Meanwhile, a third round of SALT discussions began in 1982, but was suspended a year later.

START, which began in the early 1980s, was the primary topic of discussion at the 1986 REYKJAVIK SUMMIT between President Ronald REAGAN and Premier Mikhail Gorbachev. The agreement reached at that time was that both sides would reduce their arsenal of strategic offensive weapons by 50% within five years. Reagan also agreed to hold off on deployment of the STRATEGIC DEFENSE INITIATIVE for 10 years, although he would make no other concessions in that regard.

With the dissolution of the Soviet Union in the early 1990s, the Cold War came to an end, and so did the need for SALT and START. However, concerns remain about the possession and use of nuclear weapons throughout the world, and the need to continue arms control talks is an ever-present reality.

Strategic Arms Reduction Talks (START) See
STRATEGIC ARMS LIMITATION TALKS (SALT).

Strategic Defense Initiative (SDI)

Better known by its nickname of "Star Wars," the Strategic Defense Initiative (SDI) was a controversial national defense program proposed by President Ronald REAGAN that proved to be a major factor in bringing about the end of the Cold War, even though SDI itself never came to fruition as Reagan envisioned it. In March 1983, the president presented his idea for a system designed to provide defenses against "the awesome Soviet missile threat" with laser beams or "antimissile missiles" that could be deployed from space as well as from the ground, enabling the United States to instantly destroy attack missiles before they reached their U.S. targets. The technology involved in creating SDI was so complicated that many critics thought it couldn't be done; its potential threat to worldwide security—it was just as much an offensive

system as it was defensive—was such that others thought it shouldn't be done. Reagan had no such qualms, however, and asked Congress for $26 billion over five years to develop and implement the program. (Subsequent estimates of the costs reached as high as $2 trillion.) Heated debate followed among politicians and citizens alike about the viability of SDI and the real need for such a broad and intimidating defense system. There was also concern that SDI violated the terms of the Anti-Ballistic Missile (ABM) Treaty, and to this end the Soviet Union, financially unable to develop a similar program, repeatedly pressured the United States to limit the program in the context of further arms reduction talks. Despite overwhelming objections to the program, Reagan pressed forward with it, convinced that its implementation would be "the means of rendering nuclear weapons impotent and obsolete," and thus honoring the U.S. commitment to the ABM Treaty. Left unsaid was the fact that if the program was successful, the United States would hold a monopoly in the nuclear arms race.

In April 1984, an organization to conduct SDI research was set up, and over the next several years technology was developed that brought Reagan close to the fulfillment of his dream, even as controversy and debate raged over the program. However, in late 1991, the Soviet Union finally collapsed under the weight of internal dissension and failure to keep up with the United States in the arms race. This effectively eliminated the rationale for Star Wars development, but defense research continued in the BUSH administration under a new approach entitled "Global Protection Against Limited Strikes," which was designed to protect the United States and its allies from "accidental, unauthorized ballistic missile attack." Meanwhile, technology developed as a result of Star Wars research began to find its way into other fields, including medicine, thus providing unexpected benefits from the costly program.

Student Non-violent Coordinating Committee (SNCC)

A direct product of the CIVIL RIGHTS MOVEMENT, the Student Non-violent Coordinating Committee (SNCC, often pronounced "snik") was formed in 1960 after a civil rights conference in Raleigh, North Carolina, sponsored by Martin Luther KING, Jr.'s Southern Christian Leadership Conference (SCLC). By this time, university students had become deeply involved in the movement, and felt a need to form their own organization dedicated to civil rights goals. With a founding group of 235 black students, SNCC was quickly established with King's precept of nonviolence as its central theme, as noted in its statement of purpose: "By appealing to the conscience and standing on the moral nature of human existence, nonviolence nurtures the atmosphere in which reconciliation and justice become actual possibilities." The organization had its first headquarters in the SCLC's office in Atlanta, Georgia, and soon became multiracial in nature, with many white sympathizers joining in its cause.

SNCC quickly set itself at the forefront of the civil rights movement, organizing demonstrations, marches, SIT-INS, literacy programs, voter registration drives, and "FREEDOM RIDERS" in 1961. However, as the 1960s progressed, many in the organization became increasingly dissatisfied with the movement's slow progress, as well as with SNCC leadership. In time, a growing faction within the group began to advocate stronger measures to achieve its goals, including the use of violence. This dichotomy was crystallized with the ascension of Stokely CARMICHAEL to leadership of the conference in 1966. During the course of the "March Against Fear" in Mississippi that year, Carmichael became attracted to a new slogan coined by SNCC organizer Willie Ricks: "BLACK POWER"! Carmichael began to publicly use the phrase himself, and it had the desired effect of inciting audiences to action—sometimes drastic action, much to the dismay of some civil rights leaders, such as King, who continued to advocate peaceful means of bringing about change. This turned out to be the turning point in the movement, which became increasingly splintered by infighting. By 1968 one of SNCC's leaders was H. Rap Brown, a BLACK PANTHER whose rallying cry was the exhortation to "move from resistance to aggression, from revolt to revolution!" With Brown's arrest for incitement to riot, and the national unrest of 1967–68, SNCC, which clearly had come a long way from the principles on which it had been founded, finally disbanded.

Students for a Democratic Society (SDS)

Founded in Chicago in 1960, the Students for a Democratic Society (SDS) was a radical leftist group consisting initially of white middle-class students that was created to assist in the CIVIL RIGHTS MOVEMENT and to perform community work in urban ghettos. Soon, however, the SDS membership expanded to embrace other races and radical elements and the group began to focus its atten-

tion on major societal ills, issuing calls for governmental reforms that would end poverty and create a "participatory democracy" for U.S. citizens. This mission was cemented in June 1962, with a gathering of student leaders from 59 colleges in Port Huron, Michigan, at which they adopted a statement written by Tom Hayden, a student at the University of Michigan. Among other things, the Port Huron statement condemned the U.S. government and its exacerbation of the Cold War and embraced the philosophy of the NEW LEFT. SDS activities were aimed at promoting a massive resistance to the corrupt and hypocritical ESTABLISHMENT.

By 1965, the SDS was among the leaders of the ANTIWAR MOVEMENT, conducting draft card burnings and organizing demonstrations and SIT-INS on college campuses around the country. By 1969, the group had grown to include branches in approximately 400 universities, and, partially as a result of their activities, colleges had become hotbeds of protest. Headlines were made with each seizure of a college administration building. However, internal dissension had begun to tear the organization apart. The SDS had sought to transform American society by a socialist revolution, but ideas on how to achieve that revolution differed among its various members, and it began to split into competing factions. One of these was the Weather Underground (the Weathermen), a particularly violent faction that united students, workers, and blacks in an attempt to overthrow the capitalist system by acts of terrorism and sabotage. Students opposed to the use of violence began to leave the SDS, which also lost its primary target for protest when the VIETNAM WAR was de-escalated under President Richard NIXON. The group finally disbanded in the mid-1970s.

Subversive Activities Control Board   See INTERNAL SECURITY ACT.

Symbionese Liberation Army   See HEARST, Patricia.

Symington, Stuart (1901–1988)

William Stuart Symington was a U.S. senator from Missouri who opposed the war in Vietnam despite his position as a proponent of a strong defense system for the United States. After serving in the army during World War I (enlisting at the age of 17), Symington enrolled in Yale University. He graduated in 1923 and entered the family business, the Symington Company, in Rochester, New York. Over the next few years, he worked for several different firms. In 1939, he was named president and chief executive officer of the St. Louis-based Emerson Electric Manufacturing Company, where he immediately set about appeasing the union in an effort to purge it of communist elements. His success in filling wartime contracts soon brought him to the attention of Senator Harry TRUMAN.

In 1941, the War Department sent Symington to England to study and report on airplane armament. Four years later, President Truman tapped him to chair the Surplus Property Board. Frustrated by the red tape and legal restrictions that he felt hindered his effectiveness, Symington resigned from the position in early 1946. Just a few days later, Truman named him secretary of war for air; then, he made Symington the first secretary of the air force when Congress passed the NATIONAL SECURITY ACT and established the Department of Defense. Symington served in this position from 1947 to 1950, working to desegregate the armed services and unsuccessfully attempting to expand the air force from 55 to 70 groups for reasons of national security (it was eventually reduced to 48 groups). In an address given at Baylor University in February 1950, Symington issued a warning that the Soviet Union and affiliated communist countries possessed "the world's largest ground army, air force, and undersea fleet." Alarmed by growing reductions in military armaments, which he felt sidelined national security in favor of balancing the budget, Symington resigned his position in April 1950, and immediately took up new responsibilities as chairman of the National Security Resources Board. These responsibilities included overseeing the mobilization of U.S. forces to intervene in the crisis in Korea, a task that was eventually taken over by others.

In 1952, Symington ran for office for the first time (as a Democrat) and was elected as U.S. senator; he was reelected for three successive terms. He soon acquired a reputation in the Senate for his strong position on the issue of national defense. He was named to serve on the Armed Services Committee and also served on the Government Operations Committee's permanent investigations subcommittee, from which he and two other Democratic senators resigned in July 1953, in protest over the conduct of its chairman, Senator Joseph MCCARTHY. Symington returned to the subcommittee a year later to participate in its investigation of McCarthy and the army hearings. The televised proceedings brought Symington to national attention; at one point, responding to McCarthy's accusation of cowardice, he replied, "I want you to know from the bottom of my heart that I am not afraid of anything about you or anything you've got to say any time, any place, anywhere." When the hearings ended, Symington and two other Democrats pointedly suggested that the subcommittee be reorganized and cleaned up.

In 1956, Symington led a subcommittee of the Senate Armed Services Committee to investigate the EISENHOWER administration's defense program. He continued to be alarmed by Soviet superiority in the arms race, noting that, "I don't 'believe' the Soviets are ahead of us in ballistic missiles. I state that they are." Symington forecast the Soviet Union's growing dominance in both the military and the sciences before Sputnik was launched in 1957. Nevertheless, in the 1960s, he became a vocal opponent of the escalation of U.S. military involvement in Vietnam, believing that country to be unimportant to U.S. security and the war to be too great a drain on the nation's economy. He also attacked the government's secrecy regarding the storage of U.S. nuclear weapons on foreign soil.

Symington made two unsuccessful bids for the U.S. presidency, in 1956 and in 1960. He retired from the Senate at the end of 1975.

T

Taft, Robert (1889–1953)

The son of President William Howard Taft, Robert Alphonso Taft was a U.S. senator from Ohio who became known as "Mr. Republican" due to his strong influence on party policy. A graduate of Yale University and Harvard Law School, Taft worked alongside Herbert Hoover in the U.S. Food Administration during World War I, and subsequently poured his energy into postwar relief efforts in Europe. Following in his father's footsteps, he entered politics in the 1920s. Elected to the Ohio House of Representatives, he took office in 1921 and became speaker in 1926. Taft served as a member of the Ohio State Senate in 1931 and 1932, then returned for a period to private law practice. His opposition to the New Deal programs of President Franklin D. Roosevelt led him to run for the U.S. Senate in 1938. He was elected that year, then reelected in 1944 and 1950.

A hard-line conservative, Taft became known for his advocacy of ISOLATIONISM, urging that the United States not become involved in world affairs outside the Western Hemisphere. Prior to the attack on Pearl Harbor, he argued strenuously against American intervention in World War II. With the subsequent growth of the Cold War, Taft fought many of President Harry TRUMAN's foreign policies on the grounds that they were costly and posed a threat to American security; for instance, he vigorously opposed the establishment of a NORTH ATLANTIC TREATY ORGANIZATION (NATO) army in Germany, feeling it would only invite Soviet military intervention. Nevertheless, he was in favor of attempts to contain Soviet expansion, and he backed the TRUMAN DOCTRINE of 1947, which gave U.S. aid to Greece and Turkey to combat communist aggression.

During his years in the Senate, Taft favored only limited federal programs for educational, housing, and health insurance. He also argued for a balanced budget. He was a cosponsor of the 1947 Taft-Hartley Act, which placed certain controls on labor unions (and which many labor leaders condemned as "the slave labor act"). Taft made unsuccessful bids for the Republican presidential nomination in 1940, 1948, and 1952; in all cases, his conservatism and continued opposition to U.S. internationalism were stumbling blocks he could not surmount. Nevertheless, he was a highly respected and highly influential presence within the Republican Party.

In 1951, Taft published *A Foreign Policy for Americans*. He defended the actions of Senator Joseph MCCARTHY, stating that "the pro-Communist policies of the State Department fully justified Joe McCarthy in his demand for an investigation." As McCarthy's "WITCH HUNTS" began to get out of hand, however, Taft engineered his transfer to the Government Operations Committee, incorrectly concluding that McCarthy's crusade against communism would die there. Instead, McCarthy's crusade became stronger and more rampant than ever. Taft died in July 1953, before the McCarthy era played out to its sad conclusion.

Taylor, Maxwell Davenport (1901–1987)

General Maxwell Davenport Taylor was a soldier and diplomat who served as U.S. ambassador to Vietnam during several crucial years of the Cold War. A 1922 graduate of the U.S. Military Academy at West Point, Taylor was originally commissioned into the Army Corps of Engineers as a second lieutenant. He spent the next several years in a variety of positions, finally advancing to the rank of captain and a job as a language instructor at West Point, from 1927 to 1932. He subsequently attended the Field Artillery School and the General Staff School, whereupon he was sent to Japan as an attaché at the embassy in Tokyo. He also served briefly as an assistant military attaché in Peking before being recalled to the United States in 1939, when he entered the Army War College. He subsequently held additional general staff positions, rising in rank quickly with the outbreak of World War II. By December 1942, Taylor had become a brigadier general and was made artillery commander of the 82nd Airborne Division.

Throughout the war, Taylor distinguished himself with exceptional service and decision making. In May 1944, he was promoted to major general (temporary) and given command of the 101st Airborne Division, and helped to plan the Allied invasion of France. On June 6, 1944, he parachuted into Normandy with his division, becoming the first American general to engage in battle in France. He continued to perform exceptional acts of courage under fire for the remainder of the war, in particular playing a key role in the Battle of the Bulge.

Late in 1945, Taylor became superintendent of the military academy at West Point. During his tenure, he overhauled the curriculum and created courses in military leadership, with an emphasis on building character and setting strong examples for others. He served as superintendent for four years; then, in 1949, he was appointed chief of staff of the American forces in

Europe. In September 1949, he was made the first commander of the American Military Government in Berlin. He returned to the United States in 1951 to assume duties as deputy chief of staff for operations and administration of the army. By this time he had become a permanent major general.

In February 1953, Taylor was named commander of the Eighth Army in Korea, where he supervised the last few months of the war there. In November that same year, he began implementation of a program called Armed Forces Assistance to Korea that provided aid to the war-stricken nation. A year later, he took command of ground forces in Korea, Okinawa, and Japan, and by April 1955, he had attained the rank of full general and been named commander in chief of the Far East command and the UNITED NATIONS command. He was then recalled to Washington, where he was appointed chief of staff of the United States Army. In this capacity, Taylor became a vocal proponent of an enlarged army capable of a FLEXIBLE RESPONSE to possible attack by an enemy, as opposed to the then-popular MASSIVE RETALIATION theory favored by others in the administration. When Taylor failed to achieve ratification of his military goals, he resigned his position and retired from the army, going instead into private business as chairman of the board of the Mexican Light and Power Company, Ltd. He also became president of the then-new Lincoln Center for the Performing Arts in New York City.

His 1959 book, *The Uncertain Trumpet,* brought him to the attention of a young John F. KENNEDY, who agreed with many of Taylor's arguments of flexible response for defense purposes and even used them in his 1960 presidential campaign. Taylor returned to government service following the disastrous BAY OF PIGS INVASION in April 1961, when President Kennedy asked him to undertake an investigation of the role of the CENTRAL INTELLIGENCE AGENCY (CIA) in the fiasco. Taylor concluded that the CIA should not be permitted to take part in future major operations but should be allowed to continue undercover activities on a small scale. In July 1961, he was assigned to the newly established post of military representative of the president, to advise Kennedy on military conditions as they related to foreign affairs. Later that year, in October, he and Walt Whitman ROSTOW headed a special mission to South Vietnam to study the advance of communism in the region and to determine whether U.S. troops should be sent in. They concluded in their report that a "logistic task force" of 8,000 men should be dispatched in order to maintain a flexible response to Soviet aggression in the area.

From 1962 to 1964, Taylor was chairman of the Joint Chiefs of Staff. After that, President Lyndon B. JOHNSON named him ambassador to South Vietnam. Upon witnessing the instability of the government in Saigon, Taylor made recommendations regarding the bombing of North Vietnam; he also advised that troop levels be kept at a minimum. Taylor strongly supported the president's policies, but eventually found that much of his advice was ignored as Johnson began to be influenced by the hawkish views of General William WESTMORELAND and other advisers who favored ESCALATION of the war on a larger scale than Taylor thought wise. After one year as ambassador, Taylor returned to the United States, where he served as a special counselor to President Johnson from 1965 to 1969 and also as president of the Institute of Defense Analysis, from 1966 to 1969, after which he became chairman of the Foreign Intelligence Advisory Board. In addition to *An Uncertain Trumpet,* Taylor published *Responsibility and Response* (1967), *Swords and Plowshares* (1972), and *Precarious Security* (1976).

Teller, Edward (1908–   )

Born Ede Teller in Hungary, Edward Teller is a nuclear physicist who played a leading role in the development of the HYDROGEN BOMB. He attended Budapest schools before going to Germany to study chemical engineering at the Institute of Technology in Karlsruhe. After graduation, he continued his studies in Munich and Leipzig, earning his Ph.D. degree in physical chemistry in 1930. Teller's doctoral thesis focused on the hydrogen molecular ion and provided a base for molecular orbital theory that is now commonly used. Teller then embarked on a period of study devoted to atomic physics, first with Niels Bohr in Copenhagen, Denmark, then as a professor teaching at the University of Göttingen, from 1931 to 1933.

In 1935, Teller accepted a teaching position at George Washington University in Washington, D.C., and immigrated to the United States with his wife. Together with fellow physicist George Gamow, he engaged in scientific research on subatomic particles that, together with Niels Bohr's accomplishments in uranium atom fission in 1939, led him to respond to President Roosevelt's call for a united scientific front against Nazi Germany and join in the research to develop nuclear arms. By 1941, he had become a U.S.

citizen and had joined the laboratory of Enrico Fermi at the University of Chicago, where he took part in the experiment that resulted in the first self-sustaining nuclear chain reaction. Teller then went to the University of California at Berkeley to work with J. Robert OPPENHEIMER, whom he followed to Los Alamos, New Mexico, on the first ATOMIC BOMB. As other scientists focused on building a fission bomb, he became increasingly interested in the possibility of a more powerful thermonuclear hydrogen-fusion bomb.

After the bombing of Hiroshima, Oppenheimer and other scientists lost their taste for research in nuclear weapons, but Teller continued his work. In 1946, he went to the Institute of Nuclear Studies at the University of Chicago, but continued to consult in Los Alamos. By now, he was pushing hard for U.S. development of a hydrogen bomb, especially after the Soviet Union exploded its first atomic bomb in 1949. Arguing that the United States must have nuclear weapons if the Soviet Union had them, he insisted that testing and development were necessary not only to perfect U.S. weaponry but also to create a "clean" bomb that would (supposedly) emit no radioactivity. Although the ATOMIC ENERGY COMMISSION (AEC), led by Oppenheimer, voted against it, the decision to develop a hydrogen bomb came after it was revealed that British scientist Klaus Fuchs had been transmitting American data on the hydrogen bomb to the Soviet Union since 1942. With President Truman's approval, Teller returned to Los Alamos to create the first workable hydrogen bomb. In early 1951, he and physicist Stanislaw M. Ulam worked out a solution to the ignition of a thermonuclear core and, using what has since become known as the Teller-Ulam configuration, created a nuclear device that was successfully exploded at a Pacific atoll on November 1, 1952. Despite Ulam's key contributions, Teller was given most of the credit for his stubborn pursuit of developing the world's first thermonuclear weapon against stiff scientific opposition. He was subsequently dubbed "the father of the H-bomb."

After the hydrogen bomb explosion, Teller went on to help create the second nuclear weapons laboratory in the United States in Livermore, California, in 1952. Over the next four decades, the Lawrence Livermore Laboratory became the foremost center for the creation of thermonuclear weapons. In 1954, Teller gave damaging testimony against Oppenheimer during hearings to determine the latter's security risk. After Oppenheimer was stripped of his security clearance, Teller was castigated by other scientists for betraying his former boss.

Teller served as associate director of the Lawrence Livermore Laboratory from 1954 to 1958, as director from 1958 to 1960, and again as associate director from 1960 to 1975. He also served as a member of the AEC general advisory committee from 1956 to 1958. In addition to his work at Livermore, Teller was also a professor of physics at the University of California at Berkeley from 1953 to 1960, remaining as a professor at large until 1970. Much of his work during the 1960s was devoted to the fight to maintain U.S. superiority over the Soviet Union in the development and possession of nuclear arms. He also supported Bernard Baruch's plan for international control of atomic power. Strongly anticommunist, Teller opposed the 1963 Partial Nuclear Test Ban Treaty.

Throughout his career, Teller served as an adviser to various presidential administrations on policy regarding nuclear explosives, and was highly influential in the creation of the STRATEGIC DEFENSE INITIATIVE, President REAGAN's controversial effort to build a strong defense against potential attack from the Soviet Union. Teller retired from both the Lawrence Livermore Laboratory and the University of California in 1975.

Tet offensive

The Tet offensive of 1968 was a crucial turning point in the VIETNAM WAR that turned many previously undecided Americans against U.S. military involvement in Vietnam. *Tet Nguyen-dan* is the name given to the Vietnamese New Year festival, which is celebrated during the first seven days of the first month of the lunar calendar. Ordinarily it is a time of cease-fire and celebration. In 1968, the first day of the Tet New Year was the last day of January; this was the day the Vietcong chose to launch a major offensive against U.S. and South Vietnamese troops. Much grisly battle footage was broadcast into American homes, as major cities in South Vietnam, including Saigon, crumbled under the combined effect of mortars, rockets, and gunfire, and thousands of lives were lost on both sides. One of the most traumatic images from this period—published in many newspapers and magazines—was that of a South Vietnamese officer shooting an unarmed Vietcong soldier at point-blank range in the head.

The main objective of the Tet offensive was to incite uprisings among South Vietnamese civilians and military. The North Vietnamese did not succeed in this

Saigon in ruins after the Vietcong's deadly Tet offensive (NARA STILL PHOTOS DIVISION)

goal, but still managed to score some major military and political victories throughout the long weeks of the offensive. Chief among these victories was the reaction of the American public to what they were seeing on their television screens; a typically horrifying image was that of the Vietcong attack on the U.S. embassy in Saigon. Long assured by their government leaders that they were winning the war, U.S. citizens now had visible proof that, in fact, the war was costing them dearly in the loss of both American lives and international prestige.

Thurmond, Strom (1902–   )

James Strom Thurmond is a longtime U.S. senator who has aroused extensive controversy due to his conservative views on segregation and states' rights. A 1923 graduate of Clemson College in Clemson, South Carolina, he taught school for six years before being admitted to the bar in 1930. He entered public service when he became a state senator in 1933, in addition to being a city and county attorney. In 1938, he was appointed as a circuit court judge, serving until 1942, when he enlisted for military service during World War II. He fought heroically and was discharged as a lieutenant colonel with the highest honors.

In 1946, Thurmond ran successfully for governor of South Carolina. As governor, he implemented numerous liberal reforms that included a major expansion of the state's educational system. In 1948, he was one of a group of Southerners irate over the civil rights plank in the Democratic Party's presidential platform. They broke away to form the States' Rights Democratic Party, also known as the "Dixiecrats," and nominated Thurmond as their candidate for president. He won 39 electoral votes. In 1954, he was elected to the U.S. Senate on the basis of write-in votes. He immediately gained a reputation as a die-hard Southern conservative, a vigorous supporter of increased military spending, and a foe of the civil rights movement. During hearings on the proposed CIVIL RIGHTS ACT (which became law in 1964), Thurmond suggested that, however sincere the feeling behind the demonstrations and parades of the time, they were nonetheless "inspired by communists, and I think it is part of the international conspiracy of COMMUNISM."

Thurmond was reelected to the Senate as a Democrat in 1960, but left the Democratic Party in 1964 to support Barry GOLDWATER for president. In 1966, he was again reelected, this time as a Republican, and continued to win reelection thereafter and to this day. He became chairman of the Senate Judiciary Committee in 1980, and was elected president pro tempore of the Senate in 1981, serving until 1987 and again from 1995.

Tonkin Gulf Incidents and Resolution

The events that presumably precipitated the Tonkin Gulf Resolution—and resulted in the controversial escalation of the VIETNAM WAR—took place in early August of 1964. On two separate occasions, North Vietnamese patrol boats allegedly attacked American destroyers off the coast of North Vietnam, even though the Americans claimed the destroyers were in international waters in the Gulf of Tonkin. Later information revealed that the destroyers were assisting the South Vietnamese in coastal raids and so were probably in

President Lyndon Johnson signs the Gulf of Tonkin Resolution. (JOHNSON LIBRARY)

North Vietnamese waters at the time of the attacks. Nevertheless, President Lyndon JOHNSON ordered retaliatory attacks on the North Vietnamese and subsequently sent a draft resolution to Congress authorizing "all necessary measures to repel any armed attack against the forces of the United States, and to prevent further aggression." Both houses of Congress passed the resolution overwhelmingly, with dissenting votes from only two senators, Wayne MORSE of Oregon and Ernest Gruening of Alaska.

With the passing of the Tonkin Gulf Resolution, Johnson now had congressional "permission" to escalate the war, which he proceeded to do. This move, however, increased antiwar protests and criticism of his administration to such an extent that he chose not to run for reelection in 1968. The resolution was repealed in 1970, and a few years later, publication of the PENTAGON PAPERS revealed that Johnson had prepared his draft for Congress several months before the events of August 1964 actually occurred. This revelation called into question whether the reported details of the Gulf of Tonkin incidents were accurate or manufactured for Johnson's purposes; the controversy remains to this day.

Tower Commission   See IRAN-CONTRA AFFAIR.

Truman, Harry (1884–1972)

The 33rd president of the United States, Harry Truman was a liberal Democrat who led the nation during the earliest days of the Cold War. The son of a farmer and mule trader, Truman grew up in Independence, Missouri, where he graduated from high school in 1901. He moved to Kansas City and worked as a bank clerk for several years before taking over the management of his grandmother's farm in Grandview, Missouri, where he also became the local postmaster and a road overseer, as well as a national guardsman. In 1915 and 1916, he was made a partner in a lead mine and an oil prospecting business, both of which failed. Enlisting in the military during World War I, Truman served heroically as a captain, revealing the leadership qualities that would distinguish him in years to come. Upon his return from the war, he married Bess Wallace, his childhood sweetheart from Independence. He then entered into a partnership in a Kansas City haberdashery. When it failed, he decided to go into politics under the patronage of Thomas Pendergast, the Democratic boss of Jackson County, where Kansas City is located.

President Harry Truman (NARA STILL PHOTOS DIVISION)

In 1922, Truman won election as county judge, but lost his seat two years later. For the next few years, he endured a series of business failures and also studied nights at the Kansas City Law School. In 1926, backed by Pendergast, he was elected as presiding judge of the county court. He distinguished himself during his eight years in this position, winning both Democratic and Republican support as well as a reputation for honesty and excellent managerial skills. Meanwhile, Truman found himself increasingly distanced from Pendergast. He was prevented from running for governor in 1932 and was passed over when delegates to the Democratic National Convention were named. However, in 1934, after three potential candidates had rejected Pendergast's offer of support in the Senate primary contest, Truman became the candidate of necessity and was elected soon thereafter.

Because of his association with Pendergast, Truman was initially regarded as a figurehead by many of his colleagues in the U.S. Senate, but his clear integrity and dedication to his work soon gained him friends and support. Among other accomplishments, he wrote the Civil Aeronautics Act of 1938 and led a committee investigation for two years that resulted in the Transportation Act of 1940. That same year, he narrowly won reelection. Entering into his second term as senator, Truman chaired the Special Committee Investigating National Defense, in the process exposing a large amount of graft and waste in the defense system. His work on this committee brought him public acclaim for saving millions of taxpayer dollars.

In January 1944, Robert E. Hannegan, a supporter of Truman, became chairman of the Democratic National Committee. This made it possible for Truman to replace Henry A. Wallace as the vice presidential candidate in the 1944 elections. Eighty-two days after Truman's election as vice president, he became president when Franklin D. Roosevelt died in office on April 12, 1945. (Roosevelt had met with his vice president only twice during that time.)

Despite his inexperience and unfamiliarity with the details of Roosevelt's plans and programs, Truman swiftly took charge of the administration, overseeing the conclusion of World War II. He began by arranging the final plans for a meeting in San Francisco to write the charter for what would become the UNITED NATIONS, then helped to arrange Germany's surrender in May 1945. In July of that year, he attended a summit meeting in POTSDAM, Germany, and subsequently made the decision to drop ATOMIC BOMBS on the Japan-

Harry Truman is sworn in as president following the death of Franklin D. Roosevelt (TRUMAN LIBRARY)

ese cities of Hiroshima and Nagasaki. This decision brought a quick end to the war in the Pacific, although it remains controversial to this day because of the extreme loss of Japanese civilian life.

In 1948, Truman was fully expected to lose the presidency to the more popular Republican candidate, Governor Thomas E. DEWEY of New York. However, he threw himself into the campaign with vigorous attacks on the failings of the Republicans and enjoyed an upset victory over Dewey. (The *Chicago Tribune,* counting on a Republican victory and facing a deadline, chose "Dewey Defeats Truman" as its headline for the following morning—and thus gave the president a memorable photo opportunity.) Truman began his next term in office by proposing a liberal domestic program he called the "Fair Deal." However, only one plank of the program, a measure covering low-cost housing, passed the legislative process. Foreign affairs proved to be Truman's forte, and he enthusiastically met the challenge posed by growing Soviet military power. To keep the Soviet Union from expanding its territory and influence, and acting on the advice of experts, Truman proceeded to pursue a policy of CONTAINMENT that would be followed by strategists for many years afterward. In 1947, the TRUMAN DOCTRINE was announced, with the goal of providing military aid to Greece and Turkey as protection against communist aggression. That year also saw the establishment of the CENTRAL INTELLIGENCE AGENCY (CIA). In 1948, Truman implemented an airlift to bring supplies into Berlin when the Soviets blocked land entrances (see BERLIN BLOCKADE). He also

oversaw the implementation of the MARSHALL PLAN in 1948 to assist the economic recovery in Western Europe and the creation of the 1949 NORTH ATLANTIC TREATY ORGANIZATION (NATO) pact to provide collective security to noncommunist nations. Also in 1949, he extended his containment policies to China, where the communists had taken control of the country, and instituted a program to provide aid to underdeveloped countries. Truman subsequently approved the construction of a hydrogen bomb in order to maintain U.S. nuclear superiority over the Soviet Union.

In June 1950, war broke out in Korea when communists from North Korea crossed the boundary of the 38th parallel. Truman dispatched U.S. forces under the command of General Douglas MACARTHUR to liberate the south. However, when MacArthur insisted on expanding the war into China, Truman fired him; Truman would later be criticized for having abandoned China to the communists. The president was further attacked not only for the continued U.S. military presence in Korea, but also for several scandals that had erupted among officials in his administration. The government was further weakened by Senator Joseph MCCARTHY's charges that the State Department, among other agencies, was operating under communist control.

Truman declined to run for reelection in 1952, and returned to Independence in January 1953. Although his final years in office were not very successful, he

President Truman at National Airport in Washington D.C. to see off Secretary of State George Marshall (right) and two delegates who are leaving to attend the Rio de Janeiro Conference of Foreign Ministers in Brazil. L to R: Warren Austin, U.S. representative to the United Nations, President Truman, Secretary Marshall, and Sen. Arthur Vandenberg. (TRUMAN LIBRARY)

enjoyed a renewed popularity after leaving the presidency, and later became recognized as one of the strongest presidents in history, especially for his conduct of the Cold War. He remains a favorite among Americans for his "give 'em hell" approach to political campaigning and the personal responsibility he took for the presidency, exemplified by a plaque on his desk: "The buck stops here."

Truman Doctrine

Announced to the public on March 12, 1947, the Truman Doctrine was formulated as a means of protecting the politically unstable regions around Greece and Turkey. At that time, it was evident to President Harry TRUMAN and his advisers that the Soviet Union was interested in various eastern Mediterranean countries and might even have had a hand in the eruption of a civil war in Greece being fought with communist guerrillas. After British troops withdrew from Greece, Truman feared the effects of communist subversion, and so called for immediate aid in the amount of $400 million to Greece and Turkey, as well as permission to send in U.S. troops to train local military forces and assist in postwar reconstruction efforts. The doctrine made it a principle of American policy to "support free peoples who are resisting attempted subjugation by armed minorities or by outside pressures." Although Truman's doctrine specifically identified those two countries, the idea behind it would extend to all Western European countries protected under the MARSHALL PLAN (which essentially expanded on the doctrine's goals). Underlying the Truman Doctrine was the principle of CONTAINMENT that would guide foreign policy decisions over the next several years.

U-2 affair

The notorious and embarrassing U-2 affair was a diplomatic disaster for the United States and in particular for President Dwight D. EISENHOWER. The incident began in May 1960, when a U.S. airplane piloted by Francis Gary POWERS was shot down as it was flying over the Soviet Union. Powers was captured and accused of espionage. Initially, the U.S. government denied any knowledge of Powers's existence and claimed that the plane the Soviets had shot down was a weather observation plane. However, after the Soviets produced a picture of Powers and other evidence of his espionage mission, President Eisenhower was forced to admit that the aircraft was indeed a U-2 spy plane and that he had known of Powers's flight. Soviet anger was aroused even further when it was revealed that there had been other such secret espionage flights. Eisenhower ultimately took full responsibility, publicly declaring that the Soviets had made the flights necessary due to their excessive secrecy, which had placed the United States in a state of anxiety over possible nuclear attack. UNITED NATIONS representative Henry Cabot LODGE subsequently helped to defuse public outcries over the situation by releasing clear evidence of Soviet spying.

As a result of the U-2 affair, a scheduled summit in Paris between Eisenhower and Premier Nikita Khrushchev was canceled. An angered Khrushchev loudly denounced the United States' actions, even demanding an apology, which Eisenhower refused to give. Powers, meanwhile, was tried in the USSR for espionage and sentenced to 10 years in prison, but he was later released in exchange for Soviet spy Rudolph Abel. As a result of this incident, U-2 spy flights were canceled, but they were quickly replaced by satellite surveillance that proved to be more effective than the planes had been.

United Nations

The United Nations (UN) was one of the most significant cooperative organizations to emerge in the aftermath of World War II. Established with the same idealistic principles that lay behind the earlier and defunct League of Nations, the UN was originally intended to unite the countries of the world in a collective goal of peace and international security. However, the onset of the Cold War changed that mission and turned the UN into more of a peacekeeping agency, running interference for the superpowers and guarding the interests of smaller and THIRD WORLD nations. Eventually, however, it also became a diplomatic tool in the struggles for supremacy that were to take place between the United States and the Soviet Union.

The groundwork for the establishment of the UN was laid at the Dumbarton Oaks Conference of 1944, where proposals were drafted for a later organizational conference. A year later, in San Francisco, the United Nations Conference on International Organization met from April 25 to June 26, 1945. Participants included delegates from 50 nations whose purpose was to write the UN Charter and establish the governing structure of the organization. The bipartisan U.S. delegates were Secretary of State Edward R. Stettinius, Senator Tom Connally of Texas and Senator Arthur VANDENBERG of Michigan; John Foster DULLES served as an adviser to the delegation. Numerous difficulties had to be resolved to create the charter, given the demands of so many nations, and in particular of the superpowers that comprised the Security Council. For instance, the veto power of Security Council members became a large point of contention. A compromise solution was ultimately reached, allowing for vetoes on actions taken by the council but not on topics of debate. The General Assembly was assigned greater powers than it had in its previous League of Nations incarnation, and organizations such as the International Labor Organization, the World Health Organization, and the United Nations Educational, Social, and Cultural Organization (UNESCO) were placed under the supervision of the Economic and Social Council. Also established in San Francisco were an International Court of Justice and a Trusteeship Council.

The UN mandate was soon overtaken by the events of the Cold War. As the United States was initially the largest contributor to the budget and enjoyed a majority support in the General Assembly, it was able for several years to push through its own agenda, including multilateral aid to other countries. In later years, the Soviet Union was able to gain similar leverage, and as a result the organization's foreign policy was frequently overlooked when one of the superpowers took an action that went against international agreements—i.e., U.S. intervention in Vietnam and the Soviet invasion of Czechoslovakia in 1968. These and similar incidents have led many critics to suggest that the UN is a worth-less organization and should be disbanded, or at the very least, that the United States should withdraw from membership. Nevertheless, the UN has survived and has become noted for its humanitarian work throughout the world and for its peacekeeping efforts when regional disturbances threaten world security.

United States Information Agency (USIA)

The United States Information Agency (USIA) was created in 1953 as a result of a reorganization of the government's executive branch by President Dwight D. EISENHOWER and under the directive of the United States Information and Cultural Exchange Act of 1948. Subsequent to the reorganization, the USIA took over the functions of the former International Information Administration, Mutual Security Agency, and Technical Cooperation Administration. Essentially an information service for the federal government, the USIA can also be considered a propaganda agency. One of its most notable achievements is the Voice of America radio broadcasts to innumerable countries around the world—including, at one time, nations behind the IRON CURTAIN. By 1986, the Voice of America was transmitting its programs in 42 languages to approximately 120 million listeners over 1,200 hours per week.

Headquartered in Washington, D.C., and operating independently of the State Department, the USIA performs a wide variety of informational functions intended to promote the United States and its foreign policy. In addition to the Voice of America, its other divisions are the Bureau of Programs, the Bureau of Educational and Cultural Affairs, and the Bureau of Management. The USIA also operates a satellite television network, WORLDNET, to which is attached a television and film service. The agency's best known director was George V. Allen, who led the agency from 1958 to 1961 and oversaw a restructuring of the USIA's mission, including implementing a policy of "gentle persuasion" and cultural exchanges between the United States and the Soviet Union, as well as other nations. Since Allen's time, the USIA has seen a number of changes, including a merger with the Bureau of Educational and Cultural Affairs that resulted in the formation of the International Communications Agency. However, in 1982, the original name was restored to the USIA, as it has been known ever since.

Vance, Cyrus (1917–   )

Cyrus Roberts Vance is a U.S. diplomat and government official who has distinguished himself under three U.S. presidents as well as in his service for the United Nations. Vance attended Yale University, receiving his B.A. degree in 1939 and his law degree in 1942. He thereupon enlisted in the military, serving in the U.S. Navy during World War II and achieving the rank of lieutenant before he was honorably discharged in 1946. Upon his return from the war, he went into private law practice in New York City.

In 1957, Vance was named as special counsel to the Senate Armed Services Committee, beginning a career in government service and quickly acquiring a reputation as an outstanding negotiator. During the years of 1961 to 1967, he became, in succession, general counsel to the Department of Defense, secretary of the army, and deputy secretary of defense, serving under Presidents John F. KENNEDY and Lyndon JOHNSON and playing a role in the handling of the DOMINICAN CRISIS. Vance also represented President Johnson in a number of crises, domestic and international, although he was not an enthusiastic supporter of Johnson's foreign policies. In 1968, Vance was sent to Korea to negotiate the release of the USS *Pueblo,* and subsequently to Paris to act as deputy chief negotiator in the Vietnam peace talks. Upon his return to the United States, he went back to private law practice.

After Jimmy CARTER's election as president in 1976, Vance was appointed secretary of state. Generally taking a noninterventionist approach in world affairs, he nevertheless supported the president's commitment to

Secretary of State Cyrus Vance confers with President Jimmy Carter. (CARTER LIBRARY)

ensuring the observance of human rights in other countries. He supported the policy of DÉTENTE with the Soviet Union and encouraged peaceful negotiations with that country. In addition, he worked toward U.S. recognition of Communist China as well as the passage of the Panama Canal treaties, and also played a role in the 1978 Camp David Accord. One of Vance's greatest accomplishments was bringing about the SALT II agreement between the United States and the Soviet Union that was signed in Vienna in June 1979, and which resulted in small reductions in launchers and ceilings on other military arsenals.

Vance was frequently at odds with Carter's national security advisor, Zbigniew BRZEZINSKI, who was more fiercely anti-Soviet than the moderate Vance and who ultimately began to have more influence over the president. In April 1980, after President Carter authorized the use of force to free U.S. hostages in Iran against Vance's advice, he resigned as secretary of state and returned once again to his law practice. He was recalled to public service in 1991, when he served for two years as a special envoy for the United Nations, negotiating cease-fires between warring factions in Bosnia, Croatia, and Nagorno-Karabakh. In 1983, he published his memoirs, *Hard Choices*.

Vandenberg, Arthur (1884–1951)

Arthur Hendrick Vandenberg was a Republican senator from Michigan who organized bipartisan support for a spirit of international cooperation and for the postwar foreign policy of the Truman administration. The son of a harnessmaker, Vandenberg began his career as a journalist, reporting for the *Grand Rapids Herald* from 1906 until his election to the U.S. Senate in 1928. He was continually reelected thereafter, until his death in 1951.

A conservative regarding domestic affairs, Vandenberg poured much of his energy into criticizing President Franklin D. Roosevelt's conduct of foreign affairs. Throughout the 1930s, he maintained a strong isolationist position, but changed his mind after the Japanese attack on Pearl Harbor in December 1941. By the end of the war, Vandenberg had reached the conclusion that the United States should become an active participant in an international organization, expressing this view in a highly lauded speech before the Senate in January 1945. That same year, President Roosevelt appointed him as a delegate to the UNITED NATIONS Conference on International Organization meeting in San Francisco. Vandenberg proved to be a force not only for the formation of the UN, but also for winning Senate approval for U.S. participation in the organization, which he saw as a hopeful means of bringing peace to the world. In addition to these duties, he also served as an adviser to secretaries of state James BYRNES and George C. MARSHALL.

In 1946, Vandenberg became chairman of the Senate Foreign Relations Committee, a position he held until the Democrats took over Congress in the 1948 elections. In 1947, he participated in an Inter-American Conference on Hemispheric Defense in Rio de Janeiro, where he was instrumental in formulating a pact that provided for the collective defense of countries within the Western Hemisphere. He also provided important support for the TRUMAN DOCTRINE of 1947 and the MARSHALL PLAN of 1948. Dedicated to preventing the spread of COMMUNISM, Vandenberg proposed, through a report from the Foreign Relations Committee, that the United States be committed "to the principle of military aid to self-defense groups." In early 1948, when several European countries (including Great Britain, France, Belgium, the Netherlands, and Luxembourg) sought the U.S. government's endorsement for a regional mutual defense agreement among those nations, President Harry TRUMAN turned to Vandenberg, his longtime friend, for help. The Michigan senator promptly put together a resolution, subsequently passed by Congress, that supported U.S. participation in regional security and defense arrangements, and agreed to provide aid as needed in case of aggression from other countries in those regions. This became known as the Vandenberg Resolution, and although it had no legal force, it provided the stimulus needed for the 1949 creation of the NORTH ATLANTIC TREATY ORGANIZATION, wherein each participating country agreed to provide military assistance to the others as needed.

Vandenberg became an unwilling dark horse candidate for the Republican nomination for president in 1948; he gave his unequivocal support to the eventual winner of the nomination, Thomas E. DEWEY, and helped to draft the party's platform at the Republican national convention. He was a widely admired and respected figure within the party and within Congress. As a member of the Senate-House Atomic Energy Committee, he supported nuclear disarmament, if a suitable agreement regarding international controls could be agreed upon with the Soviets. Vandenberg received the Collier's Award for Distinguished Congressional Service in 1946 and the Roosevelt Medal of Honor in 1948.

Vietnam War

The Cold War event that probably had the greatest impact on the United States and its citizens was the Vietnam War, which lasted from approximately 1957 to 1973, when a cease-fire was finally signed and U.S. military troops were fully withdrawn. However, for the citizens of North and South Vietnam (respectively, the Democratic Republic of Vietnam and the Republic of Vietnam), the war lasted much longer than that. The roots of the war lay in the FRENCH INDOCHINA WAR of 1946–54. After the armistice ending that war was signed and French troops had withdrawn, Vietnam was divided in two, with the northern section (capital: Hanoi) controlled by Ho Chi Minh and his communist regime, and the southern section (capital: Saigon) governed by the anticommunist Ngo Dinh Diem. According to the 1954 Geneva Agreement, the division was to be temporary until 1956, when general elections would be held and the nation would become unified again. However, it soon became evident to both Diem and the U.S. government that the communists would win the election and take full control of the country. Believers in CONTAINMENT and the DOMINO THEORY saw this as dangerous to the region's political stability; therefore, the United States helped to stymie the communists by backing Diem's successful efforts to block the elections. In South Vietnam in 1957, a series of terrorist incidents occurred that were led by the National Liberation Front (rebels also called the Vietcong), whose intent was to overthrow the Diem government and install a new regime sympathetic to unification with the northern communists. Soon Ho Chi Minh sent North Vietnamese military forces to join the rebels in the south.

Initial U.S. involvement in the Vietnam conflict was minimal; President Dwight D. EISENHOWER and, subsequently, President John F. KENNEDY sought only to supply military advisers to assist the Diem government in fighting the rebellion. However, as the war continued and North Vietnamese guerrilla tactics indicated the imminent defeat of Saigon, U.S. military involvement gradually increased, reaching a level of 16,000 advisers (some of whom had seen combat) by early November 1963. At that point, the Saigon government was overthrown and Diem assassinated, probably with U.S. knowledge. (President Kennedy was also assassinated, later that same month.) A series of inept administra-

A U.S. soldier guards a captured Vietcong guerrilla. (NARA STILL PHOTOS DIVISION)

tions followed, all of which were unable to deal with the advancing communist threat from the north.

The course of U.S. involvement in the war changed irrevocably with the passage of the TONKIN GULF RESOLUTION in August 1964. It allowed President Lyndon JOHNSON to order direct involvement of U.S. combat troops in Vietnam, and thereby led to a controversial ESCALATION of the war (which was never officially declared as a war). Subsequently, the number of American troops rose from 23,000 in late 1965 to more than 500,000 by the time Johnson stepped down as president in January 1969. The war escalated in other ways, as well: With the beginning of U.S. bombing over North Vietnam in 1965, the war's cost for American taxpayers began to increase dramatically. By 1969, more than $28 billion was being appropriated for the war effort. In addition, other countries were drawn into the conflict, with Australia, New Zealand, the Philippines, South Korea, and Thailand joining the U.S. as allies.

Politically, the Vietnam War was hampered by stubbornness on both sides that prolonged the fighting. The United States engaged in extensive bombing campaigns in hopes of forcing the North Vietnamese into peace negotiations. Ho Chi Minh, however, refused to engage in any discussions until the United States had withdrawn from the country, something it was not willing to do, given the instability of the Saigon government. The two sides were in a stalemate. Nevertheless, peace talks finally began in Paris in May 1968; they would continue for the next several years. By the early 1970s, no apparent progress had been made in bringing about a mutually agreeable settlement. However, President Richard NIXON managed to reduce U.S. troop levels to 184,000 by December 1971—a significant difference from the 1969 peak of over 543,000. He had also implemented his program of VIETNAMIZATION, to turn control and conduct of the ground fighting almost completely over to the South Vietnamese, while the United States maintained an air presence.

Between March and December 1972, peace talks in Paris led by Secretary of State Henry KISSINGER stalled repeatedly, the negotiations marred by accusations of bad faith and U.S. mining and bombing raids on North Vietnam. However, a series of intense air attacks in December finally brought about an agreement, which was signed on January 27, 1973. The armistice consisted of four primary points: (1) the complete withdrawal of U.S. troops from South Vietnam (this took place by March); (2) the release of all prisoners of war; (3) the installation of an international peacekeeping force; and (4) the right of the South Vietnamese to political self-determination. The North Vietnamese were not required to withdraw their troops from South Vietnam, but were prohibited from sending additional troops.

To nobody's surprise, fighting in Vietnam did not end after the U.S. withdrawal. Communist forces con-

Soldiers conduct a search-and-destroy mission in Vietnam. (NARA STILL PHOTOS DIVISION)

tinued their drive to overthrow the government of President Nguyen Van Thieu, and finally accomplished their goal with the capture of Saigon on April 30, 1975, by which time most of the anticommunist leaders had left the country with the few remaining American civilians. The communist unification of the country had finally taken place.

The effect of the Vietnam War on the United States was devastating. In addition to the more than $200 billion that was spent on the war between 1957 and 1975, 57,605 American lives were lost in the fighting. Domestically, the country was nearly torn apart by rampant opposition to the war (see ANTIWAR MOVEMENT) and the polarization of much of the nation's youth against the government. A benchmark was the publication, in 1971, of the PENTAGON PAPERS, which revealed the innumerable lies that had been told to both the public and to Congress over the years in order to bolster support for the undeclared and unpopular war. On an international level, the United States had lost a great deal of credibility as an ally, and many nations chose to become less dependent on its power and accordingly became less willing to align themselves with the United States in other conflicts.

Vietnamization

"Vietnamization" was an idealistic plan to gradually remove U.S. forces from the fighting in Vietnam while at

The war in Vietnam saw increasing use of helicopters for transportation and military operations. (NARA STILL PHOTOS DIVISION)

the same time training and building up South Vietnamese forces to be able to adequately fight their own war on their own. This was also known at one time as "de-Americanization." President Richard NIXON described it in this way: ". . . a plan in which we will withdraw all of our forces from Vietnam on a schedule in accordance with our program, as the South Vietnamese become strong enough to defend their freedom." The word quickly gained popular use in the United States, although officials in South Vietnam didn't care for it, thinking it implied a weakness in South Vietnamese troops. Nevertheless, implementation of the policy began in 1969 and proceeded over the next four years, as 540,000 U.S. troops were slowly withdrawn from the country. For some, this was a little too slow, but it was a sure path, and eventually Nixon achieved his long-term goal of full withdrawal of American troops from Vietnam.

Voorhis, Jerry (1901–1984)

Horace Jeremiah Voorhis was the Democratic U.S. representative from California who was unseated by an opponent, the ambitious young Richard NIXON, who accused him of ties to communism. After his graduation from Yale in 1923, Voorhis represented the YMCA on a goodwill tour to Germany. He returned to the United States, married, and pursued a number of differing occupations. In 1928, he received his M.A. degree from Claremont College. He also became headmaster and trustee of the Voorhis School for Boys in San Dimas, California. By this time he had registered as a socialist, and between 1930 and 1935, Voorhis lectured on labor problems at Pomona College. With the advent of the administration of President Franklin Roosevelt in Washington, Voorhis became a committed New Dealer, noting that Roosevelt had made it possible for him to be "a Democrat with a clear conscience."

Voorhis first ran for office in 1934, but was not elected to the House of Representatives until 1936. As a congressman, he fought against relief cuts and unemployment, and supported the deportation of any aliens pledging allegiance to a foreign government. He served for five terms before facing Richard Nixon in the 1946 congressional race. Determined to win the seat, Nixon seized upon growing American fears of COMMUNISM, and accused Voorhis of having communist ties due to an endorsement he received from CIO-PAC, a political labor organization that was suspected of communist infiltration. Voorhis denied the charge, but Nixon went on to establish links between Voorhis and another communist-influenced group, the National Citizens Political Action Committee. Cashing in on the prevailing American anticommunist feeling, Nixon also distributed flyers that exaggerated Voorhis's voting record. He won the seat, and thereafter Voorhis left national politics, although he remained active in local politics for many years. He also worked for 20 years as head of the Cooperative League of the U.S.A. In 1972, Voorhis wrote and published *The Strange Case of Richard Milhous Nixon*.

Wallace, George (1919–1998)

George Corley Wallace, a four-time governor of Alabama, was notorious for his vigorous stand against civil rights and court-ordered integration during the 1960s. The son of a farmer, Wallace graduated from the University of Alabama Law School in 1942, then served in World War II as a flight engineer for the U.S. Army Air Force. In 1946, he became a Democratic assistant attorney general for Alabama, then served in the state legislature from 1947 to 1953.

Wallace first came to national attention in 1948 as one of the dissenters against the civil rights plank in the Democratic Party's presidential platform. In 1953 he was elected as a judge in the Third Judicial Circuit, in which role he made prosegregation rulings that defied the U.S. Civil Rights Commission and earned him the nickname of the "Fighting Judge." Wallace ran for governor of Alabama in 1958, but lost, whereupon he returned to private law practice. Four years later, in 1963, he again ran for governor of Alabama this time successfully, on the slogan "segregation forever."

Wallace was a fervent anti-integrationist, sharing the belief of his fellow Southerner Strom Thurmond that the CIVIL RIGHTS MOVEMENT of the 1960s was fueled by communist influences. He even accused Martin Luther King, Jr., of harboring communists and felt the federal government was not doing enough to investigate COM-MUNISM in King's entourage. Wallace gained critical national attention in 1963, when he stood in the doorway of the University of Alabama's administration building to prevent the admission of two black students. He backed down after President John F. KENNEDY sent in the NATIONAL GUARD, but proceeded to provoke further confrontations in Tuskegee, Birmingham, Huntsville, and Mobile, making him a national symbol of Southern resistance to racial integration.

In 1966, Wallace was succeeded as governor by his first wife, Lurleen. After she died in 1968, he ran as an independent candidate for president. A champion of states' rights and Southern conservatism, he continued to campaign vigorously against busing and integration and also denounced the civil rights movement and antiwar demonstrations then at their peak. In the general election, Wallace won five states in the South and 46 electoral votes, placing a strong third in the presidential race and siphoning enough conservative support that he almost cost Richard NIXON the election.

In 1970, Wallace was reelected as Alabama's governor. The following year, during his campaign for the Democratic presidential nomination, he was shot in an assassination attempt. The attack removed him from the race and left him paralyzed and confined to a wheelchair for the rest of his life. Nevertheless, he continued to serve as governor through 1978, then won reelection four years later, finally retiring from politics due to ill health in 1987. In his later years, he softened his views on civil rights, and insisted he was never a racist.

Wallace, Henry (1888–1965)

Vice president of the United States under President Franklin D. Roosevelt, Henry Agard Wallace would become known over time as the man who was dropped from the ticket in 1944. Wallace received his B.S. degree in agriculture from Iowa State College in 1910, whereupon he went into agricultural research. He also wrote for the family-run agricultural newspaper, *Wallace's Farmer.* Upon the death of his father in 1924, Secretary of Agriculture Henry Cantwell Wallace, he took over the running of the paper. In 1926, he founded a company to market the seed for a hybrid corn that he had developed.

Initially a Republican, Wallace's concern for the downtrodden farmers of the Midwest led him to switch to the Democratic Party during the 1920s. In 1933, he was appointed secretary of agriculture by President Franklin D. Roosevelt and proceeded to supervise the implementation of New Deal programs that provided assistance to farmers under the Agriculture Adjustment Act of 1933. In 1940, he was chosen by Roosevelt to be his running mate in the presidential election. Over the next four years, he alienated many leading Democrats, and as a result was dropped from the 1944 ticket (he was replaced by Harry TRUMAN). In January 1945, Roosevelt appointed Wallace secretary of commerce, but he was fired by President Truman in September 1946 after he publicly criticized Truman's Cold War policies.

In 1948, Wallace ran for president as the Progressive Party candidate, but won only 2% of the popular vote and no electoral votes, in part because of accusations that he was supported by communists. He abandoned the Progressive Party in 1950 after it refused to support the war in Korea. Although he had once advocated friendship with the Soviet Union, Wallace later published a sharply worded criticism of the Soviets. After he left politics, he returned to agriculture. Among his many books are *New Frontiers* (1934), *Democracy Reborn* (1944), and *Why I Was Wrong* (1952), in which he explained his revised view and distrust of the USSR.

War Powers Resolution

With the end of the VIETNAM WAR came renewed concerns within Congress about the extent of presidential powers in regard to foreign policy, and specifically to declaring and carrying out acts of war. In an attempt to assert legislative control over that process, the War Powers Resolution was passed in November 1973 over President NIXON's veto. While not restricting the president's authority to make decisions in the event of a crisis, the resolution does prevent him from fully committing U.S. forces to overseas military operations without congressional approval. Specifically, the War Powers Resolution requires the president to report to Congress when he has ordered the use of armed forces for combat purposes, and, unless Congress authorizes otherwise, to withdraw U.S. troops within 60 days. Congress may also force troop withdrawal at any time by passing another resolution. Although all presidents since Nixon (with rare exceptions) have complied with the War Powers Resolution, they have invariably objected to it as an unnecessary (and possibly unconstitutional) restraint on their power to create and conduct foreign policy, a major concern especially during the volatile years of the Cold War, when instant decisions were often necessary. Congress has on occasion invoked the resolution, as in the Lebanon crisis of 1983, and presidents have reported to Congress as required in such instances as the hostage crisis in Iran and the GRENADA INVASION. Nevertheless, congressional ability to enforce its provisions would be negligible in the event of an emergency that would make the commitment of U.S. troops an inevitability.

Warsaw Pact

The Warsaw Pact was a military and political alliance between the Soviet Union and its satellite nations in Eastern Europe. Signed in Warsaw, Poland, in 1955, the purpose of the pact was to provide a defensive response to the NORTH ATLANTIC TREATY ORGANIZATION, which had just admitted West Germany, now rearmed, into the organization. It was initially a strong alliance, but in the waning years of the Cold War, the member nations became increasingly at odds with the Soviet Union, whose treasury had been depleted over time by its financial support of the pact and the costs of keeping up in the arms race. With the dissolution of the Union of Soviet Socialist Republics came the dissolution of the Warsaw Pact, in 1991.

Watergate

The scandal that defined the first half of the 1970s began with a burglary and ended with the downfall of President Richard M. NIXON. But the precipitating events and the aftereffects of the Watergate revelations resounded in the American consciousness for decades to come.

In many ways, Watergate (the name of the apartment complex where the break-in occurred) had its roots in Nixon's insecurity. After the 1971 publication of the PENTAGON PAPERS, the president, angered over information leaks in his administration, ordered investigations and surveillance to plug up the holes. A team of "PLUMBERS" was set in place for this purpose, and in time their mission expanded to include involvement in Nixon's 1972 reelection campaign. Their tactics included lies, manipulations, and "DIRTY TRICKS" carried out in an effort to discredit the president's political opponents, even though public opinion polls indicated that Nixon would most likely enjoy an easy victory over the probable Democratic nominee, Senator George MCGOVERN. The president, however, wanted to take no chances with his reelection. Thus, his staff on the Committee for the Re-election of the President (CREEP) determined to learn as much as possible about the opposition strategy by conducting illegal surveillance of the Democratic Party's national headquarters, located in the Watergate Hotel in Washington, D.C.

Early in the morning on Saturday, June 18, 1972, seven burglars were caught breaking into Democratic headquarters. Four were Cubans; the other three were James McCord, G. GORDON LIDDY, and E. Howard Hunt, White House "plumbers" who worked for CREEP. Initially, the burglary was overlooked by the press, until investigations by reporters Bob Woodward and Carl Bernstein of the *Washington Post* began to uncover a trail of lies and illegal activities that connected the break-in to top officials in the Nixon administration, including John EHRLICHMAN and H. R. HALDEMAN.

Nixon won the 1972 election in a landslide. In the ensuing months, however, publication of more details relating to Watergate and the Nixon administration's attempts to cover up the scandal belied Nixon's public denials of any involvement in the break-in. In 1973, the seven burglary defendants were found guilty (two had admitted their guilt); a special Senate investigating committee (chaired by Sam ERVIN) was formed; Ehrlichman, Haldeman, Nixon's personal counsel John DEAN, and Attorney General Richard Kleindienst all resigned due to their roles in the cover-up; and newly appointed attorney general Elliot RICHARDSON hired a special prosecutor, Archibald Cox, to investigate the scandal. Nixon apparently thought he could control Cox's investigation, but this proved not to be the case. When Cox and the Senate committee, backed by federal district judge John Sirica, ordered Nixon to turn over secret tapes of Oval Office conversations, the president, balking, ordered Richardson to fire Cox. When Richardson and Assistant Attorney General William Ruckelshaus refused to do so, they were both fired and the U.S. solicitor general, Robert Bork, carried out Nixon's order to fire Cox; these events came to be known as the "Saturday Night Massacre." Subsequently, William Saxbe was appointed the new attorney general and Leon Jaworski became the new special prosecutor. But Nixon's attempts to subvert the investigative processes of the Justice Department ultimately failed. The U.S. Supreme Court upheld the order to turn over the tapes to Jaworski on July 24, 1974. Their revelations were sensational, and Nixon's clear involvement in the Watergate cover-up resulted in a House of Representatives vote to impeach him. Lacking any significant support from Republicans in either house of Congress, the president elected to resign rather than submit himself to impeachment. His resignation took effect on August 9, 1974, whereupon Vice President Gerald R. FORD was sworn in as the new president. One month later, Ford pardoned Nixon for all crimes committed during his presidency, a controversial move that he had intended as a way to bring closure to the scandal that had rocked the nation. Meanwhile, the

President Gerald Ford issues his controversial pardon of Richard Nixon for his role in Watergate. (FORD LIBRARY)

majority of Nixon's staff that had been implicated in Watergate and CREEP illegal activities were convicted and sentenced to prison terms. Meanwhile, Richard Nixon's accomplishments as one of the greatest leaders of the Cold War were forever obscured by the humiliating events of Watergate.

Watergate proved to be a watershed moment in the Cold War years, creating a period of political instability that could have proved fatal to the U.S. government were it not for the system of executive, legislative, and judicial checks and balances provided by the Constitution. Among the aftereffects of the scandal were the appointments of special prosecutors to investigate other possible instances of wrongdoing in presidential administrations, leading to black marks against the Reagan and Bush presidencies (the IRAN-CONTRA AFFAIR) and against Bill Clinton (the Whitewater and Monica Lewinsky scandals). As Watergate has revealed, however, it is sometimes necessary to put checks on the powers of the president in order to keep the democratic system balanced and the American people confident in their leadership.

Weather Underground/Weathermen   See STUDENTS FOR A DEMOCRATIC SOCIETY.

Weavers, The   See SEEGER, Pete.

Weinberger, Caspar (1917–)

Caspar Willard Weinberger was the secretary of defense under President Ronald REAGAN who supervised a controversial buildup of U.S. military forces as a defense against possible aggression from the Soviet Union. The son of a lawyer, Weinberger received his law degree from Harvard University and then entered private practice. He served in the infantry during World War II and rose to the rank of captain. After the war, he returned to San Francisco, his hometown, where he practiced corporate law from 1947 to 1969. He also became very active in state Republican politics, serving both in the legislature and as director of finance under Ronald Reagan, then governor of California.

In 1970, Weinberger moved to Washington, D.C., where he was appointed to a number of high-level posts in both the NIXON and the FORD administrations. From 1973 to 1975, he served as secretary of health, education and welfare. For the next five years, he

remained in the private sector as president of the Bechtel Power Corporation, then returned to government service after Ronald Reagan's election to the presidency in 1980.

As secretary of defense, Weinberger demonstrated a profound distrust and dislike of the Soviet Union, and committed himself fully to the Cold War. In addition to overseeing the buildup of U.S. defenses, he also counseled the president against taking any steps toward an agreement with the Soviets. After Reagan was reelected in 1984, Weinberger issued a set of six conditions that he considered to be necessary for committing U.S. forces to military action. Although the last of these conditions was that sending troops overseas should be a last resort only, Weinberger's statement was a forceful indication to American citizens and to the world that the Reagan administration would not hesitate to take action in world affairs if it was deemed necessary. However, Weinberger apparently contradicted himself, on the one hand advocating a buildup of arms to strengthen the U.S. position, on the other hand hesitating to use them. His unequivocal support for the STRATEGIC DEFENSE INITIATIVE ("Star Wars") led him to write a letter to the president prior to a 1985 summit meeting with Soviet president Mikhail Gorbachev in Geneva. Portions of this letter were deliberately leaked to the press, effectively ruining the negotiations between the two leaders and enabling the United States to press forward with its arms buildup.

Weinberger expressed strong opposition to the covert IRAN-CONTRA operation, and initially believed he had squashed the idea when it first came up. However, on orders from President Reagan, National Security Advisor Robert MacFarlane had instructed Colonel Oliver NORTH to proceed with the operation. After the Iran-Contra affair became a public scandal, casting a negative light on the later years of the Reagan administration, Weinberger stepped down as secretary of state in November 1987, citing his wife's health as the reason for his resignation. In 1992, he was indicted for lying to Congress in previous testimony regarding the Iran-Contra scandal.

Welch, Robert (1899–1985)

Robert Henry Winborne Welch, Jr., was the noted and often notorious ultra-conservative founder of the controversial John Birch Society. An extremely intelligent individual, Welch graduated from high school at the age of 12. He did well in college and graduated from the University of North Carolina in 1916, although by that time he had become bored with school; he subsequently dropped his studies for a master's degree and took up clerical work for a time. He was appointed to the U.S. Naval Academy in 1917, but failed to adjust to military life and left the academy two years later. Welch then began writing summaries of the headlines in verse; his column entitled "Headline Jingles" was published in numerous North Carolina newspapers, one of which offered him a full-time job. However, he decided instead to go to law school, and enrolled at Harvard, where he met Felix Frankfurter, a professor of labor who often found himself in disputes with Welch regarding marxist theories of labor.

Still unable to adjust to academic life, Welch left school again in 1921, this time to go into business for himself as a candy manufacturer. He established the Oxford Candy Company in Cambridge, Massachusetts. In time, the company prospered, particularly due to sales of Avalon Fudge, Sugar Daddy, and Tar Baby. However, the company suffered during the Depression and was eventually sold, whereupon Welch went to work for E. J. Brach and Sons. In 1934, after two years with Brach, Welch became the sales manager for his younger brother's candy operation, the James O. Welch Company, boosting sales from $200,000 in 1935 to $20 million in 1956. He also worked as the director of a local bank and for a number of business organizations. His income soared during this time, enabling him to pursue other interests, mostly intellectual. A creative writer, Welch began writing short stories (unpublished) and an allegorical novel that drew an unflattering portrait of the New Deal, effectively comparing it to an anthill.

During the late 1940s, Welch began studying socialism and concluded that a change in government was necessary to prevent socialism from infecting society. In September 1949, he became a candidate for the Republican nomination for lieutenant governor in Massachusetts; he came in second in a field of six. Two years later he began airing a series of radio broadcasts and making speeches in support of the presidential candidacy of Ohio senator Robert A. TAFT. During one of these speeches, Welch criticized the U.S. government for betraying Nationalist China and Eastern Europe and accused it of harboring communists and communist sympathizers, noting the possibility that many were "men of great standing, in high places." The speech, which caused a sensation, was published in 1952 under the title *May God Forgive Us.*

Welch proceeded to become increasingly involved in political issues and began publishing a magazine entitled *One Man's Opinion* (subsequently *American Opinion*). In researching one article, he uncovered information about John Birch, an American military intelligence officer who was murdered by Chinese communists in 1945. Welch ended up writing a book about Birch, whom he lionized as a martyr and whose life and death he used to depict the need for a total defeat of COMMUNISM in the world; the book was published in 1954. In 1958, he published *The Politician,* an unflattering portrait of President Dwight EISENHOWER, who was, he wrote, "a dedicated, conscious agent of the communist conspiracy." He also accused Eisenhower's brother and administration officials John Foster DULLES and Allen DULLES of being members of the communist underground. When portions of *The Politician* were made public outside conservative circles in 1961, Welch was forced to clarify what he wrote, saying Eisenhower and others were not communists themselves but had simply been used by communists. He subsequently published the book for the general public.

Meanwhile, Welch had also founded the John Birch Society. The date chosen for the founding was December 9, 1958—the anniversary of John Birch's death. Welch made himself an absolute ruler of his organization, allowing little room for disagreement, and created a 10-point program for the defeat of world communism. With the idea that the communist conspiracy existed within the federal administration, Welch encouraged his followers to become "conspirators against established government" and to fight the growth of government interference in American society. He even propounded the idea that the nation's Founding Fathers had never intended for the United States to be a democracy. He also set up a publishing network to disseminate the society's ideas and ideals through bookstores and other means.

Over the years, the John Birch Society opposed summit meetings between President Eisenhower and Soviet Premier Nikita Khrushchev, the initiatives of the CIVIL RIGHTS MOVEMENT, aid to foreign nations, social security, the NORTH ATLANTIC TREATY ORGANIZATION, and the UNITED NATIONS, along with numerous political and social issues of the day. Because of its extreme views and methods of making those views heard, the John Birch Society came under sharp attack from others. However, a Senate investigation came to the conclusion that the society was nothing more than "a conservative, anticommunist organization." Within its own ranks, society members frequently objected to Welch's tight-fisted control and refusal to accede to a more moderate standpoint on certain matters. Nevertheless, by 1975 the group had grown to over 80,000 members and its publications, including *American Opinion* and the monthly *Birch Bulletin,* enjoyed healthy sales. Welch retained control over the organization until his death.

Westmoreland, William (1914–)

General William Childs Westmoreland was the commander of U.S. forces in Vietnam who was recalled to the United States after the failure of his controversial "search and destroy" missions. He graduated from the United States Military Academy at West Point in 1936, and saw extensive military action during both World War II, when he participated in the invasion at Normandy, and the KOREAN WAR. In 1960, Westmoreland was appointed superintendent of the academy at West Point, in which capacity he served until 1963, when he was sent to Vietnam. During the years of his command, the U.S. presence grew from a few thousand "advisers" to more than 500,000 troops by 1968. With the failure of his military strategies and the TET OFFENSIVE of 1968, he was called back to the United States, where he served as army chief of staff under President Richard NIXON from 1968 to 1972. He retired from the army in 1972. In 1974, Westmoreland ran as a Republican for governor of South Carolina, but lost the race. After a television documentary suggested that he had deliberately misreported the strength of enemy troops during

General William Westmoreland thanks entertainer Bob Hope for his service to U.S. troops. (NARA STILL PHOTOS DIVISION)

the Vietnam War, Westmoreland brought suit against CBS. However, he dropped the suit in February 1985, just days before the case was to go to the jury.

"winning the peace"

Late in the 1960s, it became clear that the United States would not be able to win the war in Vietnam without considerable expense and sacrifice of its troops. This was clearly an unthinkable option for a government that had already taken a public battering for its conduct of the war. Thus, other alternatives for ending the conflict were considered, but there was a catch: the United States had to appear victorious. In 1968, presidential candidate Richard NIXON promised to "end the war and win the peace." This statement held tremendous appeal for many voters, who attached themselves to the words "win" and "peace" as proof that Nixon meant to achieve an honorable settlement of the war without giving the impression that the United States had lost anything. Others feared that what Nixon meant by the phrase was massive military action with potentially damaging consequences.

Nixon was subsequently elected, and he put into motion his plans to win the peace, which included VIETNAMIZATION; this policy slowed down the withdrawal of U.S. troops from Vietnam at a pace that many protesters found to be far too slow. It wasn't until 1973 that a peace settlement was reached and the United States finally withdrew entirely from the country. By that time, it was clear to all observers that nothing had been won and a great deal had been lost.

witch hunts

Evoking the 17th century, when people (mostly women) believed to be witches were tried and executed in Salem, Massachusetts, the term *witch hunt* as used in the 1950s aptly described the mass hysteria provoked by Senator Joseph MCCARTHY and others in their attempts to root out and discredit communists in American government and industry. The practice often resulted in ruined careers and wrecked reputations, and eventually caused a backlash against those who saw a communist in every corner. Just prior to his 1952 election, Dwight D. EISENHOWER promised to prevent communist infiltration into his administration while at the same time promising not to engage in any "witch hunts or character assassination." Arthur Miller's play *The Crucible,* a dramatic exploration of the historical Salem witch trials, was also a veiled commentary on the moral issues of the McCarthy era.

women's movement

While the battle for women's rights known popularly as *feminism* had been an ongoing campaign in the United States for well over a century, it was during the turbulent years of the Cold War that the greatest strides were made in achieving rights for women that put them on a more equitable plane with men, socially, economically, and politically. The roots of the modern women's movement can be traced back to the late 1700s, when such early feminists as Abigail Adams and others urged the Founding Fathers to address the issue of female emancipation in the Constitution. However, it was not until 1848 that American women started to become publicly active in their demands for more access to the privileges of citizenship, such as the right to vote and own property. Leaders of the movement included such pioneers as Susan B. Anthony, Elizabeth Cady Stanton, Lucretia Mott, and Margaret Sanger; it is due in large part to their efforts that women made small but significant advances over the ensuing years. In time, more and more American females began to eschew traditional roles, going on to higher education and entering fields and professions previously reserved for men. One of the movement's greatest victories was attained in 1920 with the passage of the 19th Amendment, granting suffrage to women. Nevertheless, there were still a number of barriers to be overcome. As early as 1923, feminist leaders had introduced the idea of an amendment to the Constitution that would give legal backing to their desired goal of complete equal treatment and opportunities for all women. However, others in the movement were concerned about the inherent physical differences between men and women that would, they felt, make it necessary to pass legislation to provide certain protections to women under certain circumstances; in fact, the 19th amendment included a provision limiting the number of hours per week that women could work. As these two views were at odds with each other—women could not be considered equal to men if they could not do the same physical tasks and had to be "protected"—the movement stalled for the next three decades.

In 1946, the UNITED NATIONS Commission on the Status of Women was founded, with the goal of achieving equal rights for women worldwide in the political,

economic, and educational arenas. With this, and with other changes taking place in the world, the women's movement once again began to find its voice and to gather steam. One catalyzing event was the 1963 publication of Betty Friedan's pivotal book, *The Feminine Mystique,* which argued for female advancement in the workplace as a means of achieving greater fulfillment; this set the wheels in motion for what became known as the second wave of American feminism. Subsequently, leaders such as Friedan, Bella Abzug, and Gloria STEINEM emerged to take the movement in new directions and bring the word feminism to the forefront of the national consciousness. In many ways, this revitalization was influenced by the CIVIL RIGHTS MOVEMENT, which had been making such headway in obtaining legal rights for blacks that many felt an urgent need to apply those same goals to women—i.e., removing all barriers still in existence that prevented women from achieving parity with men in business, education, politics, and so on. "Equal pay for equal work" became an oft-repeated rallying cry, and many feminists also targeted such issues as abortion rights, the need for federally-funded child care centers, improved health care for women, and the elimination of prejudicial attitudes and practices against females in modern society, including hiring and wage discrimination in the workplace.

In 1966, Betty Friedan and others formed the National Organization for Women (NOW), joining women and men together to take action in order to realize "full equality for women in truly equal partnership with men" and to end all forms of discrimination against women. While NOW drew upon many of the techniques used in the civil rights movement—i.e., organized demonstrations and marches—its primary tactic was political, focusing on legislative avenues to attain its goals. For example, NOW was the primary proponent behind the ratification of the Equal Rights Amendment, a campaign begun in the 1970s that was defeated in 1982 (although hopes of passing the amendment persist to this day). Overall, the organization's work has resulted in sweeping changes in laws and social attitudes, particularly in the areas of political and economic equality, sexual harassment and violence against women, affirmative action, and abortion rights. NOW also promotes diversity, with calls for an end to racism, and it has been among the country's leaders in supporting lesbian rights. The organization currently numbers 500,000 members and boasts 550 chapters in every state in the union, as well as the District of Columbia.

One of the best-known victories of the women's movement was the 1973 *Roe v. Wade* Supreme Court decision that granted women the right to an abortion. This decision set off an ongoing controversy over the legality and morality of abortion that has resulted in numerous challenges to the law (*Casey v. Planned Parenthood* in 1992 limited abortion rights to an extent), as well as antiabortion demonstrations and even bombings of abortion clinics. Another achievement was the 1972 passage of Title IX of the Education Amendments, which prohibited sex discrimination in federally funded schools.

Throughout the 1970s and 1980s, many barriers were broken and many firsts were achieved, including the appointment of the first female justice to the Supreme Court, Sandra Day O'Connor. Yet even as the feminist movement effected tremendous changes in the status of women in the United States, it also affected the status of men, and many new problems arose in the wake of the old ones. Chief among these was an antifeminist backlash (particularly during the REAGAN presidency), which advocated a return to more strictly defined male and female roles. Nevertheless, women have persisted in their fight for equality; for instance, by 1984, 63% of women over the age of 16 had entered the workplace, and since then large numbers of women have moved into leadership positions in industry, government, and education. Thus, the women's movement, which experienced some of its greatest advances during the past three decades, is sure to have a long-lasting effect on the country's post-Cold War future.

Woodstock   See HIPPIES.

Yalta Conference

A wartime meeting of Allied leaders Franklin D. Roosevelt, Winston Churchill, and Joseph Stalin, the Yalta Conference of February 1945 was one of the factors that set the stage for later Cold War tensions between the Soviet Union and its former Allies. The "Big Three," as Roosevelt, Churchill, and Stalin came to be called, met in Yalta, a Crimean resort, to discuss details concerning postwar "division of the spoils," as well as Soviet entry into the war in the Pacific. Chief among their concerns was the nature and voting rights of the Security Council in the forthcoming UNITED NATIONS, the status of postwar Germany, and agreement over the governance of Poland. Stalin eventually acceded to a more democratic reorganization of Poland's then-current procommunist government, and the Polish boundaries were redrawn to give more territory to the Soviet Union. The Declaration on Liberated Europe, urged on the others by Roosevelt, was a pledge to ensure free elections of representative governments in the former Axis nations. The only agreement reached on Germany was that it would be divided into four zones of occupation (the French were to occupy the fourth zone). Stalin's insistence that Germany be forced to pay large war reparations was opposed by Roosevelt and Churchill, who were mindful of the effect of that very action after World War I (i.e., popular German resentment leading to the rise of Adolf Hitler). In the end, the Big Three agreed to allow a reparations commission to make the final decision on what Germany should pay.

The most controversial aspect of the Yalta Conference concerned Soviet entry into the Pacific war. In a secret agreement between Stalin and Roosevelt, the Soviet leader agreed to join the conflict after the German surrender; however, in return he wanted (and got) control or ceding of certain key areas in the Far East, including the Kuril Islands, lower Sakhalin, leaseholds at Port Arthur and Dairen, and the main Manchurian railroads. In addition, he demanded recognition of Outer Mongolia's independence from China, which was granted. Critics of the Yalta Conference accuse Roosevelt of selling out China and creating a tenuous situation for Eastern Europe as a result of his concessions. However, the areas in question were already under Soviet influence, and therefore nothing was really lost, according to many historians. Nevertheless, tensions between the United States and Soviet superpowers were readily apparent during the Yalta Conference, and many issues discussed there (particularly the German

The "Big Three"—Winston Churchill, Franklin D. Roosevelt, and Joseph Stalin—at Yalta (ROOSEVELT LIBRARY)

question) became major points of contention in the Cold War.

Yippies

The Yippies were members of the "Youth International Party," a more radical element of HIPPIES who took an "anti-" stance on almost any issue, as long as it was basically anti-ESTABLISHMENT. Two prominent Yippie leaders were Jerry RUBIN and Abbie HOFFMAN, who sought to publicize their message by way of theatrical displays that gained the attention of the MEDIA. They delighted in inciting antisocial behavior such as telling students to disobey their parents and burn their money and their draft cards. Above all, said Hoffman, "ques-

tion authority!" Yippies distrusted all kinds of government and espoused no particular political philosophy; everyone was suspect, from Republicans and Democrats to communists.

Frequently active in the ANTIWAR MOVEMENT, the Yippies were also frequently arrested for demonstrating or rioting. They often turned their subsequent courtroom trials into media spectacles, loudly proclaiming themselves to be political prisoners of a corrupt system. Their antics during the 1968 trial of the CHICAGO SEVEN, of which Hoffman and Rubin were members, riveted the nation. The Yippies' primary duty seemed to be to mock everybody and everything, as they showed during the Democratic National Convention, when they promoted a pig as the Yippie candidate of choice.

SELECTED BIBLIOGRAPHY

Archer, Jules. *Watergate: America in Crisis.* New York: Thomas Y. Crowell Company, 1975.

————. *The Incredible Sixties.* San Diego: Harcourt Brace Jovanovich, 1986.

Bernhard, Nacy E. *U.S. Television News and Cold War Propaganda. 1947–1960.* (Cambridge Studies in History of Mass Communications). Cambridge, England: Cambridge University press, 1999.

Bessette, Joseph M. *The Mild Voice of Reason: Deliberative Democracy and American National Government.* Chicago: University of Chicago Press, 1997.

Bessette, Joseph M., ed. *Encyclopedia of American Government.* 4 vols. Pasadena, Calif.: Salem Press, Inc., 1998.

Bowman, John S., editor. *The Cambridge Dictionary of American Biography.* Cambridge, England: Cambridge University Press, 1995.

Brands, H. W. *The Devil We Knew: Americans and the Cold War.* New York: Oxford University Press, 1993.

————. *Inside the Cold War: Loy Henderson and the Rise of the American Empire, 1918–1961.* New York: Oxford University Press, 1991.

Brinkley, Alan. *The Unfinished Nation: A Concise History of the American People.* 2d ed. New York: McGraw-Hill, 1997.

Ceaser, James W., Joseph M. Bessette, Laurence J. O'Toole, eds. *American Government.* Dubuque, Iowa: Kendall/Hunt Publishing Company, 1998.

Cohen, Warren I. *The Cambridge History of American Foreign Relations. America in the Age of Soviet Power, 1945–1991.* Cambridge, England: Cambridge University Press, 1995.

Cook, Fred J. *The Nightmare Decade: The Life and Times of Senator Joe McCarthy.* New York: Random House, 1971.

Crockett, Richard. *The Fifty Years War: The United States and the Soviet Union in World Politics, 1941–1991.* New York: Routledge, 1995.

Current Biography series. Bronx, N.Y.: H. W. Wilson, 1940– .

Denton, Robert E., ed. *The Cold War as Rhetoric.* Westport, Conn.: Praeger, 1991.

Encyclopedia Americana (International edition). Danbury, Conn.: Grolier, 1998.

Findling, John E. *Dictionary of American Diplomatic History.* New York: Greenwood Press, 1989.

Frankel, Benjamin. *The Cold War, 1945–1991.* Farmington Hills, Mich.: Gale, 1992.

Friedman, Norman. *The Fifty-Year War: Conflict and Strategy in the Cold War.* Annapolis, Md.: United States Naval Institution, 1999.

Gates, Robert M. *From the Shadows: The Ultimate Insider's Story of Five Presidents and How They Won the Cold War.* New York: Simon & Schuster, 1996.

Gitlin, Todd. *The Sixties: Years of Hope, Days of Rage.* New York: Bantam Books, 1987.

Glynn, Patrick. *Closing Pandora's Box: Arms Races, Arms Control, and the History of the Cold War.* New York: Basic Books, 1992.

Goldston, Robert. *The American Nightmare: Senator Joseph R. McCarthy and the Politics of Hate.* Indianapolis: Bobbs-Merrill, 1973.

Graff, Henry F. *The Presidents: A Reference History.* New York: Macmillan, 1996.

Havel, James T. *U.S. Presidential Candidates and the Elections: A Biographical and Historical Guide: The Elections, 1789–1992.* New York: Macmillan, 1996.

Issacs, Jeremy. *Cold War: An Illustrated History 1945–1991.* Boston: Little, Brown & Company, 1998.

Judge, Edward. *The Cold War: A History through Documents.* Upper Saddle River, N.J.: Prentice Hall, 1998.

Kasher, Steven. *The Civil Rights Movement: A Photographic History, 1954–68.* New York: Abbeville, 1996.

Kolko, Gabriel. *Century of War: Politics, Conflicts and Society Since 1914.* New York: New Press, 1995.

Lafeber, Walter. *America, Russia, and the Cold War 1945–1996* (America in Crisis). New York: McGraw-Hill College Division, 1996.

Leuchtenburg, William E. *In the Shadow of FDR: From Harry Truman to Ronald Reagan.* Ithaca, N.Y.: Cornell University Press, 1983.

Levy, Peter, ed. *America in the Sixties–Right, Left, and Center: A Documentary History.* Westport, Conn.: Praeger, 1998.

Lews, Lionel S. *The Cold War and Academic Governance: The Lattimore Case at Johns Hopkins* (SUNY Series, Frontiers in Education.) Albany: State University of New York Press, 1993.

McCauley, Martin. *The Origins of the Cold War 1941–1949* (Seminar Studies in History.) Reading, Mass.: Addison-Wesley, 1996.

———. *Russia, America and the Cold War, 1949–1991* (Seminar Studies in History). New York: Longman Publishing Group, 1998.

Marwick, Arthur. *Cultural Revolution in Britain, France, Italy, and the United States. c. 1958–c. 1974.* New York: Oxford University Press, 1998.

Nelson, Michael, ed. *The Presidency A to Z.* 2d ed. Washington, D.C.: Congressional Quarterly, 1998.

Neville, John F. *The Press, the Rosenbergs, and the Cold War.* Westport, Conn.: Praeger, 1995.

Safire, William. *Safire's New Political Dictionary.* New York: Random House, 1993.

Shafritz, Jay M. *International Encyclopedia of Public Policy and Administration.* Boulder, Colo.: Westview Press, 1997.

Silbey, Joel H. *The Modern American Congress 1963–1989.* Brooklyn, N.Y.: Carlson Publications, 1991.

Unger, Irwin, and Unger, Debi, eds. *The Times Were a Changin': The Sixties Reader.* Three Rivers, Mich.: Three Rivers Press, 1998.

Walker, Martin. *The Cold War: A History.* New York: Henry Holt, 1993.

Whitcomb, Roger S. *The Cold War in Retrospect.* Westport, Conn.: Praeger, 1998.

Wilcox, Fred A. *Uncommon Martyrs: The Plowshares Movement and the Catholic Left.* Reading, Mass.: Addison-Wesley, 1991.

Zinn, Howard. *A People's History of the United States, 1492–Present.* 2d edition. New York: HarperPerennial, 1995.

INDEX